PAPER PELLETS

Paper Pellets

British Literary Culture
after Waterloo

RICHARD CRONIN

OXFORD
UNIVERSITY PRESS

OXFORD

UNIVERSITY PRESS

Great Clarendon Street, Oxford OX2 6DP

Oxford University Press is a department of the University of Oxford.
It furthers the University's objective of excellence in research, scholarship,
and education by publishing worldwide in

Oxford New York

Auckland Cape Town Dar es Salaam Hong Kong Karachi
Kuala Lumpur Madrid Melbourne Mexico City Nairobi
New Delhi Shanghai Taipei Toronto

With offices in

Argentina Austria Brazil Chile Czech Republic France Greece
Guatemala Hungary Italy Japan Poland Portugal Singapore
South Korea Switzerland Thailand Turkey Ukraine Vietnam

Oxford is a registered trade mark of Oxford University Press
in the UK and in certain other countries

Published in the United States
by Oxford University Press Inc., New York

British Library Cataloguing in Publication Data

Data available

Library of Congress Cataloging in Publication Data

Library of Congress Control Number: 2009944015

Typeset by SPI Publisher Services, Pondicherry, India
Printed in Great Britain
on acid-free paper by
MPG Biddles Ltd, King's Lynn, Norfolk

ISBN 978–0–19–958253–2

1 3 5 7 9 10 8 6 4 2

For Sophie

Acknowledgements

My greatest debt is to the Leverhulme Trust. Without the award of a Senior Research Fellowship releasing me for two years from all undergraduate teaching and administrative responsibilities I do not believe that this book would ever have been completed. I am grateful, too, to the staff of the Special Collections department of Glasgow University library, where I carried out the bulk of the research for this book. They were unfailingly helpful to me. So too were the staff of the British Library on my several visits there. I am grateful to all the fellow-academics who invited me to give papers in which I tried out my arguments; to Nicholas Grene of Trinity College, Dublin; to Simon Hull, then of Bristol University, who invited me to speak at the conference he organized on the Romantic periodical; to Rolf Lesenich and Roswitha Simons of the University of Bonn who invited me to speak at their conference on *streitkultur*, to Malabika Sarkar for her invitation to lecture at the Centre for Romantic Studies in Kolkata, and to her colleagues at Jadevpur University; to Jane Stabler and Gavin Hopps who invited me to address the International Byron Conference at St Andrews in 2008; to Richard Gravil and Nicholas Roe who invited me to speak to the Wordsworth Summer Conference (I am grateful to Nick, too, for being such splendid company in Kolkata); and to Rosa Florou and Peter Graham of the Byron Society of Messolonghi, who allowed me to address them on no fewer than three occasions. I am grateful, too, to those who read my manuscript for Oxford University Press, to Tim Fulford and to the American reader whose anonymity I have failed to penetrate. I have shamelessly incorporated a number of their suggestions, and, though this may not be quite the book that they would have had me write, it is the better for their reports. The staff at the Press, first Andrew McNeillie and latterly Jacqueline Baker, have been warmly encouraging. This book would not have been as it is had I not for a number of years had the opportunity to work closely at Glasgow University with Clifford Siskin. I do not flatter myself that Cliff will much approve of the results, but he changed the way in which I think about literature. I have benefited, too, from having at the same period colleagues just as brilliant who looked at literature very differently. I am grateful to Seamus Perry, Janet Todd, Nicola Trott, and Duncan Wu. All these have left Glasgow for other if not better things, but the university is a different and a better place for the time they spent here, and, thanks to Alex Benchimol, Nigel Leask, Murray Pittock, and David Shuttleton, this remains a very congenial place for a Romanticist to work. As the only university in the world to boast a Department of Scottish Literature, it has proved an ideal base from which to explore the literary relations between England and Scotland. I am grateful to Stuart Curran for pointing out that my taste in literature was rather too solemn, and for recommending that I read *Life in London*. I would also like to acknowledge my debt to Timothy Webb and to Michael O'Neill for their intellectual companionship over many years. I had the good fortune to be writing my book at the same time as I was supervising a superb doctoral thesis, 'The Age of the Magazine: Literary Consumption and Metropolitan Culture', by David Stewart, now at the University of Northumbria. I can only hope that David learned nearly as much from me as I did from him. As my career approaches its end I find myself more and more conscious of my indebtedness to those senior colleagues who welcomed me to Glasgow at its very beginning. In particular, I am grateful to Bob Cummings, Philip Drew, and Jack Rillie. These were my real teachers. Last, and most of all, I am grateful to Dorothy McMillan, who, despite reading more drafts of this book than I had any right to impose on her, continues to share her life with me.

Contents

1

Introduction: Two Duels

I begin with two duels, both of them fatal. On 16 February 1821, John Scott, editor of the *London Magazine*, left his wife at her father's house in Cockspur Street saying that he was to dine with a friend (her father was Paul Colnaghi, the best-known print-seller of Regency London).[1] Instead John Scott joined Peter George Patmore, a journalist like Scott and later the father of the poet, Coventry Patmore. The two men took a post-chaise to Chalk Farm. It was where Londoners went to fight duels. Chalk Farm was only a mile from the city, but it was secluded, there were fields, and there was the Chalk Farm Tavern where they understood all about such things. Scott and Patmore ordered a bottle of wine there before making their way out to the field. It was a cold night, close to freezing, and foggy. Scott wore a cloak, Patmore a white greatcoat. It was unusual to fight a duel by moonlight. Most were fought early in the morning. Scott, I suspect, was anxious to avoid a long night's reflection on what the morning would bring. He was soon joined by the man he had challenged, Jonathan Henry Christie. Like Scott, Christie was an Aberdonian. He brought with him as his second, James Traill. They were Balliol men, bachelors in their twenties, both lawyers, both of Scottish families. Christie and Traill went on to make successful careers, Traill as the Metropolitan Police Magistrate, and Christie as head of a London law firm that specialized in property, but that was long after they had been acquitted of John Scott's murder.

Christie and Scott had met for the first time a little more than a month before, on 10 January. Christie was acting for John Gibson Lockhart, who had decided to resent Scott's references to him in the *London Magazine* in the course of two vigorous assaults on *Blackwood's*, the magazine for which Lockhart wrote. On 10 January Christie simply called on Scott to ask whether he acknowledged that the articles were his. Scott refused to answer unless Lockhart himself were at

---

[1] I base my account of the duel in which Scott died on the report of the trial of Christie and Traill in *The Times* for Friday 13 April 1821; Andrew Lang, *The Life and Letters of John Gibson Lockhart*, 2 vols. (London: Nimmo, 1897), 1, 250–82; Marion Lochhead, *John Gibson Lockhart* (London: John Murray, 1954), 82–5; Patrick O'Leary, *Regency Editor: Life of John Scott* (Aberdeen: Aberdeen University Press, 1983); two accounts by Leonidas Jones, 'The Scott–Christie Duel,' *Texas Studies in Literature and Language*, 12 (Winter 1971), 605–29, and *The Life of John Hamilton Reynolds* (Hanover and London: The University Press of New England, 1984), 217–25; and the account by Roger Sale, *John Clare: A Literary Life* (Houndsmills: Palgrave, 2002), 30–9.

hand and would acknowledge his own relationship to *Blackwood's*. Lockhart
hurried down from Scotland to London, and on 18 January Christie called on
Scott again. This time Scott admitted that he was the editor of the *London
Magazine* and had written the offending papers, but said that he would not
accept a challenge from Lockhart unless Lockhart would first deny that he had
any role in the '*management*' of *Blackwood's* and that he had any 'pecuniary
interest in its sale'. Lockhart would not give any such assurance, and Scott refused
his challenge, on the rather odd ground, given that Scott was himself a magazine
editor, that if Lockhart were involved in the management of *Blackwood's* he was
not entitled to the satisfaction of a gentleman. Lockhart wrote a formal note
informing 'Mr Scott, that he, Mr Lockhart, considers him as a liar and scoundrel', and returned to Scotland.

Both men published statements justifying their conduct. Lockhart's published
statement began with a denial that he had any role in the management of
Blackwood's Magazine. This prompted Scott to a second statement in which he
pointed out that no such denial had been included in the version of the statement
given by Lockhart to him. This was crucial because it was Lockhart's failure to
offer this assurance that had, according to Scott, made him unable to accept the
challenge.[2] Christie then wrote a letter to Horace Smith, who had preceded
Patmore in the role of Scott's 'friend', assuring him that, if Scott were to travel to
Scotland, Lockhart would 'give him a meeting instantly'. Horace Smith was
ready to help the two combatants to reach an accommodation, but he disapproved of duelling. After he read Christie's letter, he forwarded it to Scott,
together with a note in which he told Scott that he had written to Christie to
say that he would take no further part in the quarrel. Any further communications should be addressed to Scott directly. This time it was Christie who
published a statement (he had presumably been infected by the example of the
journalists). He explained that Lockhart had offered his denial that he had any
role in the management of *Blackwood's*, not to Scott, but to the public at large,
and by an entirely innocent oversight he had not made it clear that this denial was
not included in the version of the statement shown to Scott. He concluded
pugnaciously: 'If, after this statement, Mr Scott can find any persons who believe
that there was any thing more atrocious than an oversight in the circumstances of
the two statements, Mr Scott is perfectly welcome to the weight of their good
opinion.'

The various statements, taken together, read like an impossibly long-winded
version of one of those ill-tempered correspondences that occasionally flare up in
the letters column of the *Times Literary Supplement*, but things were about to
become serious. Lockhart had publicly charged Scott with cowardice, which, as

---

[2] *Statement, etc. by Mr John Scott in his dispute with Mr John Gibson Lockhart* (London: 1821),
*Statement: Mr Lockhart very unwillingly feels himself again under the necessity of obtruding himself upon
the public notice* (Edinburgh: 1821); *Mr Scott's Second Statement, February 2, 1821* (London: 1821).

The Scotsman pointed out, would have left Scott feeling for the time 'exceedingly tender'.[3] Scott sent his new 'friend', Patmore, to Christie's house to demand that Christie publicly acknowledge that he had intended in his own statement no reflection on Scott's character. Christie refused to offer any such assurance, Scott challenged him and, a fortnight later, John Scott was dead.

Lockhart's biographers go dewy-eyed over Christie. For Andrew Lang, Lockhart and his closest college friends were the Musketeers and Christie was D'Artagnan, 'a better friend no man ever had'. For Marion Lochhead he was Lockhart's *'fidus Achates'* and emerged quite unstained from a duel that he was forced to fight on a point of honour.[4] In fact, Christie could easily have offered Scott the assurance he demanded. Three years before, his friend Lockhart had given just such an assurance to Leigh Hunt: 'When I charged you with depraved morality, obscenity, and indecency, I spoke not of Leigh Hunt as a man. I deny the fact,—I have no reason to doubt that your private character is respectable, but I judged of you from your works.'[5] I suspect that Christie accepted Scott's challenge out of a romantic attachment to Lockhart. Lockhart was about to become a father: his son John Hugh was born on 14 February, just two days before the duel. By taking the quarrel upon himself, Christie was protecting his friend. He was also, on the morning of 14 February, breakfasting with Lockhart's father-in-law Walter Scott at his London hotel in Jermyn Street. Christie had once tried to write a novel himself.[6] It must have been especially gratifying that his involvement in the affair brought him into intimacy with the great novelist of the age. No doubt both thoughts sustained him on that cold evening at Chalk Farm.

Christie behaved very well throughout—like, as Keats would say, a picture of a man behaving well. When Scott took up his position, Christie called out, 'Mr Scott, you must not stand there: I see your head above the horizon; you give me an advantage.' In the first exchange he fired 'down the field', and only aimed at Scott after Traill protested that he should not expose himself a second time to Scott's pistol without defending himself. When Scott fell, Christie knelt by him, grasped his hand and said, 'I would rather that I was in your situation and that you were in mine.' Scott's surgeon, Dr Darling, reported Scott saying, in the days during which he lay dying in a room at the Chalk Farm Tavern, that Christie had been 'very kind to him after he was wounded'. After the duel Christie withdrew to France, from where he wrote to Walter Scott on 23 February, assuring him, 'my own conscience acquits me'.[7] In this he accurately anticipated the verdict of

---

[3] *The Scotsman*, no. 214, 24 February 1821, 62.

[4] Andrew Lang, *The Life and Letters of John Gibson Lockhart*, 1, 34 and 36; Marion Lochhead, *John Gibson Lockhart*, 80.

[5] *Blackwood's Edinburgh Magazine*, 2, January 1818, 416.

[6] Andrew Lang, *The Life and Letters of John Gibson Lockhart*, 1, 71.

[7] It was customary for those in Christie's position to go abroad and return to stand trial, thus avoiding the disgrace of being remanded in prison.

the jury, who on 13 April found Christie and Traill not guilty of murder after deliberating for forty-five minutes.

John Scott was thirty-six, with a wife and two children, ten-year-old Caroline, and John Anthony, who was only seven. He left his young family quite unprovided for. After his death a public subscription raised several hundred pounds for their support. Byron, who had been John Scott's junior by three years at Aberdeen Grammar School, contributed £30 anonymously.[8] Scott must have had feelings a good deal more mixed than Christie's as he shared his bottle of wine with Patmore at the Chalk Farm Tavern. Writing years after the event but, it may be, recalling the sad events of that day, De Quincey speaks of the duellist creeping 'stealthily, and like a guilty thing, to the bedside of his sleeping wife and child' to kiss them goodbye before leaving for Chalk Farm. Such a man experienced a 'conflict with himself that defied all rehearsal'.[9] Scott was determined to act out the part he had chosen as well as he could, but he surely cannot quite have suppressed the thought that it was a rather silly part, and one that a professional man with a young family had no business taking. He might have taken a lesson from Robert Southey. After exchanging insults with Brougham during the Westmoreland election campaign of 1818 Southey expected to receive a challenge and drafted a reply. In a duel, he wrote, 'the parties ought to meet on equal terms', but that would be possible only if Brougham were first to 'marry & have four children'. 'Please to be particular', he added 'in having them all girls.'[10] But Scott seems not to have thought the matter through so clearly. He got through the night of the duel, and the next eleven days that he lay dying, by reducing himself, or trying to reduce himself, into a man punctiliously following a code. As De Quincey puts it, the duellist is 'bound hand and foot', rendered by his decision to offer or accept a challenge utterly 'passive to the law of social usage'.[11] The code did more than regulate the manner in which fire should be exchanged: it prescribed how the combatants should behave to each other should one of them fall. When Scott fell, and Christie took his hand, Scott spoke as he should: 'Whatever may be the issue of this case, I beg you all to bear in remembrance that every thing has been fair and honourable.' He bore the operation to remove the bullet on 18 February with impressive staunchness and to the very end he insisted that he was quite satisfied with Christie's conduct.

---

[8] *Byron's Letters and Journals*, ed. Leslie A. Marchand, 8 (London: John Murray, 1978), 99.

[9] 'Sketches of Life and Manners', *Tait's Edinburgh Magazine*, n.s. 8 (February 1841), 100; *Works of Thomas De Quincey*, 21 vols., gen. ed. Grevel Lindop (London: Pickering and Chatto, 2000–3), 11, 289 (hereafter Lindop).

[10] Among Southey's other conditions was that Brougham should first 'convert [him] from the Christian religion'. I quote Southey's letter, which is in the library of the University of Rochester, from a transcript supplied by the editor of Southey's letters, Professor Timothy Fulford, to whom I am most grateful for drawing it to my attention.

[11] 'Sketches of Life and Manners', *Tait's Edinburgh Magazine*, n.s. 8 (February 1841), 108; Lindop, 11, 305.

But John Scott was also a man who found it difficult to accept either the fact that he was dying or the way in which his death had come about.

On the morning after the duel, in the dingy room of the Chalk Farm Tavern where he had been carried, he raised his head as he was being examined, and said, 'I have only one question to ask, is my wound necessarily mortal?' The bullet had entered his right side, just above the hipbone, and penetrated ten inches into the body. His doctors were not hopeful. After the bullet was successfully removed, they became more so, but on Monday 26 February, it became clear that infection had set in, and the following night Scott died. Repeatedly, in the days that he lay in the inn room, tended by his wife and by his doctors, Scott voiced his belief that the affair had been mismanaged. He did not blame Christie, but he did blame his second, P. G. Patmore. After the first exchange, Scott recalled, he heard Traill say, 'Now Mr Christie, take your aim, and do not throw away your advantage as you did last time.' He had himself immediately called out, 'What! Did not Mr Christie fire at me?', but had been interrupted by Patmore, 'You must not speak; it is now of no use to talk; you have nothing for it now but firing.' The exchange was reported at the trial by Scott's surgeon, George Darling. It may have been what De Quincey remembered in 1841 when he wrote that in many duels the true murderer is not either of the principals but the second who 'has cruelly thought fit' just for the sake of 'decorating himself with the name of an energetic man, and of producing a public "*sensation*"' to 'goad on the tremulous sensibility of a mind distracted between the sense of honour on the one hand, and the agonizing claims of a family on the other, into fatal extremities that might, by a slight concession have been avoided'.[12] In the circumstances that Scott describes, the code was clear. Once it was known that in the first exchange Christie had not taken aim, Scott could and should have pronounced himself satisfied, and the two men shaken hands. Patmore realized at once how damaging Darling's evidence was, and responded by publishing a statement. Publication came naturally to him. He was after all, like Scott and like Lockhart himself, a man of print, a prolific writer for the periodicals. He had been a contributor to *Blackwood's* himself before transferring his allegiance to the *London*, a decision which prompted the *Blackwood's* writers to retaliate by christening him Cockney Tims. Patmore's statement is a notably shuffling performance. He claims first that Traill had addressed Christie '*by name*', and so Patmore thought himself 'not entitled, much less called upon', to pay attention to anything that he said, and second that Traill's words had been 'wholly unintelligible'. John Scott died at 9.30 in the evening of Tuesday 27 February, the *Morning Chronicle* reported, 'with apparent ease, and without a groan', but his calmness, I suspect, was a symptom of septicaemia rather than an indication that he had found peace of mind.

---

[12] *Tait's Edinburgh Magazine*, n.s. 8 (February 1841), 107; Lindop, 11, 303.

John Scott was a casualty in the magazine war that broke out as more and more magazines were launched to compete for their share of the lucrative new magazine market. Sir Alexander Boswell, son of the great biographer, who was shot by James Stuart of Dunearn on 26 March 1822, and died the following day, was a casualty in a war between the political parties, a war that was fiercely fought throughout Britain in the post-war decade, but nowhere more fiercely than in Edinburgh.[13] But the two wars were not always easy to distinguish. Lockhart's quarrel with John Scott after all was a quarrel between rival journalists but also between a Tory and a radical Whig. James Stuart was a prominent Whig and Sir Alexander Boswell an enthusiastic Tory, but both made frequent appearances in print.

James Stuart was an Edinburgh lawyer, bred cattle on his Fifeshire estate, and was a Whig activist of unflagging energy, much of which he expended in publishing his correspondence with the various public figures that he engaged in dispute. He published his correspondence with the Earl of Morton, the colonel of the Royal Fifeshire Yeomanry Cavalry, whose reprimand had provoked Stuart to resign his commission, he published his correspondence with the printer of the scandalous Edinburgh Tory newspaper, *The Beacon*, and he published his correspondence with the Lord Advocate, Sir William Rae, who, along with Walter Scott, was one of a number of prominent Tories who had given the newspaper their financial backing.[14] A letter from James Stuart would have made any Tory's heart sink, it being impossible to frame any reply, as the Lord Advocate found, that did not prompt from Stuart yet another letter. Stuart's irritating pertinacity, his lumbering appearance, and his interest in cattle-breeding made him a figure of fun among the Edinburgh Tories, fun that was sharpened by a feeling that Stuart's gentlemanly status was not quite so secure as he pretended. His counsel may have claimed at his trial that he was 'blood relation to some of the first families in Scotland', but his father had practised as an Edinburgh doctor. His dispute with *The Beacon* and its printer seems to have come to a head when the newspaper observed that if, as reported, Queen Caroline, the new King's wife, were to make a visit to Scotland, 'we do believe that none above the rank of the Scotsman, or Mr James Stuart, would commit such an outrage on decency and good manners' as to receive her (the reference to 'the Scotsman' is to J. R. McCulloch, the political economist, who

[13] My account of the duel between Boswell and Stuart is drawn from *A Full Report of the Trial of James Stuart, Esq. younger of Dunearn, before the High Court of Justiciary, 10th June 1822; with an appendix containing documents, etc.* (Edinburgh, 1823); and the memoir prefixing *The Poetical Works of Alexander Boswell*, ed. Robert Howie (Glasgow: Maurice Ogle and Co., 1871).
[14] See *Correspondence between James Stuart, Esq. younger of Dunearn, and the Earl of Morton, Lord Lieutenant of the county of Fife: relative to Mr. Stuart's resignation of his commission in the Royal Fifeshire Yeomanry Cavalry* (Edinburgh, 1822); *Correspondence between James Stuart, Esq. and the printer of the Beacon* (Edinburgh, 1821); *Correspondence between James Stuart, Esq. younger of Dunearn, and the Lord Advocate* (Edinburgh, 1821).

edited the principal Whig Edinburgh newspaper until 1821).[15] Even when he was tried for murder Stuart kept up his association with the periodical press. He was defended by Henry Cockburn, the leading Whig lawyer in Edinburgh, and Cockburn was seconded in court by his close friend, Francis Jeffrey, editor of the *Edinburgh Review*.[16]

Stuart's victim, Sir Alexander Boswell, was still more a man of print than James Stuart. He was so 'infected with the *type*-fever', to use his own words, that he set up his own printing press, and 'commenced compositor'. He published antiquarian rarities, many of them from his own Auchinleck library, and he published his own work. Boswell was an accomplished minor poet and he wrote songs, both public songs such as the popular 'Jenny's Bawbee' and 'Jenny Dang the Weaver', and the private songs with which he entertained the company at the public dinners that he loved, songs that his friends described as ribald, and his enemies as obscene. He was the man principally responsible for the erection of the Burns monument on the banks of the Doon, Burns being dear to him as an Ayrshireman, as a poet, and as a fellow mason. He was six feet two and devoted to country sports, and his biographer could think of only one man who was his peer 'in robustness and elasticity of intellect, as well as in fineness of physique'—John Wilson, Lockhart's chief coadjutor on *Blackwood's Magazine*. Like Wilson, Boswell wrote for the periodicals. It led directly to his death.

Boswell was a man proud of his lineage and of Auchinleck, the estate that had remained in the family ever since 1504 when it was granted by James IV to Thomas Boswell, who proved his gratitude by dying on Flodden Field in the service of his royal master. According to J. W. Croker, Sir Alexander regretted his father's hero-worship of Johnson, considering it 'a kind of derogation'. Perhaps he selected Stuart as his butt because he thought him socially inferior. But ranks were less rigidly separated in Scotland than in England. Boswell married the daughter of an Edinburgh banker and, like James Stuart, he took an active part in farming his estate. The two men were even distantly related, though that could be said of almost any two members of the Scottish gentry. I think it likely that Boswell directed his squibs at Stuart not because he felt any particular animus against him but just because Stuart had become a standing joke among the Scottish Tories.

In July 1821, Stuart responded to the attacks on him in *The Beacon* by demanding that the printer of the newspaper, Duncan Stevenson, reveal the name of their author. Stevenson said that he would do so 'on the usual terms', that is, he would name the author provided that Stuart promised not to seek redress in the courts. This Stuart refused and, according to his own account,

[15] *The Beacon*, 30 (28 July 1821), 287.
[16] Christie and Traill did not employ periodical writers to defend them in court, but when John Scott's second, Patmore, stood trial for John Scott's murder, his defence was ably led by John Hamilton Reynolds, the poet and prominent contributor to the *London Magazine*.

repeated by Cockburn at his trial, punished the printer for his impertinence by horsewhipping him. Cockburn admitted that there might be 'some doubt of the judgement and good taste' he displayed in doing so. There was also a doubt as to the accuracy of the story. *The Beacon* reported that Stuart, assisted by two of his farm labourers, had attempted to horsewhip Stevenson, and found himself on the receiving end of a sound cudgelling. It seems likely that Stuart had intended a firm and dignified assertion of his social superiority, but Stevenson failed to respond passively to the attack and an undignified scuffle ensued. Stevenson then sent Stuart a challenge, which was refused on the ground that Stevenson was not of gentlemanly rank. Stevenson protested in the pages of *The Beacon* for 18 August that he was 'a Deputy-Lieutenant and Justice of the Peace for the county of Argyle, and [had] been so for nearly twenty years; and that, in short, he [held] a situation in society at least equal to that which James Stuart held till now'. 'Till now' because, when Stuart refused his challenge, Stevenson 'posted' him. He distributed through Edinburgh placards denouncing him as a coward.[17]

Just a week later on 25 August, *The Beacon* published its last issue. The newspaper's financial backers, chief among them the Lord Advocate, Sir William Rae and Walter Scott, had withdrawn after they found themselves named in Stuart's published correspondence with Rae. Scott wrote to his friend, William Erskine:

I am terribly malcontent about the Beacon. I was dragged into the bond against all remonstrances I could make and now they have allowed me no vote with regard to standing or flying. *Entre nous*, our friends went into the thing like fools and have come out very like cowards. I was never so sick of a transaction in my life, though I thank God I have very little to do with it.

The public will think, he wrote to Constable, that 'we approved personal abuse so long as it suited our purpose and so long as we were free from the consequence but not a jot further'.[18]

The first issue of the Glasgow *Sentinel* appeared on 10 October 1821. It announced itself as a continuation of the *Clydeside Journal*, but its true ambition was to take the place of the defunct *Beacon*. It certainly continued the *Beacon*'s campaign against James Stuart. Stuart raised an action for damages, but that served only to fuel the attacks on him. Learning that the paper's printer, William Borthwick, was imprisoned for debt, Stuart and his Whig colleagues secured his release on condition that he revealed the authorship of *The Sentinel*'s most offensive articles. The attacks on Stuart, it emerged, had been contributed by Sir Alexander Boswell. Boswell was in England, burying his much-loved younger brother, James. He arrived back in Edinburgh on the night of Saturday

---

[17] Stevenson gives his own account of the affair in *The Beacon*, 33 (18 August 1821) 252.
[18] *The Letters of Sir Walter Scott*, ed. H. J. C Grierson, 12 vols. (London: Constable, 1932–7), 7, 11–12, and 20.

23 March 1822 and, on the Monday morning, Stuart's 'friend', the Earl of Rosslyn, called on him, and demanded that Boswell deny authorship of the attacks on Stuart, or give his assurance that he had not intended any reflection on Stuart's character. The first assurance Boswell could not give, and the second he would not. A challenge followed immediately and was accepted.

That same evening Boswell and Stuart were bound over by the Sheriff to keep the peace. A friend of one of the two men had informed on them (at Stuart's trial Cockburn reported that it was a relation of Boswell's), anxious to prevent bloodshed. The only effect was to precipitate the meeting. Boswell had wanted time to settle his affairs, but the principals and their seconds agreed that this was no longer possible. The Sheriff's jurisdiction was confined to the city of Edinburgh. On 26 March Boswell was wakened at five in the morning, crossed the Forth at Queensferry with his second, John Douglas, and met James Stuart at twelve paces in a field outside the village of Auchtertool. Boswell, as he had agreed with his second on their way to the field, fired in the air. Stuart's bullet shattered Boswell's shoulder blade, and came to rest against his spine. Stuart's doctor and Boswell's own doctor tended the wound on the spot, and Boswell was then carried to the house of his cousin and close friend, Lord Balmuto. He died the next day. His wife and one of his daughters had time to reach his bedside, but his son arrived half an hour too late. That morning, Boswell was asked how he felt, and he replied, 'I feel exactly what I am—a man with a living head and a *dead* body mysteriously joined together.' They are chilling words, and yet oddly fitting, because Boswell, like John Scott, had acted all the way through the affair as if he had two quite separate identities.

Boswell was forty-six, married for twenty-two years, with a son and two daughters. He was a man who, having buried his brother so recently, must have been feeling his own mortality. He was addicted to all kinds of field sports, and he seems to have counted politics amongst them. He pursued James Stuart with the same gusto with which he hunted foxes and coursed hares. Three of his contributions to *The Sentinel*, Cockburn and Rosslyn revealed at the trial, were thought particularly offensive.[19] All three implied that Stuart had refused the printer Duncan Stevenson's challenge out of cowardice. A letter appeared in the issue for 20 February, 1822, headed 'The Late Lieutenant James Stuart'. It began by suggesting that, had the writer known all there was to know about Stuart he would never have attacked him but would 'have left his conduct to himself as the more successful satirist'. The letter then offered a jocose account of Stuart's resignation from the Fifeshire Yeomanry Cavalry. The sting was in the astonishment that the writer registers at learning that Stuart could have 'actually enrolled

---

[19] The University of Glasgow Library holds in its David Murray Collection the volume of *The Sentinel* that seems to have been used by James Stuart's defence team. The volume is marked up, Sir Alexander Boswell's contributions identified, and the most offensive have crosses written alongside them.

as a fighting man' in the troop. Boswell had contributed two still more offensive pieces to the issue for 26 December 1821. In a letter signed 'Ignotus' he commiserated with *The Sentinel* on the action brought against the newspaper by Stuart. The letter includes an apparently gratuitous reference to Henry Hunt, the radical orator whose attempt to address a reform meeting in Manchester precipitated the Peterloo massacre. After he had threatened to thrash a man, Hunt had 'showed, in the cant language, the white feather, and *refused to fight him*': 'If Mr Stuart had done this, the parallel would have been perfect.' Most offensive of all was the 'Whig Song':

> There's stot-feeder Stuart,
> Kent for that fat cow-art,
> How glegly he kicks any ba' man.

Boswell was so pleased with his rhyme that he repeated it on 20 February: 'Who's this too but Stuart, well known for the *Cow-art*.[20] On 25 March Stuart's second, the Earl of Rosslyn, invited Boswell to acknowledge that he had intended the attacks only as a 'bad joke', which is surely just what they were. But it was a joke that was about to turn extremely sour. Boswell's first thought had been to fight the duel in France. Only after taking legal advice did he decide that it might as well take place in Scotland. Clearly he had it in mind that he might kill his man. But then, on the morning of 26 March, as he was travelling towards the field, he told his second, Douglas, that it was his intention to fire in the air. Boswell could not bring himself to live consistently like the sensible man he showed himself to be at the last, but at least he died in his proper character.

Studies of the writing of the post-war decade have always been preoccupied with deaths: Jane Austen dying at College Street in Winchester, her beloved sister Cassandra closing her eyes, Keats in his rooms on the Spanish Steps in Rome, Shelley drowned in the Bay of Lerici, and Byron killed by fever and heavy-handed doctors at Missolonghi. But I choose to begin my study of the period with the less celebrated, sad, unnecessary deaths of John Scott and Alexander Boswell. These deaths give me the angle from which I view the literature of the period—an angle from which, as I hope, a rather familiar literary landscape will appear interestingly different.

Both duels had their origin in writing, but writing of a particular kind—what De Quincey describes as 'writing for the current press'.[21] It is a term that certainly includes the periodical writing in magazines such as the *London* or in newspapers such as *The Sentinel* that gave the immediate provocation in the duels in which Scott and Boswell died, but De Quincey understands the term more widely. It seems to accommodate all writing that successfully addresses itself to

---

[20] *The Sentinel*, no. 12, 26 December 1821, 94, and no. 20, 20 February 1822, 156.
[21] *Tait's Edinburgh Magazine*, n.s. 6 (April 1839), 248; Lindop, 11, 98.

the existing reading public. It is a kind of writing that De Quincey finds it easiest to define negatively, as that kind for which Wordsworth had no talent.[22] It might be described more positively by indicating the three literary phenomena that dominated publishing in the post-war decade. First there was the development of a new and distinctively modern variety of literary magazine, the best examples of which are *Blackwood's Edinburgh Magazine*, Baldwin's *London Magazine*, and Colburn's *New Monthly*, a phenomenon that has prompted Mark Parker to claim that the magazine was 'the preeminent literary form of the 1820s and 1830s in Britain'.[23] The second was the extraordinary celebrity of Lord Byron, who, as John Scott put it, had 'awakened, by literary exertion, a more intense interest in his person than ever before resulted from literature', and was 'thought of a hundred times, in the breasts of young and old, men and women, for once that any other author [was]'.[24] Byron's *Don Juan*, in large part because its publishers were not confident that the courts would uphold their copyright, became, in the words of William St Clair, the first work in English literary history that was 'designed, manufactured, and priced, so as to be able to address the whole reading nation simultaneously'.[25] Third, there were the 'Scotch novels', the series of novels by 'the Author of Waverley', that, according to William St Clair's extraordinary calculation, outsold the work of all other novelists put together.[26] The series began before Waterloo, with the publication of *Waverley* in 1814, but it was *Rob Roy*, the fifth of the novels, published in 1818 in a first edition of 10,000, that has claims to be 'the first regular best-seller in the history of the novel'.[27] All three phenomena have, as one would expect, caught the attention of recent critics,[28] but I do not believe that there has been

[22] 'Lake Reminiscences, No. III', *Tait's Edinburgh Magazine*, n.s. 6 (April 1839), 248–50.
[23] Mark Parker, *Literary Magazines and British Romanticism* (Cambridge: Cambridge University Press, 2000), 1.
[24] *London Magazine*, 3 (January 1821), 59.
[25] William St Clair, *The Reading Nation in the Romantic Period* (Cambridge: Cambridge University Press, 2004), 327. As Southey discovered when he tried to prevent the publication of a pirated version of *Wat Tyler*, an embarrassingly radical production of his youth, copyright protection was not extended to works held to be seditious. Neither was it extended to works deemed obscene. The consequence was that the publishers of *Don Juan*, Murray and later John Hunt, could only protect themselves against pirates by selling the poem at prices that made it very widely affordable.
[26] William St Clair, *The Reading Nation in the Romantic Period*, 221.
[27] *The English Novel 1770–1829: A Bibliographical Survey of Prose Fiction Published in the British Isles*, 2 vols., ed. Peter Garside and Rainer Schöwerling (Oxford: Oxford University Press, 2000), 2, 45.
[28] The current interest in magazines of the period has its origin in Jon P. Klancher's seminal *The Making of English Reading Audiences, 1790–1832* (Madison: University of Wisconsin Press, 1987), was developed by Lee Erickson, *The Economy of Literary Form* (Baltimore and London: Johns Hopkins University Press, 1996), 71–103, and has culminated in three recent studies: Mark Parker, *Literary Magazines and British Romanticism*; David Higgins, *Romantic Genius and the Literary Magazine: Biography, Celebrity, Politics* (London and New York: Routledge, 2005); and David Stewart, *The Age of the Magazine: Literary Consumption and Metropolitan Culture, 1815–1825* (forthcoming). Byron's celebrity has been the subject of important recent studies by Jerome Christensen, *Lord Byron's Strength: Romantic Writing and Commercial Society* (Baltimore and London: John Hopkins University Press, 1993); and Tom

before this a study of the period that takes as its premise the notion that these are the writings that best exemplify the 'current press' in the decade after Waterloo.

I choose to begin with the two duels partly because they are associated with all three publishing phenomena. John Scott died as a result of his quarrel with another magazine writer, and Alexander Boswell died as a direct result of his contributions to weekly newspapers. Byron's is an unobtrusive presence in the story of John Scott's death. He donated anonymously to the subscription to Scott's family, and in 1832 his tribute to his 'schoolfellow' was finally published: 'he died like a brave man—and he lived as an able one'.[29] Walter Scott, on the other hand, was a more substantial if still shadowy presence in both deaths. He breakfasted with Christie two days before his meeting with John Scott, and had dinner with Boswell a few weeks before the duel in which Boswell met his death, but he was more deeply involved in both affairs than this. Lockhart seems to have been provoked into issuing his challenge when he decided that John Scott's attacks on him were beginning to implicate his father-in-law. Walter Scott claimed that Lockhart had gone too far for retreat before he knew anything of the matter, but he seems on the whole to have approved of Lockhart's journey to London. He took the view that John Scott was 'such a dish of skim'd milk' that Lockhart risked nothing. Even when John Scott died, Walter Scott remained unrelenting: 'He has got exactly what he was long fishing for and I think it probable the incident will diminish the license of the periodical press so far as private character is concerned.' That last claim is rich coming from Scott, who, in the very same letter calls to Lockhart's attention 'a capital song in John Bull this morning' (*John Bull*, edited by Theodore Hook, was the most scandalous as well as the funniest of the London Tory newspapers): it will 'make the Whigs grind their teeth to powder'. Ten days later he regretted to Lockhart the 'party rancour' that the Edinburgh newspaper, *The Beacon*, was exhibiting in its coverage of the affair, but he neglects to mention that he had himself been one of *The Beacon*'s chief architects. In November 1819 he had written to Lord Melville about the plans to launch an aggressively Tory Edinburgh newspaper, and suggested a title: 'I think the Beacon would have a more original sound than the Guardian.'[30]

Mole, *Byron's Romantic Celebrity: Industrial Culture and the Hermeneutic of Intimacy* (Basingstoke: Palgrave Macmillan, 2007). See also *Byromania: Portraits of the Artist in Nineteenth- and Twentieth-Century Culture*, ed. Frances Wilson (London: Macmillan, 1999); and Nicholas Mason, 'Building Brand Byron: Early Nineteenth-Century Advertising and the Marketing of *Childe Harold's Pilgrimage*', *Modern Language Quarterly*, 63 (December, 2002), 411–40. Scott's overwhelming presence in the period has been most recently and most brilliantly studied by Ian Duncan, *Scott's Shadow: The Novel in Romantic Edinburgh* (Princeton: Princeton University Press, 2007).

[29] Lord Byron, *The Complete Miscellaneous Prose*, ed. Andrew Nicholson (Oxford: Clarendon Press, 1991), 171.

[30] *The Letters of Sir Walter Scott*, 6, 342, 348, 342, 374, 375, 377, 24.

It was the lampooning of James Stuart in *The Beacon*, continued in *The Sentinel*, that led directly to the death of Alexander Boswell.

Looking at the writing of the period from the fields in which John Scott and Boswell fell reveals a period constituted not, as has sometimes been suggested, by the doctrine of sympathy that its leading writers held in common but by the antagonisms that divided them. It is a decade remarkable for the number and the intensity of its literary feuds, a decade appropriately introduced by Isaac D'Israeli's publication in 1814 of his *Quarrels of Authors*. D'Israeli's book is much concerned with the writers of the previous century, with Warburton and Pope and Colley Cibber and Addison and Bolingbroke, but when he published it in 1814, he was implying, I suspect, a correspondence between the literary antagonisms of his own literary moment and those of the previous century. He was one of a number of writers who saw his contemporaries as engaged in a Queen Anne revival. All accounts of the Romantic period have registered how disputatious its leading figures might be, but those disputes, except when they can be construed as expressing ideological difference, usually understood in narrowly political terms, have remained peripheral to an understanding of its literature.[31] I argue that they are central, and also that they share a particular character. Duellists meet prepared to kill one another, and yet theirs is a cooperative antagonism, in which each confirms his opponent's proper title to masculine character and gentlemanly status. It is a period in which acceptance and rejection might be closely akin, a time when, as Jerome Christensen puts it, opposition was always apt to become apposition.[32]

All four of my duellists and three of their seconds were Scots. This may simply be a coincidence but duelling does seem to have been more prevalent among the Scots and the Irish than their English contemporaries, perhaps because citizens of nations bound in unequal partnership with England were more likely to prove, to borrow the phrase that *The Scotsman* uses of John Scott, 'exceedingly tender' if their gentlemanly status was called into question.[33] Even if this is not granted it remains, I think, a valuable coincidence because it so powerfully brings to mind the quite disproportionate importance of Scotland in the literature of the decade.[34] A very large majority of books in this as in every other decade of the

---

[31] My own approach has more in common with critics such as Kim Wheatley, who in *Shelley and His Readers: Beyond Paranoid Politics* (Columbia and London: University of Missouri Press, 1999), argues for the symbiotic relationship between Shelley and his Tory reviewers, by Steven E. Jones, who in *Satire and Romanticism* (New York: St Martin's Press, 2000) argues that Romantic and satiric modes of writing in the period are mutually defining, and by Andrew M. Stauffer, who in *Anger, Revolution, and Romanticism* (Cambridge: Cambridge University Press, 2005) argues that 'Romanticism was shaped by its struggle with anger.'

[32] Jerome Christensen, *Lord Byron's Strength*, 218–19.

[33] A suggestion rather borne out by James Landale's fascinating account of a Scottish duel of the period. See James Landale, *Duel: A True Story of Death and Honour* (Edinburgh: Canongate, 2005).

[34] A point emphasized in a number of recent studies that explore the importance of Scotland for Romanticism, among them *English Romanticism and the Celtic World*, ed. Gerard

century was published in London, but the city that was most closely identified
with the industrialization of print was Edinburgh. As a correspondent to the
London Magazine put it, 'book-making' is '*the manufacture* of the place'. A book
from Edinburgh was 'like a razor from Birmingham', and the Matthew Boulton
of book production was Walter Scott.[35]

The literary relations between Scotland and England were often aggressive,
a state of affairs rather nicely exemplified by Lockhart when he hurried down
to London intent on challenging John Scott. In *English Bards and Scotch
Reviewers* Byron suggests that the time-worn hostility between poets and their
critics was itself inflected by nationality, and he spoke for many of his English
contemporaries—for John Hamilton Reynolds who commented after the attack
on Keats in *Blackwood's* on 'the ignorant malevolence of cold lying Scotchmen',
for Charles Lamb, who had, he claimed, 'been trying all [his] life to like Scotchmen' but had been 'obliged to desist from the experiment in despair', and for
Hazlitt: 'Their impudence is extreme, their malice is cold-blooded, covert,
crawling, deliberate, without the frailty or excuse of passion.'[36] But the relationship between the two nations, like the relationship between duellists, was much
more ambivalent than such quotations suggest. Byron, who attacked Scotch
Reviewers on behalf of English Bards was himself, as he confessed, 'half a Scot
by birth, and bred / A whole one' (*Don Juan*, 10, 17, 7–8).[37] The editor of the
English magazine that Lockhart hurried to London to challenge was the Aberdonian, John Scott. The great Edinburgh publishers, Constable and Blackwood,
seemed far more conscious of their rivalry with one another than with their
English counterparts, and several of those counterparts were themselves Scots, or,
like John Murray II, the sons of Scottish fathers.[38] Constable and Blackwood
were both fully aware that they relied for their prosperity on cultivating relationships with London publishing houses. It was the same for the English. Samuel

Carruthers and Alan Rawes (Cambridge: Cambridge University Press, 2003); *Scotland and the
Borders of Romanticism*, ed. Leith Davis, Ian Duncan, and Janet Sorensen (Cambridge: Cambridge
University Press, 2004); and Murray Pittock, *Scottish and Irish Romanticism* (Oxford: Oxford
University Press, 2008).

[35] *London Magazine*, 3 (May 1821), 34. Like Matthew Boulton, of course, Scott worked with
partners, with his publisher, Archibald Constable, and with his printer, James Ballantyne.

[36] Quoted by Leonidas Jones, *The Life of John Hamilton Reynolds*, 154; 'Jews, Quakers,
Scotchmen, and Other Imperfect Sympathies', *London Magazine*, 4 (August 1821), 152; 'On the
Scotch Character', *The Liberal: Verse and Prose from the South*, 1 (January 1823), 367–8; *The
Complete Works of William Hazlitt*, ed. P. P. Howe, 21 vols. (London and Toronto: J. M. Dent and
Sons, 1930–4), 17, 105, henceforward and throughout the book, Howe. Contributors to the
London Magazine are identified here and throughout by reference to Frank P. Riga and Claude
A. France, *Index of the London Magazine* (New York and London: Garland Publishing, 1978).

[37] Quotations from Byron's poems are taken from Lord Byron, *The Complete Poetical Works*, ed.
Jerome J. McGann (Oxford: Clarendon Press, 1980–1993).

[38] On the disproportionate number of London publishers who were either Scots or of Scottish
descent, see Richard Sher, *The Enlightenment and the Book: Scottish Authors and Their Publishers in
Eighteenth-Century Britain, Ireland, and America* (Chicago and London: University of Chicago
Press, 2006), 265–440.

Smiles was glad that John Murray never lived to see the time when 'the coopera-
tion between the booksellers of London and Edinburgh was no more than a
memory'.[39] The decade on which I focus was the decade in which that coopera-
tion was at its most intense, the period that began when Constable, the publisher
of the *Edinburgh Review* and of the Scotch novels, established himself as the most
powerful literary publisher in Britain, rivalled only by John Murray, publisher of
the *Quarterly* and of Byron, and ended in 1826, when the bankruptcy of Hurst
and Robinson, his London partners, brought Constable's firm down. Literary
relations between Scotland and England were never to be quite so close again.

In the following chapters I focus on what I take to be the distinctive features of
the literary culture of the decade, features that are brought into sharp focus by the
decision to look at that culture as it appears from Chalk Farm and from that
lonely field outside the village of Auchtertool. In the first, I focus on the volatile
relationship in the period between literature and politics without which neither
duel would have taken place. In the second and third I turn to 'personality', a key
term in the period. It named at once the practice of making public attacks on
private character, and the power to persuade readers that they were granted access
to the writer's private self. The first was widely regarded as the besetting sin of the
public press of the period. The second was almost as widely agreed to be the
presiding virtue of its literature. The two senses of the word were, I argue, in
uncomfortably close association.

Both duels were a product of a sudden and significant expansion of the print
industry, as a consequence of which those like John Scott and James Stuart who
found themselves involved in journalistic quarrels were unsure whether the dispute
was public or personal. That anxiety was not misplaced, but a symptom of a
distinctive rhetoric that can be identified not just in the periodical writing but in
the novels and the poetry of the period. Writers who knew themselves to be
addressing an anonymous mass readership responded by developing in prose or
in verse a manner that suggested intimate address. This is the topic of my fourth
chapter, and it is developed in my fifth which focuses more directly on the early
nineteenth century as the age of print. When Sir Alexander Boswell admitted that
he was a man 'infected with the *type*-fever', he revealed his representative status.
This was a decade when, for the first time, literature was decisively identified with
printed language, not with language spoken or inscribed with a pen.

John Scott challenged Christie, and James Stuart challenged Boswell, because
both had been publicly branded as cowards. It was a way—the only way available
to them, it must have seemed—of ratifying their masculinity. But both men
were, I suspect, almost as anxious to demonstrate their gentlemanliness as their
manliness. I doubt whether either duel would have occurred if all the combatants

---

[39] Samuel Smiles, *A Publisher and His Friends: Memoir and Correspondence of the Late John Murray, with an account of the Origin and Progress of the House, 1768–1884*, 2 vols. (London: John Murray, 1891), 2, 516.

had been free from class insecurities, and these are the focus in the sixth chapter. Such insecurities were, I shall suggest, inevitable in the decade in which literature finally established itself as a professional occupation rather than a gentlemanly vocation. The duel was, I think, so seductive for a brief period because it was an institution that allowed literary men at once to express towards one another a murderous aggression and to ratify each on the other's behalf the right of professional writers to gentlemanly status. Writers in very many periods have been only too willing to engage in bitter disputes with their colleagues. The violent antagonisms that mark the literary relations between writers at this time are distinctive, I argue, because they function also as a means by which the writers of the time constituted themselves as a professional group.

In my seventh and eighth chapters I turn to generic questions. The duel, like the Italian sonnet, is a genre. Its practitioners secure prestige by their obedience to a demanding system of rules. But all those who engage in duels may not be perfectly familiar with the manner in which they are supposed to behave, which, I rather suspect, was the wholly forgivable error for which poor Patmore found himself all through his life stigmatized as the man responsible for John Scott's death. It is also the case that old rules may no longer be appropriate to new realities. By 1820 it already seemed an all but absurd anachronism for a magazine war, a dispute that represented itself as a contest of principle but which, as those engaged in it knew very well, was more pertinently a contest for circulation, should result in the spilling of blood rather than printer's ink. The outrage that John Scott registered at the manner in which *Blackwood's* was conducted, like the outrage that Lockhart expressed at Leigh Hunt's literary character, was, after all, in a strange and distinctively modern way impersonal, a matter to do with the relationship between publications rather than between individuals. But *Blackwood's* and the *London* were magazines of a radically new kind, and even those like Lockhart and John Scott who were principally responsible for their newness seemed to have only a shaky grasp of quite what it was that they had done. Magazines had always been miscellaneous, but the new magazine was in addition volatile. Its facts and its fictions, its solemnities and its absurdities, were not decorously separated but allowed to jostle against one another with excitingly unpredictable consequences. One of those consequences was the duel in which John Scott died. It was a horrible and yet an impressive demonstration of the power of the literary genre that Scott had helped to develop, and, as I argue in these two chapters, it became the dominant genre of the period. It was a decade in which novels and poems both aspired to be like magazines.

In my ninth chapter I address the puzzling question of why apparently decent people should have allowed themselves on occasion to behave and to write in a way that seems so unfeeling. Again it is a question prompted by the duels. How could Christie have taken aim when he knew that John Scott had children of ten and of seven at home waiting for him? How could Walter Scott, a decent and a kindly man, write, just after he had heard of John Scott's death, 'He has got exactly what he was long fishing for'?[40] How could the reviewers of the period, Lockhart not least among them, write in ways so evidently designed to cause pain? The three men, one might say, demonstrated a lack of imagination, but it is a lack that, I argue in this chapter, is rather widespread in the literature of the decade, and is not wholly to be reprehended. Even heartlessness, I suggest, has its virtues.

Finally, I turn to De Quincey's haunting picture of the agonized duellist kissing his wife and children goodbye, and ask what an exclusively male institution such as the duel has to tell us about the literary character of the period. It seems wholly incongruous with the domestic ideal that was already so powerful, and that was to become very shortly the ideal by which the British chose to define their national character. It is an incongruity that brings into sharp focus one of the more striking episodes of the literary culture of the decade, the determined and flamboyant campaign to reassert the masculine character of the republic of letters.

These, then, are the salient characteristics of the literary culture that this book attempts to define. It is a picture that will seem quite alien to many—to those for example for whom the decade marks the emergence as major poets of Felicia Hemans and Letitia Landon. It will be less strange, but still not easily recognizable, to those used to thinking of these years as belonging to the second-generation Romantics. In my conclusion I examine the relationship between the writers on whom I have focused, those who wrote for the 'current press', and the writers who have usually figured more largely in literary histories, those who preferred to address a reading public of the future, confident in the belief that the 'loftiest minds outrun their tardy ages' (*Don Juan*, 17, 9, 5). But that was not consistently Byron's view. In *Don Juan*, he is rather more likely to mock the claims of those who founded their faith in the value of their writings on an 'appeal to the unborn' that they 'baptize Posterity' (*Don Juan*, 12, 18, 2–4). For Byron as for most of his contemporaries this was a group most powerfully represented by Wordsworth, and in my conclusion I examine Wordsworth's irritable relationship with his natural adversaries, the periodical writers who had no alternative but to address the reading public that Wordsworth professed to despise. It was, I argue, a more ambivalent relationship than is commonly supposed, a relationship in which rejection was in closer relation to recognition than might have been expected. It was, in other words, a relationship rather like that between duellists. Duellists engage in a ritual that, even as each attempts to kill the other, forges a bond between them. The literary antagonisms of the period shared, I suggest, this ritualistic quality. As with the duel it was a ritual that centred on an aggressive public confrontation, and hence a ritual from which women, with rare exceptions, were excluded. That exclusion had longer lasting consequences than might have been expected. It helps to explain, I think, why, even in the early 1970s, the Romantic literature to which I was introduced as a student had so dominantly masculine a character.

---

[40] *The Letters of Sir Walter Scott*, 6, 374.

2

Two Dinners

The duels in which John Scott and Alexander Boswell died had their origins in the unusually bitter party conflicts that marked the post-war years, and in the intense literary antagonisms that festered in the same period. Both conflicts were even fiercer in Scotland than in England. Saddened by the death of Alexander Boswell, Walter Scott wrote, 'This fatal duel will probably be followed by others, for the rump of either faction endeavour to distinguish themselves by personal inveteracy and violence while Lord Liverpool and Lord Holland [the acknow-ledged leaders of the Whig and Tory parties] are quietly drinking their coffee together and going to the opera in the same carriage.'[1] He distinguishes here between the leadership of the two parties and their rank and file, but it was also a national difference. Lockhart had remarked it in 1819, when he wrote, in the character of a disinterested Welsh observer, Peter Morris, 'I had no conception previously of the real extent to which, in this country [he means Scotland] of political strife, the absurdities of party spleen are carried.'[2] In 1825, the *London Magazine* put it more forcefully. Edinburgh is 'an arena of gladiators' in which a man 'cannot have friends in both parties; nay, he cannot go from a Whig ball to a Tory one'. In London 'a man dines with his bitterest political opponent, all meet at the same tables at least, and society is not interrupted', whereas in Edinburgh 'a man must eat Whig diet or Tory diet, for it is certain that he cannot eat both'.[3]

Scott regretted that politics had descended into 'personal inveteracy and vio-lence' in a letter to Byron. The two were, as Scott must have known, as securely established at the head of the literary profession as were Liverpool and Holland at the head of the parliamentary profession, and like Liverpool and Holland they maintained, despite their political differences, entirely cordial relations one with another. Scott insists on the distinction between the great men and their followers, the *London Magazine* on the distinction between London and Edinburgh, but neither distinction was secure. Scott was after all deeply implicated in the factional journalism that led to Boswell's death, and Byron, by 1822, was embroiled in literary disputes that he conducted both in prose and in verse, and had parted

---

[1] *The Letters of Sir Walter Scott*, ed. H. J. C Grierson, 10 vols. (London: Constable, 1932–7), 7, 119.

[2] J. G. Lockhart, *Peter's Letters to his Kinsfolk*, 3 vols. (Edinburgh: Blackwood, 1819), 1, 123–4.

[3] *London Magazine*, n.s. 2 (August 1825), 498, in a paper entitled 'The Modern Athens'.

company from John Murray, the gentleman publisher, and thrown in his lot with the Hunt brothers. In such an atmosphere, political and literary relationships were unusually fraught, and they were also difficult to distinguish. Two Edinburgh anecdotes will serve to make the point.

On 22 February 1819, the triennial Burns dinner was held in the Assembly Rooms in Edinburgh's George Street. In *Peter's Letters to his Kinsfolk*, Lockhart describes the event as teaching him for the first time how, in Scotland, literary judgement had become the servant of political prejudice.[4] Those who 'took the chief direction in the affair were all keen Whigs', and in consequence, although 'the healths of Crabbe, Rogers, nay even Montgomery' were proposed, 'not one of these Edinburgh Reviewers had the common candour or manliness, in a meeting, the object of which was so purely to do honour to poetical genius, to propose the health either of Wordsworth, or of Southey, or of Coleridge', 'three of the greatest poetical geniuses our island ever has produced'. The only reason for the neglect of the three poets, according to Lockhart, was political: they supported the wrong party. Literature and politics are defined by Lockhart as mutually exclusive, distinguished one from another like the sabbath from the rest of the week. When politics impose themselves on literature, literature is 'pro-faned' by the 'poisonous sprinklings of the week-day paltriness of life'.[5] In the Assembly Rooms, a literary dinner was contaminated by politics. But political dinners posed their own problems.

In 1821 the annual Pitt dinner in Edinburgh was held not as usual in May, the month of Pitt's birthday, but in January, the month of Fox's birth, when the Edinburgh Whigs met annually to celebrate the memory of their great leader. It was a deliberately provocative piece of timetabling.[6] The dinner guests were divided between two rooms. In an inner room were the Tory grandees of Edinburgh, among them Sir William Rae, the Lord Advocate, the political leader of the Edinburgh Tories, and their spiritual and cultural leader, Sir Walter Scott (Scott had been unable to attend the Burns dinner two years before because of illness). The young men of the party dined in an outer room where they might be unconstrained by their elders' presence, and could be entertained by the likes of Sir Alexander Boswell. 'Many of the songs and toasts', it was reported in the Whig *Scotsman*, which was not a light-hearted newspaper, 'would have reflected disgrace on the inmates of a brothel'.[7] The Edinburgh Tory newspaper, *The*

---

[4] This was only the second dinner in the series. The dinner, and Lockhart's account of it, both indicate that the struggle to appropriate Burns had already become crucial to those contesting the right to define the character of the nation. The Whig-organized dinner should be compared with the campaign to raise a Burns monument led by the fiercely partisan Tory, Sir Alexander Boswell.

[5] J. G. Lockhart, *Peter's Letters to his Kinsfolk*, 1, 122–5.

[6] As Ian Duncan notes, in Edinburgh 'banquets in honour of Burns and Fox', became 'battlefields between the entrenched Tory administration and the Whigs'. Ian Duncan, *Scott's Shadow: The Novel in Romantic Edinburgh* (Princeton, NJ: Princeton University Press, 2007), 27.

[7] *The Scotsman*, no. 209, 20 January 1821, 22.

Beacon, gave a more cordial notice of the occasion and was particularly happy to record that towards the end of the evening Scott himself had emerged from his inner sanctum and joined the young men in the outer room.[8] The two rooms and Scott's passage between them constitute a key emblem of many of this book's concerns. They represent, for example, both the difference and the relationship not just between two kinds of Tory but between two kinds of Tory periodical, between the dignified *Quarterly* that Scott had helped to institute and its livelier, more scandalous counterparts with some of which Scott was also closely involved, among them *Blackwood's*, *The Beacon*, *The Sentinel*. The evening also confirmed that it was not just the Whigs who failed to maintain the distinction between literature and politics. *The Scotsman* was scandalized to learn that in the Lord Advocate's speech he had seen fit to compliment Scott's son-in-law, 'in the full knowledge that Mr John Lockhart was not known to be connected with any useful or respectable work, but that, on the contrary, he had rendered himself notorious as conductor, or conductor-in-chief to Blackwood's Magazine'.[9] It was not simply that literature was degraded by being associated with politics. Politics, it seems, could just as easily be contaminated by being brought into contact with literature, especially periodical literature. Scott and the Lord Advocate were close associates, but it was a dangerous association, even more dangerous for Scott than for Sir William Rae.

In September of the same year the two men were publicly named as members of a consortium of Edinburgh Tories who had entered into a bond guaranteeing against loss *The Beacon*, a scandalous Tory newspaper described in *The Scotsman* as 'a college of professed libellists and duellists'.[10] Against Scott's wishes the bondholders withdrew from their guarantee as soon as their names were exposed in the public press. As Scott commented to his friend, Erskine, '*Entre nous*, our friends went into the thing like fools and have come out very like cowards'.[11] Scott's exposure was more than an irritation, because it threatened his unique status in the literary world. Lady Morgan, Sydney Owenson, had been a particular target of the *Quarterly* ever since its notice of her novel *Woman, or, Ida of Athens* in its first issue. The attack culminated in the unusually severe review of her travel book, *France*, that appeared in September 1817.[12] She did not respond publicly until 1822 when she published anonymously a verse satire, *The Mohawks*, in which she made full use of the recent revelations. In

---

[8] *The Beacon*, 1 (13 January 1821), 15.
[9] *The Scotsman*, no. 208, 13 January 1821, 16.
[10] *The Scotsman*, no. 244, 22 September 1821, 297.
[11] *The Letters of Sir Walter Scott*, 7, 11–12.
[12] *The Quarterly Review*, 1 (February 1809), 50–2, and 17 (April 1817), 280–6. The earlier review was written by Gifford himself, the second by J. W. Croker with contributions, it may be, from Gifford and John Hookham Frere. Here, and throughout, contributors to the *Quarterly Review* are identified by reference to the *Quarterly Review Archive*, ed. Jonathan Cutmore, http://www.rc.umd.edu/reference/qr/index.html

her understanding of them, they served to expose the murky, covert links between literature and party politics of which she had been a victim. She notes, for example that the exposure of Scott and Sir William Rae as bond-holders had put an abrupt stop to their gloating pleasure in the scandalous activities of *The Beacon*:

> But long the man of song and legal knight,
> Like giants, in their course could not rejoice:
> The bond discover'd, dragg'd to day each name,
> They've only to divide the costs and shame.[13]

It was embarrassing for Sir William Rae that his name should be 'dragg'd to day' in this manner because the Lord Advocate is the principal law officer of the Crown in Scotland, and it was clearly inappropriate that a man in such a position should involve himself in political in-fighting, particularly of the kind favoured by *The Beacon*. Scott's case might seem to be different: he was after all a private gentleman. But Lady Morgan identifies his offence as still more grievous:

> Mourn, all ye Muses! Veil your conscious tears,
> Lo! The scorch'd laurel feels the lightning's blast!
> How fades that glory, nurseling of your cares!
> How sinks that name that should for ever last!
> In vain thy son his hundred triumphs bears,
> Disgrace and vengeance hold their victim fast.
> 'Who but must laugh, if such a man there be,
> Who would not weep, if *Marmion* were he?'
>
> (129)

Lady Morgan's sly insinuation is that the periodicals with which Scott is associated, the scandalous *Beacon* and *Blackwood's* and the supposedly dignified *Quarterly Review*, have more in common than is generally granted. But she also insists that the discovery does not just change the perception of Scott's private character, it changes the character of his writings. The Waverley novels were famous for their power to unite a readership that in all other respects seemed characterized only by its diversity, but that power was contingent on Scott's wizardry, that is, on his agreeing and being agreed to inhabit a sphere far removed from the rather muddy arena in which party politics were disputed. The narrator of *Waverley* offers a suave apology when he is obliged to describe the state of the parties at the time of the '45: 'I beg pardon, once and for all, of those readers who take up novels merely for amusement, for plaguing them so long with old-fashioned politics, and Whig and Tory, and Hanoverians and Jacobites.'[14] His authorial self would

[13] [Lady Morgan (Sydney Owenson)], *The Mohawks: A Satirical Poem with Notes* (London: Colburn, 1822), 128. The lines of the poem are not numbered. Subsequent page references are included in the text.
[14] Walter Scott, *Waverley*, ed. Peter D. Garside (Edinburgh: Edinburgh University Press, 2007), 26.

not have admitted to his implication in new-fashioned politics with such unruffled geniality. For Lady Morgan the new knowledge impels a new understanding
of the novels:

> Those tomes, whose sale we're told is so immense,
> Indited by the fluent muse of Waverly,
> Where pure description holds the place of sense,
> And ghosts and warlocks visit us so neighbourly,—
> Where Whigs to malice ever are prepense,
> And Tories preach their abject creed so cleverly,
> Might still have had their vogue: spite of abusing,
> We needs must own the novels are amusing.

(42)

Scott is revealed as a black magician whose art lies in the skill with which he
disguises the partisan character of the novels.

The Scotsman too argued that Scott's character as a writer had changed: Scott
had become 'responsible now, not only for what he writes himself, but for all that
must be held as coming forth under his auspices'.[15] That is, he must now be
regarded not only as the author of the poems and the Waverley novels but of *The
Beacon* and *Blackwood's*. Scott was revealed not just as a co-signator to the bond but
as an author of a very different kind from the author he had been taken to be. His
association with scandalous periodicals was represented by Macvey Napier as 'one
of those perplexing moral aberrations for which it is scarcely possible to account'.[16]
It threatened his place as the kingdom's leading man of letters, in Byron's phrase,
the monarch of Parnassus. By the time that Hazlitt came to write his essay on Scott
for *The Spirit of the Age*, Scott's involvement with a newspaper such as *The Beacon*
and with *Blackwood's* had become a measure of his limitations as an author.
Though 'praised, admired by men of all parties alike', he is a man who

repaid the public liberality by striking a secret and envenomed blow at the reputation of
every one who was not the ready tool of power—who strewed the slime of rankling malice
and mercenary scorn over the bud and promise of genius, because it was not fostered in
the hot-bed of corruption, or warped by the trammels of servility—who supported the
worst abuses of authority in the worst spirit—who joined a gang of desperadoes to spread
calumny, contempt, infamy, wherever they were merited by honesty or talent on a
different side—who officiously undertook to decide public questions by private insinu-
ations, to prop the throne by nicknames, and the altar by lies—who being (by common

---

[15] *The Scotsman*, no. 190, 9 September 1820, 295.
[16] *Hypocrisy Unveiled and Calumny Detected in a Review of Blackwood's Magazine* (Edinburgh:
1818), 38. This anonymous pamphlet is commonly ascribed to Macvey Napier, who was a
contributor to the *Edinburgh Review*, succeeding Jeffery as editor in 1829, editor of the
supplement to the sixth edition of *Encyclopaedia Britannica*, a prominent Edinburgh Whig, and a
frequent *Blackwood's* target. The attribution has been contested, and the pamphlet has alternatively
been attributed to James Grahame, an Edinburgh advocate.

consent) the finest, the most humane and accomplished writer of his age, associated himself with and encouraged the lowest panders of a venal press; deluging, nauseating the public mind with the offal and garbage of Billingsgate abuse and vulgar *slang*, showing no remorse, no relenting or compassion towards the victims of this nefarious and organized system of party-proscription, carried on under the mask of literary criticism and fair discussion, insulting the misfortunes of some, and trampling on the early grave of others.[17]

Hazlitt's pent-up outrage is released in a sentence that sweeps onwards so irresistibly that it seems unable to come to a close. Just as, at the Pitt dinner, Scott moved between the two rooms, so, it began to be suggested, he moved between two literary spheres: one was the domain of imaginative literature, the other was an arena occupied by violently partisan political journalism. For Ian Duncan, Scott's decision to write fiction rather than history allowed the novels 'to float above local partisan alignments (however embroiled their author) and invoke a national public'.[18] But they floated only so long as their fictional status was agreed to free them from Scott's sectarian prejudices, and by 1820 that agreement began more and more frequently to be withheld.

The mutterings about Walter Scott, when they became louder, played their part in bringing about John Scott's death. Lockhart himself claimed that it was the introduction of his father-in-law's name into the dispute that had impelled him to take action.[19] Most commentators have refused to believe him, but it does at least provide an explanation of why Lockhart behaved so differently in this instance from the way in which he had responded to similar situations before. In April 1818, John Hunt had published his opinion that if Lockhart refused to reveal himself as the author of the articles on the Cockney School of Poetry he would, in addition to demonstrating 'an utter disregard of all truth and Decency', show himself as capable of 'the height of meanness and COWARDICE'. On the face of it, Lockhart was moved only to laughter.[20] The reason that he

[17] The essay on Scott appeared as the fourth in the series 'Spirits of the Age' in the *New Monthly Magazine*, 10 (April 1824), 297–34. *The Spirit of the Age* was published as a volume by Henry Colburn the following year. This passage was added when the essay was published in book form. Howe, 11, 68.

[18] Ian Duncan, *Scott's Shadow: The Novel in Romantic Edinburgh*, xiv.

[19] In a letter to Christie dated 6 January 1821, Lockhart writes that the second of John Scott's attacks on *Blackwood's* particularly distressed him 'not on account of myself, but of Scott, of whose hitherto unprofaned name such base use was made in it'. See Andrew Lang, *The Life and Letters of John Gibson Lockhart*, 2 vols. (London: John C. Nimmo, 1907), 1, 250–1.

[20] *The Examiner*, no. 516, Sunday, 16 November 1817, 729. Lockhart replied in *Blackwood's*: 'When you tell me I have submitted to be called a liar and a coward, I must ask you in my turn, whether you seriously think it in any way incumbent on me to take notice of the silly invectives of every simpleton who writes in a newspaper; and what opinion you would have formed of my discretion, if I had suffered myself to be the dupe of so shallow an artifice?' *Blackwood's Edinburgh Magazine*, 2 (January 1818), 417. Contributors to *Blackwood's* here and throughout are identified by reference to Alan Lang Strout, *A Bibliography of Articles in Blackwood's Magazine* (Lubbock, Texas: Texas Tech Press, 1959).

responded so differently to the milder accusations brought against him by John
Scott is suggested, perhaps, by John Scott's punning on his own name:

woe betide *any* SCOTT who permits himself to become too closely connected with
magazine brutalities. He is sure to have good cause given him to repent the degrading
association.[21]

John Scott was as much an admirer of his namesake, Sir Walter, as everyone else. In
the very first issue of the *London Magazine* he launched the series 'Living Authors'
with an account of Walter Scott that recognized him as distinguished from his
contemporaries by a Shakespearean breadth of sympathy. Byron, Wordsworth,
and Moore seem, by contrast, marked by 'particular *Veins* of thought or language'.
He repeats the point even in his attack on *Blackwood's*. Writers such as Byron,
Shelley, Leigh Hunt, and John Wilson, though 'all of them are men of eminent
talent', remain 'sectaries in literature—wonders of the day rather than lights for all
time'. Only Scott's writings will remain to 'furnish the fascination of the fireside,
and topics of cheerful and social converse, when the discords and profligacies of
the living generation are laid quiet and forgotten in their tombs'.[22] Walter Scott's
ability to survive his own age is, then, dependent on his remaining free from the
sectarianism which is produced by the 'discords' of the present, and clearly
amongst these discords the bitter party politics of the time figure largely. But
Walter Scott had put his own status at risk by identifying himself with 'these men
[Lockhart and Wilson], and their scandalous publication'.

Walter Scott, the man, never made any secret of his Tory principles, but as a
novelist he felt less free to assert his own opinions. He was by 1820 widely
identified as 'the Great Unknown', 'the author of *Waverley*', and he was just as
widely known to be a Tory, but his status was dependent on his maintaining a
distinction between his personal and his authorial politics. His special literary
status, one might say, had the same source as the electoral success of Provost
Crosbie in *Redgauntlet*, who had been elected Provost three times because
'nobody could ever find out whether he is Whig or Tory'.[23] From time to time
the mask slips, as for example in *The Fortunes of Nigel* when Scott explains Nigel's
pride of birth by adducing a famous passage from Tom Paine's *Rights of Man*.
France, Paine boasts,

has outgrown the baby clothes of Count and Duke, and breeched itself in manhood.
France has not levelled, it has exalted. It has put down the dwarf, to set up the man. The
punyism of a senseless word like Duke, Count or Earl has ceased to please. Even those
who possessed them have disowned the gibberish, and as they outgrew the rickets, have
despised the rattle. The genuine mind of man, thirsting for its native home, society,

[21] *London Magazine*, 2 (November 1820), 510.
[22] *London Magazine*, 1 (January 1820), 12 and 2 (November 1820), 515–16.
[23] Walter Scott, *Redgauntlet*, ed. G. A. M. Wood with David Hewitt (Edinburgh: Edinburgh
University Press, 1997), 88.

contemns the gewgaws that separate him from it. Titles are like circles drawn by the magician's wand, to contract the sphere of man's felicity. He lives immured within the Bastille of a word, and surveys at a distance the envied life of man.[24]

Scott's prose becomes especially silky and urbane as he turns Paine's thought on its head: 'But Nigel was somewhat immured within the Bastile of his rank, as some philosopher (Tom Paine, we think) has happily enough expressed that sort of shyness which men of dignified situations are apt to be beset with, rather from not exactly knowing how far or with whom they ought to be familiar than from any real touch of aristocratic pride.'[25] It is a shrewd cut, but it is also a lapse, a momentary abandonment of the pose of political neutrality that Scott is usually careful to maintain. As Hazlitt puts it, it is one of those moments at which 'Sir Walter *stops the press* to have a sneer at the people.'[26] Much more typical is the ridicule of a character such as Sir Robert Hazlewood in *Guy Mannering*, a stereotypical Tory, who can scarcely credit that there are lawyers in Edinburgh who believe that justice should be administered 'without respect to rank and family': 'How, sir, without respect to rank and family? Will you tell me *that* doctrine can be held by men of birth and education?'[27]

Scott's third novel, *The Antiquary*, is representative. He introduced it as the third in a trilogy of novels 'intended to illustrate the manners of Scotland at three different periods'. It seems an oddly academic intention for a novelist, but in voicing it Scott distinguishes his tale, as his reviewers obediently followed him in doing, from 'the crowd of modern novels'.[28] Scott is claiming for himself not only the dignity of the historian but, by implication, the historian's disinterestedness, and this is the more necessary because *The Antiquary* is not in any ordinary sense a historical novel at all. The action takes place in 'the last ten years of the eighteenth century'.[29] The novel deals with the period during which Scott completed his studies at Edinburgh University and was received into the Faculty of Advocates, which was also the period in the recent past when ideological divisions had been at their fiercest. The novel was published in 1816, when the return of peace after a war that had lasted with only a short interruption for more than twenty years allowed the British once again to focus on their differences. Scott is even prepared teasingly to acknowledge how tales of the past might serve to point a moral for the present. Jonathan Oldbuck encourages Lovel, the novel's young hero, to compose a poem under the title

[24] Thomas Paine, *Rights of Man* (Harmondsworth: Penguin, 1985), 80.
[25] Walter Scott, *The Fortunes of Nigel*, ed. Frank Jordan (Edinburgh: Edinburgh University Press, 2004), 293.
[26] *New Monthly Magazine*, 10 (April 1824), 233; Howe, 11, 66.
[27] Walter Scott, *Guy Mannering*, ed. P. D. Garside (Edinburgh: Edinburgh University Press, 1999), 254.
[28] *Quarterly Review*, 15 (April 1816), 125.
[29] 'Advertisement', Walter Scott, *The Antiquary*, ed. David Hewitt (Edinburgh: Edinburgh University Press, 1995). Subsequent page references are included in the text.

26   *Paper Pellets*

'The Caledoniad; or, Invasion Repelled'. Such a poem, he knows, will catch the attention of readers alarmed by frequent invasion scares: 'it will suit the present taste, and you may throw in a touch of the times' (107). Scott seems equally ready to throw a touch of the times into *The Antiquary*. Lord Glenallan, Oldbuck's Catholic neighbour, pays him a visit in order to propose, as rumour has it, 'bringing doun his hill-lads and Highland tenantry to break up the meetings of the Friends o' the People' (285). The rumour is reported by the local wigmaker who has little time for the 'democraws' who seem to him as reprehensibly 'again' the king and the law, and hair powder and dressing o' gentlemen's wigs' as they would have seemed to Scott himself. Even Edie Ochiltree, the beggar (he is also an old soldier who has served with the Forty-Second), is outraged by the suggestion that in the event of an invasion he would not have much to fight for: '*Me* no muckle to fight for, sir?—is na there the kintra to fight for, and the burnsides that I gang dandering beside, and the hearths o' the gudewives that gie me my bit bread, and the bits o' weans that come toddling to play wi' me when I come about a landward town?' Oldbuck draws the proper conclusion: 'the country's in little ultimate danger, when the beggar's as ready to fight for his dish as the laird for his land' (346).

At such moments Oldbuck seems the mouthpiece for Scott's own Tory complacency. Oldbuck has after all often been identified as, of all Scott's characters, the closest to the author. Even Scott's own son-in-law recognized 'a quaint caricature of the founder of the Abbotsford Museum, in the inimitable portraiture of the Laird of Monkbarns'.[30] The links between the two go beyond the biographical. Oldbuck and the novel's narrator share an education. Both sprinkle their sentences with classical tags, both reveal close knowledge of arcane points of Scots law as well as a range of antiquarian knowledge, and, more significantly, both are so steeped in the older literature of England, and in Shakespeare's plays in particular, that their almost every sentence accommodates an echo. All this makes it the more remarkable that Oldbuck is a Whig, and a Whig very ready to voice his sympathy with the French Revolutionaries. He meets even their worst excesses with a measured understanding: if 'a set of furious madmen were now in possession of the government', this is simply 'what often happened in great revolutions, where extreme measures are adopted in the fury of the moment, and the state resembles an agitated pendulum which swings from side to side for some time ere it can acquire its due and perpendicular station' (277). It is a stance very much closer to James Mackintosh's, before his recantation, than it is to Burke's.

In allowing Oldbuck to adopt and defend such a view, Scott seems to be displaying a surprising, even an extravagant, disinterestedness, an appearance

---

[30] J. G. Lockhart, *Memoirs of the Life of Sir Walter Scott, Bart*, 7 vols. (Edinburgh: Robert Cadell, 1837), 4, 12. John Sutherland has pointed out the many links between Oldbuck's history and Scott's own life in *The Life of Walter Scott: A Critical Biography* (Oxford: Blackwell, 1995), 190–1.

which is, of course, entirely to his purpose. It is one of the means by which Scott establishes 'the Author of Waverley' as writing from a vantage point detached from and superior to the party politics in which lesser writers (Walter Scott among them, no doubt) remained embroiled. Scott's novels find their subject matter in the most uncompromising ideological conflicts, between Jacobite and Hanoverian, Covenanter and Episcopalian, Saxon and Norman, because Scott— and it was his most influential innovation—grounded the authority of the novelist in his ability to rise above them. The novelist achieves his unique authority by maintaining a political position so determined to distance itself from faction that it refuses any political content. As Peter Garside wittily puts it, Scott speaks as a member of a 'silent minority', as spokesman for a viewpoint so unpartisan that it cannot be put into words.[31] Garside is less willing to concede how far this is just a matter of show. After all, looked at another way, *The Antiquary* executes an extreme and provocative re-writing of the 1790s. In the 1790s the Home Office spy system was so alert that, just one week after the Duke of Portland received a letter reporting the suspicious activities of the Wordsworths, Coleridge, and their visitor, John Thelwall, the Duke's agent, James Walsh, had taken a room in the Globe Inn at Stowey.[32] In *The Antiquary*, when Lovel is seen to indulge in very similar activities, making 'free use of his pencil in his solitary walks', neighbourhood rumour has it that he is 'certainly a French spy'. But the only consequence is a short interview with the Sheriff, after which Lovel is 'suffered to remain undisturbed in his retirement', pursued only by two dinner invitations (35). The Home Office maintained its surveillance by the widespread practice of opening and reading private correspondence, a habit that Scott outrageously reproduces in the goings-on at the Fairport post office where no letter is safe from the postmistress, Mrs Mailsetter and her friends, the butcher's wife and the baker's wife (109–15). The disturbing paranoia that grips all states at war is benignly transformed into feminine curiosity. The economic distress that encouraged sympathy with France is registered in the person of Edie Ochiltree, a beggar so happy in his wandering life and so free from the fear of indigence, that he refuses any piece of gold offered him on the ground that, if he were to become wealthy, he would lose his way of life.

Given all this, it comes as no surprise, when the watchfires are lit to signal a French invasion, that the whole neighbourhood unites to repel it; Saunders Mucklebackit, the fisherman, the Whig antiquary Jonathan Oldbuck, Lord Glenallan, the Catholic aristocrat, and Sir Arthur Wardour, the Tory Squire. It proves a false alarm, as it must, because Scott's Britain is under real threat not from invasion by foreign troops, but from contamination by foreign manners.

---

[31] Peter D. Garside, '*Old Mortality*'s Silent Minority', in *Critical Essays on Sir Walter Scott: The Waverley Novels*, ed. Harry E. Shaw (New York: G. K. Hall, 1996), 149–64.

[32] Kenneth R. Johnston, *The Hidden Wordsworth: Poet, Lover, Rebel Spy* (London and New York: W. W. Norton and Co., 1998), 382–3.

The German fraudster, Herman Dousterswivel, whispered by a naive young man
to be an '*Illuminé*' (101) (the Illuminati were the members of a secret society
founded in Germany that was imagined by conspiracy theorists such as the Abbé
Barruel and John Robison to have instigated the French Revolution) almost
bankrupts Sir Arthur Wardour by involving him in his alchemical schemes.
The Antiquary offers a picture of 'the last ten years of the eighteenth century'
in which history is magically transformed into nonsense, in which the badge of
revolutionary sentiment is a change in hairdressing fashions that threatens the
livelihood of the local wig-maker: 'Hegh, sirs! nae wonder the commons will
be discontent and rise against the law, when they see magistrates and baillies,
and deacons, and the provost himself, wi' heads as bald and as bare as ane o' my
blocks!' (36). It is a world in which any 'ganging to raise up the puir folk against
the gentles', will find that the poor will jump to the defence of the wealthy, and a
world in which they are right to do so, because the wealthy are always prepared to
recognize that they share with their poor neighbours a common humanity. When
the young fisherman Steenie Mucklebackit is drowned Jonathan Oldbuck takes
his place as a pall-bearer and helps to carry the coffin to its grave.

It is a novel very different from the anti-Jacobin fictions of the 1790s, but
different from them principally because they present Jacobinism as a potent
threat whereas Scott represents it as not much different from all the other bogles,
brownies, and worricows with which the superstitious idly terrify themselves. It is
a picture of the decade that finds no room for Thomas Muir, Joseph Gerrald, and
the other Scottish Radicals transported to Botany Bay in those years. The war
that had so triumphantly concluded just a year before Scott published his novel
had proved their irrelevance. But Scott's novel is not simply retrospective. In
October 1816, just five months after its publication, a mass meeting of 40,000,
many of them unemployed textile workers, assembled at Thrushgrove outside
Glasgow to demand redress for their grievances. It was the beginning of the west
of Scotland radical movement. In *The Antiquary* Scott contrives to hold such a
movement up to ridicule even before it can be said properly to have begun.[33]

The Antiquary, like most of Scott's novels, is co-written by two authors, one of
whom rises serenely above party politics, while the other remains decidedly, even
extravagantly, partisan. Scott's more acute contemporaries recognized as much,
and their recognition was sharpened when such matters as Scott's association
with *The Beacon* became public knowledge. By 1824, in a notice of *Redgauntlet*
in the *New Monthly*, the reviewer identified a single plot that was repeated in all
of the novels, a plot designed 'to disgust the people with the turmoil inseparable

---

[33] Nicola J. Watson points out that 'the novel's virtuous beggar, the loyal king's-bedesman Edie
Ochiltree, is transparently a wish-fulfilling fiction produced in the face of the mass vagrancy
occasioned by the demobilisation of 1815, when starving, disaffected, unemployed, and begging
soldiers and sailors were flooding the countryside.' See *The Antiquary*, ed. Nicola J. Watson
(Oxford: Oxford University Press, 2002), xvi.

from the assertion of rights, and to recommend a political quietism, which leaves every thing to chance, and finds in every abuse its own compensation and cure'.[34] Similar suspicions explain why, in almost all his remarks about Scott, Hazlitt performs rapid pirouettes, twirling between admiration and contempt. When it seems to him that Scott 'sees fair play between Roundheads and Cavaliers, between Protestant and Papist', and does not 'enter into the distinctions of hostile sects or parties', Hazlitt recognizes him as Shakespeare's true heir, treating of 'the strength or the infirmity of the human mind, of the virtues and the vices of the human breast, as they are to be found blended in the whole race of mankind'. But in the very same paragraph Hazlitt splenetically asks, 'Is he infatuated enough, or does he so dote and drivel over his own slothful and self-willed prejudices, as to believe' that his novels will make 'a single convert to the beauty of Legitimacy, that is, of lawless power and savage bigotry?' In an effort to resolve the discrepancy Hazlitt is driven, like Lukacs after him, to the view that Scott is unaware of the purport of his own fiction, that he is 'besotted as to the moral of his own story',[35] but it would be more persuasive to claim that his stories very often have rival morals.

In *The Antiquary*, for example, the plot is familiar from many other novels. Scott's young hero believes himself to be illegitimate, and the young woman he loves knows that he will for this reason be unacceptable to her father. He discovers at the last that he is the legitimate heir of a Catholic peer, Lord Glenallan, and has the additional good fortune that his education had been supervised by Glenallan's brother, who had converted to Protestantism. Novel heroines are more often than novel heroes suspected of illegitimacy, but Scott has simply taken a plot familiar from novels by Ann Radcliffe, Frances Burney, and Charlotte Smith, and cross-dressed it. There is one slightly fresher addition. Glenallan's life has been soured because he has been misled by his mother into believing that his bride was the illegitimate daughter of his own father, so that his son was born of an incestuous union. As Fiona Robertson remarks, the son's recovery of his birthright reflects the restoration of legitimate monarchies all over Europe in the year before the novel's publication. But the restored heir has already proved himself by making a successful career in the army through the exercise of his own talent, and he has also changed his religion. For Robertson this signals Scott's attachment to a 'dynastic legitimacy' that is also both 'Protestant and progressive'. It is, she recognizes, an oddly paradoxical political ideal, that can best be embodied in a hero who, because he is 'brought up in ignorance of his own identity and heritage' can function at once as 'a legitimate representative' and as 'an ideological opponent of the dead past which he alone can

---

[34] *New Monthly Magazine*, 11 (July 1824), 94. The reviewer was T. N. Talfourd. Here and throughout contributors to the *New Monthly Magazine* are identified by reference to the *Wellesley Index to Victorian Periodicals, 1824–1900*, ed. Walter E. Houghton, Esther Roads Houghton, and Jean Slingerland, 5 vols. (Toronto, Ontario and London: University of Toronto Press and Routledge and Kegan Paul, 1966–89).

[35] *New Monthly Magazine*, 10 (April 1824), 203; Howe, 11, 65.

revitalize'.[36] So, when the young hero is restored to his birthright, the Catholic Earldom of Glenallan is secured, but it is secured when the heir is recognized to be a young man who is a Protestant and whose whole career underwrites the notion that the respect in which a person is held properly depends on merit rather than birth. Or, to put this another way, an effete, inbred aristocracy must be revitalized by the introduction of new blood, but the legitimacy of the new order will only be secured if after all it emerges that the new blood is in fact identical with the old.

This seems more like a self-contradictory position than a complex one, which perhaps helps to explain why the young hero of *The Antiquary*, like several other of Scott's young heroes, has a multiple rather than a single identity. When he first travels to Fairport, in forlorn pursuit of Isabella Wardour, he assumes the name of Mr Lovel (for obvious reasons a rather common name for the hero in sentimental fiction), but he is, in fact, an officer in the army on furlough, and in the regiment he styles himself Major Neville. He believes himself to be the natural son of Lord Glenallan's brother, Edward Geraldin Neville, although he is quite aware that he has 'no better right to the name of Neville, by which [he has] been generally distinguished, than to that of Lovel' (353). After Glenallan recognizes him as his son, he becomes Lord Geraldin, heir to his father's earldom. It is conventional enough, of course, for a hero or heroine to discover a lost name, but for Scott the device is particularly useful. His hero needs more than one name because he has more than one identity.

One of the novel's minor characters is Richard Taffril, a native of Fairport, who has risen to become a lieutenant in the navy, and is so clearly a gentleman that Lovel, when he is challenged by Captain M'Intyre, asks him to act as his second. The postmistress and her gossips are particularly excited when a letter arrives from the Lieutenant for Jennie Caxon, the wigmaker's daughter, because 'one report stated that Taffril had acknowledged a private marriage with Jenny Caxon—another that he had sent her a letter, upbraiding her with the lowness of her birth and education, and bidding her an eternal adieu' (114). Taffril remains true to Jennie, and the novel makes it clear that by virtue of his gallant service as an officer in the navy his title to be a gentleman is quite unaffected by his choice of bride. One reason that his fellow-officer, Major Neville, assumes the name of Lovel when he comes into the neighbourhood is that under the name of Neville he is rather well known. Sir Arthur Wardour is surprised that Oldbuck has never heard of him: "'O, Mr. Oldbuck,'" said Sir Arthur, "you must remember his name frequently in the newspapers—a very distinguished young officer indeed'" (340). When Neville marries his daughter, Sir Arthur learns, as Sir Walter Elliot learns in *Persuasion*, that in Britain at the end of the Napoleonic wars men of ability outrank men of birth. But this is a lesson that the novel contrives at once

---

[36] Fiona Robertson, *Legitimate Histories: Scott, Gothic and the Authorities of Fiction* (Oxford: Clarendon Press, 1994), 197–205.

to teach and not to teach, because, in the event, Isabella Wardour does not marry Major Neville but Lord Geraldin. Having several names can be very useful, as Scott, who wrote novels as 'the Author of Waverley', as Peter Pattieson, as Lawrence Templeton, as Chrystal Croftangry, and, at last, as Sir Walter Scott, was particularly well placed to understand. In this as in so much else Jonathan Oldbuck reveals his kinship with his creator. He explains to Lovel that his two essays in the Antiquarian Repository were the one 'signed *Scrutator*, and the other *Indagator*', and that for his essay in the *Gentleman's Magazine* he chose yet another pseudonym: it was 'subscribed Oedipus' (106).

In 1821 one of Scott's concealed identities came to light when he was revealed as a financial backer of *The Beacon*. In the *London Magazine*, John Scott was even more anxious to expose his relationship, through Lockhart, with *Blackwood's*. In his 'Second Statement', for example, John Scott compared Lockhart to Sir Richard Varney in Scott's recently published *Kenilworth*, a hit so telling that it was immediately taken up in *The Scotsman*.[37] Varney is the supreme villain of the novel, and the murderer of Amy Robsart. It is presumably his 'habitual expression of sneering sarcasm'[38] which makes him the fit counterpart of Lockhart, the Scorpion, but it is the unspoken implication that is the more damaging. The Earl of Leicester is the Queen's favourite and the people's darling, but his association with Varney results first in his corruption and then in his downfall. As Amy Robsart says, 'who would mention the illustrious Dudley as the accomplice of such a wretch as Varney?' (235). The clear implication is that the complicity between Walter Scott and Lockhart was just as surprising and might prove just as damaging.

As the novels followed one another so rapidly in the years following the publication of *Waverley*, readers gradually began to be increasingly suspicious that their author might occasionally 'throw in a touch of the times'. *The Abbot*, for example, was published on 2 September 1820, in the midst of the crisis prompted by Queen Caroline's return to England on her husband's accession to the throne. The treatment of Mary Queen of Scots in the novel raised the suspicion that an innuendo was intended against the wife of the new King: 'Some of the allusions to the charges brought against her have been strained to bear an intended reference to the inquiry which now attracts so large a share of public attention; and it does seem scarcely possible, that the author should not have foreseen that they would be so construed.'[39] *The Abbot* had been written in the months during which the whole of Britain was divided between those who supported the Regent who in January 1820, became George IV, and those

[37] *Second Statement by Mr John Scott in his Dispute with Mr John Gibson Lockhart* (London, 1821), 5; *The Scotsman*, no. 212, 10 February 1821, 46.
[38] Walter Scott, *Kenilworth*, ed. J. H. Alexander (Edinburgh: Edinburgh University Press, 1993), 391. Subsequent page references are included in the text.
[39] *London Magazine*, 2 (October 1820), 428. The review is by John Scott.

who supported the wife that George was desperate should not be crowned as his Queen. Scott's novel, which climaxes in Mary Stuart's defeat in the Battle of Langside, describes a Scotland divided between those who recognized Mary as sovereign, and those who recognized her infant son and the regency of the Earl of Murray. It is a Scotland in which every citizen, like Scott's hero Roland Graeme, must decide whether he is 'kingsman or queensman'[40] (181). In her imprisonment in Lochleven Mary amuses herself with a series of witty innuendoes aimed at the lady of the castle, the mother of the Regent through her liaison with Mary's father. This may seem unwise given the charges of 'murder and adultery', dismissed by her followers as 'foul and odious calumnies', that had been brought against Mary herself (203), and given that the novel was being written while George's wife, Caroline, was herself on trial for adultery before the House of Lords, reviewers might be forgiven for suspecting that it was not only Mary Queen of Scots who had a penchant for malicious gossip.

Lockhart's account of the Edinburgh Burns dinner reveals how important it was felt to be that the literary should be separated from the political. The Whig organizers disgraced themselves by failing to toast the Lake Poets, an omission that, Lockhart suggests, can be explained only as an entirely inappropriate expression of party feeling. Jeffrey was present at the dinner, and, according to *The Beacon*, Jeffrey had himself been largely responsible for the contamination of literature by politics. *The Beacon* quoted with approval an allegation made in the *New Times*:

The Edinburgh Review is 'a periodical political pamphlet', and assumes the garb of a literary work, perhaps allowably, but certainly with no other object than to infuse the more easily into the minds of its readers the political opinions to which it is devoted.[41]

It was not a complaint that was only made by Tories. For Hazlitt it was the Tories, aided and abetted by Walter Scott, who practised a 'nefarious and organized system of party-proscription, carried on under the mask of literary criticism'. The practice is so destructive because politics, as John Scott put it, concern only the 'living generation' whereas it is the defining quality of literature that it should provide 'lights for all time'.[42] This was the distinction that Hazlitt had in mind when he told Jeffrey, who had offered to introduce him to Scott, 'I should be willing to kneel to him, but I could not take him by the hand.'[43] The friendships that Scott studiously maintained with Jeffrey and with Byron were a true reflection of the anxiety of leading literary figures publicly to demonstrate

---

[40] Walter Scott, *The Abbot*, ed. Christopher Johnson (Edinburgh: Edinburgh University Press, 2000), 181. Subsequent page references are included in the text.

[41] *The Beacon*, 1 (6 January 1821), 5.

[42] Howe, 11, 68 (the passage is not included in the essay on Scott in Hazlitt's series 'The Spirits of the Age' in the *New Monthly Magazine*), and *London Magazine*, 2 (November 1820), 516.

[43] The comment is reported by P. G. Patmore, *My Friends and Acquaintances* (London: Saunders and Otley, 1854), 22.

their readiness to transcend political differences. It was an anxiety registered in the magazines, too. *Blackwood's*, for example, consistently pointed to its own willingness to recognize Shelley's talents (often pointedly contrasted with Jeffrey's refusal to notice him in the *Edinburgh*) as clinching evidence of its own ability to keep literary judgement independent of political opinion.[44] Reformist periodicals such as *The Scotsman* and the *London Magazine* vied with each other in the extravagance of the plaudits they offered Walter Scott in part, perhaps, as evidence that they could achieve a similar disinterestedness, and Tory journals were so ready to recognize Byron's genius, it may be, for the same reason.

The same principle seems to have informed literary production as well as reception. Lockhart pointed out, only half in jest, that 'it seems to be the rule that a literary man should publish with a bookseller attached to the opposite political party—a Tory with a Whig, and *vice versa*'.[45] He had principally in mind the two greatest literary men of the day, Byron published by the Tory John Murray, and Scott published by the Whig Archibald Constable. No doubt both arrangements were fortuitous. Scott felt free to make arrangements with other publishers, bringing out his second novel with Longman, and his fourth with William Blackwood, and Byron, in 1822, transferred his allegiance from Murray to Leigh Hunt's radical brother, John. And yet it is hard not to feel that the political differences that separated the writers from their publishers served a deeper purpose. At James Stuart's trial the judge praised the 'great good taste' shown by Stuart's defence counsel, Cockburn and Jeffrey, in confining their choice of character witnesses to 'gentlemen of opposite politics to the panel'.[46] By only inviting Tories to speak on Stuart's behalf, Cockburn and Jeffrey were enforcing a distinction between moral and political principle that was crucial to the defence that they were mounting. It may be that in choosing publishers 'of opposite politics', Scott and Byron, whether by accident or design, were upholding a similar distinction between literary and political principle. The attacks on Byron's politics, as opposed to his profligacy, were oddly muted even in Tory reviews until rather late in his career. *Cain* came out under Murray's imprint, but Byron was already associated with the Hunts in *The Liberal*, and it is surely not a coincidence that it was only at this juncture that the *British Critic* was moved to wonderment: 'It is a marvellous thing indeed, that a Peer of England, the first of nations upon earth, should wish for a revolution which would dash him into the

[44] This is more questionable than it might seem, because, as Charles Robinson has argued, it is possible to explain the surprisingly favourable reviews of Shelley by reference not to Lockhart's disinterest but to Blackwood's partnership with Shelley's publisher, Charles Ollier. See Charles E. Robinson, 'Percy Bysshe Shelley, Charles Ollier, and William Blackwood', in *Shelley Revalued: Essays from the Gregynog Conference* (Leicester: Leicester University Press, 1983), 183–226. In the same way, Byron was so favourably reviewed in the Tory *Quarterly*, surely because its owner, John Murray, was Byron's publisher.

[45] *Blackwood's Edinburgh Magazine*, 17 (February 1825), 132 (footnote).

[46] *A full report of the trial of James Stuart, Esq. younger of Dunearn, before the High Court of Justiciary*, 10 June 1822 (Edinburgh: 1822), 83.

dirt; so is it marvellous that he should hate his own native land, fly from the sight of his fellow countrymen, and permit the dregs of London only to call him friend.'[47] In its notice of the first instalment of *Don Juan*, *Blackwood's* carefully distinguished between the poem's literary and moral character: the 'moral strain of the poem' may be 'pitched in the lowest key', but it remains the case that 'Lord Byron has never written any thing more decisively and triumphantly expressive of the greatness of his genius.' But such distinctions could not survive Byron's change of publishers, and Cantos VI–VII were received very differently: 'Alas! that one so gifted . . . should descend to the composition of heartless, heavy, dull, anti-British garbage, to be printed by the Cockneys, and puffed in the Examin-er.—Alas! alas! that he should stoop to the miserable degradation of being extolled by Hunt.'[48] It is as if it was a poem's imprint rather than its content that determined its political character. But it was not just that.

On the one hand there was the pressure to distinguish between literature and politics, on the other there was a pressure to distinguish between one kind of politics and another. The Whig organizers of the Burns dinner threatened the former distinction by refusing to toast Wordsworth, and at the Pitt dinner Walter Scott refused the latter when he emerged from the inner room and joined the young Tories gathered in the outer. In the inner room Edinburgh's Tory leadership shared a dignified intimacy that, on other occasions, might readily be extended to Whigs. No doubt most of those in the inner room, like Walter Scott, numbered Francis Jeffrey amongst their friends. Lords Liverpool and Holland, Scott assures us, thinking sadly of the death of Alexander Boswell, would happily accompany each other to the opera, and Scott and Jeffrey would have done the same, showing that, although they differed in politics, they continued to share a social code, an ideal of gentlemanly behaviour. But the young men in the outer room vented their high spirits in coarse lampoons on their political adversaries that precluded the possibility that they might mix elsewhere on friendly terms:

> There's stot-feeder Stuart,
> Kent for that fat cow-art,
> How glegly he kicks any ba' man.

When Walter Scott went to sit in the outer room he threatened a distinction Byron recognized well enough. Byron responded with horror to the Cato Street Conspiracy in part because the Tory cabinet that the conspirators planned to assassinate included those that Byron thought of as friends: 'And if they had killed poor Harrowby—in whose house I have been five hundred times—at dinners and parties—his wife is one of "the Exquisites"—and t'other fellows what end would it have answered?'[49] His friend John Cam Hobhouse threatened

[47] *British Critic*, second series, 17 (May 1822), 538.
[48] *Blackwood's Edinburgh Magazine*, 5 (August 1819), 512–13; and 14 (July 1823), 88.
[49] *Byron's Letters and Journals*, ed. Leslie A. Marchand, 7 (London: John Murray, 1977), 62.

the same distinction less violently when he attended the dinner to congratulate 'Orator' Hunt on his return to London after Peterloo. Byron, as he put it in the Dedication to *Don Juan*, still retained his 'buff and blue'. He was a friend to reform, but allied himself only with 'the genteel part of the reformers'.[50] Hobhouse, on the other hand, had parted company with the Whigs, and showed himself ready to mix socially with those such as Henry Hunt considered by Byron to be 'blackguards'. He responded with a squib that wounded Hobhouse when Murray had it placed in the *Morning Post*, just before Hobhouse stood for election to one of the Westminster seats, as the comment of 'a noble poet . . . on his *quondam friend* and annotator':[51]

> Who are now the people's men,
> My boy Hobbie O?
> There's I and Burdett—Gentlemen
> And blackguard Hunt and Cobby O.

By taking his place with Hunt and Cobbett rather than Byron and Sir Francis Burdett Hobhouse had passed from one room to another. Byron was to do the same when he parted company with John Murray and set up with John Hunt.

The division between the two rooms was mirrored in the periodical market. The inner room was occupied by the great reviews, the *Edinburgh* and *Quarterly*, both of which claimed a dignity to which the monthly magazines such as *Blackwood's*, the *London*, and the *New Monthly* were not admitted, still less weeklies such as *The Examiner*, *The Beacon*, and *The Sentinel*. While John Scott lay dying at the Chalk Farm Tavern, Walter Scott wrote to his son-in-law offering fatherly advice: 'You have now the best possible opportunity to break off with the Magazine, which will otherwise remain a snare and temptation to your love of satire and I must needs say that you will not have public feeling nor the regard of your friends with you should you be speedily the hero of such another scene.'[52] He urged Lockhart to break with *Blackwood's* in order to safeguard his reputation. But the distinction that Scott appealed to between respectable and disreputable publications was much less stable than he implied, a fact of which Scott, who was at once a founder of the *Quarterly*, a contributor to *Blackwood's*, and a co-signator of the bond insuring *The Beacon* against loss,

---

[50] *Byron's Letters and Journals*, 7, 44.
[51] See *Byron's Bulldog: The Letters of John Cam Hobhouse to Lord Byron*, ed. Peter W. Graham (Columbus, Ohio: Ohio University Press, 1984), 290–3. Byron's defence, that he had intended Murray to show the squib only to Hobhouse, is disingenuous. The satirical verses that he was in the habit of enclosing in his letters to Murray were Byron's means of commenting on topical matters and were clearly intended for circulation. Hobhouse's relationship with Byron was a matter of political importance. In his first attempt to win the Westminster seat he had been attacked for his association with the licentious poet. To be publicly disowned by that same poet during the second campaign must have been irksome. For an interesting discussion of this, see John Gardner, 'Hobhouse, Cato Street, and *Marino Faliero*', *Byron Journal*, 31 (2003), 23–37.
[52] *The Letters of Sir Walter Scott*, 6, 363.

should have been only too aware. It was not only Lady Morgan who felt that Croker's abusive review of her *France* eliminated any distinction between the *Quarterly* and *Blackwood's* (her poem *The Mohawks* echoes in its title John Scott's attack on *Blackwood's* as 'The Mohock Magazine').[53] Southey, the *Quarterly's* most prolific contributor agreed with her. He protested loudly against the rumour that he was himself responsible for the review: 'I would rather have cut off my right hand than have written anything so unmanly and disagreeable as that criticism.'[54]

It proved equally difficult to maintain a firm distinction between literature and politics. In his Preface to the *New Monthly Magazine*, Thomas Campbell argued that it does not follow from 'the general utility of political discussion, that it should invariably pervade every species of literary compilation, or that there should be no calm spot in the world of periodical literature where all minds of common charity and candour may meet without the asperities of party feeling'. His own journal would therefore be 'literary and not political'.[55] It was a principle that he took very far. When a scheme to establish a Royal Society for Literature was published, the magazine opposed it, because, it argued, it was inevitable that in such a body literary judgement would be subordinated to political judgement, and only those writers prepared to give their support to the government be rewarded.[56] But Campbell's distrust of faction was less a repudiation of party politics than an indication of the particular party to which his magazine lent its support. As Nanora Sweet has argued, Campbell's claim to be apolitical masked his formation, with his proprietor Colburn, and his radical sub-editor Cyrus Redding, of a coalition, liberal in its political character, which expressed itself most comfortably in support for the similar coalition of moderate Tories and liberals headed by George Canning.[57] John Scott, by contrast, pooh-poohed his publisher's advice that he should keep the *London Magazine* free from politics: 'If it were said that a Literary work has nothing to do with Politics,—the answer would be, that a Magazine has much to do with Politics—that English Literature is closely connected with Politics—as are English trade, English amusements, Manners, thought, and happiness.'[58]

[53] *London Magazine*, 2 (December 1820), 666–85.
[54] *Selections from the Letters of Robert Southey*, ed. J. W. Warter, 4 vols. (London: Longman, 1856), 3, 79.
[55] *New Monthly Magazine*, 1, v–vi. Such magazine prefaces were usually written, as Campbell notes, 'at the close of a year's labour' (iii) and inserted in the bound volume.
[56] See 'New Society of Literature', *New Monthly Magazine*, 8 (August 1823), 97–104. The piece was written by Cyrus Redding.
[57] Nanora Sweet, 'The *New Monthly Magazine* and the Liberalism of the 1820s', in *Romantic Periodicals and Print Culture*, ed. Kim Wheatley (London and Portland, Oregon: Frank Cass, 2002), 147–62.
[58] From a letter by John Scott to the proprietor of the *London*, Robert Baldwin, quoted by Mark Parker, *Literary Magazines and British Romanticism* (Cambridge: Cambridge University Press, 2000), 35.

Campbell insists on separating literature and politics because he is concerned at the danger that literary judgement might become merely an indirect expression of political sympathy, and it is an anxiety that many of his contemporaries shared, but it was the alternative possibility countenanced by John Scott, that politics might be subsumed into literature, that proved the more dangerous.

It was predictable that James Stuart should have found Boswell's 'Whig Song' peculiarly offensive. The charge of cowardice stung more when written out in verse, just as Byron's comments on his separation from his wife provoked more outrage when they were delivered in rhyme. It was the collapse of generic boundaries that generated so much heat. John Scott's attacks on *Blackwood's* constituted a back-handed compliment, modelled as they clearly were on the series of articles that Lockhart contributed to *Blackwood's* on 'The Cockney School of Poetry'. John Scott christened *Blackwood's* 'the *Reekie Magazine*': its attacks on the Cockneys exemplified the '*reeky* school of reviewing'.[59] John Scott was retaliating in kind, but also attempting to repeat the achievement of *Blackwood's* in building its commercial success on the notoriety it earned by the Cockney School articles, and by the pieces furiously assailing Wordsworth and Coleridge that accompanied them. 'Wordsworth', Scott complains, 'has been outrageously vilified, and zealously defended by the same individual' (John Scott seems mistakenly to have believed that the pieces in question were written by Lockhart rather than John Wilson). Oddly, in the very same edition of the *London* Scott had included the paper, 'Christ's Hospital Five and Thirty Years Ago', in which Elia refutes the 'magnificent eulogy' of his old school that 'Mr Lamb' had reprinted in his '"Works", published a year or two since'.[60] For Scott, of course, Lamb's duplicity was quite innocent, a playfulness entirely appropriate in a literary paper. But *Blackwood's*—and it was one of its most daring innovations—refused to maintain clear distinctions between literary papers and papers that were critical or political. In his 'Cockney School' articles Lockhart reinvents criticism as a kind of poetry, a variety of flyting, a literary kind closely associated with Scotland (see 'The Flyting of Dunbar and Kennedie'), that contrives to exhilarate through the intensity and the ingenuity of the insults to which it subjects its victims. As the *Blackwood's* writers knew, and as John Scott knew well enough when he dismissed Baldwin's suggestion that he keep the *London* free from politics, the new magazines had made their established rivals such as the *Gentleman's* seem so old-fashioned precisely by refusing to maintain clear distinctions between material of different kinds. But when politics, criticism, and literature were allowed to converge the effects were unpredictable, and might even, as in John Scott's case, prove fatal.

At the Edinburgh Burns dinner in 1819, in Lockhart's account of it, party feeling was disgracefully allowed to inform an occasion that ought to have

---

[59] 'The Lion's Head', *London Magazine*, 11 (November 1820), 476.
[60] *London Magazine*, 11 (November 1820), 512 and 483.

remained purely literary. At the Pitt dinner two years later, Walter Scott, by leaving his peers and going to join the younger men in the outer room, threatened the distinction between dignified and scandalous expression of political opinion. The two dinners are true emblems of the literary culture of a post-war decade that was peculiarly volatile precisely because it failed to maintain that careful separation between respectable and unrespectable opinion, and between literature and politics that allowed those who differed in their politics, or who were divided in their literary tastes, to maintain the cordial social relations that Lord Liverpool maintained with Lord Holland, and Francis Jeffrey kept up with Walter Scott.

3

Personalities

The Scott and the Boswell duels both pitted Whig against Tory, and in both cases the immediate provocation was not political difference in itself, but rather the rhetoric in which that difference was expressed. The Whig press all through these years charged the Tory press with contaminating political life by introducing into political discussion 'personalities', that is, attacks on the personal appearance and the private lives of political opponents, attacks on, as it may be, Hazlitt for having pimples or on Leigh Hunt as a man unnaturally fond of his sister-in-law. John Scott's death, it seemed to J. R. McCulloch in *The Scotsman*, was a direct and predictable consequence of this unfortunate innovation: 'It is nearly three years since it was prophesied that the "ordinary business of life could not proceed if it became general"':

we should have nothing but a perpetual round of cudgelling, duelling, and stabbing, if every weak, odd, or even vicious *private act* of every individual were to be published, with all the circumstances of name, time, and place, for the general amusement.[1]

The Tory press retorted that it was a practice that had been instituted by Whigs. Theodore Hook, for example, editor of *John Bull*, claimed that he was guiltless in comparison with Thomas Moore: 'Let any man take up either of these works, the *Twopenny Post Bag*, or the *Fudge Family*, and read it, and then say whether in JOHN BULL from the first hour of its establishment to this moment, there has ever appeared in its pages articles so grossly personal or so shamefully scandalous, as the libels which appeared in those *classics* of the opposition:—the truth is, we have taken them at their own weapons, and beat them at them—and they are savage: this is the greatest compliment they can pay us'.[2]

It was a practice most closely associated with the periodical press, but not confined to it. Benjamin Haydon, for example, was convicted by John Scott in the *London* of an outrageous 'personality' in an epic painting when he introduced the head of the sceptic Voltaire looking sardonically over Wordsworth's piously bowed left shoulder in his 'Christ's Entry into Jerusalem': 'In this age of personalities, this is positively the worst personality we have yet witnessed, for it has the treble bad effect of injuring the effect of the composition as a piece of

---

[1] *The Scotsman*, no. 214, 24 February 1821, 62.
[2] *John Bull*, no. 22, 17 May 1821, 173.

art; of providing a ready substitute for want of skill in the artist, who has only to copy a portrait when he cannot imagine a head; and, of forming a precedent for the most scandalous violations of decency.'[3] Jeffrey in the *Edinburgh Review* claimed that it was Byron in *Don Juan* who must bear the chief responsibility for popularizing the practice:

> If his Lordship's sense of propriety does not cure him of this propensity, we hope his pride may. For the practice has gone down to such imitators, as can do him no honour in pointing to him as their original. We rather think it would be better, after all, to be called the founder of the Satanic School, than the Master of the John Bulls, Beacons, and Sentinels.[4]

The surprising omission from the list is *Blackwood's*, but this, I suspect, is simply a measure of Jeffrey's disinclination even to allow the magazine's name to appear within the pages of his own journal. It did not prevent *Blackwood's* from responding to the charge. In the episode of the *Noctes Ambrosianae* for May 1822, Dr Wodrow begins the discussion by saying how pleased he had been by Jeffrey's attack on Byron:

> Well, now, I must say that I read that passage with delight: there is no doubt that Lord Byron is very much to blame, if it really be so, which I am no judge of, that he was the first who wrote in a personal manner. It was introducing a dangerous—a deadly trick. There's no saying where it may end yet. Christian folk should dwell together like brethren in unity.—Oh! sirs, there's a deal of needless heart-burning and hot water among you literary folk of this time, take ye my word for that.

Sir Andrew Wylie is more sceptical—'Does Mr Jeffrey really charge Lord Byron with being the author and instigator of the sin of personality?'—and Pen Owen returns the charge against Jeffrey himself: 'Has he forgot how he lashed his friend TOMMY MOORE? Was it no *Personality* that pointed the path to Chalk Farm?'[5]

The dispute about who had begun the practice sometimes widens to become a long history of 'personality'. Most commonly, a precedent was sought in the writers of the Restoration and early eighteenth century, in Pope's *Dunciad*, or in Dryden's *Absalom and Achitophel*, 'every verse of which is a drop of the genuine aquafortis of personality'.[6] But perspectives are sometimes much longer. It may have been a device that passed down to Milton, Dryden, Butler, Swift, Pope, and Arbuthnot, but, Christopher North claims, it passed down to them from Aristophanes, Horace, and Cicero.[7] In such readings the history of personality

---

[3] *London Magazine*, 1 (May 1820), 585–6.
[4] *Edinburgh Review*, 36 (February 1822), 452.
[5] *Blackwood's Edinburgh Magazine*, 11 (May 1822), 601–18, 608. This, the third episode of the *Noctes*, was supplied by Lockhart. Chalk Farm was the site of Moore's aborted duel with Francis Jeffrey, for a full discussion of which see the Conclusion to this book. Sir Andrew Wylie and Pen Owen are the eponymous heroes of novels by John Galt and James Hook. They owe their appearances in the *Noctes* to the fact that both novels were published by Blackwood.
[6] *Blackwood's Edinburgh Magazine*, 10 (October 1821), 312.
[7] *Blackwood's Edinburgh Magazine*, 11 (May 1822), 612.

becomes identical with the history of satire, but that still left the problem of how personality was to be defined. When Pen Owen is asked what is meant by the term he is puzzled:

I don't know—I can't well say. I suppose Jeffrey means, when he accuses Lord Byron of it, to allude to his cuts at Coleridge, and Southey, and Sotheby, and Wordsworth, and Bowles, and Sam Rogers, and the King, and so forth.[8]

But not all 'cuts' counted as 'personalities'. Jeffrey, after all, had allowed Byron's right to take a cut at Southey:

We have already noticed the ferocity of his attack on Mr Southey. The Laureate had railed at him indeed before; but he had railed 'in good set terms';—and, if we recollect right, had not even mentioned his Lordship's name. It was all, in his exquisite way, by innuendo. In spite of this, we do not mean to deny that Lord B. had a right to name Mr Southey—but he had no right to say any thing of Mr Southey's wife; and the mention of her, and of many other people, is cruel, and unhandsome.[9]

Naming was, in itself, a sensitive matter, even for politically active men such as the Edinburgh Whigs, James Gibson and James Stuart, whose 'names', as *The Scotsman* complained, 'have been hawked about the streets in the doggerel verse of Tory libellists and defamers'.[10] Before he accepted Lockhart's challenge, John Scott required that Lockhart should prove that he was 'a gentleman assailed in his honourable feelings by an indecent use of his name in print' rather than a '*professional scandal-monger*'.[11] John Murray, complaining that Leigh Hunt had 'had the baseness to enter upon a Series of Abuse of me', objected that Hunt's behaviour was inappropriate because Murray 'never did give [his] name to the Public, except in a business advertisement'.[12] His name remained private, it seems, even though it was also the name of his publishing firm. It was common to object to the public use of a name almost as if one's name was an aspect of a private self that is defiled by being printed and published to the world, which is why naming is so central to the notion of 'personalities'. As Peter Murphy notes, the objection to 'personality' is a way of 'insisting on privacy: persons have a part that is theirs alone, and decency requires that we leave personalities to their owners'.[13] But this view was rapidly being supplanted by a new understanding

---

[8] *Blackwood's Edinburgh Magazine*, 11 (May 1822), 609.

[9] *Edinburgh Review*, 36 (February 1822), 452. In the preface to his *Vision of Judgement* (1821) Southey had denounced those responsible for the establishment of a 'Satanic school' of English poets for polluting English poetry with 'monstrous combinations of horrors and mockery, lewdness and impiety'. He clearly has chiefly in mind Byron and *Don Juan*, but neither is directly named. Byron retaliated in an appendix to *The Two Foscari*.

[10] *The Scotsman*, no. 208, 13 January 1821, 17–18.

[11] *Statement, etc. by Mr John Scott in his dispute with Mr John Gibson Lockhart* (London: 1821), 3.

[12] *The Letters of John Murray to Lord Byron*, ed. Andrew Nicholson (Liverpool: Liverpool University Press, 2007), 229.

[13] Peter Murphy, 'Impersonation and Authorship in Romantic Britain', *English Literary History*, 59 (1992), 625–49, 631–2.

that a name was what marked and secured a professional identity. Hence both *Blackwood's* defence of its own practice of referring by name to its antagonists, and the impish manner in which the defence was couched: 'We maintain, then, that unless in cases of horrific, or repulsive, or ludicrous names, such as have a tendency to render their owners either objects of fear, disgust, or laughter—there is no guilt in mentioning an individual either by Christian or surname—and it is a practice to which we mean rigidly to adhere.'[14] Jeffrey accepts the point. If Southey conducted his assault on Byron without once mentioning 'his Lordship's name', this was just an example of Southey's 'exquisite way'. Since there was no doubt that Byron was Southey's target there was no reason at all why Byron should not 'name Mr Southey' in his retaliation. The real distinction is between Byron's references to Southey and his references to Southey's wife. Edith Southey's sex, one feels, counts for something, but the crucial difference is that Southey and Byron both inhabit a public arena whereas Southey's wife occupies an entirely private station, which should protect her from Byron's revealing to all his readers that, before they married Coleridge and Southey, she and her sister had been 'milliners of Bath' (*Don Juan*, 3, 93, 8).

Distinguishing between the public and the private components of a single individual might be a good deal trickier. *The Scotsman* confidently protested its innocence: 'from first to last we have deprecated and avoided personalities, that is, attacks upon individuals on account of personal appearance, or of conduct, habits, connexions, or circumstances, affecting private life'.[15] But its condemnations of those guilty of the practice come very close to constituting personalities in their own right, as when John Wilson is denounced as a '*Convicted slanderer*', a 'libeller' who had 'assailed the character of the late Mr Playfair with a rancour and malignity unparalleled in the annals of literature'.[16] Nor is it always easy to distinguish between public and private life. In a politician, for example, one might reasonably insist on the necessary 'connexion between private character and public conduct':[17] truthfulness, to offer just one instance, is a virtue that seems to span the two. The distinction might seem easier to make in the case of writers, whose public life extends no further than their publications. In fact, it remained problematic. As Lockhart pointed out when reflecting on Byron's career, a writer's 'personal character' is a composite, made up of 'two widely different matters' which are 'generally, we might say universally, mixed up here—the personal character of the man as proved by his course of life, and his

---

[14] *Blackwood's Edinburgh Magazine*, 8 (October 1820), 100/104. The pagination is faulty at this point.

[15] *The Scotsman*, no. 227, 13 October 1821, 321.

[16] *The Scotsman*, no. 156, 10 June 1820, 189. John Playfair, who had died in 1819, had been Professor of Natural Philosophy at Edinburgh University, and a chief target for *Blackwood's* because he was, together with Dugald Stewart, the leading Whig in the Edinburgh professoriate and as a frequent contributor to the *Edinburgh Review*.

[17] *The Sentinel*, no. 27, 10 April 1822, 209.

personal character as revealed in, or guessed from, his books'. Although it would be 'absurd' to claim that there is no connection between the man and the author, the conflation of the two is unwarranted and has been particularly damaging in Byron's case. It has produced a vicious circle in which 'the poet damns the man, and the man the poet'.[18] But in the case of Byron, it was rather generally agreed, man and poet were especially hard to distinguish, and it was this more than any exclusively literary quality that had made him the most popular poet of the day.

The literary form that takes the relationship between authors and persons as its special topic is literary biography. Lockhart was himself to become a celebrated practitioner of the form, but, for the very reason that he pointed out himself, that it was a form that tended to assume the identity of the man and the author, it was controversial.[19] In 1791 Boswell's *Life of Johnson* had radically transformed the character of the genre by exploiting so fully Boswell's records of Johnson's private conversations. In a review of Spence's *Anecdotes* Isaac D'Israeli pointed out that collections of anecdotes, or 'anas' [the term derives from the suffix in expressions such as 'Burnsiana'], had been more popular with the French than the English until all earlier examples were 'eclipsed by the singular splendour of Boswell's Johnson'. It was, as Southey put it, 'the *Ana* of all *Anas*'.[20] But Boswell's achievement was not welcomed by everyone. Wordsworth, for example, in his 'Letter to a Friend of Robert Burns', regretted that Boswell had 'broken through many pre-existing delicacies, and afforded the British public an opportunity of acquiring experience, which before it had happily wanted'.[21] Lockhart, too, ironically, since in his life of his father-in-law, Walter Scott, he was to establish himself as Boswell's only serious rival as the great British biographer, spoke of the life of Johnson as constituting something like tasting the fruit of the tree of knowledge: 'the evil, if evil it were, was done, and could not be repaired'.[22] It was Boswell who had licensed 'the coarse intrusions into the recesses, the gross breaches upon the sanctities, of domestic life'[23] perpetrated by the biographers who succeeded him. After Boswell no aspect of a subject's life was safe from biographical scrutiny. Boswell included, for example, a story derived from Garrick of how, when Johnson kept a school, his pupils would 'listen at the door of his bed-chamber, and peep

[18] *Blackwood's Edinburgh Magazine*, 17 (February 1825), 133.
[19] For an informed and shrewd account of literary biography and its discussion in the period, and of Lockhart in particular, see Francis R. Hart, *Lockhart as Romantic Biographer* (Edinburgh: Edinburgh University Press, 1971), especially 1–45. See also Annette Wheeler Cafarelli, *Prose in the Age of Poets: Romanticism and Biographical Narrative from Johnson to De Quincey* (Philadelphia: University of Pennsylvania Press, 1990), *Romantic Biography*, ed. Arthur Bradley and Alan Rawes (Aldershot: Ashgate, 2003), and David Higgins, *Romantic Genius and the Literary Magazine: Biography, Celebrity, Politics* (London and New York: Routledge, 2005), 46–89.
[20] *Quarterly Review*, 23 (July 1820), 400–34, 402; Robert Southey, *The Doctor* (London: Longman, Brown, Green and Longmans, 1849), 627.
[21] *Prose Works of William Wordsworth*, ed. W. J. B. Owen and Jane Worthington Smyser, 3 vols. (Oxford: Clarendon Press, 1974), 3, 120.
[22] *Quarterly Review*, 46 (November 1831), 18.
[23] *Prose Works of William Wordsworth*, 3, 122.

through the key-hole, that they might turn into ridicule his tumultuous and awkward fondness' for his wife, Tetty.[24] After Boswell, biographers, like Johnson's pupils, felt free to peep through whatever keyholes they could find into the bedrooms of their subjects.

The debate focused on biographies of Burns and Pope. Burns's biographer, James Currie, had seen fit to chronicle rather fully Burns's decline into alcoholism as well as intimating more indirectly his lapses from strict chastity. Bowles, in the life prefixed to his edition of Pope, speculated about the precise nature of Pope's relationship with Martha Blount. Undergarments came to feature prominently in biographical discussion, and again it was Boswell who had given the lead. Johnson, Boswell reports, forswore his visits to the Green Room of Drury Lane because he found that 'the silk stockings and white bosoms' of the actresses excited his 'amorous propensities'.[25] According to Maria Edgeworth, the attraction of biography was precisely the promise it offered of allowing the reader to glimpse 'great minds in undress'.[26] After all, Johnson had himself located the peculiar value of biography in the access it gave to the great 'in their private apartments, in their careless hours',[27] where we are allowed, as in his 'Life of Pope', to see such things as the poet's legs—so thin that he wore three pairs of stockings which, such was his debility, had to be pulled on and off by his maid.[28] The biographical promise to reveal the great 'in undress' was, as in this instance, often fulfilled literally. Bowles offered as evidence of Pope's licentiousness a letter to Lady Mary Wortley Montague in which Pope suggested that, since he was travelling abroad, they might write to each other with less restraint: 'Let us be like *modest* people, who, when they are close together, keep all *decorum*; but if they step a little aside, or get to the other end of a room, can *untie garters,* or TAKE OFF SHIFTS, without scruple.' To his rival editor, William Roscoe's, objection that 'the *nakedness* to which Pope there alludes' has reference 'not to the body, but to the mind', Bowles retorted that Pope's expression constituted 'a disgusting equivoque, of which he was conscious'.[29]

Of course, such charges were apt to rebound against the accuser. As Octavius Gilchrist noted in the *London Magazine*, in detecting Pope's licentiousness, Bowles revealed his own prurience:

---

[24] *Boswell's Life of Johnson*, ed. G. B. Hill, revised L. F. Powell, 3 vols. (Oxford: Clarendon Press, 1934–50), 1, 98.

[25] *Boswell's Life of Johnson*, 1, 201.

[26] Quoted in Francis R. Hart, *Lockhart as Romantic Biographer*, 36. Edgeworth went on to note the possibility that the publication of letters may allow us to see 'minds like Byron's' only 'in prepared undress'.

[27] In Johnson's 'Review of the Memoirs of the Duchess Dowager of Marlborough', *Samuel Johnson: The Major Works*, ed. Donald Greene (Oxford: Oxford University Press, 2000), 114.

[28] Samuel Johnson, *Lives of the English Poets*, ed. Roger Lonsdale, 4 vols. (Oxford: Clarendon Press, 2006), 4, 55.

[29] William Lisle Bowles, *The Invariable Principles of Poetry* (London: Longman, Hurst, Rees, Orme and Brown, 1819), 9–10, and 2.

the inquisition which he has instituted into the poet's attachment to Martha Blount, is eminently his own; and though the pruriency with which his nose is laid to the ground, to scent some taint in their connexion, and the anatomical minuteness with which he examines and determines on the physical constitution of Pope, might, in charity, be deemed only unseemly or unbecoming in a layman, and occasional critic,—in an editor and a clergyman such conduct appears to us indecent and insufferably disgusting.[30]

To Bowles, predictably, it was Gilchrist's choice of metaphor that was insufferably disgusting. There is no end to such disputes because it is scarcely possible to document a charge of obscenity without repeating the offence. But there were more serious issues at stake.

Poets were often suspicious of biography, anxious, perhaps, that biography might serve to make of the poet's life, to adapt Wordsworth's metaphor, 'the gothic church' in which the poems are accommodated as so many subsidiary chapels, with the inevitable result that the poet is supplanted by the biographer as the principal architect of the entire oeuvre.[31] John Hamilton Reynolds shrewdly suggested that there was a natural war between the 'children of genius' and 'the malice of a biographer', though he made the point, it has to be admitted, in the course of a biographical sketch of the actor, John Kemble.[32] In his *Letter to a Friend of Robert Burns* Wordsworth looked back fondly to a time when a writer was a private person. He could see 'no cause why the lives of that class of men should be pried into with the same diligent curiosity, and laid open with the same disregard of reserve, which may sometimes be expedient in composing the history of men who have borne an active part in the world'. The 'private lives' of public men might help to explain their 'public conduct', but this was not the case with writers in general, and with poets in particular: 'of poets more especially, it is true—that, if their works be good, they contain within themselves all that is necessary to their being comprehended and relished'.[33] Shelley insisted on a still more decisive separation between the man and the poet. Evidence that 'Homer was a drunkard, that Virgil was a flatterer, that Horace was a coward, that Tasso was a madman, that Lord Bacon was a peculator, that Raphael was a libertine' and 'that Spenser was a poet laureate' (he resists the temptation to 'cite living poets') would not threaten his conviction that the poet 'inasmuch as he is a poet' is 'the wisest, the happiest, and the best' of men.[34] Keats, still more radically,

---

[30] *London Magazine*, 1 (February 1820), 193–4.

[31] A position taken to its logical conclusion by Carlyle when he asserts that Burns's writings afford only 'brief broken glimpses of a genius that could never show itself complete'. Hence it is 'not chiefly as a poet, but as a man, that he interests and affects us'. Burns is best known, it follows, not by readers of his poems but of his biography, in this case Lockhart's. See *The Works of Thomas Carlyle*, 29 vols. (London: Chapman and Hall, 1896–9), 26, 266 and 264.

[32] *London Magazine*, 7 (April 1823), 450.

[33] *Prose Works of William Wordsworth*, 3, 122.

[34] *Shelley's Poetry and Prose*, ed. Donald H. Reiman and Neil Fraistat (New York: Norton, 2002), 533–4.

claimed that the poet, at any rate the kind of poet that he aspired to be, was distinguished by having 'no self', 'no identity', 'no nature'. But even Keats accepted that there was another kind of poet who had a rather emphatic sense of his own identity: he distinguishes the poetical character that he takes to himself from 'the wordsworthian or egotistical sublime; which is a thing per se and stands alone'.[35] Wordsworth was himself ready to admit that, although it was of 'comparatively little importance' to their rank as poets whether Homer, Virgil and Shakespeare were 'good or bad men', 'far otherwise is it with that class of poets, the principal charm of whose writings depends upon the familiar knowledge which they convey of the personal feelings of their authors'. Wordsworth does not say whether he places his own poems in this category, but it is 'eminently the case with the effusions of Burns'.[36]

It was not clear, then, whether or not the character of the poet was relevant to the character of the poems, and it was equally unclear what evidence as to the character of the poet was admissible. When Wordsworth recalled 'the black things which have been written' of Burns 'and the frightful ones that have been insinuated against him', he was inclined to think that the best policy might be 'explicitly to declare to what degree Robert Burns had given way to pernicious habits, and, as nearly as may be, to fix the point to which his moral character had been degraded'.[37] An *Edinburgh* reviewer made a similar point when he remarked, 'Surely society is entitled, on occasions like the life of Burns and Byron—if to any thing—to the *truth*, and to that most solemn of all warnings which the errors of genius convey.'[38] The lives of writers such as this are, it seems, themselves exemplary texts of greater authority than any poem that they may have written.

The thought would seem to underwrite a policy of full disclosure, but not everyone agreed. D'Israeli, for example, objected to editors such as Bowles who 'gratify their own pruriency, or that of those who buy their books, by reviving pieces written in the levity of youth or exuberance of wit, but suppressed in maturer age and by improved judgement' and who make available to the public 'the productions of inconsiderate gaiety, never meant for indiscriminate perusal'.[39] He is equally uncertain whether biographers should permit themselves 'the liberty of chronicling conversations, or perpetuating domestic incidents', and doubts whether things spoken while the bottle circulates, 'our unpremeditated thoughts, our negligent assertions, and our playful deceptions, the mere odds and ends of our fancy, all our humours, good and evil' ought to be 'permanently

---

[35] *The Letters of John Keats*, ed. Hyder Edward Rollins, 2 vols. (Cambridge: Cambridge University Press, 1958), 1, 387.
[36] *Prose Works of William Wordsworth*, 3, 123.
[37] *Prose Works of William Wordsworth*, 3, 118.
[38] *Edinburgh Review*, 55 (January 1832), 141.
[39] *Quarterly Review*, 32 (October 1825), 273–4.

recorded'.[40] The argument could be taken further. Walter Scott approved of Currie's exclusion from his edition of Burns of 'every thing approaching to licence, whether in morals or in religion', so that the poet's works in Currie's edition of them approached a form 'such as doubtless Burns himself, in his moments of sober reflection, would have most highly approved'.[41] It was the editor's business, it seems, to present a writer not as he was but as he would like to have been.

The view shared by Scott and D'Israeli seems founded on the old-fashioned notion that the self was consciously fashioned by the individual, so that an editor should present a writer's life, in exactly the same way as he should present the writings, in the form that corresponded as nearly as possible to the writer's best intentions. Bowles was so anxious to demonstrate that Pope had himself tricked Curl into publishing his correspondence because, if this were the case, the publication of the letters had been sanctioned by Pope himself, which left Bowles free to make what use of them he chose. Typically, Bowles is not quite consistent. He wishes that the letters to Lady Mary Wortley Montagu had never been published, or that 'like Lord Byron's life of himself, they had met with some kind friend to consign them to the flames',[42] and yet he cites them rather eagerly as evidence of Pope's depravity. Burns had no hand in the publication of his letters, which left his friend, Alexander Peterkin, free to ask, 'Is an author to be held strictly accountable at the bar of the public, for his careless private letters, published after he is dead, by third persons, for the sake of profit?'[43] Bowles defended himself against such charges by claiming that he had, in using manuscript evidence, followed the principle of never admitting 'one word which could be thought *more offensive* to good morals and decency, than any *which Pope himself had published*'.[44] This allowed—at least it claimed to—Pope's right as a biographical subject himself to determine the limits within which his biographer should operate. But in practice it was a principle that allowed the biographer to substitute innuendo for evidence. Byron pointed out Bowles's habit of alluding to letters by Pope too disgusting to cite, but it was a practice that Byron did not disapprove of strongly enough not to imitate. He went on to remark that he had seen 'a collection of letters by another eminent—nay—pre-eminent poet [he has in mind Burns]—so abominably gross—and elaborately coarse, that I do not

---

[40] *Quarterly Review*, 23 (July 1820), 403. D'Israeli was writing anonymously, which made it possible for him to espouse a principle that seems radically at odds with his practice in the books he published under his own name, the *Quarrels of Authors*, for example. But the discrepancy is in itself revealing of the double-mindedness of the period on these matters.

[41] *Quarterly Review*, 1 (February 1809), 19–20.

[42] William Lisle Bowles, *A Final Appeal to the Literary Public, relative to Pope, in reply to certain observations of Mr. Roscoe, in his edition of that poet's works* (London: Hurst, Robinson and Co., 1825), 12.

[43] Alexander Peterkin, *Review of the Life of Robert Burns and of Various Criticisms on His Character and Writings* (Edinburgh: Macredie, Skelly, and Mackersy, 1815), 97–8, from a letter written by George Thomson.

[44] William Lisle Bowles, *The Invariable Principles of Poetry*, 62.

believe they could be paralleled in our language'. An editor of Burns, he claims in a rich inconsistency, should not think of 'even alluding to them'.[45]

The inconsistency reveals that Byron was as undecided as his contemporaries as to where the line should be drawn between the public and the private. He castigates Bowles for repeating Cibber's claim that when he and Pope were inveigled into a brothel he rescued Pope from a prostitute out of concern for his health, and retorts that he knows 'a much better story of Mr B.' Byron recounted the anecdote in a letter to Murray. Bowles, on his first visit to Paris, intent on verifying a friend's opinion that 'Paris contained the *finest women in the world*', propositioned a woman on the streets, 'caught a rousing pox—was laid up for two months—& returned perfectly persuaded that there were the finest women in the world at Paris'.[46] It was a tale likely to damage a clergyman's reputation, and Byron told Murray that it was 'of course *not* for the public'. But all letters are documents unstably placed between the public and private worlds, and letters to Murray were especially insecure. Byron must have known very well that it was Murray's practice to show around Byron's letters rather widely. When Thomas Moore read Byron's pamphlet he was put out, because he had himself told the anecdote about Bowles to Byron in what he had thought a private communication, but Byron 'had had the bad taste to allude' to it. It was, Moore wrote, 'even worse than Bowles in his pamphlet quoting me as entirely agreeing in the system he is combating for' (Moore, it seems, thought the opinion he had given Bowles a private one too).[47] What all this shows is that the line between writing that might be made public and writing that must remain private was unclear and rather fiercely disputed.

The division between the public and the private became still more insecure for all those who recognized that selfhood could no longer be regarded simply as an attribute of individuals. Wordsworth might wish to 'fix the point to which [Burns's] moral character had been degraded', but this, it was more and more widely believed, required not simply an examination of Burns's individual self, but a knowledge of the class of society to which he belonged and the period in which he lived. Peterkin complains that Currie's assessment of Burns's moral character had been decisively influenced by his sense of Burns's class. Poets of high rank might be entitled to their failings, 'but Burns was a poor ploughman— a humble excise-officer'.[48] For Jeffrey and Scott on the other hand this was exactly the point: Burns's vices were those of his class. For Jeffrey, his personal as much as his poetic failings were best explained by 'the lowness of his origin'. For

[45] Lord Byron, *The Complete Miscellaneous Prose*, ed. Andrew Nicholson (Oxford: Clarendon Press, 1991), 126–7.

[46] *Byron's Letters and Journals*, ed. Leslie A. Marchand, 8 (London: John Murray, 1978), 111.

[47] *Memoirs, Journal, and Correspondence of Thomas Moore*, ed. Lord John Russell, 8 vols. (London, Longmans, 1853–6), 3, 222.

[48] Alexander Peterkin, *Review of the Life of Robert Burns and of Various Criticisms on His Character and Writings*, 50.

Scott, Burns had the soul of 'a plebeian, of a high-souled plebeian indeed, of a citizen of Rome or Athens, but still of a plebeian untinged with the slightest shade of that spirit of chivalry which since the feudal times has pervaded the higher ranks of European society'.[49] Not to take account of a writer's rank in life will lead to a mistaken view of his character, and it is equally misleading to ignore a writer's place in history. D'Israeli points out that 'Pope's youth was passed in an age, which was not yet refined from the vices of the second Charles's court',[50] and Byron similarly insists that Pope's occasional indecency represented 'less the tone of Pope—than the tone of the *time*'.[51] It is hard to see how the self, once it is understood as a function of class and history, can remain in any ordinary sense private.

Bowles and Byron both pretend that writers should be characterized only by reference to their published writings. If their practice is always likely to contradict their principles, it is because they are also sympathetic to the more recent notion that people are best revealed in their unguarded moments. One view supposes that individuals fashion the selves by which they are known, the other that their authentic selves are precisely those aspects of their identity that have escaped fashioning. Boswell writes on the principle that Johnson is most himself in his private conversation, when he can be spied on by his biographer in much the same way that his pupils spied on his nuptial intimacies. Peterkin may regret the publication of Burns's letters because they were private documents, but Jeffrey regretted their publication because so many of them were 'composed as exercises and for display', and hence are a less reliable guide to the man than the poems which were 'almost all written primarily from feeling'.[52]

Wordsworth had divided poets into two classes: poets such as Homer, Virgil, and Shakespeare, whose characters were irrelevant to their works, and those poets in whom the man and his work are inseparable. Burns is emphatically to be placed in the second category, but so, it seemed to some, was Pope. Aaron Hill had complained that he found '*in Mr Pope, too much of Mr Pope*'. He disliked that Pope 'should *poke himself, at every turn, betwixt his readers and his subject*', but for Isaac D'Israeli, and he claims to speak not just for himself but for his generation, 'these personalities are delightful': they serve to 'admit us into the privacy of friendship'.[53] How was it possible to sustain the distinction between a writer and his work if what was most valuable in the work was the fullness with which it revealed the personality of the writer? Poets might complain of such assumptions. Byron, for example, thought his 'case as an Author' was 'peculiarly

---

[49] *Edinburgh Review*, 26 (January 1809), 252; *Quarterly Review*, 1 (February 1809), 26.
[50] *Quarterly Review*, 32 (October 1825), 284.
[51] Lord Byron, *The Complete Miscellaneous Prose*, 169.
[52] *Edinburgh Review*, 26 (January 1809), 256.
[53] *Quarterly Review*, 23, (July 1820), 431–2.

hard in being everlastingly taken or mistaken for [his] own Protagonist'.[54] But it was clearly a readerly habit that the poems themselves invited. Gilbert Burns, in defending his brother, suggests more subtly that in his poems Burns offers 'a kind of mock-heroic account of himself and his opinions which he never supposed could be taken literally'.[55] Jeffrey, for example, regrets that Burns is so given to 'ravings about sensibility and imprudence,—in common swearing, and in professions of love for whisky',[56] but, his brother suggests, this is to misread a poem such as 'Scotch Drink', to disregard its 'mock-heroic' character:

> Fortune! if thou'll but gie me still
> Hale breeks, a scone, an' whisky gill,
> An' rowth o' rhyme to rave at will,
>   Tak a' the rest,
> An' deal't about as thy blind skill
>   Directs thee best.

(121–6)

Lines such as these clearly 'admit the reader into the privacy of friendship'—the reader is enrolled as the poet's drinking companion—but the personality that the lines express is itself a product of Burns's stanza. Even those who agreed that poets like Burns and Byron expressed in their poems their own personalities might insist that those personalities were themselves poetic fictions rather than biographical truths. It was, after all, precisely Lockhart's defence when accused by Leigh Hunt of a particularly gross personality:

When I charged you with depraved morality, obscenity, and indecency, I spoke not of Leigh Hunt as a man. I deny the fact,—I have no reason to doubt that your private character is respectable, but I judged of you from your works.[57]

The controversy about personalities in the period had its origin in a newly vexed relationship between the public and the private, and also in a new way of writing. Commentators seem agreed that it was egotism that best defined the literature of the age: 'This is confessedly the age of confessions,—the era of individuality—the triumphant reign of the first person singular . . . Egotism has become as endemical to English literature as the plague to Egypt, or the scurvy to the northern climes.'[58] It was a state of affairs that most claimed to regret. Thomas Hope, for example, wrote *Anastasius* in the form of a confession, but finds it refreshing to introduce a short third-person history of an especially savage warlord if only to 'get rid, during a few pages of that eternal I which haunts all the rest of [his]

[54] Lord Byron, *The Complete Miscellaneous Prose*, 90.
[55] From a letter from Gilbert Burns quoted in Alexander Peterkin, *Review of the Life of Robert Burns and of Various Criticisms on His Character and Writings*, 81.
[56] *Edinburgh Review*, 13 (January 1809), 272.
[57] *Blackwood's Edinburgh Magazine*, 2 (January 1818), 416.
[58] *Blackwood's Edinburgh Magazine*, 13 (January 1823), 86.

narrative'.[59] *Blackwood's* praises the writers who manage to stay aloof from the confessional fashion:

Throughout all the works of Scott, the most original-minded man of his generation of Poets, scarcely a single allusion is made to himself . . . What has Campbell ever obtruded on the Public of his private history? Yet his is a name that will be hallowed forever . . . And finally, who more gracefully unostentatious than Moore?[60]

But these are rare exceptions. The 'two greatest egotists of the present day,' writes *Blackwood's* confidently are 'Mr Wordsworth and Mr Leigh Hunt',[61] but elsewhere it identifies as still more flagrant exponents of the first person Byron, Coleridge, Hazlitt, and Hogg. Wilson wonders of Hogg with some asperity, 'how many lives of himself does the swine-herd intend to put forth?'[62] Coleridge's *Biographia Literaria* reveals Coleridge's 'inveterate and diseased egotism': 'no sound is so sweet to him as that of his own voice'.[63] Byron, almost whenever his poems are mentioned, in *Blackwood's* or elsewhere, attracts the judgement that he is 'the vainest and most egotistical of poets', and for that very reason cannot complain if his critics choose to comment on his private life, although 'any other poet might complain with justice, should he see remarks of a personal nature mixed up with a criticism upon his writings'.[64] Similarly, it is Hazlitt's own egotism that at least mitigates the offensiveness of the scurrilous attacks on him such as the piece for which he sued *Blackwood's*, 'Hazlitt Cross-Examined'. In Hazlitt, it is a quality so pronounced that it offers itself to the parodist:

It is vulgarly supposed, that man, who is always thinking and talking of himself, is an egotist. He is no such thing; he is the least egotistical of all men. It is the world he is studying all the time, and self is but the glass through which he views and speculates upon nature. People call me egotist; they don't know what they say. I never think of myself, but as one among the many—a drop in the ocean of life. If I anatomise my own heart 'tis that I can lay hands on no other so conveniently; and when I do even make use of the letter *I*, I merely mean by it any highly-gifted and originally-minded individual. I have always thought myself very like Rousseau, except in one thing, that I hate 'the womankind'.[65]

Such complaints, appearing in *Blackwood's*, carry their own irony, because, as *Gold's London Magazine* remarks 'there are none who possess the power of excessive

[59] Thomas Hope, *Anastasius, or, Memoirs of a Greek: Written at the Close of the Eighteenth Century*, 3 vols. (London: John Murray, 1820), 3, 219.
[60] 'Some Observations on the Biographia Literaria of S. T. Coleridge', *Blackwood's Edinburgh Magazine*, 2 (October 1817), *Blackwood's Edinburgh Magazine*, 2 (October 1817), 3–18, 6–7.
[61] *Blackwood's Edinburgh Magazine*, 5 (April 1819), 97.
[62] *Blackwood's Edinburgh Magazine*, 10 (August 1821), 43.
[63] 'Some Observations on the Biographia Literaria of S. T. Coleridge', *Blackwood's Edinburgh Magazine*, 2 (October 1817), 5.
[64] *Blackwood's Edinburgh Magazine*, 3 (June 1818), 327, in Lockhart's review of *Beppo*.
[65] *Blackwood's Edinburgh Magazine*, 10 (August 1821), 69.

egotism, and introduce it with such humorous effect, as the writers in Blackwood's Magazine'.[66] But writers in other magazines eagerly competed with them. Lamb, in his epitaph for Elia, admits of the essays, 'Egotistical they have been pronounced by some',[67] and defends them on the ground that Elia's first-person is unusually flexible, capable, for example, of presenting Coleridge's memories of school as his own. But egotism was not peculiar to Lamb's essays: it was characteristic of magazines in general. When *The Etonian* tries to capture the special quality of magazine writing it arrives at the expression 'scribbling egotism'.[68] It was a thought that had been anticipated by T. G. Wainewright who chose as one of the flamboyant array of pseudonyms under which he wrote the name 'Egomet Bonmot'.

Egotism had become so endemic that the pressing need was to discriminate between its different kinds, in particular between the acceptable and the unacceptable varieties. For John Scott, the distinction was clearly indicated by the difference between Cobbett and Leigh Hunt:

No man ever better understood the art and mystery of egotism than the Editor of the Political Register,—as no man seems to understand it less than the Editor of the Examiner. The former always secures his reader's attention and sympathy when he speaks of himself,—the latter never fails to disgust his reader when he does so: we wish the author of our TABLE TALK would take up the difference as a subject for one of his Essays— for we cannot exactly hit upon the cause of this effect, which is so obvious to us,—and are perfectly sure he could make it plain in a very few sentences.[69]

Egotism seemed at once irritating and inescapable. The objection is in part to the new prevalence of literary kinds concerned with self-examination; Coleridge's *Biographia Literaria*, which prompted Wilson to remind Coleridge that 'the true confessional is not the bar of the public',[70] Wordsworth's rumoured *Prelude*, De Quincey's *Confessions of an English Opium-Eater*, and, for *Blackwood's* the absolute nadir of works of this kind, Hazlitt's *Liber Amoris*.[71] But the 'egotism' objected to was not just a matter of genre, it was also a matter of style.

In poetry its most adept exponent was Byron. John Scott identified as the great defect of Byron's poetry that it occupied a kind of no-man's-land between the lyric and the narrative. 'Childe Harold' is neither a self-portrait nor a character wholly separate from Byron himself. It was this that had made him so popular. It had given

---

[66] *Gold's London Magazine and Theatrical Inquisitor*, 3 (January 1821), 18.

[67] 'A Character of the Late Elia', *London Magazine*, 7 (January 1823), 19–21.

[68] *The Etonian* (London: Henry Colburn, 1824), 1, 320.

[69] *London Magazine*, 2 (December 1820), 636. Hazlitt does take the matter up in the *Conversations of Northcote* in which he argues that it was precisely because of the 'excess of his egotism' that Rousseau 'found a corresponding sympathy in the conscious feelings of every human breast'. Egotism such as Hunt's, by contrast, is alienating. Howe, 11, 278.

[70] *Blackwood's Edinburgh Magazine*, 2 (October 1817), 4.

[71] For the best account of the fashion, see James Treadwell, *Autobiographical Writing and British Literature, 1783–1834* (Oxford: Oxford University Press, 2005). See also Susan M. Levin, *The Romantic Art of Confession* (Columbia SC: Camden House, 1998).

his poetry a salacious interest that brought it close to gossip, but it was an aesthetic flaw: Byron's poems are inadequately dramatized. Kemble, the actor, lost himself in the part he was playing. 'Beyond an occasional cough, which he could not restrain', nothing of the actor survived in the performance. The reader of Byron's poetry, by contrast, is gripped not by the poem but by the person of the poet.[72] John Scott is disapproving: Walter Scott took a more benign view. For him, at least by implication, Byron's peculiar virtue is that he undoes the distinction between the dramatic and the lyric: he is, since the time of Cowper 'the first poet who, either in his own person, or covered by no very thick disguise, has directly appeared before the public, an actual living man, expressing his own sentiments, thoughts, hopes and fears'.[73] Scott seems to understand Byron's verse as a transparent medium through which the poet's beating heart is plainly visible, except that the phrase, appearing before the public, is taken from the theatre: Byron's verse, he suggests, stages its own sincerity. This is exactly what prompted John Scott's disapproval, but his sensitivity to the manner in which Byron's poems play between the public and the private, his alertness to how in Byron's verse intimate self-exposure itself becomes theatrical, is entirely predictable in the editor of a magazine, as is his awareness of the commercial power of the device. Byron 'has awakened, by literary exertion, a more intense interest in his person than ever before resulted from literature'. The effect is produced by 'literary exertion': the fact that he is 'thought of a hundred times, in the breasts of young and old, men and women, for once that any other author is'[74] is an achievement of style.

Personalities, *Blackwood's* insisted, entered literature with Aristophanes, but they are especially characteristic of the modern period: 'reviews and magazines' arrived 'and personality, which no literature ever was without, blended itself with them *ab ovo*'.[75] The great reviews were stamped with the personality of their editors, Jeffrey of the *Edinburgh*, and Gifford of the *Quarterly*. So too were the political weeklies. The *Political Register* was an expression of Cobbett's personality even more thoroughly than *The Examiner* was an expression of Leigh Hunt's. Personality was at once the most widely deprecated resource of those engaged in political and literary controversy and the most valued characteristic of modern writing. That is at any rate Christopher North's view: 'In reviewing, in particular, what can be done without personality? Nothing, nothing.' And that is because of the nature of the books that are currently offered for review: 'What are books that don't express the personal characters of their authors?' he asks, and another rhetorical question inevitably follows: 'Who can review books without reviewing those that wrote them?' A just literary criticism becomes inevitably an exercise in personalities: 'Can a man read Burns without having the idea of a great and a

[72] 'Living Authors, No. IV, Lord Byron', *London Magazine*, 3 (January 1821), 50–61.
[73] *Quarterly Review*, 19 (April 1818), 217–18.
[74] *London Magazine*, 3 (January 1821), 59.
[75] *Blackwood's Edinburgh Magazine*, 3 (May 1822), 612–13.

bold man—or Barry Cornwall, without the very uncomfortable feeling of a little man and a timid one?' Hence North's feigned astonishment at the furore that the magazine's indulgence in personalities has provoked.[76] Even *Blackwood's* seems pettishly to accept that criticism that strays into extra-literary areas is likely to arouse resentment: 'Were anyone, for instance, to drop a word about Hazlitt's face being as thick-studded with pimples as a tumbler of soda water is with air-bubbles, or to hint that John Keates was a smart hand at a glister, you have no notion what a lamentable squeaking would be sent forth.'[77] If it should be objected that timidity is a defect that characterizes at once a person and a literary style whereas pimples are defects that attach only to the complexion, *Blackwood's* had a response to hand. Allusions to Hazlitt's pimples, as to Leigh Hunt's 'depraved morality, obscenity, and indecency', had reference to qualities of the writing: 'what designation could be more apt to mark the scurvy, uneven, foully-heated, disordered, and repulsive style of the man?'[78] This might seem a rather obvious case of special pleading, but, when Hazlitt's 'On the Old Age of Artists' was published in the *New Monthly*, *Blackwood's* itself squeaked: 'Let me ask you, Mr Thomas Campbell, why you permit Mr William Hazlitt, the modern Pygmalion, to fill your pages with gross scurrilous, and low-lived abuse of people, whom such a man should not be permitted to name.'[79] Maginn's point (the piece is his) is that in Hazlitt's essays just as much as in the *Blackwood's* attacks on the Cockney School, style is represented as imprinted on the physical body of the stylist. So, Hazlitt writes of Fuseli:

His ideas are gnarled, hard, and distorted, like his features—his theories stalking and straddle-legged, like his gait—his projects aspiring and gigantic, like his gestures—his performance uncouth and dwarfish, like his person. His pictures are also like himself, with eye-balls of stone stuck in rims of tin, and muscles twisted together like ropes or wires.[80]

The artist's body becomes an allegorical representation of his paintings, and the same technique might serve to characterize a writer. In a later essay Hazlitt would make much of Coleridge's snub nose, which is 'small, feeble, nothing—like what he has done'.[81] It was a mark of the new prose that it searched the body for

[76] *Blackwood's Edinburgh Magazine*, 11 (March 1822), 362.
[77] *Blackwood's Edinburgh Magazine*, 8 (March 1821), 674–5.
[78] *Blackwood's Edinburgh Magazine*, 14 (September 1823), 311.
[79] *Blackwood's Edinburgh Magazine*, 14 (September 1823), 309.
[80] 'On the Old Age of Artists', *New Monthly Magazine*, 8 (September 1823), 214; Howe, 12, 94.
[81] 'My First Acquaintance with Poets', *The Liberal: Verse and Prose from the South*, 2 (April 1823), 27. Howe, 17, 109. A reviewer judged the reference to Coleridge's nose 'as shameful and contemptible as it is improper and absurd', *Literary Register*, 44 (May 1823), 275. It was a personal remark that Hazlitt had made before, in a review of Coleridge's *Lay Sermon*, when he imagines how Walter Shandy would have explained Coleridge's character defects, 'You have little or no nose, sir,' *The Examiner*, 9. no. 454, 8 September 1816, 571; Howe, 7, 381. Charles Lamb commented in a letter to Wordsworth, 'Have you read the review of Coleridge's character, person, physiognomy &c. in the Examiner—his features even to his *nose*—O horrible license beyond the old Comedy.' *The*

indicators of the moral character of its subjects: it was one of the ways in which a magazine paper sought to become as readable as a novel.

As Lockhart himself pointed out, all writers maintain two distinct identities, as men (the gender exclusivity is Lockhart's) and as authors. That Hazlitt the man, as his friends protested, had a clear complexion was no proof that Hazlitt the author might not be pimpled. The distinction in this period became unusually important and unusually volatile. John Scott was so outraged by the possibility that the attacks and defences in *Blackwood's* of Wordsworth and Coleridge were the work of the same man (in this case John Wilson rather than, as Scott believed, Lockhart) because he could not entertain the possibility that an anonymous magazine writer might feel freed from a duty of consistency that the same writer might acknowledge when writing in his own person. Ironically (perhaps deliberately so) Lamb writing as Elia contrasts his own personality with the national character of the Scots: Scots are 'plain and ingenuous in their mode of proceeding', whereas 'anti-Caledonians' such as himself 'cannot speak always as if they were upon oath—but must be understood, speaking or writing, with some abatement'.[82] Periodical writing was especially dependent on abatements of that kind: columns, as even Hazlitt recognized, would never get written if writers had to pause before expressing an opinion to decide whether they really held it. The games with signature that *Blackwood's* delighted in, and that so outraged John Scott—it offered the 'names of Odoherty, Kempferhausen, Wastle, Timothy Tickler, and Lauerwinckel' as proof that its writers scorned anonymity[83]—are, looked at from a different point of view, simply an acknowledgement of the conditions under which magazines are produced, conditions which do not permit writers to restrict themselves to the expression of opinions that they would be prepared to voice 'under oath'.

As 'Z' Lockhart voiced opinions about Leigh Hunt, Hazlitt, and Keats that he refused to own, and this was not simply an instance of his insincerity. 'Z', like Ensign Odoherty, Timothy Tickler, or Christopher North himself, was a *Blackwood's* character rather than a pseudonym. He was sometimes whimsically identified with General Izzard, who commanded the army of the United States in the war of 1812. John Wilson became nearly deranged with anxiety when he feared that it might become known to Wordsworth that he was the author not only of the defences of Wordsworth in *Blackwood's* but the attacks because Wilson, too, even when he used no by-line, had assimilated the magazine habit of writing in character. It was a habit that John Scott recognized even as he

Works of Charles and Mary Lamb, ed. E. V. Lucas, 7 vols. (London: Methuen, 1905), 6, 491. David Higgins relates the use of physical characteristics to delineate moral character to the popularity of phrenology in the period. See his *Romantic Genius and the Literary Magazine: Biography, Celebrity and Politics*, 53–4.

[82] 'Jews, Quakers, Scotchmen and other Imperfect Sympathies', *London Magazine*, 4 (August 1821), 152–6.

[83] *Blackwood's Edinburgh Magazine*, 10 (August 1821), 104.

denounced the use to which it was put in the rival magazine. And it was not a habit confined to periodical writers. Walter Scott wrote under various signatures, and seems to have felt able without compromising his principles to deny his authorship of the Waverley novels. 'There was an innate predilection in the mind of Lord Byron' as John Galt pointed out, repeating an observation made by almost every other contemporary commentator, 'to mystify everything about himself',[84] but it was not a habit peculiar to Byron: it was distinctive of the cultural moment. Byron began his 'Observations' on an article in *Blackwood's* that had attacked *Don Juan* by demanding to know 'by what right—the Writer assumes this work which is anonymous to be my production'.[85] For Shelley, the distinction between the writer and his work was not an expedient but an aesthetic principle: 'The poet & the man are two different natures: though they exist together they may be unconscious of each other, & incapable of deciding on each other's powers & effects by any reflex act.'[86] To dramatize the point he too often published anonymously, or under an assumed character such as Julian, 'an Englishman of good family', but 'a complete infidel, and a scoffer at all things reputed holy', or as a man who had 'died at Florence, as he was preparing for a voyage to one of the wildest of the Sporades' where he had planned to set up home.[87] Print, as I will argue in a later chapter, is an uncanny medium: it severs the connection between a writer and his writing, so that the writing becomes less an expression of the self than a weird doppelgänger.

In a print culture an author's name serves two very different functions: it may denote a particular individual, or it may serve as a metonym, denoting not a person but a body of writing. The ambiguity might be life-saving. In July 1806, after their duel had been interrupted, Jeffrey and Moore were reconciled when Jeffrey claimed and Moore accepted that the strictures he had made against Moore's poems did not implicate the man. Neither John Scott and Lockhart nor James Stuart and Alexander Boswell managed as dextrously to separate the body of the writer from the body of the text and the consequences in both cases were fatal. It was not a difficulty peculiar to magazines—it was symptomatic of the entire literary culture of the period—but it is nevertheless predictable that the elusiveness of authorial identity became such a prominent topic in the magazines, one that the precocious schoolboys who wrote *The Etonian* immediately

---

[84] John Galt, *Life of Lord Byron* (London: Colburn and Bentley, 1830), 159–60. Compare Lady Blessington, who writes that Byron admits 'that it amuses him to *hoax* people, and that when each person, at some future day, will give their different statements of him, they will be so contradictory, that *all* will be doubted,—an idea that gratifies him exceedingly'. See *Conversations of Lord Byron with the Countess of Blessington* (London: Henry Colburn, 1834), 47.

[85] Lord Byron, *The Complete Miscellaneous Prose*, 89.

[86] *The Letters of Percy Bysshe Shelley*, ed. F. L. Jones, 2 vols. (Oxford: Clarendon Press, 1964), 2, 310.

[87] From the prefaces to *Julian and Maddalo* and *Epipsychidion*, *Shelley's Poetry and Prose*, 113 and 373.

assimilated. The magazine's fictional editor is not believed when he introduces himself to two old Etonians as Peregrine Courtenay:

One of them asserted that he had been an intimate friend of Courtenay's these last six years, and that he had parted with him not two minutes ago at the Christopher. The other laid claim to an acquaintance with Peregrine of equal standing, but maintained that the worthy Chairman had gone off to King's College four years ago.

As Peregrine comments, 'This is damnable.—I begin to doubt my own existence.'[88] Fictional characters like Courtenay flicker in magazines into a spectral life of their own. More disturbingly, real people might be reduced to fictions. Dr Scott, an obscure Glasgow dentist, was celebrated in *Blackwood's* as 'the Odontist', a writer of various facetious songs (the real Scott seems to have rather enjoyed his unearned celebrity). More worryingly, James Hogg found himself occupying a dual role as at once a contributor to the magazine and one of its chief characters, transformed by Wilson and Lockhart, as John Scott charged, into 'the *regular fool-capped, bell-coated Zany of their Magazine*'[89] It was a role that Hogg himself did not always relish, but neither did the painter, James Northcote, when he found himself translated by Hazlitt into a character of his own invention.[90]

In a later chapter I shall argue that the distinction between the man and the writer that Lockhart insisted upon becomes both more pronounced and more volatile when it is fixed in print. Here I wish only to insist on the connection between the twin senses in the period of the word 'personality', as a word signifying at once an attack on private character and a word naming a distinctive identity that exists prior to and independent of any particular example of behaviour. If writing is most valued for its personality, if Barry Cornwall's defects are fixed by the impossibility of reading him 'without the very uncomfortable feeling of a little man and a timid one', then all literary criticism is bound to constitute a personality in the first sense. But there is a further difficulty. Barry Cornwall was the pen name of Bryan Procter: author and man were nominally distinguished, but it was radically unclear to which of the two the character of littleness and timidity attached. In a brilliant article, Peter Murphy has represented John Scott as the victim of his own conservative reading practices, killed because of his inability to distinguish between the signature and the body of the writer. But Lockhart was no more capable of maintaining that distinction

---

[88] *The Etonian*, 2, 312–13. For a deft examination of the kind of *Blackwood's* ploy that *The Etonian* is imitating, see Nicola Z. Trott, 'North of the Border: Cultural Crossing in the *Noctes Ambrosianæ*. *Romanticism On the Net*, 20 (November 2000) [accessed 22 January 2009] http://users.ox.ac.uk/~scat0385/20trott.html

[89] *London Magazine*, 2 (December 1820), 678.

[90] Northcote strongly objected to personal details that Hazlitt divulged in the conversations with him that appeared in the *New Monthly* in 1826–7 in the series 'Boswell redivivus', and later in the *Court Journal*, the *London Weekly Review*, and *The Atlas*. The conversations were published in book form in 1830 as *Conversations of James Northcote, Esq., R. A.* See Duncan Wu, *Hazlitt: The First Modern Man* (Oxford: Oxford University Press, 2008), 395–6 and 425–6.

himself. If it had been otherwise he would not have rushed down to London to demand that John Scott acknowledge or deny the authorship of the articles in the *London Magazine* that had offended him. Alexander Boswell's case was much the same. In the months in which he baited James Stuart, in the columns of news-papers and at political dinners, I doubt whether he felt any rancour against the man. In those months Stuart would have separated in Boswell's mind into two people, one of them a farmer like himself, a distant relation, a man he might have mixed with politely enough when the social occasion demanded it, and the other a caricature of the Edinburgh Whig, an entirely proper object of ridicule. As Peter Murphy points out, *Blackwood's* had 'a nearly obsessive interest in the interaction, attachment and slippage between authors (published names) and persons (bodies indicated by names)'.[91] But it was not just a single magazine but much of the writing of the period that focused repeatedly on the mysterious connection between writers' minds and writers' bodies.

[91] Peter Murphy, 'Impersonation and Authorship in Romantic Britain', 626.

4

Flesh-Coloured Silk

All tragedies are finish'd by a death,
All comedies are ended by a marriage. (*Don Juan*, 3, 39, 1–2)

So Byron writes, before going on to question whether there is very much difference between the two outcomes. The deaths of John Scott and Alexander Boswell may not have elevated them into tragic figures, but they served at least to lend them a certain dignity. William Lennox, when he visited the field where Boswell fell, was moved to produce a ballad:

> I strew'd the spot where the Baron fell
>   With his bonnie yellow gowan,
> And I wish'd his departed spirit well,
>   While my very soul was glowing.
>
> I tried to sing as I turn'd away,
>   But it dwindl'd down to sighing.
> 'Brave Boswell,' I said, 'Thou art gone for aye,'
>   And I scarce could help from crying.[1]

The Scotsman was similarly moved by the death of John Scott, though the newspaper was not quite successful in hiding its satisfaction at the discomfiture of *Blackwood's*:

> Away! For in his bosom he
>   Must bear a heart of stone
> Who could a single moment pause
> Ere he resolv'd the guilty cause
>   Of murder to disown.
>
> Away! Thy wit is pointless now,
>   Thy muse has lost her charms—
> And when to her I lend my ear
> 'Tis but the groan of death I hear,
>   'Tis but the din of arms.

---

[1] *The Poetical Works of Sir Alexander Boswell*, ed. Robert Howie Smith (Glasgow: Maurice Ogle and Co., 1871), lxi.

> Away! In hours of joy and grief
> I oft have conn'd thee o'er;
> But from my heart I tear thee now,
> And here inscribe the solemn vow,
> I'LL NEVER READ THEE MORE![2]

But both of these catastrophes were exclusively masculine affairs. When the failure to respect the boundary separating the public from the private involved women as well as men, tragedy, as Byron intimates, descended to comedy, or, perhaps it would be more accurate to say, melodrama tumbled into farce.

Hazlitt was exposed as the author of 'a nasty book called "LIBER AMORIS, or, the NEW PYGMALION" in *John Bull* in the issue for 16 June 1823. On the following Sunday *John Bull* clinched the case by printing a letter from Hazlitt to Sarah Walker, an edited version of which he had included in the book. It was, of course, wholly improper for a weekly newspaper to publish a private letter without its author's consent, but, in this case, *John Bull* claimed, its decision was defensible: 'if [Hazlitt] feels offended or sore that his letters are thus made public, he must reconcile himself by recollecting that it is he himself who has given publicity to the affair altogether'.[3] Hazlitt could not expect *John Bull* to respect the barrier between the public and the private when he had himself flouted it. He could not accuse *John Bull* of a 'personality' when he was himself guilty of traducing in print a young woman who had never ventured into public life.

Hazlitt's foolhardy decision to publish his book was only the last stage in a long-drawn-out process throughout which, as he confessed to his friend Bryan Procter, he seems to have felt under a compulsion to expose himself:

'I am a cursed fool' said he to me. 'I saw J——going into Will's Coffee-house yesterday morning; he spoke to me. I followed him into the house; and whilst he lunched I told him the whole story.' 'Then' (said he) 'I wandered into Regent's Park, where I met one of M——'s sons. I walked with him some time, and on his using some civil expression, by God! Sir, I told him the whole story.' . . . 'Well, sir' (he went on) 'I then went to Haydon; but he was out. There was only his man, Salmon, there: but, by God! I could not help myself. It all came out: the whole cursed story! Afterwards I went to look at some lodgings in Pimlico. The landlady at one place, after some explanations as to rent, etc. said to me very kindly, 'I'm afraid you are not well, sir?'—'No, ma'am,' said I, 'I am not well;' and on inquiring further, the devil take me if I did not let out the whole story, from beginning to end!'[4]

Is it Procter or Hazlitt himself who was responsible for giving this anecdote so deft a comic turn? Hazlitt is scarcely more discreet in the text than he was in the town. An advertisement may claim that the book is based on a manuscript

---

[2] *The Scotsman*, no. 217, 17 March 1821, 86.

[3] *John Bull*, no. 131, 16 June 1823, 189 and no. 132, 23 June 1823, 197–8.

[4] Bryan Procter (Barry Cornwall), *An autobiographical fragment and biographical notes, with . . . sketches of contemporaries, unpublished lyrics, etc.* (London: Bell, 1877), 180–1.

written by a 'native of North Britain', who died in the Netherlands soon after the termination of the romantic attachment that it records, but the text reveals that the author is a writer, who refers to himself under the initial 'H——'. As Lamb points out, journalistic conventions dictate that people are referred to by their initials when engaged in illicit or unbecoming sexual activities:

> Nor with less lustre have initials shone
> To grace the gentler annals of crim. con.,
> Where the dispensers of the public lash
> Soft penance give; a letter and a dash——
> Where vice reduced in size sinks to a failing,
> And loses half her grossness by curtailing.
> Faux pas are told in such a modest way,——
> You must forgive them——for what is there, say,
> Which such a pliant Vowel must not grant
> To such a very pressing Consonant?

Interestingly, the other use of the convention picked out by Lamb is in the reporting of duels ('How fierce the shock, how fatal is the jar, / When Ensign W. meets Lieutenant R.'), but when Hazlitt borrows it the effect is at once decorous (the participants in the affair are not given by name) and salacious.

Lamb makes his comments on the use of initials in the prologue to *Mr H——*, an afterpiece which was unsuccessfully performed at Drury Lane in December 1806.[5] Hazlitt had been present, and he associates the evening with his affair with Sarah Walker. He recalls both, for example, in his essay 'On Great and Little Things', which was published in February 1822, when the affair was at its height.[6] Lamb's play is slight enough. Mr H——, who is known only by his initial, is the most eligible bachelor in Bath until it is revealed that the initial stands for Hogsflesh, at which point he becomes a social pariah and decides to change his name by royal warrant to Bacon. Hazlitt associates his affair with the play because of the coincidence of the initial, of course, but also perhaps because its subtitle registers Hazlitt's mordant sense of the figure he cuts in the affair: it is *Mr H——; A Farce*.

Like the newspapers Hazlitt chooses an initial that seems designed at once to conceal and to reveal his identity. One is reminded of Hogg's Robert Wringhim or Colwan disguising his name as Cowan, or of Byron complimenting Don Juan on his swimming in the second canto of that anonymous poem by recalling a feat of his own that he advertised almost as widely as did Hazlitt, his unhappy affair with his landlady's daughter:

---

[5] *The Works of Charles and Mary Lamb*, ed. E. V. Lucas, 7 vols. (London: Methuen and Co., 1903), 5, 180–1.
[6] *New Monthly Magazine*, 4 (February 1822), 127–34; Howe, 8, 226–42.

He could, perhaps, have pass'd the Hellespont,
As once (a feat on which ourselves we prided)
Leander, Mr. Ekenhead, and I did.

(2, 105, 6–8)[7]

Walter Scott himself maintained for much of his career a similarly odd anonymity, an anonymity so imperfect that the *British Critic* could choose as the running-title of its review of his very first novel, 'Waverley: supposed by W. Scott'.[8]

Liber Amoris is, as Jonathan Gross puts it, a 'pathological work', by which he means that it is a work that 'reveals a strain in Hazlitt's identity'.[9] But such strains may characterize cultures as much as individuals. The boarding house kept by Sarah Walker's parents at 9 Southampton Buildings in Holborn is a representative space. Hazlitt moved there on 13 August 1820, because his marriage had broken down and he had become once more one of the single young men the building catered for, like the apothecary Mr Griffiths, of whom Hazlitt overheard Sarah Walker's brother say to his mother and sisters, 'he must be seven inches',[10] or Robert Roscoe, the young lawyer who married Sarah's older sister after entering the house as a lodger, or like another trainee lawyer, John Tomkins, who was to become Hazlitt's successful rival for the affections of Sarah Walker.[11] Boarding houses attracted men like these, young men training for one of the professions, or older men who belonged to professions that were not yet quite secure, such as Griffiths the apothecary or Hazlitt the periodical writer. In such a house the status of the Walkers was oddly unfixed. They were at once landlords and servants. Hazlitt thought better of recording the conversation about Mr Griffiths's dimensions in the published version of *Liber Amoris* (though it is included in the printer's copy), but he refers to it in his letter to J. S. K— as 'the conversation below stairs (which I told you of when I saw you)'.[12] Here the floor inhabited by the Walkers is clearly referred to as the servants' quarters. When Hazlitt's feelings about Sarah are different, at one of the moments when he 'worshipped her' rather than when he remembered how he had eavesdropped on her engaged with her family in a coarse conversation, the room she sits in at the window seat sewing becomes 'the front parlour', and Hazlitt feels free to enter only when he has her permission (154).

---

[7] A point made by John Thelwall, who quotes these lines to demonstrate that Byron, for all that he 'withholds his name from the title page, stamps the broad seal of his acknowledgement' upon the poem. See *The Champion* (1 August 1819), 490. Byron had advertised his feat most widely in the circumstantial note to his poem 'Written after swimming from Sestos to Abydos May 9 1810', published with the first two cantos of *Childe Harold's Pilgrimage* in 1812.

[8] *British Critic*, 2 (August 1814), 189–211.

[9] Jonathan Gross, 'Hazlitt's Worshipping Practice in *Liber Amoris*', *SEL*, 35 (1995), 707–21, 708.

[10] This detail, deleted from the manuscript, is recorded by Duncan Wu, *The Selected Writings of William Hazlitt*, ed. Duncan Wu, 9 vols. (London: Pickering and Chatto, 1998), 7, 264.

[11] There was also a married couple, the Folletts, lodging in the house.

[12] Howe, 9, 95–162, 152. All subsequent quotations from *Liber Amoris* are taken from this edition and page references are included in the text.

As all readers of *Liber Amoris* have noted, Sarah's status swings dizzyingly throughout the text between virgin and whore before Hazlitt assigns her firmly at last to the latter category. She resembles in his eyes a copy of a 'fine old Italian picture', 'some say it is a Madona; others call it a Magdalen' (100), but her unfixed moral status is closely tied to the uncertain place she has in an increasingly complex class structure. Had Hazlitt met her thirty years before he would not have been shocked by overhearing her conversation. Like Francis Place, the radical, she was a member of the lower middle class. But Place had been born in 1771, and in his childhood, as he remembers it in his autobiography, domestic conversation was 'remarkably gross'. He supports his point by recalling the songs sung at domestic parties. He has in mind, it seems, songs such as 'The Morgan Rattler', which unblushingly celebrates the size of a male member.[13] A generation later stricter codes of propriety had filtered down from the upper to the lower middle class so effectively that even a man as independent as Hazlitt had been infected.

At 9 Southampton Buildings, as in Elsinore Castle in a play that Hazlitt more than once echoes in the text, no space was securely private, which explains how Sarah Walker's brother came by his unusually intimate knowledge of Mr Griffiths's anatomy, and how Hazlitt came to overhear him discussing it with his family. Sarah's father, when challenged by Hazlitt, confirms that he once passed Hazlitt's door, 'which stood a-jar' and revealed his daughter and Hazlitt in a compromising position, Sarah 'sitting in my lap, with her arms round my neck, and mine twined round her in the fondest manner' (146). In a particularly fraught moment, Hazlitt emits a scream that 'brought the whole house, father, mother, lodgers and all' into his room (145). It is a house of thin walls, a house where doors seem always to be unlocked and ajar. Hazlitt's response to his public humiliation is to rush out of the house 'thinking to quit it forever', but he is 'no sooner in the street' than he is overpowered by a sense of 'the desolation and the darkness' and goes back. (146). Throughout the text Hazlitt represents himself as unable to stay in the building or to leave it. Whenever he leaves he makes an abrupt, unplanned return, once from as far away as Scotland, where he had planned to stay until he was granted his divorce. It is a habit that gives a kind of appropriateness to one of the odder episodes in this odd narrative. Hazlitt demands an interview with Sarah who is understandably reluctant to come into his room, and so he 'sat down in a chair near the door, and took her hand, and talked to her for three quarters of an hour,' while she remained in the corridor outside (144). *Liber Amoris* is quite literally a liminal romance.

When he took his rooms in the building on 13 August Hazlitt entered into an economic relationship with the Walkers. His affective relationship with Sarah began three days later, on 16 August, when Sarah for the first time brought him

[13] *The Autobiography of Francis Place*, ed. Mary Thrale (Cambridge: Cambridge University Press, 1972), 58–9. See also Ben Wilson, *Decency and Disorder: The Age of Cant 1789–1837* (London: Faber and Faber, 2007), 63–4.

his breakfast, turned at the door, and fixed her eyes full upon him. Hazlitt never succeeds in disentangling the two kinds of relationship. He signals his affection for Sarah by giving her presents; a flageolet, his prized bronze bust of Napoleon, books, among them 'a little Prayer-Book, bound in crimson velvet, with green silk linings; she kissed it twenty times when she received it' (149). 'You sit on my knee and put your arms round my neck, and feed me with kisses', Hazlitt reminds Sarah, and wonders whether all this might be for her just a 'regular task' that she goes through 'without one natural feeling' (106), a suspicion fuelled perhaps by the way in which people and commodities in this text melt together. She kisses the prayer-book as readily as she kisses its donor, and the two are even dressed rather like one another (Hazlitt's friends noted how during his relationship with Sarah Walker he fitted himself out with a fashionable new wardrobe). If Hazlitt suspects that Sarah's displays of affection might just be designed to 'get a few presents out of [him]' (107), his suspicion is justified by his own habit of measuring his affection by the value of the gifts he offers her. In a note added to the manuscript Hazlitt carefully assesses the value of the 'few presents' as 'upwards of 30£. worth—a trifle', among them a trinket 'set down in the Jeweller's bill' as 'a gold chased heart', a description which prompts some predictable puns.[14] It is almost exactly the sum that Hazlitt calculated (surely optimistically) that he could earn in a week's hard writing. In a letter sent to Sarah from a Scottish inn he claims, 'I regularly do ten pages a day, which mounts up to thirty guineas' worth a week, so that you see I should grow rich at this rate, if I could keep on so; *and I could keep on so*, if I had you with me to encourage me with your sweet smiles, and share my lot' (112). Hazlitt claims later that he once offered to spare Sarah work by taking 'nearly the whole of the lodgings at a hundred guineas a year' (156), a sum very close to the £100 for which Hazlitt sold the copyright of *Liber Amoris* to John Hunt. These are revealing coincidences. Money, sex, and writing in this text consistently tend to converge.

Boarding house keepers at once rent out rooms and invite their lodgers into their homes. They offer an experience of domesticity that can be secured for so much a week. Their earnings depend on the skill with which they can elide the difference between economic and social relationships. Hazlitt was left at the end of the affair bitterly suspecting that his mistake had been to conduct a sentimental relationship with Sarah rather than forcing himself upon her. In an episode he chose not to include in *Liber Amoris* he persuaded an acquaintance to take rooms in the building, and make the experiment (one is pleased to learn that the attempt failed).[15] Had it been a hotel, or had the class difference between

---

[14] 'A *chased* heart indeed, but not given for a *chaste* heart!' The manuscript is quoted by Duncan Wu, *The Selected Writings of William Hazlitt*, 7, 264.

[15] In Hazlitt's journal the friend is referred to only as 'Mr F.', who may have been Albany Fonblanque. The episode is recounted by Jon Cook, *Hazlitt in Love: A Fatal Attachment* (London: Short Books, 2007), 189–91. Cook's is the most incisive biographical account of Hazlitt's relationship with Sarah Walker.

Sarah and Hazlitt been greater, it would have been different. Polidori noted how Byron, on landing at Ostend, took rooms at the Cour Impériale and 'fell like a thunderbolt upon the chambermaid'.[16] But it is also the case that had Hazlitt been a guest in a private home he would have understood clearly that he had to court Sarah rather than rape her. A boarding house was an in-between place, a place it seemed to Hazlitt in his frequent moments of bitterness that offered an ersatz domesticity for sale, and hence a place that most closely resembled a brothel. The suspicion seems confirmed when he interrogates his successful rival and finds that 'she had been playing the same game with him as with me'. He 'breakfasted first, and enjoyed an hour of her society, and then I took my turn, so that we never jostled; and this explained why, when he came back sometimes and passed my door, as she was sitting in my lap, she coloured violently, thinking, if her lover looked in, what a *denouement* there would be' (158). Sarah is, he decides, 'a regular lodging house decoy, played off by her mother upon the lodgers, one after another', which is scarcely distinct from 'a common courtesan who *bilks* a customer, and passes him, leering up at her bully, the moment after' (160). The connection between Sarah, suspected of deploying her caresses in order to meet the economic needs of her family, and Hazlitt, who sells transcriptions of his conversations with her and of his love letters to her to the publisher, John Hunt, is unexplored in the text, but for all that it is hard to ignore.

Liber Amoris has usually been described as an extreme, utterly eccentric, text, but in subjecting a woman to an elaborate public exposure—Hazlitt puts it gloatingly, 'a more complete experiment on character was never made' (160)—it might be thought of as oddly representative. In July 1819, Byron had published the first canto of *Don Juan*, in which his wife is pilloried as a prude. It was only the latest episode in the history of a marital breakdown that had from the first taken the form of a public relations contest between Byron and his wife. In March 1816, Byron, like most husbands when their wives first leave them, found himself torn between tender regret and atrabilious resentment, but he decorously separated the two responses. He expressed the first in a courtly lyric addressed to his wife, and the second in a verse imprecation of Juvenalian violence directed against her maid, whom he blames for poisoning his marriage but refuses to name out of respect for his wife:

> But for the love I bore, and still must bear,
> To her thy malice from all ties would tear—
> Thy name,—thy human name—to every eye
> The climax of all scorn should hang on high,
> Exalted o'er thy less abhorred compeers—
> And festering in the infamy of years.
>
> ('A Sketch', 99–104)

---

[16] Leslie A. Marchand, *Byron: A Biography*, 3 vols. (New York: Albert A. Knopf, 1954), 2, 610.

In thrall to his own better nature, he spares the maid the publication of her name to the world that she so richly deserves. In the lyric 'Fare Thee Well!' by contrast he represents 'the world' as callously prying into a marital relationship the value of which is located in moments of enclosed intimacy, as when his wife had laid her head on his breast as she fell asleep, or in that future moment when she will gaze at her daughter's face:

> Should her lineaments resemble
> Those thou never more may'st see—
> Then thy heart will softly tremble
> With a pulse yet true to me.

(41–4)

But Byron was not content just to write these poems. He had fifty copies printed by Murray for private circulation. On 16 April 1816 both poems were printed in *The Champion*, edited at the time by John Scott, under the title 'Lord Byron's Poems On His Own Domestic Circumstances', after which they were widely circulated in pirated editions. The attack on his wife's maid was entitled 'A Sketch from Private Life'.[17] As almost all commentators pointed out, Byron seemed to have taken a very odd view of how a private life was constituted.

Still more spectacularly, in July 1821, proceedings began in the trial before the House of Lords of George IV's wife, Caroline, for adultery. *John Bull* was launched as a weekly newspaper almost solely dedicated to traducing the Queen and her supporters, which gives a certain irony to its defence of Sarah Walker against Hazlitt's attacks on her character. In all three cases the scandal had to do with the exposure before the public gaze of intimate details of women's private lives, whether they had to do with Lady Byron's disapproval of sex or Queen Caroline's appetite for it. The green bag, the mysterious container which was supposed to contain the evidence gathered by the committee appointed to look into the charges of adultery brought against the Queen, became a particular object of fascination, repeatedly alluded to in cartoons, songs, and poems, presumably because it came to represent the threat or promise that shameful, private experience was about to be exposed to the public eye.

The scandal of the separation of Britain's foremost poet from his wife began in January 1816. It was nine years later that scandal engulfed the nation's greatest actor. In January 1825, Edmund Kean was the defendant in a crim. con. case brought against him by Alderman Cox for the seduction of his wife, Charlotte. The jury found for the plaintiff and set the damages at £800, leaving Kean to discover to his cost that, as Byron explained in *Don Juan*, in 'the nations of the moral north' where it is the custom for juries to 'cast up what a wife is worth', impoverished husbands like Alderman Cox might conclude that the adultery of their wives was a 'marketable vice' (*Don Juan*, 1, 64). Byron never himself

---

[17] These occurrences are sharply recorded by Fiona MacCarthy, *Byron: Life and Legend* (New York: Farrar, Strauss and Giroux, 2002), 273–5.

incurred such a penalty, but, unsurprisingly, it did not escape his attention. When he ogles the women in the harem Juan risks a fate still worse than the 'damages men pay / In moral England where the thing's a tax' (6, 29, 6–7), and when he arrives in England his looks are admired '*Nem. con.* among the women, which I grieve / To say leads oft to *crim. con.* with the married' (15, 84, 2–3). But Byron and Kean were linked by more than their sexual errancy.

When Byron first saw Kean as Richard III he wrote in his journal

By Jove, he is a soul! Life—nature—truth without exaggeration or diminution. Kemble's Hamlet is perfect;—but Hamlet is not Nature. Richard is a man; and Kean is Richard.[18]

Moore reports that Byron was so affected by Kean's Sir Giles Overreach that he was 'seized with a sort of convulsive fit'.[19] He marked his admiration by presenting Kean with gifts; fifty guineas, 'a handsome snuff-box and a costly Turkish sword'. When he first visited his future wife in her family home she remembered of their conversation only that he talked of Kean.[20] It seems that Byron recognized a kinship between the actor's talent and his own, and so did others. When John Scott contrasts Byron's poems with Kemble, who disappeared in the characters he played, Kean is surely the suppressed term that explains the thought. Scott is implicitly comparing the innovation Byron made in poetry with the innovation that Kean brought to the stage.[21] Caroline Lamb, who is an even more powerful authority than John Scott, ends her own continuation of *Don Juan*, 'A New Canto', by explaining that Byron's poem is explicable only as an antidote to boredom and as a symptom of his morbid desire for fame, and again, she insinuates, the proper comparison is with Kean:

> But something must be done to cure the spleen,
> And keep my name in capitals, like Kean.
>
> (215–16)[22]

There was, no doubt, a range of qualities that the two shared, but John Scott was, I think, right to suggest that the power they exerted over their contemporaries had its origin in the manner in which both confounded the distinction between private character and public performance. Both men were particularly vulnerable to scandalous revelations about their private lives, not by chance, but as a consequence of the kind of performance that made both men famous, a performance in which self and role were blended indistinguishably.

Kean's case came to court on 17 January 1825. The court became a theatre for the day. The gallery was crowded, and those who filled it were rebuked more than

---

[18] *Byron's Letters and Journals,* ed. Leslie A. Marchand, 3 (London: John Murray, 1974), 244.

[19] As reported by Moore, Leslie A. Marchand, *Byron: A Biography,* 1, 452 (note).

[20] Leslie A. Marchand, *Byron: A Biography,* 1, 244, 451–2, 490.

[21] 'Living Authors, No. IV, Lord Byron', *London Magazine,* 3 (January 1821), 50–61.

[22] Quoted from Peter Cochran's online edition of the poem at http://www.hobby-o.com/newcanto.php, consulted [25 November 2008].

once by the Lord Chief Justice for behaving as if they had been at Drury Lane rather than the Court of Chancery. The noise from the gallery, *The Times* reported, 'resembled that of the over-crowded pit of the theatre'.[23] The lawyers seemed to share the delusion of the spectators. The Common Sergeant, appearing for Cox, asked whether a passage from a letter from Kean to Mrs Cox did not 'denote a foregone conclusion,' echoing Othello (III, iii, 434), which, surely not by coincidence, was one of Kean's most famous roles. In one of his letters Kean reported that he would be later than usual in meeting Mrs Cox, 'Welcome, my life, my love, my soul, I cannot see you till after the farce which I act in to-night for my benefit.' The lawyers were as eager to match him in his comic as in his tragic performances. Cox had a black servant, who reported that Mrs Cox was 'a good-sized woman... about my size'. This gave the Common Sergeant the opportunity to provoke 'loud laughter' by retorting, 'I hope she is not a good-coloured woman, according to the same criterion.'

The highpoint of the proceedings was the reading in open court of a selection of letters from Kean to Mrs Cox that had been discovered by the Alderman after he had ordered his wife out of the family home. Private letters read in court, and transcribed by shorthand writers so that they could be reproduced at length in the next day's newspapers, had much more than simply evidential value. Like the contents of the green bag in the trial of Queen Caroline they had a metonymic power, focusing the prurient spectacle of intimate private doings dragged before the public gaze that gave the trial its unseemly glamour. A carnival was held on 17 January, in which the barriers that separated the law from the theatre, and intimate private life from public spectacle were removed for a day but, unlike carnival, the effect was potentially genuinely subversive. It raised the suspicion that those barriers might only ever have been illusory.

Kean's love letters were so potent by virtue of their authenticity, but it was an authenticity guaranteed by their ineptness. Leigh Hunt, it is worth noting, offered the high quality of the verse as decisive proof that the tenderness that Byron expresses for his wife in 'Fare Thee Well!' was insincere.[24] No one who loved truly could have written so well. Kean's letters by contrast fail even for a moment to produce that powerful illusion of psychological depth that novelists writing within the Richardsonian tradition could so readily command. Instead, Kean offers a weak impersonation of himself. He reprises his own performances—Macbeth, for example: in Cox's absence he would 'hold [his] little darling to [his] heart, and "sleep in spite of thunder"' (IV, i, 86)—or Hamlet. Kean is so fond of the quatrain that Hamlet speaks to Ophelia in Act II, scene ii

[23] On the day after the trial, Tuesday, 18 January 1825, *The Times*, like several other newspapers, offered a full transcript of the proceedings, on which I have drawn in the account that follows. I have supplemented this with the account of the trial and its aftermath by Giles Playfair. See Giles Playfair, *The Flash of Lightning: A Portrait of Edward Kean* (London: Kimber, 1983).

[24] Leigh Hunt, *Lord Byron and Some of his Contemporaries* (London: Henry Colburn, 1828), 111.

that he quotes it in two separate letters, prompting his counsel, James Scarlett, to suggest a little desperately that the letters must have been written to different people: 'It was not likely that a man of Mr Kean's talents would have had the bad taste to make the same quotation twice over to the same woman.' Kean diverges wildly between registers. 'My Heart-Strings' is his address to Charlotte Cox in a letter of 8 August 1822, and he goes on in similar vein, 'The world without you appears one vast and gloomy dungeon, and your letters are as sunbeams through the grating of the prison-house.' But then he commissions her to act for him in a financial transaction involving a fellow actor, 'Now, little bitch, obey the following injunctions about Hughes.' The letters are so bad that they can only be real, and there is another effect equally disconcerting.

When actors in their most private moments are subjected to the full glare of publicity, privacy itself comes to seem theatrical, as if it were a quality produced only by the spotlight. Scarlett tried to show that Alderman Cox, by encouraging his wife's admiration of Kean's acting, had been complicit in his own cuckolding. He had allowed her to witness 'delineations of tenderness, with a truth of feeling which no other man could equal'. The grammatical awkwardness may be only a slip of the shorthand writer, but a refusal to distinguish between feelings and their representation, between reality and dramatic illusion, marked the whole of the court's proceedings. Scarlett made much of Cox's permitting his wife to visit Kean in his dressing room. Kean's dresser gave evidence that she had seen him without his breeches, wearing only 'silk leggings', which were 'flesh coloured' and 'intended to represent flesh'. The court was presented with a strange world in which to reveal 'flesh coloured' silk was no less provocative than to reveal flesh, a world in which the dramatic illusion of nudity seemed somehow more flagrant than its reality.

On 24 January, a week after the trial, Kean returned to the stage, a decision which *The Times* described the following day as constituting 'as great an outrage to decency, as if he were to walk naked through the streets at mid-day'. Every night that he took the stage the audience divided raucously between his defenders, who shouted 'Down with Cant', and his assailants who were determined to drown out his every speech. On 28 January, Kean addressed the audience, and tried to distinguish between his 'private conduct', which he did not attempt to vindicate, and his professional identity. 'I stand before you', he said 'as the representative of Shakespeare's heroes', the representative that night of Othello. To respond to him not as Othello but as Edmund Kean was to deny the premise on which theatre is founded. *The Times* retorted that by his 'very extraordinary appearance on another stage' Kean had surrendered this argument.[25] He had by his own actions contrived that his private character had become a matter of public spectacle. The audience at Drury Lane seemed to side with the newspaper, shouting out all through the performance phrases from his love letters thought particularly risible, 'Heart-Strings', 'Little Breeches', and hooting at any line that might be thought to

[25] *The Times*, Tuesday, 25 January 1825, 2.

carry a double entendre. The audience created its own coarse, popular theatre and, throughout that London spring, drowned out the more traditional programme that Elliston, the manager of Drury Lane, had planned for them. But their refusal to distinguish between Kean and his roles was surely not just naive. It might even be understood as a backhanded compliment, because the popular theatre that the audience substituted for the advertised offerings had at least a kinship with the new kind of theatre that Kean had introduced to the London stage. Even in its derision, it may be, the audience signalled its recognition that Kean was an actor of a new kind, an actor whose power derived precisely from his refusal to allow a distinction between himself and the character he was playing. That, surely, is what had prompted Byron to note of his most famous performance, 'Richard is a man; and Kean is Richard.' It was a thought on which Byron mused for good reason: Kean exhibited on stage precisely the quality on which, as many of his readers noted, the still more phenomenal success of Byron's poetry was founded. It is in this, I want to suggest, that Byron and Kean are revealed as the two most able exponents of a new kind of performance, the power of which derives from its refusal to allow a distinction between role and reality.

Kean could be grandiose. In a revealingly Byronic moment he remarked, in a letter to Charlotte Cox, that he was 'watched more closely than Buonaparte at St Helena'. He saw himself heroically, and it is hard to believe that he could have become the great tragic actor that he was had he not done so. But in the Court of Chancery his life was revealed not as high tragedy but as bedroom farce. Scarlett revived an old rumour that Mrs Cox had, long before her relationship with Kean, been surprised by her husband with another lover. Before Cox came into the bedroom, the lover took refuge in the closet, only for his presence to be exposed by Mrs Cox's lapdog's furious barking. Scarlett himself acknowledged the theatricality of the anecdote: 'It was only according to dramatic rule, that the husband should disturb the gallant—that the gallant should walk into the closet—that the lap-dog should lead to the discovery of the gallant.' Farce was the genre that continued to organize the court proceedings. The Common Sergeant was careful, when he examined Cox's niece, to cast doubt upon a still more extravagant rumour, that when Mrs Cox had been surprised by her husband in bed with Kean she had successfully concealed him beneath the blankets. The rumour surely had its origin in one particular bedroom farce, the scene in Canto I of *Don Juan*, when Don Alfonso bursts into Donna Julia's bedroom and she triumphantly protests her innocence when all the while Juan is hiding, 'half-smothered', beneath the bedclothes:

> He had been hid—I don't pretend to say
>   How nor can I indeed describe the where.
> Young, slender, and packed easily, he lay
>   No doubt in little compass, round or square.
> But pity him I neither must nor may
>   His suffocation by that pretty pair . . .
>
> (*Don Juan*, 1, 166, 1–6)

Something about Kean's predicament seemed to bring *Don Juan* to mind. *The Times* dismissed the speech with which Elliston tried to appease those barracking Kean as 'a specimen of that description of eloquence, which 'the learn'd call *rigmarole*',[26] quoting, possibly unconsciously, Byron's description of the speech in which Don Alfonso offers a stiff apology for having falsely suspected his wife (1, 174, 8). In the weeks that followed the court case the Drury Lane audiences, one might say, travestied Shakespearean tragedy in much the same way that *Don Juan* travestied epic poetry. In both cases plot was subordinated to a volatile, precarious exchange between the audience and their star performer. But there remains a crucial difference. In *Don Juan* the exchange is orchestrated by Byron: his audience is summoned into existence by the poet himself, textually produced, ushered within the poem into the author's own affable but unquestionably aristocratic presence. Byron also had a readership outside the poem that proved far less easily suborned by the poet's rhetorical skills, but the audience produced by the poem remains virtual. Kean's audience by contrast materialized threateningly every evening on which he took the stage. It is a difference, it might seem, between the poet who is read in his absence, and the actor, whose performance demands the physical presence of his admirers. But it was not just that, as becomes clear when one considers the consequences that befell Hazlitt when he took the fateful decision not to leave it to his enemies, as Kean left it to *The Times* and the other periodicals, to publish to the world his own recent sexual history, but to write up the affair himself and publish it as *Liber Amoris*, the scandalous nature of the narrative thinly disguised by the use in the title of a respectably dead language.

Hazlitt understands himself and Sarah Walker as engaged in a joint endeavour to bring shameful attention upon themselves. Hazlitt seems to be the principal in this enterprise. In *Liber Amoris* he represents himself as discussing Sarah's behaviour in indecorous detail with her father, her mother, her brother-in-law, and John Tomkins, the preferred suitor, as well as speaking and writing about her to his own friends. When his scream 'brought the whole house, father, mother, lodgers and all' into his room, the reader has every reason to suspect that he screamed, although he might not have been aware of it, in order to summon them. He represents himself and Sarah as petting each other while the door of Hazlitt's room remains half-open, not just once but repeatedly, so that they are glimpsed by Sarah's father, by Sarah's servant Maria who 'looked in' and saw Sarah sitting in Hazlitt's lap (106), and narrowly escape discovery by Tomkins (158). Spying on lovers' endearments is represented as a family custom. Sarah reports that her 'sister Betsey was always watching' when her elder sister was courting (106). It is as if neither Hazlitt nor Sarah can appreciate the intimacy

---

[26] *The Times*, Saturday, 29 January 1825, 3.

that they share unless there is a third party to witness it, as if their most private
emotions must be ratified by spectators if they are to be persuaded of their reality.
Hazlitt's concern throughout is that in her displays of affection for him Sarah
may only be 'acting a part, a vile part' (106). He fears that she may have 'two
characters, one that you palm off upon me, and another, your natural one, that
you resume when you get out of the room, like an actress who throws aside her
artificial part behind the scenes' (109). He concludes at last that her whole
behaviour is best understood as 'one faultless, undeviating, consistent, consummate piece of acting' (161). Hazlitt attempts on such occasions to maintain
a distinction between the authentic and the inauthentic, between the real and the
sham, but the distinction is unstable because Hazlitt loves Sarah, as Dorian Gray
loves Sybil Vane, precisely because of her theatricality. The serpentine, lamia-like
quality that entrances him has its origin, he confesses, in a play, in the lines from
Barry Cornwall's *Mirandola* that he repeatedly associates with Sarah, 'see with
what a waving air she goes / Along the corridor'.[27] Hazlitt suggests that the
character was based upon Sarah, which seems unlikely, except that years later in
his autobiography Procter offers a description of Sarah that seems quite clearly
founded on the lines from his own play:

Her movements in walking were very remarkable, for I never observed her to make a step.
She went onwards in a sort of wavy, sinuous manner, like the movement of a snake.[28]

Significantly, the happiest time that Hazlitt can remember spending in her
company was an evening when he took her and her mother to watch Macready
in *Romeo and Juliet*. *Liber Amoris* is liberally seeded with references to plays, to
Dekker's *The Honest Whore* from which Hazlitt borrows one of his names for
Sarah, Infelice, to Byron's *Sardanapalus*, in which the hero's love for Myrrha
echoes, Hazlitt imagines, his own for Sarah, to *Women Beware Women*, *The Plain
Dealer*, *Henry IV, Part One*, *King Lear*, *Macbeth*, and *The Merry Wives of Wind-
sor*, in addition to the more pressingly pertinent texts, *Hamlet* and *Troilus and
Cressida*, and the play referred to most frequently of all, *Othello*. The point is,
I take it, that the reality that plays conjure is like the reality of Hazlitt's love for
Sarah in that both depend on the presence of an audience.

The most persuasive evidence of this is, of course, *Liber Amoris* itself. Hazlitt
began to write it when the affair was at its most intense, and he even notes his
decision in the published text. He reports in a footnote to a letter to his friend,
Patmore, written from Scotland where he has gone to secure a divorce, 'N.B.
I have begun a book of our conversations (I mean mine and the statue's) which

[27] The passage is quoted both in *Liber Amoris*, 143, and in 'On Living to One's Self', in which it
is followed by the sardonic remark: 'however beautiful the description, defend me from meeting
with the original!', Howe, 8, 96.
[28] Barry Procter, *An autobiographical fragment and biographical notes, with…sketches of
contemporaries, unpublished lyrics, etc.*, 181.

I call LIBER AMORIS. I was detained at Stamford and found myself dull, and could hit upon no other way of employing my time so agreeably' (117). It is as if he can authenticate his love for Sarah only by transforming it from an experience into a text, and then by publishing it, bringing it before a readership.

Almost all of the book's critics have focused on the paradox that *Liber Amoris*, a text that seems to transcribe raw experience, should be at the same time so intensely literary. Most of the text consists of a sequence of transcribed conversations and letters, and yet, as John Barnard notes, in its first edition the book emphatically asserts its printed status. It includes, for example, a section consisting of two sentences, which are headed 'Written in a Blank Leaf of Endymion', and yet the lines, represented as a handwritten inscription in a book, are printed enclosed in a neat rectangular box and given a page all to themselves. They are presented, that is, in a way that is only possible in a printed text.[29] It is a device that seems designed to direct the reader's attention to the relationship between manuscript and print. Readers of *Liber Amoris* have divided between those who understand the text as a symptom and those—a rather smaller group—who insist on its artifice, between those who conceive of it as an episode in Hazlitt's biography and those who try to place the book among his works. For one group of readers 'H—' is indistinguishable from Hazlitt; for the other the two are distinguished by an ironic self-consciousness which allows Hazlitt to expose 'H—' to his reader's critical scrutiny. But the possibility remains that the difference between the two kinds of reading might be more apparent than real.

Liber Amoris is an unusually knowing text. The allusions to *Othello*, the decision to represent H—as writing his thoughts on a blank leaf of *Endymion*, Keats's poem of obsessive passion, and in one of those thoughts to describe Sarah as equipped with 'dove's eyes and serpent-shape' (114) in a manner that so evidently echoes another of Keats's poems, the use made of the bronze statue of Napoleon, who resembles Sarah's former lover—'How odd it was that the God of my idolatry should turn out to be like her Idol' (112)—seem all of them uncomfortably willed. They invest the whole text with the crippling self-consciousness, which is, Hazlitt claims in his essay 'On the Conduct of Life', peculiar to writers, because writers 'feel nothing spontaneously'. In an earlier essay, 'On the Literary Character', published in *The Round Table*, he makes a similar point: in the case of writers such as himself 'those whom we love best, take nearly the same rank in our estimation as the heroine of a favourite novel!'[30] For writers, he implies, experience is authenticated only insofar as it is, or may be, printed and published, which is why real women can never appeal quite so

---

[29] John Barnard, 'Hazlitt's *Liber Amoris; or, the New Pygmalion* (1823): Conversations and the Statue', in *Translating Life: Studies in Transpositional Aesthetics*, ed. Shirley Chew and Alistair Stead (Liverpool: Liverpool University Press, 1988), 181–98.

[30] Howe, 17, 396 (the essay was first published in the Paris edition of *Table-Talk*, but the quoted phrase appears in the essay as printed by Hazlitt's son, with manuscript additions, in 1836), and 4, 135.

intensely as the heroine of a novel, whose only being is as print. But the condition once peculiar to writers has, Hazlitt suggests in *Liber Amoris*, become more general. Sarah is scarcely less knowing than Hazlitt himself. She is as aware as he is of what it means when he 'dashed the little Buonaparte on the ground, and stamped upon it' (145). He confesses himself 'sadly afraid the *little image* was dethroned from her heart, as I had dashed it to the ground the other night' (152), and he asks her 'if she could get *the little image* mended' (154). Sarah is a reader practised enough to understand his metaphors, able even to translate a spoken sentence into the printed form in which an italic font brings out its full meaning. In his essay 'On Great and Little Things', Hazlitt maintains that if he were united with his 'Infelice' it would prove an exception to the rule that unequal matches are miserable. He adds immediately,

I have an utter aversion to *blue-stockings*. I do not care a fig for any woman that knows what *an author* means. If I know that she has read anything I have written, I cut her acquaintance immediately. This sort of literary intercourse with me passes for nothing.[31]

But in *Liber Amoris* he reveals that, for him and even for Sarah, all intercourse is literary: there is no area of experience into which literature has not penetrated. The moment when Hazlitt comes closest to persuading himself that Sarah fully returns his affections is when her sister gives him to understand that she sets store not by his person but by his books. Sarah returns all the books he has given her, and when he explains that it was only the three written by himself that he had asked for, Betsey replies, 'AND THOSE ARE THE ONES THAT SHE PRIZES THE MOST!' (149). Again, it is the printer's convention, the capitals, that announce the importance of a remark that, Hazlitt claims, had the power to 'revive the dead'.

Tom Paulin notes of *Liber Amoris* that it 'never in all its sequence of dead surprises achieves an authentic image or cadence even for a moment'.[32] You 'resemble some graceful marble statue in the moon's pale ray!' (103), H— tells S—, and not long afterwards complains to her that in the very first week of their acquaintance she had sat on his lap, 'and I have not got much farther since' (107). It is startling to see Hazlitt writing in a manner that so closely resembles Kean's letters to Charlotte Cox. S— describes her attachment to a former lover with an awkward ingenuousness—'he used to make me read with him—and I used to be with him a good deal, though not much neither' (105)—and shortly afterwards she remarks, 'Nothing tends more to alienate friendship than insult' (109). Hazlitt seems comically unable to characterize either of his speakers consistently, and yet surely it is precisely those violent shifts of register that confer on the book its still shocking reality. Hazlitt is writing for a readership so practised, so familiar with all those techniques that novelists,

[31] *New Monthly Magazine*, 4 (February 1822), 135.
[32] Tom Paulin, *The Day-Star of Liberty: William Hazlitt's Radical Style* (London: Faber and Faber, 1988), 45.

poets, and essayists have used to body forth the reality of their inward lives upon the page that only the most patently inauthentic cadences retain the power to produce the shock of the real. It is as if, by 1823, consistency of character no longer served to confer authenticity so much as to reveal the presence of an accomplished author. It is by allowing H— and S— to remain discontinuous, jumping erratically between quite different verbal registers that they achieve their modern, paradoxical reality.

For Paulin, *Liber Amoris* stands in lamentable contrast to the essays in which Hazlitt perfects his radical style, but the barrier between the two is surely more permeable than Paulin supposes. It is not just that references to Sarah Walker intrude into almost every essay that Hazlitt wrote during the affair, into both the essays that Hazlitt contributed to the February 1822 edition of the *New Monthly Magazine*, for example, 'On Great and Little Things' and 'The Fight'. As he himself admitted, he was for a period unable to keep her out of anything that he wrote and any conversation he engaged in. It is more that the magazine essay, as the form was developed by Hazlitt, Lamb, and their contemporaries, cultivated an intimacy that was most often and most powerfully produced by admitting into the essays indecorous moments of self-revelation. The sense of intimacy might equally well be produced by indiscreet revelations about others, about the quality of the private conversation of literary figures such as Coleridge and Hunt, for example. If it was, as contemporaries were agreed, an 'age of personalities', an age in which the boundaries between public and private life were repeatedly flouted, then it seems safe to assume that such transgressions, denounced vociferously though they were, filled a public need. When *Blackwood's Magazine* published an article entitled 'Hazlitt Cross-Questioned' (August 1818), Hazlitt sued, and Blackwood settled out of court for £100. The piece put to Hazlitt a series of questions of which the second was the most inflammatory:

2. Is it, or is it not, true, that you owe all your ideas about poetry or criticism to gross misconceptions of the meaning of [Wordsworth's] conversation; and that you once owed your personal safety, perhaps existence, to the humane and firm interference of that virtuous man, who rescued you from the hands of an indignant peasantry whose ideas of purity you, a cockney visitor, had dared to outrage?[33]

The incident has so exercised Hazlitt's biographers that it is easy to be distracted from the strange manner in which the sentence segues from an accusation that Hazlitt is a clumsy plagiarist to an accusation that he had been guilty during a residence in the Lake District of a serious sexual assault. The charge makes Hazlitt's decision five years later to publish *Liber Amoris* still more inexplicable, but it works together with Hazlitt's book to suggest that this was a literary culture which understood, even though it feared, the energies that could be produced

---

[33] From John Wilson's 'Hazlitt Cross-Questioned', *Blackwood's Edinburgh Magazine*, 3 (August 1818), 550.

when 'ideas about poetry or criticism' refused to keep their distance from the physical body with all its violent and shameful importunities. It was a state of affairs of which Hazlitt became a victim, as did Sarah Walker, Charlotte Cox, Lady Byron, and Queen Caroline. All four women suffered public defamation, and it is this that makes them such fully representative women in an age of personality.

5

Remembering Peebles

In May 1820, less than a year before he was killed, John Scott wrote a piece in the *London Magazine* pointing out the failings of *Blackwood's* but conceding that it 'was, and is, a great improvement, in point of talent, on the general run of magazines'. 'Its faults, gross as they are,' he added, 'bear the character of whims, and flights, rather than of radical vices', which is why 'it would, indeed, give us some pain, to have any serious disagreement with the "Edinburgh lads"; for, whether it proceed from professional or national sympathy, we feel, after all, a sort of sneaking kindness about our heart, for them and their work'. He ends by hoping that next time he is in their city the 'Edinburgh lads' will invite him to share a dinner at Ambrose's.[1] Their affinities as fellow-Scots and fellow-writers outweighed, it seems, their differences. Who could have guessed that Scott was beginning a dispute that would end at Chalk Farm?

Blackwood's itself wondered why the 'animal boisterousness, and coarse, sanguine, vivacity' that Scott admired in the magazine should have caused such offence. If the magazine was sometimes guilty of 'personalities' they were far milder than those perpetrated in the eighteenth century and yet they were more fiercely resented. The difference lay, it suggested, in the modern magazine's wider circulation:

> But in the days of King William and Queen Anne, the circulation of satire and libel was comparatively very circumscribed, and the taste of the age in such things was much grosser than that of the present. Besides, the reciprocities of social intercourse were much more strictly confined to particular classes, and families; so that the abuse of satire was then, in fact, less mischievous. But now, when commerce has broken down the fences of the privileged classes, and mingled all orders and professions into one general multitude, the peace of society is much more endangered by the additional chance of conflicting interests and individuals coming into contact with each other.[2]

The insults traded between Pope and his dunces were circulated within a less refined world, but it was also a smaller world and a world less socially various. When James Stuart saw himself lampooned in *The Beacon* and *The Sentinel*, and

---

[1] 'Lord Byron: His French Critics: the Newspapers; and the Magazines', *London Magazine*, 1 (May 1820), 495–6.

[2] *Blackwood's Edinburgh Magazine*, 10 (October 1821), 315.

when Lockhart read Scott's attacks on him in the *London*, it was not just what was written but the thought of who was reading it, how many people and of what kind, that seemed unbearable. Boswell may well have sung his 'Whig Song' at a Pitt dinner, and had he done so Stuart would certainly have heard about it. But a lampoon that circulated only within a closed circle was very different from that same lampoon published in a newspaper.

In April 1820, *Blackwood's* printed a speech by Canning in which he represented the crowd attracted to reform meetings as constituting only an 'aggregation'. At such meetings a 'multitude of individuals' are brought together that have 'no permanent relation to each other, no common tie, but what arises from their concurrence as members of that meeting'.[3] By printing Canning's speech, the magazine implicitly contrasted its own readership with the crowds of this kind attracted by orators such as Henry Hunt. Its readers, the suggestion is, shared not only political opinions, but aesthetic principles, a love of country sports, a taste for philosophy that happily coincided with a relish for the bottle, and a cordial dislike of Whigs, prudishness, and bluestockings. And yet the *Blackwood's* writers must have been aware that its real, as opposed to its imagined readership, was just as much an aggregate as the crowds that met to petition for parliamentary reform. All the new magazines of the second decade of the century look back fondly to the periodicals of Queen Anne's day, most fondly of all to Addison and Steele's *Spectator*. It was Addison and Steele, after all, who, together with Johnson, had made periodical writing respectable, but it was also, I suspect, a tribute to the success of Addison and Steele in 'marking out a region of intimacy' into which their readers were invited.[4] It was an effect that the later magazines busily tried to imitate, but even as they did so they signalled their awareness that the intimacy that magazines offered in an age of mass production could only be illusory.

Blackwood's was in the habit of representing itself grandiosely as a publication that circulated to the farthest reaches of the empire—the natives of 'Hindostan / Read none but North—he is their only man'[5]—and throughout Europe—'We are much read at Genoa, Milan, Florence, and Rome'[6]—but such boasts were often punctuated by displays of parochial Scots feeling: 'God preserve us, but we had almost forgot to mention Peebles.'[7] It seems a typically absurd *Blackwood's* joke to represent itself as at once a global publication and as something more like a parish magazine, but it is a considered joke, a joke spelt out by Christopher North when he objects to a complaint in *John Bull* that

[3] *Blackwood's Edinburgh Magazine*, 7 (April 1820), 11–21, 15.
[4] Michael G. Ketcham, *Transparent Designs: Reading, Performance, and Form in the* Spectator *Papers* (Georgia: University of Athens Press, 1985), 163.
[5] *Blackwood's Edinburgh Magazine*, 10 (December 1821), 497.
[6] *Blackwood's Edinburgh Magazine*, 8 (October 1820), 82.
[7] *Blackwood's Edinburgh Magazine*, 8 (October 1820), 87.

Blackwood's is too much concerned with people and activities of no interest to anyone outside Edinburgh:

the London people will say it is *local*. And why not? London itself is the most provincial spot alive. Let our Magazine be read in the interior of Africa, along with either or both of the two Monthlies, and which will seem most cosmopolite to the impartial black population? Ebony. The London people, with their theatres, operas, Cockneys &c. &c. are wholly unintelligible out of their own small town. The truth must be told them— *London is a very small insignificant place.* Our ambition is that our wit shall be local all over the world.[8]

Christopher North makes the remark in an episode of the *Noctes Ambrosianae*, and, on the nights when the *Blackwood's* men meet to dine in its inner room, Ambrose's Tavern becomes a place where Edinburgh news can be canvassed, London doings mocked, and where guests such as Mr Buller, newly arrived from Oxford, Professor Feldborg from Denmark, and the German Doctor Kempferhausen might also be admitted to the company. At such moments the Edinburgh tavern became a local of a unique kind, a local where people from all over Europe if not all over the world might congregate. These dinners are presented as reproducing in little the character of the magazine in which they are recorded. The competitors of *Blackwood's* took up similar positions. The two *London Magazines*, for example, *Baldwin's* and *Gold's*, are as firmly based in London as *Blackwood's* is in Edinburgh. In his Prospectus John Scott claimed that *Baldwin's* was established so that 'the METROPOLIS' would not 'remain *unrepresented* in the new strenuous competition of Periodical Literature'.[9] His was a London magazine that covered the London theatre and the London exhibitions. It even, in a paper by Barry Cornwall, offered the 'Cider Cellar' as London's answer to Ambrose's Tavern,[10] and yet the two *London Magazines*, and the *New Monthly*, which was also a magazine closely affiliated with the capital, just as much as *Blackwood's*, had interests that extended to the whole nation and might even stretch 'all over the world'.

It was a cultural moment at which it was oddly difficult to distinguish between the local and the national. The most striking indication of this is *The Etonian*, a school magazine established by W. M. Praed who was assisted by some other senior pupils of the school such as H. N. Coleridge and John Moultrie. It was a magazine written by and for Etonians past and present. It was written, that is, for a small homogenous group many of whom would have been personally acquainted with each other. Each issue begins with the secretary's account of the meeting of the 'King of Clubs', presided over by Peregrine Courtenay, a schoolboy of alarming sophistication, who performs the same function for

---

[8] *Blackwood's Edinburgh Magazine*, 11 (April 1822), 488.
[9] *London Magazine*, 1 (January 1820), iv.
[10] *London Magazine*, 2 (October 1820), 384–8.

The Etonian as Christopher North for *Blackwood's*. The contributors write under pseudonyms: although the magazine will admit only 'the writing of Etonians, it is of course allowed them to write under whatever signature and character they think fit', since this 'has been the practice of all periodical writers'.[11] *Blackwood's* was a mass-market periodical in the guise of a club magazine: *The Etonian* was a club magazine in the guise of a mass-market periodical like *Blackwood's*. The difference between the two was so negligible that *The Etonian*, apparently effortlessly, was able to outgrow its original status: it was taken on by a major London publisher and went through several editions before fully outgrowing its origin and becoming, still under Praed's editorship, *Knight's Quarterly Magazine*, a fully-fledged London periodical. Its oddly hybrid character struck its writers as so amusing that the joke had to be shared with their readers. Peregrine Courtenay claims to have received a letter from the publisher of the *London Magazine*:

Received a letter from Baldwin, soliciting the co-operation of the Club, in the event of the discontinuance of 'The Etonian.' Shall be happy to oblige Mr Baldwin, as far as I am concerned; but Montgomery is hand and glove with Mr Christopher North; and Sir Francis and Sterling are severally under engagements to the *Edinburgh* and *Quarterly*.[12]

The major British periodicals compete to secure the services of the writers of a school magazine. This is a joke, of course, but what gives it point is that it was a joke so very close to the truth.

When *John Bull* complained that *Blackwood's* included too much material of merely local Edinburgh interest that remained incomprehensible to English readers, Christopher North retorted that there is a special pleasure to be found in not understanding. North enjoys for example *John Bull*'s 'notices to correspondents', the column of opaque responses supposedly prompted by readers' letters: 'The noble Lord's communication has been received—he will see by the leading Article of this day's Paper what very great attention we have paid to his entertaining Lecture:—we are surprised at his Lordship's meanness, which is only equalled by his stupidity.'[13] 'Is it not pleasant sometimes', North asks, 'to see things under a tender, obscure, and hazy light?'[14] The 'Notices' work by inviting readers to join a closed circle of those possessed of knowledge as yet unpublished to the world and at the same time they alert those readers to their exclusion. The whole of the *Noctes Ambrosianae* series works in a similar way. Readers are at once invited to join an intimate, convivial social group and apprised that they are excluded from it—it may be by an inadequate knowledge of Edinburgh's intellectual and social life, or it may even be by a defective knowledge of the Scots language. When Tickler describes the young Edinburgh Whigs as 'poor

---

[11] *The Etonian* (London: Henry Colburn, 1823), 1, 97.
[12] *The Etonian*, 2, 102.
[13] *John Bull*, no. 3, 31 December 1820, 20.
[14] In an episode of the *Noctes Ambrosianae*, *Blackwood's Edinburgh Magazine*, 11 (April 1822), 488.

Pow-heads', advice to the English reader unfamiliar with the Scottish term for tadpoles is enclosed in brackets '(see Dr Jamieson)'. The same advice is repeated when the *New Monthly*'s politics are said to consist of 'concealed, suppressed, discontented, yawmering (see the Dr) whiggism',[15] and can be found many more times in early issues of the magazine. It is entirely sensible advice for those English readers who possessed a copy of Jamieson's 1818 *Dictionary of the Scottish Language*, but that was surely a group so tiny that it might as well be discounted. Hazlitt complains of Hunt that he writes in *The Examiner* just as he speaks 'to a private circle round the fireside', unaware that he may not always make himself 'intelligible to the public', but Hazlitt makes the charge in an essay that ends with an affectionate portrait of the unnamed George Dyer, who, unlike 'H-yd-n', 'G-dwin', 'L—', and 'H—', his readers could not be expected to identify, and the essay includes a passage such as this:

'Mrs—'s conversation is as fine-cut as her features, and I like to sit in the room with that sort of coronet face. What she says leaves a flavour, like fine green tea.[16]

When the essay was collected in *The Plain Speaker* the name was supplied, but Anna Montagu would not have been familiar to many readers either of the magazine or the volume.[17] Hazlitt's sentences leave a flavour and that flavour surely depends on the 'tender, obscure, and hazy light' in which they are suffused.

John Galt invented for *Blackwood's* a distinctive kind of fiction that seems specifically designed to explore the possibility that writing for the magazine makes available, the possibility of being 'local all over the world'. Thomas Duffle, who describes his 'Voyages' in 'The Steam-Boat', Galt's serial for 1820, plays, in the knowing way that marks this as a *Blackwood's* production, on the defining feature of magazine serial fiction, that it tells stories that break off before they are completed. His narrator records tales told to him which, because the boat docks before the story is finished, break off never to be resumed. Duffle is a cloth-merchant trading in Glasgow's Saltmarket, and his voyages are less than grand, consisting of two day-trips down the Clyde to Greenock. He is able to escape from 'the obscurities of the Salt-market, and the manufacturing smokes and smells of Glasgow, to enjoy the hilarity of the sparkling waters of the summer sea',[18] and still return to his rented rooms well before nightfall. And yet on that Clyde paddle-steamer he meets far-travelled folk who tell him tales that encompass half the globe: a widow woman tells of her trip to Waterloo to find her son's grave; a sailor explains how he came to survive a hurricane that overtook his ship on a voyage from Trinidad to St Kitt's; a Norwegian tells a tale of Spitzbergen

[15] *Blackwood's Edinburgh Magazine*, 11 (April 1822), 485 and 486.
[16] 'On the Conversation of Authors', *London Magazine*, 2 (September 1820), 250–63; Howe, 8, 25–44.
[17] She was the third wife of Basil Montagu, illegitimate son of the Earl of Sandwich by the singer Martha Ray, lawyer, one-time Godwinian, and friend of Wordsworth and Coleridge.
[18] *Blackwood's Edinburgh Magazine*, 9 (June 1821), 258.

and the midnight sun, and a 'Yanky from Philadelphia' describes how he became 'the Deucalion of Kentucky' when his town and all its inhabitants were swept away in a flood. This is fiction that almost comically exemplifies the art of being 'local all over the world'. But Galt knows that the part of the world with which the magazine is most intensely concerned is London, a guilty knowledge that *Blackwood's* too betrays in the asperity of its response to *John Bull.*

Blackwood's, John Bull warns, risks seeming provincial, which would have annoyed those who wrote for a magazine that issued, as far as they were concerned, from a great capital city, the modern Athens. But Wilson and Lockhart, though they contested, could not deny *John Bull*'s assumption, that in Britain all places other than London were provincial because all other places defined themselves in their relation to London. So it is that Galt's Thomas Duffle supplements his voyages down the Clyde with a voyage to London. During his stay in the capital he witnesses the King's coronation, which does not much impress him, but he is gratified to find himself everywhere feted as 'Mr Duffle of Blackwood's Magazine'.[19] Duffle is only following in the footsteps of Dr Pringle, the hero of Galt's first *Blackwood's* fiction, *The Ayrshire Legatees*, which traces the adventures of Dr Pringle, the minister for Garnock in Ayrshire. Dr Pringle and his family travel to London to collect a legacy, and witness when they arrive the funeral of the old King and the trial of the new King's Queen. The Doctor and his wife display all the comical innocence of London ways that the reader expects, except that by a cunning sleight of hand the Pringles emerge from their adventures with their dignity enhanced, and the inhabitants of the sophisticated metropolis are left seeming sadly diminished. When the Pringles come back to Garnock they re-enter a solider, less trivial world. In this, the story is true to the magazine in which it appeared, and, more importantly, characteristic of much of the literature of the post-war decade.

Galt was developing a narrative strategy that had first been deployed by Scott in the first series of *Tales of My Landlord* (1816). The *Tales* are presented to the reader by Jedediah Cleishbotham, parish schoolmaster of the imaginary village of Gandercleugh, which is situated midway between Glasgow and Edinburgh. Cleishbotham, who has visited Glasgow three times and Edinburgh twice, on one of which occasions he witnessed a debate at the General Assembly of the Church of Scotland, is confident that his name on the title-page will itself be enough to secure the attention of 'the sedate and reflecting part of mankind'. He addresses the reader from a village which, far from revealing his as a provincial perspective, establishes him at the very centre, 'the navel (*si fas sit dicere*) of this our native realm of Scotland'. The forty years during which Cleishbotham has spent every evening bar the Sabbath in the common room of the Wallace Inn have allowed him a more extensive knowledge of 'the manners and customs of

---

[19] *Blackwood's Edinburgh Magazine*, 10 (August 1821), 13.

various tribes and people' than if he had been himself a traveller. Scotland would only partially be represented by Edinburgh, 'our metropolis of law', or by Glasgow 'our metropolis and mart of gain', but finds its true epitome in the entirely undistinguished village of Gandercleugh. But the implicit claim is still grander. *Tales of My Landlord*, published by Blackwood in Scotland and by John Murray in London, was a British rather than a Scottish publishing event: Gandercleugh established itself in the closing months of 1816, not at all ironically but as a fact amply borne out by the volume's sales figures, as the 'navel' of the whole of the United Kingdom.

Scott and Galt find their amusement in displacing the metropolitan by the provincial at the centre of national life. It would be hard to claim that any poem of the period was less provincial than *Don Juan*, a point rather forcefully made within the poem itself:

> You gentlemen, by dint of long seclusion
>   From better company, have kept your own
> At Keswick, and, through still continued fusion
>   Of one another's minds, at last have grown
> To deem as a most logical conclusion,
>   That Poesy has wreaths for you alone:
> There is a narrowness in such a notion,
> Which makes me wish you'd change your lakes for ocean.
>
> (*Don Juan*, Dedication, 5)

But, as Byron well knew, there were other kinds of provincialism than the kind of which the Lake Poets were guilty. There was, for example, the provincialism of the 'twenty score / Of well-bred persons, call'd "*The World*"' (*Beppo*, 59, 7–8), or of the 'twice two thousand people' in London's West End bred to 'look down on the universe with pity' (*Don Juan*, 11, 45). They share the complacent illusion that persuades Jedediah Cleishbotham that Gandercleugh is 'the navel' of the world, and Byron gently mocks them for it. But he is just as likely to share their position as to satirize it. When, in the second canto of *Don Juan*, Byron speaks of swimming the Hellespont, 'As once (a feat on which ourselves we prided) / Leander, Mr Ekenhead, and I did' (2, 105, 7–8), he seems entirely confident, as, I suppose, an aristocratic celebrity might well be, that all of his doings are familiar and of interest to the world. But, especially in the poem's English cantos, that explanation proves insufficient. In the great *ubi sunt* passage in Canto XI, for example, Byron asks, 'Where are the Lady Carolines and Franceses?' (11, 80, 1). The names refuse to remain simply generic. Lady Caroline had particularized herself, feeding the publicity that had from the first surrounded her relationship with Byron by publishing *Glenarvon* ('Some play the devil, and then write a novel' (*Don Juan*, 2, 201, 8)), and even a 'New Canto' of *Don Juan*, but Lady Frances Webster is particularized by association and her only provocation seems to have been that in 1813 Byron had forborne to complete his seduction of her even though she was 'young, and religious, and pretty' and her husband was Byron's 'particular friend'.[20] The line teasingly pretends to admit its readers to a curtained world of aristocratic dalliance only to remind them of their exclusion from it, and it can be fully appreciated only by those who enjoy both manoeuvres.

There were those who claimed that the publishing sensation of the age, the Scotch novels, was erected on similar foundations. Scott's most powerful tool was the Scots language that most of his best-loved characters spoke. In *The Antiquary* Edie Ochiltree points out that Elspeth Mucklebackit, who, before she became a fishwife was the personal servant of a Countess, can when she chooses speak standard English: 'It's fearsome baith to see and hear her when she wampishes about her arms, and gets to her English, and speaks as if she were a prent book.'[21] The use of Scots, Ochiltree implies, releases the reader from alienating print into a warmly human spoken language. It is a tactic that helps to explain the popularity in this period not just of Scott, but of Hogg and Galt, of writers whose characters might speak Irish English such as Maria Edgeworth, and of those like John Clare who used English dialectal forms. In her (mildly) amusing burlesque *Scotch Novel Reading*, Sarah Green presents as Scott's representative admirer Alice Fennel, the Cockney daughter of a retired apothecary, who affects to speak in Scots herself so great is her admiration of the novels. But Alice finds much of the language in which they are written entirely incomprehensible.[22] Scott's readers were beguiled, as it were, by being placed in the position of the readers of *Blackwood's* who were repeatedly advised to look for the meaning of a word in a dictionary that it seems impossible that any significant number of them would own. This was a readership that delighted, as Christopher North puts it, to see things 'under a tender, obscure, and hazy light'.

Scott's Jedediah Cleishbotham lies behind Galt's Thomas Duffle and Dr Pringle, and the 'Chaldee Manuscript', the most scandalous of *Blackwood's Magazine*'s ventures into local Edinburgh affairs may itself have had the same inspiration.[23] The 'Chaldee Manuscript' offers an account of how William Blackwood, 'a man clothed in plain apparel' whose 'name was as it had been the colour of ebony', established the *Edinburgh Monthly Magazine*, under the editorship of Thomas Pringle and James Cleghorn, two beasts equipped with

---

[20] *Byron's Letters and Journals*, ed. Leslie A. Marchand, 3 (London: John Murray, 1974), 122.

[21] Walter Scott, *The Antiquary*, ed. David Hewitt (Edinburgh: Edinburgh University Press, 1995), 309.

[22] Sarah Green, *Scotch Novel Reading; Or, Modern Quackery. A Novel Really Founded on Facts* (London: A. K. Newman, 1824), 1, 4–5.

[23] 'Translation from an Ancient Chaldee Manuscript' appeared in the first issue of the re-born magazine, 2 (October 1817), 89–96, but Blackwood chose to exclude the piece from all subsequent editions, so that it is absent from many library copies of the magazine. It is re-printed with introductions by Alan Lang Strout, 'James Hogg's "Chaldee Manuscript"', *Publications of the Modern Language Association of America*, 65 (1950), 695–718, and in *Blackwood's Magazine, 1817–25: Selections from Maga's Infancy*, ed. Anthony Jarrels, 6 vols. (London: Pickering and Chatto, 2006), 2, 21–37.

'staves wherewith they skipped' (Pringle and Cleghorn were lame). When Blackwood discontinued the magazine Pringle and Cleghorn joined with his principal competitor, Archibald Constable, the 'man who was crafty in counsel', to produce the *Scots Magazine* only for Blackwood triumphantly to re-launch his own magazine with the assistance of the leopard, the scorpion, and 'the great wild boar from the forest of Lebanon' (Wilson, Lockhart, and Hogg) under the title *Blackwood's Edinburgh Magazine*. The wit of the piece has not worn well, though its offensiveness remains apparent, as in the reference to John Dalyell, the antiquarian and naturalist: 'His face was like unto the face of an ape, and he chattered continually, and his nether parts were uncomely.' Hogg, Lockhart, and Wilson (the piece seems to have been a joint effort) were, I suspect, prompted by Jedediah Cleishbotham's description of how he had passed his undermaster's manuscript to John Ballantyne, Scott's own printer, 'one cunning in the trade (as it is called) of book-selling', 'a mirthful man, of small stature, cunning in counterfeiting of voices' (Ballantyne was an accomplished mimic). Scott's reference is affectionate, and he does not, like the 'Chaldee Manuscript', affect biblical parody, but both Scott's introduction and the *Blackwood's* paper wilfully choose to admit references that many of their readers must have found opaque, and it is worth considering why they should have done so.

Scott's novels brought into existence a new kind of readership, a mass readership. Even before *Tales of My Landlord* went on sale Murray had recognized that the very large first edition that he and Blackwell had agreed on would be quite inadequate. He wrote to Blackwell, 'You may go on printing as many as you can, for we certainly need not stop until we come to the end of our unfortunately limited 6000.'[24] Scott's readers no doubt relished, like Alice Fennel, the feeling that their enjoyment was shared by so many, but that sense of forming one in a faceless army of admirers is the more satisfying if it can somehow be made to coincide with a rhetoric that persuades its readers that they are enlisted in a 'little platoon', a local community made up of those who can share references to Mr Ekenhead or Lady Frances or the printer, John Ballantyne.

It was the new magazines, as they competed for their share of the new mass readership, that cultivated this rhetoric most assiduously. The great magazine of the eighteenth century, the *Gentleman's*, 'old Sylvanus', for which *Blackwood's* pretended to maintain a pious regard, had come to seem, as *Gold's* put it, 'so completely out of its element in this busy bustling scene of activity and cheerfulness, that we wonder at its being able to sustain existence'.[25] It addressed a rural squirearchy that seemed already a relic of the previous century. The new magazines were products of what had become an increasingly mechanized publishing industry. 'But ten years ago', the *Westminster Review* explained in 1824, the

---

[24] Edgar Johnson, *Sir Walter Scott: The Great Unknown*, 2 vols. (London: Hamish Hamilton, 1970), 1, 557.
[25] *Gold's London Magazine and Theatrical Inquisitor*, 3 (January 1821), 15–16.

printing presses produced 'at the ordinary rate' only '250 single impressions in an hour', with the result that large print-runs could be delivered quickly only by setting up each page twice or even three times. But Koenig's steam press, first introduced at *The Times*, made it possible to produce copy at the extraordinary rate of '25000 impressions an hour'.[26] Edinburgh, like Glasgow, its neighbour to the West, had become an industrial city, but the industry that made it famous was print. A correspondent to the *London Magazine* reported from Edinburgh: 'Literature, somehow, is degenerating into a kind of trade in Edinburgh just as calico is in Glasgow, or metal in Birmingham.—People come here to *make books*, and book-making is, consequently, *the manufacture* of the place . . . a book *published in Edinburgh* . . . is in danger of becoming like a razor from Birmingham or a printed gown-piece from the Gorbals.'[27] In Edinburgh, it seems, books were mass-produced. The effect was most marked in the production of periodicals. The same correspondent notes that whereas, twenty years ago, only one magazine was published in Edinburgh, 'there are, now, at least a dozen monthly and quarterly publications, with the contents of one or more of which you find almost the whole population acquainted'.[28] This newly mechanized industry of periodical publication was sustained by a newly created mass readership, and written by a new class of professional periodical writers. It prompted Patmore in a piece for the *London Magazine*, 'On Magazine Writers', to a comic speculation that conceals, one suspects, a real anxiety: 'I have heard that a patent has been, or is about to be, taken out for an automaton writer, the principle of which is, that after being wound up it is only necessary to fling in a certain number of pages of Johnson, or any other vocabulary, and they come out completely formed into the shape of an article'.[29] Writing periodicals was in danger of becoming as mechanized and impersonal a business as printing them. It was in reaction against the conditions that made possible their production that the new magazines encouraged a prose that fostered an illusion of personal, intimate address.[30] Essays in the new style, of which Lamb, Hazlitt, De Quincey, Leigh Hunt, and Cobbett were the masters, worked busily to realize the presence of the essayist, so that the consumption of a mass-produced pamphlet might seem to the reader an experience as intimate as being engaged in conversation by an unusually clever and entertaining friend.[31]

---

[26] *Westminster Review*, 2 (July 1824), 205.

[27] *London Magazine*, 3 (May 1821), 34.

[28] *London Magazine*, 4 (July 1821), 78.

[29] *London Magazine*, 6 (July 1822), 25.

[30] For an analysis of how in his Elia essays Lamb contrives to return to his readers 'their cherished privacy, their frail intentionality' in the face of the threat of 'mechanical reproduction' see Peter Manning, 'Detaching Lamb's Thought', in *Romantic Periodicals and Print Culture*, ed. Kim Wheatley (London and Portland, Oregon: Frank Cass, 2002), 137–46.

[31] For a suggestive discussion of writers' responses to the new phenomenon of mass production centred on Byron, see Tom Mole, *Byron's Romantic Celebrity: Industrial Culture and the Hermeneutics of Intimacy* (Basingstoke: Palgrave Macmillan, 2007).

The most brilliant tactic developed by *Blackwood's* was to cast the whole magazine as the all but accidental production of a group of companions in the habit of meeting at Ambrose's tavern in Edinburgh to eat, drink, and enjoy each other's company. John Scott insisted that he would not 'seek to impart to [his] sheets that redolency of Leith-ale, and tobacco-smoke, which floats about all the pleasantry of the magazine in question—giving one the idea of its facetious articles having been written on the slopped table of a tavern parlour in the back-wynd, after the *convives* had retired, and left the author to solitude, silence, pipe-ashes, and the dregs of *black-strap*'.[32] But despite John Scott's protest it was a 'redolency' that he and very many writers of the period seemed rather anxious to give their pages. Byron's unpublished Preface to the first two cantos of *Don Juan* parodies Wordsworth's note to 'The Thorn', but perhaps more pointedly mimics the *Blackwood's* effect by presenting the poem as narrated 'by a Spanish gentle-man in a village in the Sierra Morena on the road between Monasterio and Seville, sitting at the door of a posada with the Curate of the hamlet on his right hand, a cigar in his mouth, a jug of Malaga or perhaps "right sherries" before him on a small table, containing the relics of an *olla podrida*'. The vivacity with which John Scott describes the effect in itself betrays the envy lurking within his disapproval. It is, after all, exactly the quality that he most admires in the contributors to the rival magazine, a 'sort of animal boisterousness, and coarse, sanguine, vivacity', which 'render it impossible to be very angry with their excesses'.[33] By a benign alchemy the manner worked to transform the anony-mous consumer of the magazine into a valued member of an exclusive, brilliant, and sparklingly entertaining social circle. It is an aspect of the *Blackwood's* nostalgia for the days of Queen Anne that the magazine attempted to recreate the intimacy of address achieved by Addison and Steele, but it required a new kind of prose. Reviewing James Hogg, a member of the *Blackwood's* inner circle, the *London* described him as 'an intimate acquaintance whom we have never seen, but with whom we are on the most familiar footing'.[34] The extraordinary success of Mary Russell Mitford's *Our Village* rested on a similar basis. A fellow writer in a tribute to Mitford observes, 'I never saw you in my life' and yet 'I have walked with you, gathered your primroses', not only 'admired you, but admired your dog, which is the touchstone of true love'.[35] The need to foster that illusion became especially urgent in the years in which book production was becoming industrialized, a process that inevitably alienated the writer from the reader. Magazines were the chief symptom of the new system of production which

---

[32] *London Magazine*, 1 (May 1820), 495. Notice that Scott's description long pre-dates the first appearance in *Blackwood's* of the *Noctes Ambrosianae* in March 1822.

[33] *London Magazine*, 1 (May 1820), 496.

[34] *London Magazine*, 1 (June 1820), 666. The reviewer is probably John Scott.

[35] Lady Charlotte Bury, *Journal of the Heart* (London: Colburn and Bentley, 1830), 84. Mitford's stories, before they were collected into volumes, first appeared as papers in the *Lady's Magazine*.

makes it unsurprising that they should have prized so highly writers who could generate the illusion that their readers saw their face and heard their voice.

Lamb, Hazlitt, Leigh Hunt, and Cobbett all learned to write a prose that seemed to realize the physical presence of its writer. This is prose that seems to clap its readers on the shoulder, lean towards them confidentially: it moves between the jocular, the pathetic, and the serious in transitions so quick and so easy as to realize an ideal of social converse that its readers, poring over the magazine in their lonely rooms, are invited to share, at least by proxy. Lamb's 'New Year's Eve', for example, proved its merit by prompting from a reader a rhymed 'Epistle':

> I would that eye to eye it were my lot
> To sit with thee, the chafing world forgot;
> While the 'grape's unchecked virtue' in the cup
> 'Moved itself right,' and as the hearth blazed up,
> Ruddying our cheeks, thy witty eloquence
> Threw brighter sparkles forth than sparkled thence.[36]

Lamb is successful because he can make the readers of a mass-produced essay feel that they have been invited into his private presence. But the readership he addresses is not so unsophisticated as this would suggest. De Quincey could knowingly speak of 'the public (into whose private ear I am confidentially whispering my confessions)', and T. J. Wainewright could advertise 'Mr Weathercock's Private Correspondence, Intended for the Public Eye'. John Wilson entitles one of his most brilliantly inventive pieces for *Blackwood's* 'An Hour's Tete-a-Tete with the Public'.[37] They were addressing a readership willing at once to enjoy the illusion of intimate address and its illusoriness.

De Quincey and Wainewright are entirely typical in playfully suggesting that there might be no clear difference between public and confidential communication. They wrote for magazines and magazines were never happier than when they could dismantle the barriers separating the public from the private. Lamb's 'Christ's Hospital Five and Thirty Years Ago', to the affected horror of *Blackwood's*, recalls the private schooldays of those, like T. F. Middleton, the Bishop of Calcutta, who had since become public men.[38] Many of Lamb's essays trespass in similar ways. In 'On Some of the Old Actors', Elia sees William Dodd walking in the gardens of Gray's Inn. Dodd specialized in playing simpletons such as Sir Andrew Aguecheek: 'in expressing slowness of apprehension' he 'surpassed all others'. It is because he had so famous a public face that the sight of his 'serious,

[36] *London Magazine*, 4 (August 1821), 137. The verses are by Sir Charles Elton.
[37] *London Magazine*, 4 (October 1821), 368; Lindop, 2, 61; *London Magazine*, 2 (September 1820), 299; *Blackwood's Edinburgh Magazine*, 8 (October 1820), 78–105. Some months later Maginn published a sequel, 'Another Tete-a-Tete with the Public', *Blackwood's Edinburgh Magazine*, 8 (February 1821), 529–35.
[38] *Blackwood's Edinburgh Magazine*, 8 (November 1820), 207–9.

thoughtful' offstage countenance struck Elia as at once so sad and so strange.[39] That privileged and disconcerting glimpse of the actor at a moment when he does not know that he is being looked at offers material that is especially congenial to a magazine essayist. A similar illicit pleasure rewards the readers of the second article in the series, whose eyes, as Godwin's tragedy fails, are allowed to focus not on the stage but on the face of the blissfully unaware author and his anxiously sweating companion.[40] Hazlitt returns the compliment in 'On Great and Little Things', when Lamb attends the opening performance of his own farce, *Mr H*, and Hazlitt points his reader's attention not at the stage but at Lamb himself, sitting in the front row, listening to the prologue and roaring with laughter at his own wit, happily ignorant that his play will be damned so finally that its first will be its last performance.[41] Even more pointedly, in Hazlitt's 'On the Conversation of Authors', readers are offered the pleasure of peeping into intimate spaces where they can glimpse famous authors as they talk in private at their firesides.[42] Authors, people encountered before only in print, are given voices, social mannerisms and they are attached to bodies. Hazlitt reveals Godwin and Coleridge as they seem to those who meet them rather than read them, and John Hamilton Reynolds did the same by Hazlitt. In a piece for the *Scots Magazine* he contrasted Hazlitt's 'lion-sinewed' prose with the weakness of his handshake: 'He appears to abandon a bunch of melancholy fingers to your threatened squeeze, with some hope of their not coming to a shake.'[43]

Magazine essays cultivated a distinctive rhetoric, which they tended to describe as occupying a midway point between the public and the private. In its report of the King's coronation in the issue for August 1821, for example, the *London*, like the other magazines was conscious that it had been pre-empted. The ceremony had been exhaustively described in newspaper accounts. Its solution was to offer its own account in the form of a letter from a cit, a representative member of London's middle class, to 'a Lady in the Country'. The letter form allows hushed reverence—'such magnificence' was not made by 'mortal hands, but wrought by fairy spell out of wonders of the sea and air'—to alternate with references to the Marquis of Anglesea's ill-behaved horse and the 'confused murmur' that broke out when Queen Caroline tried to demand entry to the proceedings. The reporter, J. H. Reynolds, managed to get a ticket only the day before, and had to buy his court dress for the occasion. His ticket did not give him entry to the Abbey but Westminster Hall, from which he was able to watch the King progress to the Abbey by scratching the white paint from the great window, while his feet were trodden on and his coat scratched by women anxious to take his place. After

[39] 'On Some of The Old Actors', *London Magazine*, 5 (February 1822), 174–9, 177.
[40] 'The Old Actors,' *London Magazine*, 5 (April 1822), 303–11, 309–10. In *Essays of Elia* the revised essay was published under the title 'On the Artificial Comedy of the Last Century'.
[41] *New Monthly Magazine*, 4 (February 1822), 127–39; Howe, 8, 232.
[42] *London Magazine*, 2 (September 1820), 250–62.
[43] 'Living Authors. A Dream', *Scots Magazine*, n.s. 86 (August 1820), 133–40, 136.

the ceremony the King and his nobles returned to the Hall, and the reporter had the pleasure of watching them dine, all the while recalling that he had himself eaten nothing for fifteen hours. Once the King had eaten, had drunk a toast to his people and retired, Reynolds was allowed to share the vestiges of the feast with the other onlookers, and secured a glass of burgundy and a piece of cherry pie, not to mention a sugar dolphin that he preserves as a souvenir.[44] It is entirely appropriate that when he is reminded of a poem it should be 'Ode on a Grecian Urn' by the recently dead Cockney, Keats. The bandsmen, their music drowned by the shouts of the crowd, 'pipe to the spirit ditties of no tone'.[45] The writer deftly takes up the in-between vantage typical of the Cockney and this is the perspective from which the coronation reveals itself as offering material appropriate to a magazine.

It was a rhetoric that Hazlitt consciously set himself to learn in his early 'Table-Talk' essays for the *London Magazine*. John Scott had worked with Hazlitt before, when he edited *The Champion*. The two men had fallen out, and were reconciled early in 1820, but Scott remained suspicious. He feared, as Hazlitt must have known, that Hazlitt's 'besetting errors' and 'improper subjects' might disqualify him as a contributor to the new magazine.[46] Hazlitt's first essays are designed to allay Scott's fears by showing that he could address a readership that might not share his political sympathies. It was a task that seems to have led Hazlitt to reflect on the kind of essay that the new magazines demanded, the subjects it would be 'proper' to treat in them, and, just as important, what kind of treatment those subjects should be given. Hazlitt's essays for *The Examiner*, collected in *The Round Table* in 1817, had been abused by reviewers for their vulgarity, rancorous politics, 'blasphemous ribaldry', and disrespect for Burke.[47] Looking back on Hazlitt's career in 1819, the *British Review* concluded that his 'aim appears to be to destroy the very foundations of morality and decorum, by a series of periodical attacks upon all received opinions, and by the systematic ridicule of every thing that is serious or respectable'.[48] Attacks of this kind would not have affected his standing at *The Examiner*, which, under Leigh Hunt's editorship, had a fixed political character and a small circulation pretty much

---

[44] *London Magazine*, 4 (August 1821), 186–96. Compare Keats's *The Fall of Hyperion*. In the poem's first vision, the poet finds himself in a *forest* clearing, where a feast is spread on a mossy mound: 'Which, nearer seen, seemed refuse of a meal / By angel tasted, or our Mother Eve . . .' (30–1). The poet standing amid 'empty shells' and 'grape-stalks but half bare' is in a position very similar to the *London Magazine* correspondent, permitted to feed on the remnants of the feast after the invited guests have departed.

[45] The other quotation, 'All, all abroad to gaze!' describes the multitude gathered to witness the cremation of the Rajah Arvalan and the sati of his wives in Southey's *The Curse of Kehama*, and, just for a moment, it transforms the Coronation into a ceremony of savage and exotic oriental grandeur.

[46] Stanley Jones, *Hazlitt: A Life from Winterslow to Frith Street* (Oxford: Oxford University Press, 1989), 168–70 and 306–7.

[47] See the *Quarterly Review*, 17 (April 1817), 154–9; the *Eclectic Review*, 7 (April 1817), 385–6; and the *British Critic*, 7 (June 1817), 554–69.

[48] *British Review*, 13 (May 1819), 313–39, 313–14.

confined to those in sympathy with its politics, but would not do for the *London Magazine*. Hunt, Hazlitt observes in 'On the Conversation of Authors', needs 'a select circle of admirers and devotees to feel himself quite at home'. He is 'too confident and secure of his audience', which is why 'his hits do not tell like L—'s'.[49] He is comparing the private conversation of the two men, and his account of Lamb's 'Thursday evening parties' has never been bettered, but he is doing so in an essay that appeared in the *London Magazine* the month after Lamb had made his debut as Elia in 'Recollections of the South Sea House'.[50] It may be that the contrast between Lamb's parties, where if a person 'took snuff heartily, it was sufficient', and Hunt's dependence on a closed circle of acolytes also acknowledges the difference between *The Examiner* and the new magazine, the *London*, that had by then enlisted the services of both Hazlitt and Lamb.

The *London* happily accommodated politics but avoided partisanship. It was a posture Hazlitt experimented with in the second of his 'Table-Talk' essays, 'On the Difference between Speaking and Writing'. Hazlitt's chief exhibits in the essay are parliamentary speeches, but he maintains a studious disinterestedness. In its review of *The Round Table* the *Quarterly* had selected for particular disapproval a footnote in which Hazlitt describes Burke as 'a half poet and a half philosopher' who 'has done more mischief than perhaps any other person in the world'. In the essay for the *London* Hazlitt insists on Burke's failure to impress his fellow Parliamentarians:

He was emphatically called the *Dinner-Bell*. They went out by shoals when he began to speak. They coughed and shuffled him down.[51]

But he offers the rapidly emptying House as the decisive proof of Burke's genius, rather in the same way that Wordsworth boasted of his own poor sales, undertaking 'formally to prove, that no poet, who deserved the name of one, was ever popular in his life-time, or scarcely after his death!'[52] In the fourth of his *London* essays, 'On the Present State of Parliamentary Eloquence', he is less guarded. John Scott adds a footnote distancing himself from Hazlittt's description of Brougham as a trimmer, although he allows to pass without comment the suggestion that Canning undermines the causes he supports by defending them with 'the pertness of a school-boy, and the effrontery of a prostitute'.[53] But in these early essays Hazlitt seems less interested in voicing his opinions than in considering the nature of his own prose.

---

[49] 'On the Conversation of Authors', *London Magazine*, 2 (September 1820), 258; Howe, 12, 38.

[50] 'Recollections of the South Sea House', *London Magazine*, 2 (August 1820), 142–6; Hazlitt's 'On the Conversation of Authors', *London Magazine*, 2 (September 1820), 250–62; Howe, 12, 24–44.

[51] 'On the Difference between Writing and Speaking', *London Magazine*, 2 (July 1820), 25; Howe, 12, 266.

[52] William Hazlitt, 'On the Qualifications Necessary for Success in Life', *London Magazine*, 1 (June 1820), 646–54, 649; Howe, 12, 201.

[53] 'On the Present State of Parliamentary Eloquence', *London Magazine*, 2 (October 1820), 376 and 383; Howe, 17, 8 and 20.

In several of them Hazlitt reflects on the difference between writing and speech. The 'great leading distinction' is that 'more time is allowed for one than the other'. In speaking everything must be done 'off-hand, at a blow', whereas writing allows 'time to think and do better'.[54] It seems an obvious point but, for a periodical writer, it is a fraught one. Magazine writing, like Byron in *Don Juan* or Scott in the novels, is characteristically self-reflexive: it repeatedly pauses to reflect on its own procedures. The magazine article about writing a magazine article quickly established itself as a favourite sub-genre, especially with writers who needed to produce copy but found themselves without materials. In one such piece T. J. Wainewright represents himself attempting to write a review of the latest London exhibition while 'sitting in a church-yard, seventy-three miles from London, without a single book, either in my pocket or portmanteau'. He cannot begin until his 'smock-frocked valet-de-place, Ralph Westropp' brings, along with a delicious rustic lunch, his 'materials for writing', which turn out to consist of 'four soiled crumpled sheets of 4to': 'Where's the case-knife to cut my pencil—(N.B. neither pen nor ink) So! Now I begin.'[55] The elaborate Sternean joke lies in Wainewright's eliding the difference between narrative time and the time of composition, which in its turn elides the difference between writing and speech (according to Hazlitt, Sterne's is 'the best style that ever was written', because 'you fancy that you hear the people talking').[56]

A writer, unlike a speaker, Hazlitt claims, is allowed 'a year to think of a subject' and 'a year more to find out words for his thoughts'. He 'may turn a period in his head fifty different ways, so that it comes out smooth and round at last...we can wait'.[57] But periodical writers do not have two years to produce a paper: their editors will not wait nearly so long. Speaking and writing may 'not unusually be in direct opposition',[58] but the periodical writer must show both talents. His is, it often seems to Hazlitt, an inferior business:

I have not much pleasure in writing these Essays, or in reading them afterwards; though I own I now and then meet with a phrase that I like, or a thought that strikes me as a true one. But after I begin them, I am only anxious to get to the end of them, which I am not sure I shall do, for I seldom see my way a page, or even a sentence, beforehand; and when I have, as by a miracle, escaped, I trouble myself little more about them.[59]

[54] 'On the Difference between Writing and Speaking', *London Magazine*, 2 (July 1820), 22–33, 22; Howe, 12, 262–3.
[55] 'C. Van Vinkbooms, his Dogmas for Dilettanti', *London Magazine*, 4 (September 1821), 285–93, 285, 286, 287.
[56] 'On the Conversation of Authors', *London Magazine*, 2 (September 1820), 260; Howe, 12, 41.
[57] 'On the Difference between Writing and Speaking', *London Magazine*, 2 (July 1820), 31; Howe, 12, 277.
[58] 'On the Difference between Writing and Speaking', *London Magazine*, 2 (July 1820), 22; Howe, 12, 262.
[59] 'On the Pleasure of Painting', *London Magazine*, 2 (December 1820), 597–607, 597–8; Howe, 8, 6.

Orators enjoy an immediate reward in the applause of their audience: writers—
periodical writers included—are condemned to solitude, to 'look into their own
minds, not in the faces of a gaping multitude'.[60] This is one reason why 'persons
of rank and fortune' become orators, whereas there are 'few authors who are not
paid by the sheet!'[61] But looked at in another way, it is the writers that occupy the
prouder place: it is the men of letters who breathe the 'pure, silent air of
immortality', far above 'the dust, and smoke, and noise' of the modern
world.[62] But the periodical writer, who is bound to time, cannot hope to achieve
the rewards of the literary man any more than of the orator. The producer of
literature loses himself in his writing: 'The *personal* is to him an impertinence.'[63]
For the orator, by contrast, personal mannerisms may be all-important: 'the air
with which a celebrated barrister waved a white cambrick handkerchief passed for
eloquence'.[64] Thelwall could so hold a crowd by the 'orator's vehement gesture,
the loudness of the voice, the speaking eye, the conscious attitude' that it comes
as a surprise to read the selfsame speech and find that it amounts only to 'a few
labels, nicknames, and party watch-words'.[65] In this the periodical writer resembles Thelwall more closely than Wordsworth. Like the orator he must offer
immediate pleasure, and to do this he must cultivate the mannerisms, all the
merely '*personal*', that a writer such as Wordsworth scorns. He may write rather
than speak, but his prose, like Byron's verse in *Don Juan*, aspires to the status of
silent chat: 'I rattle on exactly as I'd talk / With anybody in a ride or walk' (*Don
Juan*, 15, 19, 7–8). The illusion of personal presence that his prose generates is
far more vital to his success than the number and quality of the ideas that he
communicates. It is because he recognizes all this that Hazlitt's contempt for
speech-makers alternates with admiration, and it is why he recognizes his
fellowship with them even when he is at his most contemptuous.

Speech-makers, for example, only at their peril reveal themselves as more
intelligent than their audience, which is one reason for Burke's failure. But
Hazlitt must have been conscious that writers for popular magazines operate
under a similar constraint. The consequence in Parliament is that the most
effective speeches consist only of 'a successful arrangement of commonplaces',
and the same might surely be said of most magazine articles. Of all parliamentarians it was William Windham who best adapted to these circumstances, and he

[60] 'On the Difference between Writing and Speaking', *London Magazine*, 2 (July 1820), 32; Howe, 12, 279.
[61] 'On the Difference between Writing and Speaking', *London Magazine*, 2 (July 1820), 30; Howe, 12, 274.
[62] 'On Reading Old Books', *London Magazine*, 3 (February 1821), 128–34, 134; Howe, 12, 221.
[63] 'On the Difference between Writing and Speaking', *London Magazine*, 2 (July 1820), 33; Howe, 12, 279.
[64] 'On the Qualifications Necessary for Success in Life', *London Magazine*, 1 (June 1820), 646; Howe, 12, 195.
[65] 'On the Difference between Writing and Speaking', *London Magazine*, 2 (July 1820), 24; Howe, 12, 263.

did so by making his speeches out of inverted commonplaces, which is to say paradoxes: 'Ask the first old woman you met, her opinion on any subject, and you could get at the statesman's; for his would be just the contrary.'[66] It can hardly have escaped Hazlitt's attention that paradox was the signature of his own magazine prose, a point very often remarked, as in a *Blackwood's* parody of Hazlitt's style: 'It is vulgarly supposed, that a man, who is always thinking and talking of himself, is an egotist. He is no such thing; he is the least egotistical of all men.'[67]

'I hate your shuffling, *shilly-shally* proceedings, and diagonal sidelong movements between right and wrong', Hazlitt writes in 'On the Present State of Parliamentary Eloquence'. He has in mind in particular Sir James Mackintosh and Henry Brougham. But if he blames Brougham because he 'trims too much between all parties', he does so in a paper for a magazine that he is fully aware demands that he exercise himself a similar tact. However much he may claim to hate 'shuffling, *shilly-shally* proceedings',[68] in these essays for the *London* Hazlitt devises procedures that are really rather similar. The essays shuffle between contrasting, even contradictory positions. In 'On the Difference between Writing and Speaking' the successful speaker simply has the knack of disguising 'the emptiness of the *matter*' by 'a certain exaggeration and extravagance of *manner*'.[69] Hazlitt affects a lofty scorn for oratory which is immediately extinguished when he thinks of Chatham whose 'short, clear, pithy, old English sentences' made him seem 'the genius of common sense personified': Chatham 'sprang out of the genius of the House of Commons, like Pallas from the head of Jupiter, completely armed'.[70] The technique is deployed most elaborately in the essay 'On the Look of a Gentleman'. Hazlitt begins by paying obsequious tribute to the gentlemanly *je ne sais quoi*. When you see 'Sir Charles B-nb-ry, as he saunters down St James's-street' he may be wearing 'a large slouched hat, a lack-lustre eye, and aquiline nose, an old shabby drab-coloured coat' and 'old top-boots' but everyone can tell 'infallibly at the first glance, or even a bow-shot off, that he is a gentleman of the first water'.[71] This is unnervingly like Byron denying that the 'shabby-genteel' of the Cockney school could ever be mistaken for true gentlemanliness even though the Cockney's boots might be the 'best-blackened of the

[66] 'On the Difference between Writing and Speaking', *London Magazine*, 2 (July 1820), 29; Howe, 12, 272–3.
[67] *Blackwood's Edinburgh Magazine*, 10 (August 1821, Part II), 69. The parodist is Eyre Evans Crowe.
[68] 'On the Present State of Parliamentary Eloquence,' *London Magazine*, 2 (October 1820), 373–84, 374; Howe, 17, 7.
[69] 'On the Difference between Writing and Speaking,' *London Magazine*, 2 (July 1820), 24; Howe, 12, 265.
[70] 'On the Difference between Writing and Speaking', *London Magazine*, 2 (July 1820), 26–7; Howe, 12, 268.
[71] 'On the Look of a Gentleman', *London Magazine*, 3 (January 1821), 39–45, 39; Howe, 12, 210–11.

two',[72] although Byron admittedly is complacent rather than obsequious. But then we are told that the gentlemanly air has almost disappeared from the modern world, surviving only in 'the butlers in old families, or the valets, and "gentlemen's gentlemen," in the younger branches'. It is seen to best advantage in the 'well-grown, comely haberdasher' who walked every day 'from Bishop's-gate-street to Pall Mall and Bond-street, with the undaunted air and strut of a general-officer'.[73] Throughout the essay Hazlitt swithers between paying respectful tribute to the gentlemanly ideal and satirizing it, and the energy of the essay has everything to do with the fine unpredictability that results. It is an effect possible because Hazlitt does not so much write as talk onto paper, so that every statement must be understood, in Lamb's phrase, 'with some abatement'. Hazlitt's essay style is digressive, like Byron's verse in *Don Juan*—'To return from this digression, which is a little out of place here', 'But to pass on to our more immediate subject'[74]—and to the same effect. Both the essays and the poem are freed from the constraints of consistency, freed from the failing that Hazlitt attributes to the conversation of authors, who tend to fasten upon a subject and will not let it go.[75]

In two of these early essays, 'On the Conversation of Authors', and 'On the Present State of Parliamentary Eloquence', Hazlitt comments on political oratory. It is a topic that allows him to sidestep ideology by focusing attention on the manner rather than the matter of the speakers, but also a topic that allows him silently to acknowledge that his own essays have more in common with the unprepared speeches that are proper to Parliament than with speeches like Canning's, who is 'not so properly an orator, as an author reciting his own compositions'.[76] The first duty of magazine writing was to seem spontaneous. A *Blackwood's* article describes itself as a 'sort of rambling article,—quite chitty-chatty and off-hand,' a description that impressed T. J. Wainewright so much that he used it as an epitaph for one of his own papers in the *London Magazine*.[77] The 'chitty-chatty' style was so important to magazines because it generated an illusion of intimacy with its unknown reader. In the House of Commons speakers addressed two audiences, their fellow Members and the nation.

---

[72] Lord Byron, *The Complete Miscellaneous Prose*, ed. Andrew Nicholson (Oxford: Clarendon Press, 1991), 159.

[73] 'On the Look of a Gentleman', *London Magazine*, 3 (January 1821), 39–40; Howe, 12, 211–12.

[74] 'On Reading Old Books', *London Magazine*, 3 (February 1821), 128–34, 132; Howe 12, 225; 'On the Conversation of Authors', *London Magazine*, 2 (September 1820), 253; Howe, 12, 29.

[75] 'On the Conversation of Authors', *London Magazine*, 2 (September, 1820), 254; Howe, 12, 32.

[76] 'On the Present State of Parliamentary Eloquence', *London Magazine*, 2 (October 1820), 381; Howe, 17, 18.

[77] 'Much Ado About Nothing', *London Magazine*, 1 (June 1820), 657–61, 657. I cannot find this phrase in *Blackwood's*, though the thought is common enough, as in D. M. Moir's ottava rima poem, 'Christmas Chit-Chat', *Blackwood's Edinburgh Magazine*, 10 (December 1821), 493–500. Compare J. H. Reynold's poem, 'A Chit Chat Letter on Men and Other Things', *London Magazine*, 8 (October 1823), 361–4.

Magazine writers did the same. They addressed an anonymous readership in the guise of addressing an intimate circle: they spoke to the reading nation under cover of addressing the inhabitants of Peebles. In the pursuit of this end the private jokes, the songs, to give just one example, that *Blackwood's* delighted to attribute to Dr James Scott, the entirely blameless Glasgow dentist nicknamed by the magazine the 'Odontist', were not a self-indulgence but a key rhetorical strategy.

Hazlitt ends his paper 'On the Conversation of Authors' with a portrait of a gentle scholar, one who 'hangs like a film and cobweb upon letters, or is like the dust upon the outside of knowledge, which should not be rudely brushed aside'. 'On the Look of Gentleman' ends with a portrait of one of 'God Almighty's gentlemen' who couples with 'absence of mind, with ignorance of forms, and frequent blunders' an unmatched natural delicacy.[78] Both are por-traits of George Dyer, though in neither essay is Dyer named. Dyer makes appearances in Lamb's essays, too, in 'Oxford in the Vacation' and in 'Amicus Redivivus', where he is identified by his initials, G. D.[79] Dyer seems to have been a man who inspired amused affection in everyone who knew him, but he was also, I think, a peculiarly congenial figure for the magazine essayist. In the 1790s he had been a public figure, a leading radical, an active member of the Constitu-tional Society, but by 1820 his fame had faded, and he eked out a precarious living working for the booksellers. He is not a figure like 'Mr H—' that magazine readers would be expected to recognize, but neither is he quite a figure from private life like 'Mrs— whose conversation leaves a flavour, like fine green tea.' He occupies that indeterminate position that magazines found so congenial, somewhere between the great world and Peebles.

[78] 'On the Look of a Gentleman', *London Magazine*, 3 (January 1821), 45; Howe, 12, 219–20.
[79] 'Oxford in the Vacation', *London Magazine*, 2 (October 1820), 365–9, and 'Amicus Redivivus', *London Magazine*, 8 (December 1823), 613–15.

6

Mr Knight's Best Small Capitals

In *The Examiner* for 16 November 1817, John Hunt quoted two of the more colourful passages on his brother, Leigh, from the first of Lockhart's pieces 'On the Cockney School of Poetry', and immediately issued a thunderous challenge:

The anonymous Author of the above atrocious attempt to destroy the personal character of the Editor of this Paper, is again called upon to avow himself: which he cannot fail to do, unless to an utter disregard of all Truth and Decency, he adds the height of Meanness and COWARDICE—Should this however be the case, those who have published the foul Scandal—if they persist in screening the Author from a just punishment,—must prepare to abide the consequences of their delinquency.[1]

The individual who wrote under the signature 'Z' should reveal himself, failing which Hunt threatens to bring a civil action against William Blackwood as publisher. According to Wilson, responding in *Blackwood's*, Hunt had succeeded only in revealing his own ignorance: 'gentlemen do not communicate private messages of that kind through the medium of the public prints'.[2] But Wilson did not stick to this position. The following year he was himself attacked by the anonymous author of *Hypocrisy Unveiled and Calumny Detected in a Review of Blackwood's Magazine*, who dwelt rather gloatingly on Lockhart's failure to respond to Hunt's challenge:

Our readers are all aware, that Mr Hunt has, in his Examiner, repeatedly called on his libeller in the Magazine to declare himself, and has again and again denominated him a liar, a coward, and a scoundrel. And they are also aware that the SCORPION (otherwise Z.) has found it convenient to take no notice of these choice epithets.[3]

Wilson responded by issuing a challenge even more thunderous than John Hunt's, and, just like John Hunt, he had it printed and published:

It is probable, however, that you will come forward from your concealment, when you feel that you cannot continue it without the consciousness of cowardice. I, therefore, request your name and address, that I may send a friend to you, to deliver my opinion of

---

[1] *The Examiner*, no. 516, 16 November 1817, 729.
[2] *Blackwood's Edinburgh Magazine*, 10 (December 1821), 575, in a piece probably by John Wilson.
[3] *Hypocrisy Unveiled and Calumny Detected in a Review of Blackwood's Magazine* (Edinburgh: printed for Francis Pillans, 1818), 23.

your character, and to settle time and place for a meeting, at which I may exact satisfaction from you for the public insult you have offered to me.[4]

Duels demand the physical presence of the combatants, which is one reason why John Scott refused to confirm that he had written the articles in the *London* attacking Lockhart until Lockhart had himself arrived in London. But the challenge that finally resulted in an exchange of fire, the challenge that John Scott issued to J. H. Christie, was the culmination of a much more extended series of exchanges delivered 'through the medium of the public prints': the articles in the *London* that began it all, the statements by John Scott and by Lockhart, comments on these statements in *The Scotsman* and various other periodicals, and statements by Christie and by Scott's second, Patmore. It was a time at which it was unusually hard to distinguish between material that ought to be confined to private communications and material that might properly be communicated by way of public prints, and this was not an incidental difficulty: it is a defining characteristic of the cultural moment.

As I showed in my last chapter it was a culture that placed an unprecedented value on writing that could produce the illusion of the speaking voice, on prose writers who could fabricate a 'chitty-chatty style', and on poets such as Byron who could give the impression of rattling on even when writing in a rather demanding verse form. But the high value accorded such writing was itself a symptom of a widespread recognition that what distinguished modern literature from the literature that had gone before it was that writing in the modern age was mass-produced. Even as Byron rattled on, he accepted that his relationship with his readers was only by a polite fiction social: their real connection was through an anonymous, economic exchange. His 'gentle reader' was in fact his 'still gentler purchaser' (*Don Juan*, 1, 221, 1–2) and what was purchased was not Byron's company but his printed words. The cases of John Scott and Alexander Boswell suggest that even the kind of personal dispute that ended in a duel no longer took the form of an exchange of spoken insults or of handwritten communications. The dispute had to be played out in print.

The duel in which John Scott died is particularly revealing because its immediate cause, it could be said, was a typographical mistake. Lockhart's first published statement began by denying that he was editor of *Blackwood's Magazine*. Scott immediately retorted by pointing out that it was precisely Lockhart's refusal to deny that he was editor of *Blackwood's* that had prevented Scott from accepting his challenge. Lockhart replied in his second statement that this was a 'very trivial mistake . . . originating in nothing more than a typographical oversight': 'a line', he wrote, had now been introduced, '(as it ought to have been at first) between Mr LOCKHART's *Introduction* to the public and the statement of fact which he thought fit to subject, in the first instance, to the notice of

---

[4] John Wilson, *Correspondence on the Subject of Blackwood's Magazine* (Edinburgh: 1818), 1–2.

Mr JOHN SCOTT'.[5] The ill-feeling between the two men, it seems, was raised to its highest pitch by the failure to follow a printer's convention: no line across the page distinguished the '*Introduction* to the public' from the statement that followed. The absence of that line in itself generated a good deal of print. The oversight had been pointed out (at his own instigation, Lockhart insisted, and before ever he had seen Scott's second statement) in the *Edinburgh Weekly Journal*, where *The Scotsman* picked it up, and ridiculed Lockhart's excuse before dryly representing his denial that he was involved with *Blackwood's Magazine* in any editorial capacity as 'a very unexpected declaration'.[6]

John Scott's death was a by-product of an odd cultural moment at which the relationship between printers' conventions and codes of behaviour was uneasy and quite likely to issue in violence. Thomas Hope's Anastasius regards his transformation from a warrior to a secretary as 'a mere trifle': 'The same turn of the wrist will do to cut a flourish on paper and on the face of the enemy; and it would be only fancying myself in the field, marshalling a parcel of soldiers, when I sat in my closet symmetrising a heap of words; and that for the same purpose too—namely of defending ourselves, and of attacking our enemies.'[7] Writing and fighting seemed scarcely distinct, and this in its turn was an accurate expression of a culture in which print and all the other business of life seemed increasingly hard to distinguish. As the *New Monthly* put it, 'print has become part of our existence—has superseded vulgar sight and fame; like to the air we breathe, it is the medium through which we receive sound and light, every idea and every feeling,—beyond whose influence we cannot get, and could not live'. As a result 'the world and books are no longer at variance,—they are one and the same thing'.[8]

Even very recently Wordsworth and Coleridge had preferred to circulate many of their most important poems in manuscript, often seeming actively to dislike the printed medium. Wordsworth's *Prelude* was known to most of those familiar with the poem before its publication in 1850 in Wordsworth's recitation, although a favoured few were allowed access to the poem in manuscript. *Peter Bell*, to the amusement of Wordsworth's younger contemporaries, remained in manuscript for twenty-one years before its publication in 1819, and Coleridge's 'Kubla Khan' and 'Christabel' had circulated in manuscript and through recitation for eighteen years before Murray finally published them in an 1816 pamphlet. 'We had frequently heard of Mr. Coleridge's manuscript of Christabel',

---

[5] See *Statement, etc. by Mr John Scott in his dispute with Mr John Gibson Lockhart* (London: 1821), and *Statement: Mr Lockhart very unwillingly feels himself again under the necessity of obtruding himself upon the public notice* (Edinburgh: 1821).

[6] *The Scotsman*, no. 211, 3 February 1821, 38.

[7] Thomas Hope, *Anastasius, or, Memoirs of a Greek: Written at the Close of the Eighteenth Century* (London: John Murray, 1820), 2, 292.

[8] *New Monthly Magazine*, 2 (August 1821), 223, in a piece by Cyrus Redding on literary women, 'Blues and Anti-Blues.'

a reviewer of the poem remarked.[9] By then Coleridge and Wordsworth were among the best-known British poets, but they were, one suspects, familiar names to many acquainted with few if any of their poems. This was partly because their volumes did not sell, but also because they published so little. Wordsworth was silent for seven years after the failure of *Poems in Two Volumes* in 1807, and it was not until the first collected edition in 1815 that his work became at all widely available. After *Poems on Various Subjects* in 1796 Coleridge did not publish a substantial collection of verse until *Sybilline Leaves* in 1817. Both men seem to have suffered from what Sara Coleridge calls 'the fear of the press'.[10] The proper contrast is with Byron. It is not just that Byron rarely allowed as many months to elapse between his various volumes as Wordsworth and Coleridge did years, but that Byron seemed as unwilling to keep a poem in manuscript as Wordsworth and Coleridge were to consign it to print. The best example is *The Giaour*, published by Murray on 5 June 1813, as a poem of 684 lines. Thereafter, as Byron pointed out to Murray, his 'snake of a poem' continued 'lengthening its rattles every month',[11] until, in its seventh edition of December 1813, it reached its final form as a poem of 1,334 lines. It was as if Byron, not content simply to publish each poem as he finished it, insisted on publishing his successive drafts, a practice which, as reviewers began more and more often to observe, worked both to his and his publisher's financial advantage. Walter J. Ong has made the bold claim that 'typography was interiorized in the Western psyche definitively at the moment in Western history known as the Romantic Movement'.[12] It seems that Wordsworth and Coleridge were situated on one side of this divide, and their younger contemporaries on the other.[13]

---

[9] *Eclectic Review*, 5 (June 1816), 565.

[10] *Notes and Lectures upon Shakespeare and Some of the Old Poets and Dramatists with Other Literary Remains of S. T. Coleridge*, ed. Mrs H. N. Coleridge, 2 vols. (London: Pickering, 1849), 1, viii.

[11] *Byron's Letters and Journals*, ed. Leslie A. Marchand, 3 (London: John Murray, 1974), 100.

[12] Walter J. Ong, *Interfaces of the Word: Studies in the Evolution and Consciousness of Culture* (Ithaca: Cornell University Press, 1977), 283. W. J. T. Mitchell usefully underwrites the pivotal nature of the cultural moment by arguing, contra Ong, that 'Wordsworth's claim that a poet is a man "speaking" (not writing) to men is no casual expression, but a symptom of what Derrida would call the "phonocentric" tendency of romantic poetics.' See W. J. T. Mitchell, *Picture Theory: Essays on Verbal and Visual Representation* (Chicago: Chicago University Press, 1994), 115.

[13] This claim has been recently and persuasively contested by Peter Simonsen in *Wordsworth and Word-Preserving Arts: Typographic Inscription, Ekphrasis and Posterity in the Later Work* (London: Palgrave Macmillan, 2007), but Simonsen recognizes that it is only the later Wordsworth, the Wordsworth of the post-war years, who may usefully be represented as a proponent of '(typo) graphocentrism' (66). Andrew Bennet in his *Wordsworth Writing* (Cambridge: Cambridge University Press, 2007) revealingly focuses on the relation in Wordsworth's poetry between speech and handwriting, scarcely addressing the relationship between handwriting and print. In fact, both Wordsworth and Coleridge, but Coleridge in particular, who was intermittently a professional journalist, maintained competing identities as professional men of letters and as poets. The first of these was wholly dependent upon print, in which both men sometimes register a keen interest, as in a letter to Joseph Cottle, in which Coleridge proposes writing an essay on 'the Metaphysics of Typography.' See *The Collected Letters of Samuel Taylor Coleridge*, ed. Earl Leslie Griggs, 6 vols. (Oxford: Clarendon Press, 1956), 1, 412.

Lamb speaks for the younger generation when, in 'Oxford in the Vacation', he confesses his distaste for the manuscripts even of great writers such as Milton:

There is something to me repugnant, at any time in written hand. The text never seems determinate. Print settles it.[14]

Manuscript is made to seem obsolete, like those great ledgers of the South-Sea House 'with their old fantastic flourishes and decorative rubric interlacings'.[15] It was a perception that had been anticipated by Frankenstein's monster. His education may begin by listening to the De Lacey family speak, but it is completed only when he finds the 'leathern portmanteau' containing '*Paradise Lost*, a volume of *Plutarch's Lives*, and the *Sorrows of Werter*'.[16] The monster is a creature of the late eighteenth-century Enlightenment, the creature of a reading world, in which citizenship is dependent on access to print.

In Scott's novels that world is projected into the distant past. In Jacobean London, for example, Nigel, Lord Glenvarloch, at a particularly low point in his fortunes is forced to seek sanctuary in the lawless London borough of White-friars. On his first evening there he finds that what most troubles him is the lack of something to read. He asks for a book.[17] In *Guy Mannering*, young Harry Bertram, confined in a provincial Scottish gaol, has the same thought and gives the maid a shilling, with which she borrows 'two odd volumes of the Newgate Kalendar' from a fellow inmate.[18] Still more remarkably, when Lockhart's Valerius sails along the Tiber into second-century Rome, he gazes at the gardens of the villas that he passes and sees 'from time to time, the figure of some stately Roman, or white-robed lady, with her favourite scroll of parchment in her hand'.[19] The culture of print had become so pervasive that, by 1821, Lockhart could quite unselfconsciously attribute it to a Roman matron who does not seem discommoded by having to make do with a scroll rather than an octavo volume. Christianity is recommended in *Valerius* as a religion of the book, a religion to which Valerius is converted when he reads the gospel given to him by the woman he will marry. In Thomas Moore's *The Epicurean* the point is made still more emphatically. Alethe is brought up as a Christian by her mother, Theora, who was herself converted when she transcribed the writings of Origen after being appointed his secretary. Alciphron, the epicurean of the novel's title, at first only

[14] 'Oxford in the Vacation', *London Magazine*, 2 (October 1820), 365–9, 367 (footnote).
[15] 'Recollections of the South Sea House', *London Magazine*, 2 (August 1820), 142–6, 143.
[16] Mary Shelley, *Frankenstein; or, the Modern Prometheus*, ed. Nora Crook (London: William Pickering, 1996), 88 and 95.
[17] Walter Scott, *The Fortunes of Nigel*, ed. Frank Jordan (Edinburgh: Edinburgh University Press, 2004), 266.
[18] Walter Scott, *Guy Mannering*, ed. P. D. Garside (Edinburgh: Edinburgh University Press, 1999), 267–8.
[19] J. G. Lockhart, *Valerius: A Roman Story* (Edinburgh: Blackwood, 1869), 12. The reviewer in *Knight's Quarterly Magazine*, 1 (June–October 1823), 30, points out 'anachronisms of sentiment' in the novel.

pretends to convert, impelled by his love for Alethe, but her spiritual protector gives him the Old Testament, which, almost as if it had been a contemporary miscellany, a Regency magazine such as *Blackwood's*, entrances him by passing so 'rapidly from annals to prophecy, from narration to song'. But the Old Testament does not offer him the hope of personal immortality that he has always craved, and his conversion is sealed only when he is given a still more valuable 'volume', the New Testament.[20]

Lockhart's *Adam Blair* is set in the mid-eighteenth century, and yet there still seems a slight anachronism when Blair, unable to sleep, takes to bed with him the Odyssey in Greek, and becomes so absorbed that he continues to read until he comes to the end of a book: he construes the Greek text as if he were reading a novel.[21] In Lockhart's next novel, *The History of Matthew Wald*, even death is figured as a scene of interrupted reading. Wald's death is brought home to his friend most feelingly when he enters his study and finds 'all the books about—his paper knife remaining in the heart of Candide—two or three Couriers and Cobbetts still lying upon the table—I confess all this was too much for me'.[22] By the early decades of the nineteenth century, it had become a world in which the one qualification for citizenship was the ability to read, and reading was increasingly not a social activity—it did not entail reading a book aloud to a family circle or a circle of friends—but a silent, solitary activity of the kind that Matthew Wald indulged in, enclosed in his lonely room. The experience of the solitary reader is mediated not through the voice but through print. Walter Scott is the representative novelist of the age of print, and his most powerful tool is the Scots that his best-loved characters speak, a language that acts so powerfully to persuade his readers that they are being initiated into a culture that is sustained by a community of speakers that they are persuaded to forget that they are sharing an experience made possible only by a sophisticated print industry. Clearly the effect the novels give of initiating their readers into an oral culture is illusory, because in the novels Scots is not really a way of speaking but a typographical phenomenon, prized not least by English readers entirely unfamiliar with the language of Scotland or its pronunciation, readers like Alice Fennel, the heroine of Sarah Green's *Scotch Novel Reading*, who finds much of what she reads incomprehensible.[23]

There were no longer any areas of experience that were not, or might not, or should not be cast into print. Hence the prevalence of 'personalities' and the even more prevalent denunciations of them. It was a state of affairs that might be regretted. James Hogg, for example, records that his mother was displeased when

---

[20] Thomas Moore, *The Epicurean: A Tale* (London: Longmans, 1827), 262.

[21] J. G. Lockhart, *Some Passages in the Life of Mr Adam Blair, Minister of the Gospel at Cross-Meikle* (Edinburgh: Edinburgh University Press, 1963), 71.

[22] J. G. Lockhart, *The History of Matthew Wald* (Edinburgh: William Blackwood, 1824), 381.

[23] Sarah Green, *Scotch Novel Reading; Or, Modern Quackery. A Novel Really Founded on Facts* (London: A. K. Newman, 1824), 2, 110.

Walter Scott's *Minstrelsy of the Scottish Border* transmuted all the border ballads that she held in her memory into print. Scott had 'broken the charm' of poems that were 'made for singing and no' for reading'. Hogg adds that his mother had been proved right, 'for from that day to this, these songs, which were the amusement of every winter evening, have never been sung more'.[24] The people's minstrelsy, like the common land, had been enclosed, by print rather than by fences, but the effect was the same: the people lost access to it. When Dr Pringle, the Church of Scotland minister of John Galt's *Ayrshire Legatees*, travels to London he is shocked by the publication of newspapers on the Sabbath, and by the conduct of the London ministers, who read their sermons, and, still worse, do not just read their prayers but read 'printed prayers'.[25] Pringle is shocked on behalf of the Presbyterian tradition of extemporary worship, but he is shocked too by being so suddenly transplanted from an Ayrshire that retains its oral traditions to a London that has become so completely a city of print.

In fact, oral traditions were highly valued by metropolitan magazines. The very first issue of the *London Magazine* carried Octavius Gilchrist's 'Some Account of John Clare, an Agricultural Labourer and Poet',[26] and Clare went on to become the most prolific contributor of verse to the new magazine. It may be that the *London* championed John Clare as an appropriate counterpart to James Hogg. *Blackwood's* might have its Ettrick Shepherd but the *London* could claim as its own the Northamptonshire peasant, and the *London* also secured, from *Blackwood's*, the services of Allan Cunningham, stonemason, neighbour of Burns and friend of Hogg. Magazines, precisely because they were so completely a product of an urban print culture, cultivated a nostalgia for the oral culture of the past. In *Blackwood's* Hogg appealed to that nostalgia in his 'Tales and Anecdotes of the Pastoral Life', and his 'Shepherd's Calendar' series in which he presented himself as the conduit through which the oral folk wisdom of the Borders might be transported into the new world of print. In the *London Magazine*, Allan Cunningham's contributions often served a similar purpose.

For Hazlitt, Scottish romance, and Scott's novels in particular, were so popular because they offered a refuge from 'the level, the littleness, the frippery of modern civilization' in the 'last skirts of ignorance and barbarism'. They offered a respite from a modern world in which characters, like all other commodities, had been flattened and regularized by the mechanical systems that produced them. England may have had 'a Parson Adams not quite a hundred years ago—a Sir Roger de Coverley rather more than a hundred', but eccentrics now are to be found only in Scotland, and even there only 'a hundred

[24] James Hogg, *Anecdotes of Scott*, ed. Jill Rubinstein (Edinburgh: Edinburgh University Press, 1999), 38.
[25] *Blackwood's Edinburgh Magazine*, 7 (September 1820), 594.
[26] *London Magazine*, 1 (January 1820), 7–11.

miles to the North of the "Modern Athens" or a century back'.[27] But this is fanciful. The secret of Scotland's popularity was not that Scotland remained untouched by the modernity that had standardized character, but that novels set in Scotland had a licence to resist standardized orthography, like the speech of the Ettrick Shepherd in the *Noctes Ambrosianae* or the diction of John Clare's poems. By preserving phonetically the speech patterns of his peasants and clansmen Scott offered his urban readership the opportunity to contact through his elegantly printed pages the oral culture that could only enter into their drawing rooms when transformed into typography. In Hogg's *The Three Perils of Woman*, Daniel Bell, the Lowland sheep-farmer claims that Scots differs from other varieties of English because it admits no difference between speech and writing:

I write Scots, my ain naiteve tongue; and there never was any reule for that. Every man writes it as he speaks it, and that's the great advantage of our language ower a' others.

He explodes in a fit of indignation when invited to call a male sheep a ram: 'It's no tupe, hinney, nor tup, nor tip, nor ram; nor ony o' thae dirty cuttit words; it's just plain downright toop, the auld Scots word, and the auld Scots way o' saying it.'[28] He demands the right to retain his own variety of spoken English, but even as he does so he reveals that in the printed world in which Hogg's book has its place, ways of speaking can only be marked by ways of spelling. Such novels seem to preserve oral culture, but they do so only by translating orality into orthography. The Shepherd of the *Noctes Ambrosianae* confesses as much when the short-hand writer, Gurney, is discovered hiding in a cupboard and transcribing the conversation of the *Blackwood's* men. Gurney, Hogg complains, has caught him 'doun to [his] verra spellin'.[29]

  Hogg and Clare were, after all, untaught poets of a new kind. Hogg edited his own magazine, *The Spy*, before joining the *Blackwood's* team. All his life he wrote for periodicals, and Clare too was, even when he worked as an agricultural labourer, already a creature of print. It is the Cambridge-educated Wordsworth a generation earlier who urges us in 'The Tables Turned' to quit our books and listen to the song of the 'woodland linnet' and the 'throstle'. Clare would never have thought that reading and birdsong might be incompatible pleasures. He consistently represents himself in his poems as a reader, as a man who, when he returns home from a walk, is apt to 'reach down a poet [he] love[s] from the shelves', a copy of Thomson or Cowper ('The Holiday Walk'), who spends his evenings 'bending oer [his] knees', reading by the light of the fire, and, when he worked in the fields, would often wish for rain so that he might get back to his

[27] 'The Spirits of the Age (No. IV): Sir Walter Scott', *New Monthly Magazine*, 10 (April 1824), 297–304; Howe, 11, 62.
[28] James Hogg, *The Three Perils of Woman, or, Love, Leasing, and Jealousy: A Series of Domestic Scotch Tales*, ed. David Groves, Antony Hasler, and Douglas S. Mack (Edinburgh: Edinburgh University Press, 1995), 42 and 7.
[29] *Blackwood's Edinburgh Magazine*, 21 (April 1827), 478.

books ('Labours Leisure'). Clare is happy to confess, as Wordsworth would never have done, to feeling the excitements of bookishness, 'cutting open with heart beating speed' the leaves of a brother poet's long-sought volume ('The Pleasures of Spring'). When he takes his walks, he takes a book with him, and if the scenery is 'delicious' enough to persuade him to 'shut and put the volume bye', it is a fact worth noting ('On Visiting a Favourite Place'). Readerly habits are dear to him, especially the habit of marking a passage by turning down the corner of a page. When he reads out of doors some 'pocket poet' a plucked primrose serves '[i]nstead of doubling down to mark the place' ('The Pleasures of Spring'), and the same habit gives Clare a metaphor to define his own poetic purpose:

> How many pages of sweet natures book
> Hath poesy doubled down as favoured things
>
> ('Nature', 1–2)[30]

Clare may not have attended a school after the age of ten, but for him just as much as for Byron, the contemporary with whom he felt so close an affinity that he produced his own versions of 'Child Harold' and 'Don Juan', poetry and print had become inseparable.

In *Blackwood's* it is not one of the contributors to the magazine, but its putative editor, Christopher North, who performs most flamboyantly the role of the author as hero, but the distinctive feature of Christopher North is that he is not so much a heroic figure as a heroic typeface. The tenth volume of the magazine begins with some dedicatory stanzas to Jeffrey in which Jeffrey is, as one would expect, belittled by comparison with the editor of *Blackwood's*. The poem ends:

> Were I forced by some dread demoniacal hand,
> To change heads (what a fate!) with *some* Whig in the land,
> I don't know but I'd swap with yourself my old Gander,
> (I should then be Diogenes—not Alexander!)
> But to shew my good will in a manner more solemn,
> I inscribe to your name (Jump for joy) this whole VOLUME,
> Being always your servant, your friend, and so forth—
> The humanest of conquerors—
>
> CHRISTOPHER NORTH[31]

North is aggrandized, quite literally, by the upper-case letters that name him. Or his dignity might be asserted by other typographical means, as when 'Byron', making a guest appearance in the *Noctes Ambrosianae*, raises his glass to the 'immortal Kit North!!! !!! !!!', a toast in which Byron's respect is precisely measured by the nine exclamation marks drawn up in three neat ranks.[32] The

---

[30] Clare's poems are quoted from John Clare, *Poems of the Middle Period*, ed. Eric Robinson, David Powell, and P. M. S. Dawson, 4 vols. (Oxford: Clarendon Press, 1996–8).

[31] *Blackwood's Edinburgh Magazine*, 10 (August 1821, Part II), 'Stanzas Dedicatory', iv.

[32] *Blackwood's Edinburgh Magazine*, 12 (July 1822), 105.

capital letters and the exclamation marks quietly remind the reader that in a print culture reality is, in the end, a matter of print: greatness is a measure of the size of the font, and the proper measure of awe is the precise number of exclamation marks that the compositor chooses to employ. It was a perception that the clever schoolboys who wrote *The Etonian* were quick to seize on. 'Morris Gowan' writes to the editor complaining, 'In despite of my repeated asseverations, no one will believe but that the Members of your Club are all fictitious personages.' His own letter will put to shame such doubters: 'Methinks their preconceived opinions will be not a little startled when they see my own real name affixed to this communication, in Mr. Knight's best small capitals.'[33]

In such a world the living man is far less real a presence than fictional characters—Odoherty, for example, does not recognize Byron at all, and has to ask who he is—because fictional characters solidly and simply exist as print. Byron's human reality is less firmly founded, and so rapidly begins to dissolve. He is reduced to the status of a character in another author's fiction, his opinions, manners, and modes of speech no longer self-generated but devised by the writer of this particular piece, William Maginn. And as if to underline the point Odoherty and Byron talk of how Byron has proved unable to exercise control over his own writings. *The Vampyre*, by his personal doctor Polidori, sold so well because it was marketed as a novel by Byron himself, and Odoherty confesses that he had himself reviewed *Anastasius* in the belief that it was written by Byron rather than by Thomas Hope.[34] The effect is to undo the distinction between fictional creations and living human beings, and it was an effect of which *Blackwood's* was very well aware: 'Our biographies of wretched persons unborn are so affecting, that the weeping public hath no tears to bestow on men and women actually in poor circumstance and bad health.'[35]

Byron's one rival as the leading literary personality of the day was, odd though it seems, officially nameless, referred to on his title pages as 'the Author of Waverley', and in other publications as 'the Great Unknown', or 'the Wizard of the North'. But Scott's anonymity was no safeguard against his 'name' being appropriated. On 19 October 1819, the *Morning Chronicle* carried an advertisement announcing the publication of 'TALES OF MY LANDLORD, collected and arranged by JEDEDIAH CLEISHBOTHAM, Schoolmaster and Parish Clerk of Gandercleugh, containing "PONTEFRACT CASTLE"'. Scott had playfully represented his *Tales of My Landlord* as sold to the publishers by Jedidiah Cleishbotham. Scott's agent, John Ballantyne, quickly intervened, and on 21 October the *Chronicle* published his letter insisting that 'this Author has no concern whatever with the catchpenny publication announced'. But on 30 October another advertisement appeared:

---

[33] *The Etonian* (London: Henry Colburn, 1823), 2, 38.

[34] See 'On Anastasius. By—Lord Byron', *Blackwood's Edinburgh Magazine*, 10 (September 1821), 200–6. The review was probably contributed by Wilson rather than Maginn.

[35] *Blackwood's Edinburgh Magazine*, 8 (October 1820), 96.

If, by the Author, you mean Jedediah Cleishbotham, I think (to say the least of it) you presume too much, when, without having read a line of the Fourth Series, you pronounce it 'spurious'. The Fourth Series, collected and arranged by Jedediah Cleishbotham, is no more spurious than the First, the Second, or the Third. It is for the Public to judge of that when they see the work, and certainly not for you, who have never seen it.[36]

Scott, the suggestion is, by refusing to write in his own name, and offering in its stead comical pseudonyms, has undermined pretensions to authenticity, for why should a character named Jedediah Cleishbotham be dismissed as a spurious version of a character named 'Jedidiah Cleishbotham': of two almost identical fictions how can one be authentic and one spurious?[37] Scott, as his namesake John Scott charged, must himself bear some responsibility for destabilizing the relationship between authorship and signature.[38]

In an age that was so conscious of itself as an age of print, it is no wonder that writers became unusually sensitive to the printed form in which they appeared before the public. Walter Scott, its first writer, is also its true representative, operating through most of his career in partnership with his printer, James Ballantyne.[39] His modern novel *Saint Ronan's Well* is set in a watering place that centres on its bookseller's shop, which serves also as its post office and circulating library, and describes a society divided between hard-drinking men and the literary set presided over by Lady Penelope Penfeather. But in some ways the historical novels are still more revealing, because the pre-print cultures that they represent are so consistently defined by their difference from the print culture of Scott's own day. In *The Monastery*, for example, the wholly benign counterpart of the odious Lady Penfeather is Alice Avenel, who has the unusual distinction for a woman of the mid-sixteenth century of being able to read and write. She possesses only one book from which she reads to the whole household until it is confiscated by a scandalized monk, the Bible in English translation.

---

[36] The story is told by Edgar Johnson, *Sir Walter Scott: The Great Unknown* (London: Hamish Hamilton, 1970), 685–6.

[37] Scott addresses the issue in the material with which he prefaced his next novel, *The Monastery*. An 'Introductory Epistle' from 'Captain Clutterbuck' presents to the 'Author of Waverley' a manuscript excavated from the ruins of Kennaqquhair Abbey. The 'Author' replies justifying his decision to exclude Captain Clutterbuck from the title page of the published text on the grounds that he recognizes that 'Captain Clutterbuck' represents not a real person but a well-established literary convention. This heavy-handed pleasantry prefaces a threat of legal action directly addressed to the author of the spurious fourth volume of *Tales of My Landlord*. The 'Author' insists, 'I will announce my property in my title-page, and put my own buist [brand] on my own cattle', a sturdy sentiment that would have been more persuasive had Scott not persisted in publishing anonymously. See the discussion of this episode by Penny Fielding, *Writing and Orality: Nationality, Culture, and Nineteenth-Century Fiction* (Oxford: Clarendon Press, 1996), 58–64.

[38] *London Magazine*, 2 (November 1820), 517.

[39] A close relationship between writers and printers was symptomatic of the period. Pierce Egan, as I have noted, was trained as a compositor. In 1819 William T. Sherwin became at once editor and printer of *Sherwin's Political Register*. Hazlitt maintained close friendship with several printers, as noted by Duncan Wu, *William Hazlitt: The First Modern Man* (Oxford: Oxford University Press, 2008), 184.

In *Kenilworth* Scott looks at the library which has been despoiled by the brutish Anthony Forster—the books are ripped apart and their pages used to scour the pewter and clean the boots—with the eye of a modern antiquarian only too aware of the prices those volumes would command in the modern market.[40] In *Guy Mannering* the same effect is achieved by describing Colonel Mannering's library, the delight of Dominie Sampson, inherited from his uncle, the Bishop, in a passage quoted from a 'modern poet', Crabbe:

> That weight of wood, with leathern coat o'erlaid;
> Those ample clasps, of solid metal made;
> The close-press'd leaves, unclosed for many an age;
> The dull red edging of the well-fill'd page;
> On the broad back the stubborn ridges roll'd
> Where yet the title stands in tarnish'd gold.[41]

Redgauntlet of all Scott's novels is perhaps most self-conscious about its printed status. The novel restlessly moves between narrative modes, often pausing to discuss these decisions with the reader. It begins as an epistolary novel, but abandons the form after the first volume, anxious to avoid 'various prolixities and redundancies' which 'would only hang as a dead weight on the progress of the narrative' (125). But the narrative is itself divided between the 'narrative of Darsie Latimer' and the 'narrative of Alan Fairford'. The effect is that the novel's readers always remain conscious of the oddity and the arbitrariness of the activity in which they are engaged, reading a novel. In *Redgauntlet* handwriting, pens, and paper are repeatedly fetishized. Darsie Latimer himself, we are told, writes in 'pigmy characters' (152), a habit he has developed as a law student 'for the purpose of transferring as many scroll sheets as possible to a huge sheet of stamped paper' (200), and hence a habit that secures a valuable economy. When the woman that Latimer later learns is his sister leaves him some verses warning him that he is in danger, we are told that 'the hand in which they are written is a beautiful Italian manuscript' (204). A village schoolmaster's limited talents are measured when we are told 'it takes him foive hours to write as mony lines' (166). When an old Jacobite, 'Pate-in-Peril', volunteers to write a letter he is offered a pen and paper. 'A pen that can write, I hope', he says, and the Provost assures him, 'It can write and spell baith in right hands' (228). These seemingly almost redundant details serve a single important purpose: they keep Scott's reader attentive to the difference between the manuscripts so often mentioned in the novel and the modern volume, finely printed in Edinburgh, in which all those scripts are encountered.

---

[40] Walter Scott, *Kenilworth: A Romance*, ed. J. H. Alexander (Edinburgh: Edinburgh University Press, 1993), 27–8.

[41] Walter Scott, *Guy Mannering*, 109; George Crabbe, *The Library*, in *The Complete Poetical Works*, ed. Norma Dalrymple-Champneys and Arthur Pollard, 3 vols. (Oxford: Oxford University Press), 145–50.

It is a concern felt in almost all the novels. *Rob Roy* begins with Frank Osbaldistone anxiously aware that 'the tale told by one friend, and listened to by another, loses half its charm when committed to paper'.[42] Frank writes his account of his early life in pen and ink for the benefit of his friend and business partner, Will Tresham, but he compares it with printed texts—Sully's Memoirs, for example, both the 'rare and original edition' (presumably the edition of 1640) that Will perversely prefers to the edition 'which is reduced to the useful and ordinary form of Memoirs' (presumably the selected edition of 1768, or even the English translation of 1812) (6). Through such references, and the description of the library at Osbaldistone-Hall, Scott places his novel within the history of the book that the library brings to mind: its

antique oaken shelves bent beneath the weight of the ponderous folios so dear to the seventeenth century, from which, under favour be it spoken, we have distilled matter for our quartos and octavos, and which, once more subjected to the alembic, may, should our sons be yet more frivolous than ourselves, be still farther reduced into duodecimos and pamphlets. (81)

Scott likes to keep in mind the material reality of the experience he offers his readers, drawing attention, for example, to his habit of introducing each chapter with a verse epigraph. He begins the third chapter of *Rob Roy* with some lines from Gay, and then points out how he has 'tagged with rhyme and blank verse the subdivisions of this important narrative, in order to seduce your continued attention by powers of composition of stronger attraction than my own' (22). He remains quite untroubled by any thought that the use of verse epigraphs seems wholly inappropriate in what purports to be a handwritten manuscript. He reminds the reader that his novels are written in chapters almost as often as Byron reminds the readers of *Don Juan* that his poem is written in rhymed stanzas: 'Here the conversation paused, until renewed in the next chapter.'[43] From the beginning, Scott offered his novels to his readers as printed objects. The very first, *Waverley*, begins with a sustained meditation on the importance of the title page, and frontispiece, and the choice of 'second or supplemental title'.[44]

Scott's own favourite of all the Waverley novels was *The Antiquary*. Jonathan Oldbuck, like Scott himself, prizes any object that has strong historical associations, but most of all he prizes books, which, in his library, are 'drawn up in ranks of two or three files deep, while numberless others littered the floor and the tables' (21). He is a bibliophile, whose favourite memories are of how he 'wheedled an old woman' out of a 'bundle of old ballads', and of haggling at bookstalls before paying

---

[42] Walter Scott, *Rob Roy*, ed. David Hewitt (Edinburgh: Edinburgh University Press, 2008), 5. Subsequent page references are included in the text.

[43] Walter Scott, *The Antiquary*, ed. David Hewitt (Edinburgh: Edinburgh University Press, 1995), 102. Subsequent page references are included in the text.

[44] Walter Scott, *Waverley; or, 'Tis Sixty Years Since*, ed. P. D. Garside (Edinburgh: Edinburgh University Press, 2007), 3–4.

the money and pocketing the book, 'affecting a cold indifference, while the hand is trembling with pleasure!' (23–4). His most prized possession is a 'rare quarto of the Augsburg Confession' (85), because it was printed by Aldobrand Oldbuck, the Westphalian printer from whom he is as proud to claim descent as is Sir Arthur Wardour from Gamelyn de Guardover, the ancestor whose name was 'written fairly with his own hand in the earliest copy of the Ragman-roll' in 1296 (50). The printer's motto, 'Kunst macht Gunst', skill wins favour, 'expressive of his indepen-dence and self-reliance, which scorned to owe anything to patronage that was not earned by desert' (85), marks Oldbuck's distance from his friend, Sir Arthur Wardour's exclusive concern for birth. It may also indicate Scott's sense that the 'author of Waverley' is a personage who might more appropriately claim descent from a fifteenth-century German printer than from a Norman knight or a Scottish lord.

One of Scott's few rivals in popularity, Pierce Egan, had been a printer's apprentice, which was no doubt why he was so attentive to the look of the page. Egan is the most typographically inventive author of the period. A sentence may be translated into a simple pictorial code in which a line drawing of a key substitutes for the word. Bob Logic's visiting card is not simply mentioned, but typographically reproduced.[45] Thackeray recalled reading *Life in London* in his youth:

How nobly those inverted commas, those italics, those capitals, bring out the writer's wit and relieve the eye. They are as good as jokes, although you mayn't quite perceive the point.[46]

In Egan's case, the frenetic typography of his novel carries the comedy, but even tragedy can become typographical. In Lockhart's *Adam Blair*, the minister falls from grace, disastrously sacrificing the respect of his community and his own self-respect for the sake of a single, momentary liaison with Charlotte Campbell, the friend of his late wife. The event is recorded in the text simply by thirty asterisks, divided between five lines.[47] It was a fateful decision. In *Knight's Quarterly Magazine* 'the thirty ill-omened stars which frown at the commence-ment of the fourteenth chapter' are identified as principally responsible for 'the outrageous abuse' to which the novel had been subjected.[48] It was, after all, a scandalous device. The ill-repute of *Don Juan* was in part secured by the frequency with which lines deemed too salacious to print were replaced by 'stanzas of asterisks'.[49]

[45] Pierce Egan, *Life in London; or, The day and night scenes of Jerry Hawthorn, esq. and his elegant friend Corinthian Tom, accompanied by Bob Logic, the Oxonian, in their rambles and sprees through the metropolis* (London: Sherwood and Jones, 1823), 36 and 87.

[46] W. M. Thackeray, 'De Juventute', *Roundabout Papers, The Works of William Makepeace Thackeray* (London: Smith, Elder and Co., 1869), 20, 69–86, 85.

[47] J. G. Lockhart, *Some Passages in the Life of Mr Adam Blair, Minister of the Gospel at Cross-Meikle* (Edinburgh: Edinburgh University Press, 1963), 160.

[48] *Knight's Quarterly Magazine*, 1 (June–October 1823), 28.

[49] See the *Literary Chronicle* (11 August 1821), 495.

Acting is a favourite topic in the magazines, perhaps, because the topic challenges the writer to find a way of writing voices, of rendering them graphically. Lamb revealingly praises Jack Palmer for the way in which he could modulate his voice so that his insincerities were 'marked out in a sort of italics to the audience'.[50] Lamb admired the way in which Palmer's acting broke the dramatic illusion by inviting the audience to recognize it as acting. In Byron a similar habit might be deplored. In his review of Byron's *Poems* of 1816, Josiah Conder detected 'the mind of the artist at leisure' who remains 'coolly detached from the passions he delineates.' He was reminded of a theatrical anecdote: 'Garrick, in the most pathetic part of King Lear had his mind sufficiently at leisure to observe the aspect of his audience, and to whisper, with a low oath to a fellow actor, "Tom, this will do."'[51] Hazlitt, reviewing *Marino Faliero* in the *London*, voiced a similar objection when he complained that Byron's characters were apt to 'describe a scene by moonlight, with a running allusion to the pending controversy between his Lordship, Mr Bowles, and Mr Campbell, on the merits of the natural and artificial style in poetry'. As Hazlitt remarked, *Marino Faliero* failed to transport its reader to the Venice of the fourteenth century. His page remains 'modern, smooth, fresh from Mr. Murray's, and does not smack of the olden time'.[52] *Don Juan* was the poem that concentrated such complaints. It was Byron's habit of calling attention to his poetry as poetry that gave it the stamp of modernity. Byron is always aware, too, of *Don Juan* as a poem in print. He reminds the reader that he has already given Lady Adeline's age in 'I forget what page' (14, 54, 5). He promises to include Lord Henry's economic advice to the government 'in a brief appendix / To come between mine epic and its index' (14, 69, 7–8). Middle age with its greying hair reminds him of the black and white of a printed page (12, 1, 6–8). The point at which a society woman irretrievably loses her reputation is something like a semi-colon, a printer's mark: society is tolerant of errant women 'up to a certain point, which point / Forms the most difficult in punctuation' (13, 81, 1–2).

Byron transmitted a similar awareness of the page on which a poem was written to the magazine writers who admired him. Poems in the modern style were not sung but printed. When *Blackwood's* versified its 'Notices to Correspondents', it made sure to mention the magazine's printers, Oliver and Boyd, and error–ridden proof sheets provide the material for one of the better jokes: 'Printr, Compositr, Pressmn, are quaking.'[53] Typography takes the place of the Muse, as in John Moultrie's couplet in *Knight's*:

[50] 'On Some of the Old Actor', *London Magazine*, 5 (February 1822), 174–9, 178.
[51] *Eclectic Review*, 5 (June 1816), 597.
[52] 'Lord Byron's Tragedy of Marino Faliero,' *London Magazine*, 3 (May 1821), 550–4, 551.
[53] 'Notices to Correspondents', *Blackwood's Edinburgh Magazine*, 2 (March 1818), on an unnumbered page between 610 and 611.

I must acknowledge, though you'll think me rash.
She was the subject of the "Lines to—."[54]

The lines conceal not a woman's name, but a printer's mark: the word necessary to complete the rhyme is 'dash'. Lockhart may even have anticipated Byron rather than followed him. 'The Mad Banker of Amsterdam,' which began to appear a few months after the publication of 'Beppo', is already wholly conscious of itself as a poem in print. Wastle calls attention to his modest insistence on writing in double rather than single columns, so that his verse does not run

> Down large resplendent pages, smooth and sleek,
>   Winding and wandering, stately, stiff, and thin.
> But as for me, when rhyming is my freak,
>   I pack my doggrell liberally in,
> I cut my page into a pair of stripes,
> And cram each column close with pica types.[55]

Pleasantries such as this are the more pointed because 'William Wastle', the signature under which Lockhart wrote the poem, like all the other *Blackwood's* signatures, like the great Christopher North himself, does not refer to a person. The name has no reality beyond its printed form: the face of the author is only an illusion fostered by a typeface. Even when, as in the case of James Hogg, a name does have a corporeal referent, it may be misleading. James Hogg was impersonated so successfully in the magazine that according to James Farrier, John Wilson's editor and son-in-law, the Ettrick Shepherd of the *Noctes Ambrosianae* bodied forth 'an ideal infinitely greater, and more real, and more original than the prototype from which it was drawn'.[56] In comparison with Wilson's fictional Shepherd, whose only being is in typescript, the real James Hogg, both the bodily man and the body of his writings, sinks into unreality.[57]

It is a world where identity can only be secured by print, and there is no space so deeply interior that it can escape the empire of the printed word. De Quincey recognizes as much when he records how, lying awake at night, almost asleep, he has a capacity for total recall of poetry: 'I become a distinguished compositor in the darkness, and with my aërial composing-stick, sometimes I "set up" half a page of verses, that would be found tolerably correct if collated with the volume that I never had in my hand but once.'[58] As he lies in the dark, and his mind withdraws into itself, he gains access to a deep inner space that reminds him,

[54] *Knight's Quarterly Magazine*, 1 (June–October 1823), 404.
[55] *Blackwood's Edinburgh Magazine*, 4 (February 1819), 563.
[56] John Wilson, *Noctes Ambrosianae*, ed. Professor James Farrier, 4 vols. (Edinburgh and London: William Blackwood and Sons, 1855), 1, xvii.
[57] For Hogg's function in the magazine as the type of bodily physicality, see Ian Duncan, 'Hogg's Body', *Studies in Hogg and His World*, 9 (1998), 1–15.
[58] 'Suspiria de Profundis: Being a Sequel to the Confessions of an English Opium-Eater, Part I', *Blackwood's Edinburgh Magazine*, 57 (April 1845), 490.

rather surprisingly, of a printer's workshop. People had become like print. In a novel of 1827, a lumbering young woman is said to have 'feet about the length of a folio, and the breadth of an octavo volume'.[59] The comparison would surely scarcely have occurred to an earlier novelist or to a later. Hazlitt, thinking of how, as one becomes older, one's impressions of people and things become fixed, finds a metaphor in a printing process that had been known for a century but had been used in book production for less than ten years, 'The mind becomes *stereo-typed*.'[60] To read the sentence is to witness the birth of a metaphor that has long since died. In the 1820s there seemed to be no escape from print.

In the magazines of the period the relationship between personality and typography was particularly close. The magazines offered their readers companionship. To buy a mass-produced commodity was to acquire, at once and at modest cost, a brilliant and fascinating circle of friends. But this virtual society was realized only in print, only by typographical means, and the magazine writers themselves were fully aware of this. This, for example, is T. J. Wainewright, writing in the *London*: 'I know where to shake my head in *italics*; utter a "MEGA THAUMA" in capitals; and, by the mere force of appropriate collocation, make a word, nay sometimes a syllable, express a start, or a shrug, or a casting up of eyes.'[61] 'Ensign and Adjutant Odoherty' is a *Blackwood's* character most closely associated with William Maginn, though he could also be impersonated by Lockhart, and was first invented by Thomas Hamilton, brother of the philosopher, William. He was common property because he was not a pseudonym but a character who, like Christopher North and all his other *Blackwood's* colleagues, from the very first had his only being in writing, in print. Thomas Hamilton seems to confess as much on Odoherty's very first appearance in the magazine when pointing out that he was an essential presence at every convivial Dublin gathering: 'In short he was like the *verb* in a sentence, quite impossible to be wanted.'[62]

The eerie Gil-Martin, the shape-shifting Satanic villain of Hogg's *Private Memoirs and Confessions of a Justified Sinner*, has his origins in the Borders folklore that Hogg absorbed in his youth, in Germanic Gothic texts such as Hoffmann's *The Devil's Elixir*, but also in a relationship with *Blackwood's Magazine* that had demonstrated to Hogg so powerfully that in the new world of print no one could command his own identity, least of all Hogg himself. It is a letter signed by Hogg that actually appeared in *Blackwood's* in August 1823, that prompts Hogg's 'editor' to ask his 'townsman and fellow-collegian, Mr L——t of C——d' (that is John Gibson Lockhart of Chiefswood) to go with him to Thirlestane to investigate the grave that Hogg had described in his letter. They

[59] Thomas Hamilton, *The Youth and Manhood of Cyril Thornton*, ed. Maurice Lindsay (Aberdeen: Association for Scottish Literary Studies, 1990), 264.
[60] 'On Antiquity,' *London Magazine*, 3 (May 1821), 527–33, 530.
[61] 'Modest Offer of Service from Mr. Bonmot to the Editor,' *London Magazine*, 1 (January 1820), 22–4, 23.
[62] *Blackwood's Edinburgh Magazine*, 2 (February 1818), 562.

take the August issue of the magazine with them, only to find that the printed letter is wilfully misleading. The grave is not in the place that Hogg had indicated. Despite this, they locate it, excavate it, and find, not the manuscript that readers familiar with the Gothic tradition would expect, but '*a printed pamphlet*' followed by a few pages in manuscript which the editor reproduces in a 'fac-simile' 'bound in with the volume'. The pamphlet records the 'private memoirs and confessions' of a man who seems to have died more than a century before, a religious maniac, an antinomian predestinarian whose false theology has bound him in league with the devil. And yet the narrative, its editor suspects, might just as easily be an 'allegory'.[63] It can be read as an allegory in which Hogg records his own experiences in the world of magazines.

Gil-Martin can assume any appearance, but most often adopts that of Robert himself or his hated brother George, alternative guises that disorient Robert much as Hogg was disoriented as he found himself, in swift alternation, the admired pet and the despised butt of Lockhart and John Wilson. Robert's bouts of amnesia, the lost weeks in which he commits, it seems, crimes of which he has no memory, similarly echo Hogg's experience. In *Blackwood's* he became not a person but a by-line, and the by-line might signal material supplied by Hogg but might just as easily be attached to material written by Lockhart or Wilson. His printed name lived a life of which its bearer might be quite unaware. In a letter to Blackwood Hogg referred to Lockhart and Wilson as 'the two devils',[64] and he slyly introduces the same thought into his novel. When Robert tells the keeper of a wretched inn at Ancrum that he is a poor student of theology on his way to Oxford, the inn-keeper and his family are horrified, because 'they had some crude conceptions that nothing was taught at Oxford but the *black arts*' (158–9). It is a conception, however crude, that may have occurred to Hogg himself when he contemplated some of the doings of the Oxford-educated Wilson and Lockhart. Soon after the publication of *Confessions*, he wrote to Blackwood, 'I have a strange indefinable sensation with regard to [Wilson], made up of a mixture of terror admiration and jealousy just such a sentiment as one deil might be supposed to have of another'.[65] Hogg's feelings about Wilson seem to have hardened after August 1821, when Wilson responded to Hogg's 'Memoir' of his own life by suggesting that when he masqueraded as an Edinburgh man of letters he appeared 'liker a swineherd in the Canongate than a shepherd in Ettrick Forest'. His illiteracy was, Wilson claimed, only hidden from the world by the conventions of a print culture in which spelling, grammar, and punctuation

[63] James Hogg, *The Private Memoirs and Confessions of a Justified Sinner*, ed. P. D. Garside (Edinburgh: Edinburgh University Press, 2002), 165–75. Subsequent page references to this edition are included in the text.
[64] Quoted in James Hogg, *The Private Memoirs and Confessions of a Justified Sinner*, xxxviii.
[65] Quoted in James Hogg, *The Private Memoirs and Confessions of a Justified Sinner*, xl.

might be supplied by the editor and compositors: 'Let Hogg publish a fac-simile of his hand-writing, and the world will be thunderstruck at the utter helplessness of his hand.'[66] It is hard not to see a retort to the jibe in the editor's description of the manuscript 'in a fine old hand, extremely small and close,' and his order to his printer to 'procure a fac-simile of it to be bound in with the volume' (174).

One of the points of origin of Hogg's great novel lies in his recognition that print can live a life of its own, independent of its reputed author, and independent too of the real world to which it claims to refer. Hogg reproduces his own letter to *Blackwood's* with its account of 'the broad blue bonnet' still sitting on the head of the suicide's corpse, and places alongside it the editor's insistence that it was 'neither a broad bonnet, nor a Border bonnet' but rather 'a Highland bonnet, worn in a flat way like a scone on the crown' (168 and 173). There is a similar but more uncanny disjuncture between Robert as he is revealed in his final panic-stricken journal entries and Robert as he is represented in Hogg's letter, a 'youth' of 'a deep, thoughtful, and sullen disposition' who had been 'a considerable time in the place' and had given no reason to anyone to doubt his 'character' (166). If the editor's account of the bonnet is more likely to be believed than Hogg's that means only that he is better able to command the rhetoric of realism. In a print culture reality becomes an adjunct of prose style, which is one of the reasons, no doubt, that Hogg located in that culture an eeriness of the kind that permeates his novel.

When Robert flees south he lodges for a night with a country weaver. When asked to identify himself he replies that his 'name is Cowan', an odd failure of invention. The weaver suspects he may be the notorious murderer 'Colwan, there being so little difference in the sound', until it occurs to him that a murderer 'wad hae taen a name wi' some gritter difference in the sound' and not have chosen simply to 'leave the L out' (146–7). Cowan is less an alias than a misprint, which explains why, when Robert escapes the weaver and makes his way to Edinburgh, he chooses the more imaginative alias of Elliot. It may also, and more interestingly, suggest why, in Edinburgh, he should find employment as a compositor with the royal printer himself, James Watson. It is at Watson's establishment in Craig's Close that Robert's manuscript is put through the press, although all copies except the copy buried with him are subsequently destroyed by Watson. When the story reaches him of 'the devil having appeared twice in the printing house, assisting the workmen at the printing' of the book, Watson reads the pamphlet and denounces it as 'a medley of lies and blasphemy' (153). The episode seems designed to insinuate a pun. In Hogg's *Confessions*, the devil, it emerges, is a printer's devil, an apprentice in a printing office.[67]

---

[66] *Blackwood's Edinburgh Magazine*, 10 (August 1821, Part II), 43–52.

[67] Ian Duncan insinuates that in Hogg's novel print culture brings about a Fall from which there is no possibility of recovery: textuality 'marks a lethal alienation from common life in its original condition of a traditional community', after which the original community may itself be recovered only 'as another text'. Ian Duncan, *Scott's Shadow* (Princeton: Princeton University Press, 2007), 286.

Private Memoirs, as has long been recognized, bears the imprint of a novel that William Blackwood had published in 1821, E. T. A. Hoffmann's *The Devil's Elixir* in the translation of R. P. Gillies, a regular *Blackwood's* contributor well known to Hogg. The elixir, a flagon of wine with which the devil had once sought to tempt St Anthony, has the power to dissolve for those who drink it any stable sense of their own identity. The monk Medardus when he tastes it is precipitated into a world in which he is repeatedly horror-struck by meetings with himself. When, in the second volume, he is awaiting trial for murder and a naked figure with matted hair breaks into his cell from the cell below and hands him the murder weapon, a stiletto, Medardus records, 'I RECOGNIZED MYSELF, and losing all consciousness and self-possession, fell in a deadly swoon on the pavement.'[68] The reader will be less astonished for there have been several earlier encounters of the same kind. Throughout the novel Medardus, 'like the fabulous knight who fought with his DOUBLE in the dark forest', is 'at variance, and combating with [him]self' (1, 138). Such experiences are produced, the novel suggests, by the magical potency of the elixir and the mysterious circumstances of Medardus's birth. The novel's power has to do with Hoffman's skill in persuading his reader to recognize that Medardus becomes through his experience of self-division a representative figure, the only character in the novel with whom the reader feels a kinship. It seems to Medardus 'as if [his] frame was split and divided an hundredfold, and every division thence arising assumed a peculiar and individual principle of life' (2, 144). He becomes in himself as large a population as his imagination can support, with the inevitable result that his world becomes solipsistic. He wanders delightedly through a town fair gazing at the commodities displayed on the stalls only to realize that the only relationships left to him are with things rather than with people (1, 213–14). Commodities are invested with the glamour that living people sadly lack.

   It is entirely consonant with this position that to have sex with someone is to be prompted to kill them. Medardus has an affair with Euphemia, and then poisons her, and he stabs his bride, Aurelia, on their wedding day. In this novel sex and murder are all but identical activities. As Euphemia herself explains, her husband became, as soon as they were married, 'a run-down piece of clock-work'. As soon as she embarks on an affair with Hermogen, her husband's son by an earlier marriage, Hermogen comes to seem 'a broken *marionett*—a worn-out play thing' (1, 157, 162–3). She invites Medardus to join her in ruling over 'the contemptible world of puppets' that they inhabit (1, 164), but, as she instructs Medardus, such power is only available to the individual who has perfected the art of self-division, and possesses 'the power of stepping, as it were, out of herself,— of contemplating her own individuality from an external point ... for our own

---

   [68] *The Devil's Elixir: from the German of E. T. A. Hofmann*, 2 vols. (Edinburgh: Blackwood, 1824), 2, 2, and 55. Subsequent page references are supplied in the text.

identity, when viewed in this manner, serves like an obedient implement—a passive means of obtaining whatever object we have proposed to ourselves' (1, 155).

Medardus represents his narrative of his own life as his confession, the task imposed on him as a penance for his sins that will issue in his forgiveness. As he writes he seems to hover 'as if on seraph's wings, above all these earthly remembrances' (2, 332). It does not seem to strike him that this seraph bears an uncanny likeness to the devil that pursues him all through his narrative: 'it seemed to me as if my most secret thoughts played false with him to whom they owed their birth—as if they departed from me, and dressed themselves up in a cursed masquerade, representing MYSELF' (2, 296). This is a diabolic masquerade, and the seraph is a figure from a divine masquerade that is its exact counterpart. Medardus understands himself as the site at which rival genes, the genes of his saintly mother and of his devilish father, do battle for his soul, but it is the fact of self-division rather than its character that seems to underlie his sinful progress.

Like Matthew Lewis's Ambrosius (*The Devil's Elixir* is strongly influenced by *The Monk*) Medardus becomes a preacher celebrated for his sanctity, but he soon begins to study his effects, endeavouring 'to give to [his] periods the proper rounding, and to adorn [his] discourses throughout, with all the flowers of eloquence' (1, 54), and as soon as he does so, his patron, the Prioress, recognizes him as a travesty of the man of God he pretends to be. He has become 'a profane actor on the stage' who has 'practised gestures and a studied mien, all for the sake of the same base meed of wonder and applause' (1, 83–4). The condition of virtue, it seems, is a perfect unselfconsciousness, and yet the whole of the novel offers an invitation to its readers to accept that in their own experience, as in the experience of Medardus, no such unselfconsciousness is possible.

Medardus tumbles into guilt as soon as he begins to compose his sermons, and he is invited to seek atonement by writing his memoirs, by engaging in an activity, writing, which, as he recognizes, can only confirm that he is a man divided from himself. As he writes he rises on wings above himself: the hand that holds the pen parts company with the hand that wielded the stiletto. Medardus leaves a manuscript, but it is an 'editor' who is responsible for the printed text. It is a worn Gothic convention but retains vestiges of vitality. At the moment, for example, when Medardus is about to consummate his relationship with Euphemia, the reader encounters a bracketed clause: '[a few sentences are here left out by the Editor]' (1, 154). It is the business of editors to prepare a text to be consumed, but even before the editor begins his task, as Medardus writes his manuscript, he seems to anticipate that his manuscript will become a commodity, consumed by a stranger, the anonymous reader of the nineteenth-century novel: 'I addressed myself to thee, oh stranger, who may one day read these pages' (2, 91). That nineteenth-century reader, as he sits in an armchair or lies on a couch, inhabits at once a safe domestic space, and wanders through a long ago Germany in which all ordinary rules seem to have been suspended. To read a novel, *The Devil's Elixir* reminds us, just as much as to write one, is to engage in an experience that demands the power of self-division. It is a power that Hogg and Hoffman seem to agree, is diabolic and yet it is the power that defines the world of print.

Gilmartin's satanic quality is most clearly revealed by his use of the Bible in his seduction of Robert Wringhim. He misleads by wrenching the sense of Scripture, or by reading passages removed from their context. He deprives Wringhim of what should be his surest stay, and he does so by offering in place of the Word of God an endlessly unstable play of textuality. The difference seems clear, except that Hogg is perfectly aware that Gilmartin's methods mimic the practices of all those preachers who pride themselves on how ingeniously they can play upon the Word of the Bible.[69] In *The Three Perils of Man* Hogg parallels the chivalric conflict that pits the Black Douglas against the Earl of Musgrave with the uncanny contest between the Wizard, Michael Scott, and Roger Bacon, who is living incognito in Scotland, known only as the Gospel Friar. The two men, Hogg explains, are quite different. Bacon 'considered the Christian Revelation as the source of all that is good, wise, or great among men', whereas Scott 'had disbelieved it from his youth upward', and had preferred to seek power through 'communion with the potent spirits of the elements'.[70] And yet the illiterate moss-troopers who travel with the Friar associate the Bible that Bacon holds in such reverence with the black arts, unable to distinguish it from Michael Scott's famous Book of Spells. In the contest that pits the Friar against the Wizard the two men seem rather like one another, equally capable of murderous supernatural violence. In the novel's last pages the King orders that Scott's body be 'reverendly deposited' in 'a vaulted aisle of the abbey of Melrose', for, as the King insists, he was, after all, the 'greatest man, and the most profound scholar of the age'.[71] Michael Scott and Roger Bacon are revealed as doubles of one another. Hogg is fascinated by the process through which this comes about, but it also fills him with a holy horror.

His supposedly more sophisticated associates seem to have shared his feelings. John Wilson, for example, quickly became addicted to the opportunities made available to him by magazine anonymity and pseudonymity, evidently taking an unholy glee in calumniating and praising Wordsworth in successive issues of *Blackwood's*, and yet he associated true piety with a capacity for innocent trust in the truthfulness of the written word. In Wilson's own most successful novel, *The Trials of Margaret Lindsay*, Margaret is sustained in all her tribulations by a simple-minded faith in a book. Cast out by the family who have adopted her,

---

[69] For a discussion of Hogg's reading of the Bible, stressing that the Bible 'remains in the *Confessions* a dangerously ambiguous book', see Alison M. Jack, *Texts Reading Texts, Sacred and Secular*, Journal for the Study of the New Testament Supplement Series 179 (Sheffield: Sheffield Academic Press, 1999), 38–74, 74.

[70] James Hogg, *The Three Perils of Man: War, Women and Witchcraft*, ed. Douglas Gifford (Edinburgh: Scottish Academic Press, 1989), 197.

[71] James Hogg, *The Three Perils of Man*, 462–3.

she rests in a pleasant rural location, takes the Bible from the small bundle that she carries, and 'in the silence of that sweet solitary spot' she reads 'two or three chapters of the New Testament', and is comforted.[72] Wilson builds his whole narrative on the absolute distinction between one book and another, between Paine's *Age of Reason* that had politically and morally corrupted Margaret's father, and the Bible that sustains Margaret herself. It is as if Wilson offers his novel as an apology for the recklessness with which in his magazine writing he had undermined any simple faith in the printed word. Still more telling is Wilson's short story 'The Forgers'. An old man learns that his brother has died. The dead man's only son had gone away to sea and, because he has not been heard of since, is believed dead. The old man and his son forge a will in which the old man is named as his brother's heir. The brother's son returns, exposes their crime, and they are executed, but on the day of execution the pastor finds 'the Bible open before them', which allows him some hope that they will find forgiveness.[73] It is a story that invests the abuse of a signature for profit with all the horror that attends a capital offence.

Lockhart was equally ready to exploit the opportunity given him in his contributions to *Blackwood's* and in *Peter's Letters to his Kinsfolk* to shift shapes as bewilderingly as Gilmartin. It must have reassured him to recall that his father-in-law had anticipated him by presenting his novels under a rich variety of signatures. But both men indicate at times their suspicion that such playfulness might be criminal. It is a kind of lying. In *Heart of Midlothian* Jeanie Deans cannot tell a lie even if that lie will save her sister's life, and Scott presents her intransigence as heroic. Her heroism is shared by Lockhart's Adam Blair, who may fall sexually, but, as his friend and colleague, Dr Muir, insists, 'even if he had been capable of offending in the manner imputed to him', he could never have been guilty of 'telling a deliberate and uncalled-for LIE'.[74] At such moments Scott and Lockhart reveal a nostalgia for an earlier age in which speech had priority over print, and words were the solemn responsibility of those who uttered them. The representative book in this earlier, more innocent age was the Bible, a book that should be read as Margaret Lindsay reads it, single-mindedly. But in Hogg's *Private Memoirs* the Bible becomes in Gilmartin's hands a quite different kind of book, a text as radically unstable, as shape-shifting, as duplicitous, as *Blackwood's Magazine* itself.

Wordsworth would not allow a copy of *Blackwood's* to 'enter [his] doors',[75] and he was surely right to recognize a radical discrepancy between his own poetry and magazine writing. His poems cultivate an aesthetics of depth, inviting the

---

[72] John Wilson, *The Trials of Margaret Lindsay* (Edinburgh: Blackwood, 1823), 236.

[73] John Wilson, 'The Forgers', *Blackwood's Edinburgh Magazine*, 9 (August 1821), 572–7. The story was re-printed in Wilson's *Lights and Shadows of Scottish Life* (Edinburgh: Blackwood, 1822).

[74] J. G. Lockhart, *Some Passages in the Life of Mr Adam Blair, Minister of the Gospel at Cross-Meikle*, 220.

[75] *The Letters of William and Dorothy Wordsworth. vol 3: The Middle Years, Part I. 1812–1820*, ed. Mary Moorman and Alan G. Hill (Oxford: Clarendon Press, 1970), 522.

reader to carry them 'far into the heart'. They invite the slow contemplation that the poems themselves devote to objects such as a ruined cottage or a half-finished sheepfold. Their forward movement is slowed by the resistance of memory, by the pressure exerted on the present by the past. Magazines, by contrast, demand to be read superficially. If magazine writing, which some magazine writers doubted, might properly be considered literature, it was literature of a new kind. It was, for example, literature designed to be read in a new way, not from beginning to end but dipped into, and not slowly digested but skimmed. Elia remembers 'poor Tobin', who when he became blind, did not so much miss 'the weightier kinds of reading', because they could be read aloud to him, 'but he missed the pleasure of skimming over with his own eye a magazine, or a light pamphlet'.[76] Part of the pleasure of this kind of reading depends on its speed. It is also, I think, characteristically a solitary kind of reading. The *New Monthly*, it is true, imagines the magazine being received into a family circle. A 'reader' writes a letter fondly recollecting the arrival of a new issue: 'the moment when, the fire stirred, the red curtains drawn, the tea-urn smoking, and the Argand Lamp gently raised—I put the paper-knife into the foldings of the first sheet of a new number, is a moment of breathless expectation and delight to every member of the fire-side'.[77] But such a scene denies the extent to which magazines are designed to be negotiated by silent individuals, who remain free to decide for themselves the order in which they consume the contents, and to skip, skim, or settle to an article as they please, rather than readers held in thrall by a speaker's voice as constraining as the ancient mariner's.[78] If the new kind of reading admits domesticity, it is domesticity of the peculiar kind described by Lamb in 'A Quaker's Meeting': 'what so pleasant as to be reading a book through a long winter evening with a friend sitting by—say, a wife—he, or she, too, (if that be probable), reading another, without interruption or oral communication?'[79]

There were novels and poems in the period that demanded to be read almost like magazines. Alice Fennel, for example, the heroine of *Scotch Novel Reading*, is a silent reader, necessarily so, because she cannot pronounce the Scots language that she so admires, and because it has not been her habit to read the novels all the way through. As soon as she does so she is disillusioned: she had 'hitherto merely skimmed over the works of her enchanting writer, as she always denominated the author of "Waverley". She had read only the romantic parts.'[80] This is

---

[76] 'Detached Thoughts on Books and Reading', *London Magazine*, 6 (July 1822), 33–6.
[77] *New Monthly Magazine*, 7 (1823), 2.
[78] Lucy Newlyn persuasively argues that the importance attached to the practice of reading aloud in the Wordsworth–Coleridge circle was itself a reaction against the commodification of print. See Lucy Newlyn, *Reading, Writing and Romanticism: The Anxiety of Reception* (Oxford: Oxford University Press, 2000), 19–20.
[79] *London Magazine*, 3 (April 1821), 385.
[80] Sarah Green, *Scotch Novel Reading*, 2, 87.

satire, of course, and yet Scott himself refers in *Redgauntlet* to 'the laudable practice of skipping',[81] and his novels increasingly seem to invite this kind of reading. When novels are as lightly organized as *The Fortunes of Nigel*, the reader's attention is scarcely distracted from the episodes to the main plot, and this was one of the pleasures that the novels offered, as a reviewer in the *New Monthly* noticed when observing that *Peveril of the Peak* was less successful than most of Scott's novels precisely because it was more nearly unified: in his best work 'each of [the scenes] has an interest of its own, independent of the links by which they are connected'.[82]

Poets, too, began to invite their readers to scan their poems much in the same way that they would scan a magazine. Henry Luttrell, for example, in *Advice to Julia*, his poem of 1820:

> So use your privilege—of dipping
> Now here, now there—of sometimes skipping;
> And if you feel your eyelids dropping
> O'er lines unreadable,—of stopping.[83]

But the poem of the period that most winningly invites a reading of this kind is *Don Juan*. This is partly because it is a poem so alert to the delights of speed:[84]

> On with the horses! Off to Canterbury!
>   Tramp, tramp, o'er pebble, and splash, splash, thro' puddle;
> Hurrah! how swiftly speeds the post so merry!
>   Not like slow Germany, wherein they muddle
> Along the road, as if they went to bury
>   Their fare; and also pause besides, to fuddle
> With 'schnapps'—sad dogs! whom 'Hundsfot' or 'Ferflucter'
> Affect no more than lightning a conductor.
>
> (10, 71)

Byron invites his reader to share the exhilaration of speed by allowing the eye to dash through the stanzas. The inferiority of ponderous German traffic is deftly communicated through those verbal borrowings that irritate English readers by slowing them down. It is a poem that resists the voice because the tongue moves so much more slowly than the more nimble eye, and it sometimes resists the voice still more emphatically, as in the prescription stanza:

[81] Walter Scott, *Redgauntlet*, ed. G. A. M. Wood with David Hewitt (Edinburgh: Edinburgh University Press, 1997), 126. Subsequent page references are included in the text.
[82] *New Monthly Magazine*, 7 (March 1823), 273.
[83] [Henry Luttrell], *Advice to Julia: A Letter in Rhyme. A New Edition* (London: John Murray, 1820), 171. The lines are not numbered.
[84] For John Wilson speed is an integral aspect of modern print culture: reading 'subjects the mind to a crowd of thoughts, which of old could only have been gathered slowly, and separately, during the course of a whole existence', *Blackwood's Edinburgh Magazine*, 4 (October 1818), 83. As Jane Stabler remarks, 'Skimming the surface is the readerly process that Byron's poetry usually invites.' See *Byron, Poetics and History* (Cambridge: Cambridge University Press, 2002), 186.

But here is one prescription out of many:
   'Sodae-Sulphat. 3vi. 3. s. mannae optim.
Aq. fervent. F. 3iss. 3ij. tinct. sennae
   Haustus.' (And here the surgeon came and cupped him)
'R. Pulv. Com. gr. iij. Ipecacuanhae'
   (With more beside, if Juan had not stopped 'em).
'Bolus potassae sulphuret. sumendus,
Et haustus ter in die capiendus.'

(10, 41)

It is possible to recite the stanza, and it is even possible to recite it metrically,[85] but it is a feat that no reader could perform on sight. *Don Juan* may be the first major English poem designed from the first to be read silently, to be encountered not through the voice, but on the page, as type. A word, according to Byron, has the capacity to make 'thousands, perhaps millions, think', but only when life is bestowed upon it by 'a small drop' of printer's ink. It is the 'letter', the printed word, not 'speech' that forms the 'lasting link / Of ages' (*Don Juan*, 3, 88). *Don Juan* is the poem that best characterizes the cultural moment that I have been describing: it is the primary epic of the age of print.

[85] See Lord Byron, *The Complete Poetical Works*, ed. Jerome J. McGann, 7 vols. (Oxford: Clarendon Press, 1980–93), 5, 744 (note).

7

Pistols and Horsewhips

When James Stuart discovered that Alexander Boswell was responsible for the attacks on him in the *Sentinel*, he straight away issued a challenge. It was partly a matter of demonstrating his courage, but it was also important for him as an assertion of his social position. The duel between John Scott and Christie seems to have been prompted in much the same way. The quarrel with Lockhart left Scott anxious to prove at the first possible opportunity both his manliness and his gentlemanliness. It was a time when the distinction between gentlemen and non-gentlemen might be violently contested. When Stuart found himself libelled in the Edinburgh newspaper, *The Beacon*, he had responded by horsewhipping the newspaper's printer, Duncan Stevenson, at least he had tried to, and had then contemptuously refused Stevenson's challenge on the grounds that Stevenson was not entitled to the satisfaction of a gentleman. Stevenson protested that 'he [held] a situation in society at least equal to that which James Stuart held'.[1] Stuart had assumed that a printer could not be a gentleman, but the printer disagreed. A rather similar incident had taken place in Edinburgh in 1818, when a man who thought himself defamed in *Blackwood's* burst into William Blackwood's shop, and 'laid his whip across his shoulder'. Blackwood bought a stick, took James Hogg with him, and went in search of his assailant. He found him boarding the Glasgow coach and gave him a severe drubbing.[2]

Issuing a challenge and administering a whipping are both of them aggressive acts, but the duelling pistol acknowledges the right of the man who is challenged to be admitted within the same social circles as the challenger, whereas the horsewhip violently proclaims its victim's social inferiority. Hence, looked at in another way, the two acts are antithetical. To issue a challenge, however unfortunate the consequences may be, is in some sense an act of inclusion. As Peter Murphy puts it, 'Duels celebrate the strength of the agreements and acknowledgements between the antagonists, the rules which have brought them peaceably together in murderous antagonism.'[3] According to Walter Scott—although one may suspect

---

[1] *The Beacon*, 33 (18 August 1821), 252.

[2] Mary Wilson Gordon, *'Christopher North': A Memoir of John Wilson* (Edinburgh: Edmonston and Douglas, 1862), 1, 278–9.

[3] Peter Murphy, 'Impersonation and Authorship in Romantic Britain', *English Literary History*, 59 (Autumn 1992), 625–49, 626. For the best account of duelling and its relation to class, see

an anachronism—the subtleties of the code were as absorbing for men of the mid-sixteenth century as for those of his own day. In *The Monastery*, Sir Piercie Shafton, the Euphuistic English knight, is perplexed as to how he should respond when he is insulted by Halbert Glendinning. Were he to issue a challenge Sir Piercie fears that he would 'derogate from [his] sphere' by 'indulging the right of a gentleman to the son of a clod-breaking peasant'.[4] Halbert himself is uncertain of his social station, and can voice his 'distant pretensions' to descent from an ancient family only 'with a faltering and uncertain voice' (324). In the end Sir Piercie's resentment proves more powerful than his scruples, and he delivers his challenge, but he recognizes that in doing so he has effected an 'unnatural equality' between the two men, which he acknowledges on the morning of the duel by doffing his hat to Halbert (198). Horsewhipping, by contrast, is an act of exclusion, a denial of the victim's right to claim equality with the perpetrator.

From time to time, men without the proper status would duel, and when they did they were likely to become the objects of public mirth. When a man who was a dyer by trade was found to have engaged in a duel, for example, newspapers found punning references to 'dying duellists' irresistible.[5] As De Quincey observed, 'a ridicule . . . everywhere attaches to many of the less elevated or liberal modes of exercising trade in going out to fight with sword and pistol'.[6] This was why Walter Scott was so amused when there seemed a prospect that Hogg, who was after all only a shepherd, might receive a challenge from John Douglas, editor of the *Glasgow Chronicle*: 'Our poor friend Hogg has had an *affair of honour* or a something tending that way which is too whimsical to suppress.'[7] Scott seems, like his own Mr Touchstone, to have been nostalgic for the time when 'men who had no grandfathers never dreamt of such folly'.[8] Burns, Scott observed, 'did not see anything so rational in the practice of duelling, as afterwards to adopt or to affect the sentiments of the higher ranks upon that subject', but this was a proof, it emerges, not of his good sense but of his 'plebeian spirit'.[9] The ethics of duelling were, Scott assumed like most of his contemporaries, inseparable from questions of class, which is why Henry Cockburn, the leading defence counsel when Stuart was tried for Boswell's murder, for all that he was, like Stuart, a Whig and a champion of the rights of the people, took pains to establish that

V. G. Kiernan, *The Duel in European History: Honour and the Reign of Aristocracy* (Oxford: Oxford University Press, 1988).

[4] Walter Scott, *The Monastery*, ed. Penny Fielding (Edinburgh: Edinburgh University Press, 2000), 187. Subsequent page references are included in the text.

[5] See *The Sentinel*, no. 4, 31 October 1821, 31.

[6] *Tait's Edinburgh* Magazine, n.s. 8 (February 1841), 106; Lindop, 11, 301.

[7] *The Letters of Sir Walter Scott*, ed. H. J. C. Grierson, 12 vols. (London: Constable, 1932–7), 5, 154. Scott was writing to the Duke of Buccleuch.

[8] Walter Scott, *Saint Ronan's Well*, ed. Mark A. Weinstein (Edinburgh: Edinburgh University Press, 1995), 140.

[9] *Quarterly Review*, 1 (February 1809), 27.

Stuart belonged to the class that might properly expect and be expected to fight duels: he was 'blood relation to some of the first families in Scotland'.[10]

As a novelist, if not as a man, Scott affects to rise above the class system. In *The Antiquary*, for example, the antiquary himself, consistently understood by Scott's readers to be a mocking self-portrait of the author, was 'no friend to the *monomachia* or duel' even in his younger days, and is glad that he is now old enough to 'indulge [his] irritabilities without the necessity of supporting them by cold steel'.[11] He consistently tries to appease the belligerent instincts of his fiery Highland nephew Hector M'Intyre. But that is because Oldbuck, unlike his nephew, is freed by his unaristocratic lineage from the full rigour of the code of honour: he traces his descent only from a Westphalian printer. That code acts with double force on M'Intyre, who has the Highlander's pride in his lineage and is also a serving soldier. So, too, is the man he knows as Lovel, and when M'Intyre doubts Lovel's word, a challenge immediately follows. This raises a difficulty. Lovel has assumed a false name, prompting M'Intyre's second to observes that 'many persons will even consider it as a piece of Quixotry in M'Intyre to give [him] a meeting, while [Lovel's] character and circumstances are involved in such obscurity' (157). But the business goes ahead. Even the objections of the beggar, Edie Ochiltree, who, although an ex-soldier, has the ethics of a thoroughgoing plebeian, fail to deter the combatants. Ochiltree points out that duelling is an offence against the laws of God, and against the duellists' families and friends. It is 'an ill fight whar he that wins has the warst o't', and when the duel brings together two army officers in a nation under threat of invasion, it constitutes a breach of loyalty to king and country (161–2). His argument is unanswerable, but it is also entirely unavailing. The two men fight, M'Intyre falls, and Lovel flees, suddenly aware that he would even give up the hand of the woman he loves to regain 'the conscious freedom from blood-guiltiness which he possessed in the morning' (164). Happily, M'Intyre recovers, Lovel is revealed as the gallant Major Neville, and when the two men meet again they seal a fast friendship, but the incident serves to illustrate that by 1816, when *The Antiquary* was published, ethical codes and social codes coexisted uneasily, and that in the practice of duelling the awkwardness became especially apparent.

Hogg might be expected to be particularly sensitive to social distinctions of the kind highlighted by the duelling code. In his *Private Memoirs and Confessions of a Justified Sinner*, the brothers, or half-brothers, George Colwan and Robert Wringhim, are placed on either side of a class divide. George is an enthusiast for sports of all kinds, tennis and cricket among them. Wringhim despises such

---

[10] *A full report of the trial of James Stuart, Esq. younger of Dunearn, before the High Court of Justiciary, 10th June 1822* (Edinburgh: 1822), 10.

[11] Walter Scott, *The Antiquary*, ed. David Hewitt (Edinburgh: Edinburgh University Press, 1995), 70. Subsequent page references are included in the text.

activities. When he disrupts a cricket match in which his brother is engaged, one
of his brother's friends, Adam Gordon, delivers the ultimate insult, 'You are no
gentleman, Sir.' But for Wringhim the gentlemanly code has exactly the same
status as ungodly sports such as tennis and cricket: 'If *one* of the party be a
gentleman, *I do hope in God I am not.*'[12] The code of honour required the
distinction between gentlemen and others to be clear and recognized even by
those it excluded, but in Edinburgh in the early nineteenth century, as Hogg's
novel and the dispute between James Stuart and Duncan Stephenson both
indicate, this was not at all the case.

By 1821, the fashion for duelling was on the decline. Duelling was, until mid-
century, tolerated in the armed services because refusing a challenge was believed
to compromise the honour of the regiment, and it was common, too, among
politicians, presumably because the professional status of politicians is inseparable from their private reputations. Men of letters had no *esprit de corps* to
defend, and their professional success was independent of their private character,
which makes it at first sight odd that they should have become in the second
decade of the nineteenth century, after soldiers and politicians, the professional
group most given to duelling. It was not just a penchant of Irishmen like Thomas
Moore or aristocrats like Byron (who despite rather often challenging or being
challenged seems never actually to have fought). Coleridge, Leigh Hunt, Keats
and Hazlitt, as well as Lockhart, John Wilson, James Hogg, and John Scott all of
them at one time or another received, issued, or threatened to issue a challenge,
although none of them could claim, as Cockburn claimed on behalf of James
Stuart, to be blood relation to some of the first families in the land. Thomas
Moore was the son of a grocer, born above the shop in Aungier-Street, Dublin.
John Scott's father owned a furniture shop in Aberdeen, John Wilson's father was
a tradesman, too, though in a grander way, Keats was the son of an inn-keeper,
and the fathers of Coleridge, Hazlitt, Leigh Hunt, and Lockhart were all church-
men of one persuasion or another.[13] It was not, then, their family backgrounds
that predisposed these men to belligerence.

It seemed strange that literary men should be so bellicose even to the literary
men themselves. As John Scott himself pointed out in the *London*, the 'idea of
changing "ink for blood"' had become so prevalent that reviewers nowadays
needed unusual qualifications: 'when able to snuff a candle at ten paces, any
reviewer might safely enough, we apprehend, undertake the works of the most
irascible of our writers'.[14] Scott's quarrel with *Blackwood's* was to end in his
death, but even after that event *Blackwood's*, in an episode of the *Noctes* written

---

[12] James Hogg, *The Private Memoirs and Confessions of a Justified Sinner*, ed. P. D. Garside
(Edinburgh: Edinburgh University Press, 2002), 26.
[13] See Mark Parker, *Literary Magazines and British Romanticism* (Cambridge: Cambridge
University Press, 2000), 26.
[14] A remark Scott makes in a comparison between the actor, Elliston, and the Emperor Nero.
See the *London Magazine*, 1 (June 1820), 610.

by Lockhart himself, was just as willing as Scott had been to register the absurdity of magazine disputes:

Nothing amuses me more than to see Magazines—which, after all, are not living beings, but just so many stitched sheets of letter-press, *going to loggerheads* and *becoming personal.* Up jumps Ebony's Magazine, and plants a left-handed lounge on the bread-basket of Taylor and Hessey. That periodical strips *instanter,* a ring is formed, and the Numbers are piping hot as mutton-pies. Can any thing be more ridiculous?[15]

The writers of the period were almost all of them members of a middle class much given to cultural mimicry of its social superiors, but their fellow professionals rarely took mimicry so far as to engage in duels, and this suggests that an explanation must be sought in the circumstances of the particular profession to which writers belong.

THE SEMIOTICS OF CLASS

When Christie first carried Lockhart's challenge to John Scott, Scott demanded to know 'in which of two capacities Mr. Lockhart should be regarded—whether as a *gentleman* assailed in his honourable feelings by an indecent use of his name in print; or as a *professional scandal-monger,* who had long profited by fraudulent and cowardly concealment'.[16] It was a tricky question, because if Lockhart agreed that he was a paid journalist he might be taken to have disclaimed the gentlemanly status that would oblige Scott to respond to his challenge, and if he denied it then Scott might reasonably claim that Lockhart was not implicated in strictures made against the editor and chief contributor to *Blackwood's.* As John Murray explained the matter in a letter to Byron: 'If you wont answer this question I shall not fight— and if you do—in the affirmative—I cant fight you.'[17] Scott would probably have known that Macvey Napier, when threatened by John Wilson for his attack on *Blackwood's,* had pointed out that if Wilson did not write the offending articles 'then you have nothing to say to me', and if he did, his writing of such articles showed that he had 'lost every claim to the character of a gentleman, and [had] no right whatsoever to demand that satisfaction which is due only to one who has been unjustly accused'.[18] But it is the oddity rather than the trickiness of the question that strikes, because Scott, who earned his living as a journalist and editor, seems hardly the appropriate person to insist on a distinction between a gentleman

---

[15] *Blackwood's Edinburgh Magazine,* 11 (April 1822), 487. The speaker is Thomas Tickler. Taylor and Hessey bought the *London Magazine* from Baldwin after Scott's death.

[16] *Statement, etc. by Mr John Scott in his dispute with Mr. John Gibson Lockhart* (London: 1821), 3.

[17] *The Letters of John Murray to Lord Byron,* ed. Andrew Nicholson (Liverpool: Liverpool University Press, 2007), 379.

[18] *Correspondence on the Subject of Blackwood's Magazine,* bound up with *Hypocrisy Unveiled and Calumny Detected in a Review of Blackwood's Magazine,* 2nd edn (Edinburgh: 1818), 3.

and a professional writer. Yet Scott repeatedly makes such distinctions, as when he registers a lofty conviction that it is 'more than ridiculous to see the regular trader in anonymous lampoons and scandals, when worsted in print, affecting to put himself on the footing of a private gentleman'.[19] Macvey Napier's situation was very similar. He was an Edinburgh lawyer who earned his living as a professional writer—he was Constable's choice to edit the supplement to the *Encyclopaedia Britannica*, and much later succeeded Jeffrey as editor of the *Edinburgh Review*—and he was himself the son of a tradesman. Yet Napier remained confident that the pernicious effect of *Blackwood's* would cease when it was recognized that the motives of its editors were mercenary: 'their malice' would be rendered 'impotent' as soon as it was known that it was 'exerted to purchase bread'.[20] It is predictable that the old notion that those who wrote for money forfeited their gentlemanly status should have survived into the early decades of the nineteenth century: it is a good deal more surprising that it should have survived amongst professional journalists.

One reason that *Blackwood's* provoked unusually strident attacks was its readiness to boast jocularly of the profits the magazine made. In October 1820, for example, just before John Scott launched his campaign against the magazine, Christopher North elaborately computed how much he made a year from his work for *Blackwood's*, beginning with £4,000 and repeatedly adjusting the figure upwards to nearly £7,000 before concluding that he made more money from literature than anyone 'with the exception of the author of the novels, whoever he may be'.[21] The piece is written by John Wilson in cheerful mockery of the affectation of writers who still clung to the notion that men of letters were distinguished from Grub Street hacks because they could claim a disinterested-ness only proper to those who wrote without financial motives. Lockhart too was perfectly capable of sensibly accepting that professional writers might properly hope to make a living from their writing. He dismissed Byron's pretensions to be above writing for gain: 'Now, Sir Walter has made a fortune by his books, and you will do so in good season too; and nothing can be more proper, because, if you did not, your booksellers would sell your books just as dear as they do, and pocket double as much as they do; whereas, all the world knows they have pocketed, and are pocketing, by both of you, quite as much as is at all good for them.'[22] In 1824 James Mill, writing in the *Westminster Review*, robustly reminded his readers that in a periodical 'every thing is paid for—from the accounts of pugilistic fights, to Mr Irving's sermons,' and that 'it is an axiom which the experience of all periodical works establishes beyond question, that

---

[19] *Statement, etc. by Mr John Scott in his dispute with Mr. John Gibson Lockhart*, 7.
[20] *Hypocrisy Unveiled and Calumny Detected in a Review of Blackwood's Magazine* (Edinburgh: 1818), 10.
[21] *Blackwood's Edinburgh Magazine*, 8 (October 1820), 86–8.
[22] *John Bull's Letter to Lord Byron*, ed. Alan Lang Strout (Norman: University of Oklahoma Press, 1947), 103.

every unpaid contributor was an ass'.[23] In 1826 the *New Monthly* derided Sir Egerton Brydges for persisting in the belief that literature should be an occupation of the amateur: 'Authors are paid for the talent and time which they choose to employ in producing books, instead of employing those in painting, or agriculture, or any thing else, which would otherwise produce them money.'[24] By then, the matter seems to have been settled, but in the preceding decade things were not so clear. The duel in which Scott received his death-wound was the outcome of a particular moment in the growth of the print industry. Lockhart and Scott, as principals of two of the leading British magazines, were competing for their share of a rapidly expanding market, and yet both men remained wedded to a notion of themselves as literary men and literature as a kind of writing produced disinterestedly by gentlemen rather than writing produced for money. They had, despite all their experience to the contrary, still not wholly rid themselves of the belief that, like the *Gentleman's Magazine* in the eighteenth century, their own magazines might, and in some sense should, still be compiled from the contributions supplied by their gentlemen readers rather than by the professional men of letters, Scott and Lockhart among them, who had taken their place.

Christopher North's boasts of his income are funny because they so flamboyantly refuse the rather absurd delicacy that in literary circles tended to invest references to money matters. This is Jeffrey in October 1818 writing to John Wilson, enclosing payment for a contribution to the *Edinburgh Review*:

MY DEAR SIR,—I take the liberty of enclosing a draft for a very inconsiderable sum, which is the remuneration our publisher enables me to make for your valuable contribution to the last number of the *Edinburgh Review*; and though nobody can know better than I do, that nothing was less in your contemplation in writing that article, it is a consequence to which you must resign yourself, as all other regular contributors have done before you.

And now having acquitted myself of the awkward part of my office with my usual awkwardness, I should proceed to talk to you of further contributions...[25]

This is smooth enough, but, as Jeffrey acknowledges, what is being smoothed over is an awkwardness. De Quincey insists that in 1812 he was a gentleman, a claim he makes 'as a scholar and a man of learned education' but also because, 'from my having no visible calling or business, it is rightly judged that I must be living on my private fortune'.[26] But could he continue to make this claim in 1821, that is, at the time of writing? He was, after all, recalling his residence in Grasmere in a paid article contributed to the *London Magazine*. J. G. Lockhart,

---

[23] *Westminster Review*, 2 (July 1824), 202.
[24] *New Monthly Magazine*, 6 (January 1826), 60.
[25] Quoted in Mary Wilson Gordon, *'Christopher North': A Memoir of John Wilson*, 1, 293.
[26] 'Confessions of an English Opium-Eater,' Part II, *London Magazine*, 4 (October 1821), 353–79, 362–3; Lindop, 2, 52–3.

writing in *Blackwood's Magazine*, coined the term 'the Cockney School of Poetry', inaugurating a new kind of literary criticism that understood poems as the expression of the class status of their authors. The Cockney poets, in Marjorie Levinson's phrase, occupied the 'neither/nor' position that defined a social class that had no attributes other than its difference.[27] But one reason that Lockhart, despite his Oxford education, could describe that position with such feline accuracy is that periodical writers such as himself occupied an indeterminate position in the literary world uncomfortably analogous to the position that he attributed to poets such as Keats and Leigh Hunt.

Lockhart began his furious, disgraceful, and funny series in the inaugural number of *Blackwood's*. His attack on the Cockneys was a crucial element in the new magazine's forging of its own identity. Christopher North, whose habit was to meet with his coadjutors in an inner room of Ambrose's Tavern in Edinburgh's Gideon Street, was from the first defined by his contrast with Leigh Hunt taking tea with his young acolytes in his Hampstead living room with its pianoforte, its books, and its plaster bust of Homer. The raucous male fellowship of the Edinburgh tavern exposes the Hampstead scene as precariously genteel, peopled by those whose social and cultural pretensions are laughably insecure. Lockhart invented the Cockney school of poetry as the opening gambit in a bold campaign designed to represent the metropolis of London as itself provincial, absurdly unqualified to sustain its boast of cultural centrality. The charge, as Lockhart must have foreseen, immediately rebounded against the young Scots who levelled it, Scots, even Edinburgh Scots, being traditionally more vulnerable to charges of provincialism than Londoners.

Hazlitt together with Hunt was the chief target of the Cockney School attacks, which makes it unsurprising that he should dispute the *Blackwood's* notion of what a Cockney might be. The magazine believed that a Cockney was someone 'who has happened at any time to live in London, and who is not a Tory', whereas Hazlitt understands a Cockney to be 'a person who has never lived out of London, and who has got all his ideas from it'. 'Cockneyism', for Hazlitt 'is a ground of native shallowness mounted with pertness and conceit', a description that outdoes Lockhart in the fierceness of its contempt. By his own definition, of course, Hazlitt could not be counted a Cockney, and yet he can hardly have been unaware that 'pertness and conceit' are qualities that the *Blackwood's* writers believed peculiarly characteristic of Hazlitt's prose. The Cockney, according to Hazlitt, 'takes the wall of a Lord, and fancies himself as good as he'. He regards even the most distinguished of his fellows with contemptuous familiarity. But familiarity of exactly that kind was what *Blackwood's* detected in his own essays, in *The Spirit of the Age*, for example, when he notes Lord Eldon's 'fine oiliness',

---

[27] Marjorie Levinson, *Keats's Life of Allegory: The Origins of a Style* (Oxford: Oxford University Press, 1989), 5.

and recalls 'the cordial squeeze' of his hand.[28] The Cockney lives, according to Hazlitt, in 'a go-cart of local prejudices', has an opinion on every subject, and 'loves a tea-garden in summer, as he loves the play or the Cider-Cellar in winter', two of which tastes Hazlitt shared (the Cider-Cellar was his favourite tavern). The essay registers at once Hazlitt's contempt for the Cockney, and his affinity with him, which is why it does not amount to a complete volte-face when the essay ends by embracing the very Cockneyism that for most of its length it has held up to disdain. There is something admirable in the Cockney's refusal to be impressed: '*Your true Cockney is your only true leveller.*' The Cockney assumption that he shares the greatness of the city in which he lives requires an effort of the imagination of the kind that only 'a Scotchman', 'that pragmatical sort of personage', could disapprove. Even the Cockney's membership of 'a strange sort of society' in which 'a man does not know his next-door neighbour' has its advantages: it makes of the Cockney 'a public creature', someone who 'lives in the eye of the world, and the world in his'.

Hazlitt's essay first appeared in the *New Monthly Magazine*,[29] which, as Jon Klancher and Mark Parker have shown, was especially interested in presenting the streets of London as a system of signs and in instructing its readers how they should be read. For Klancher it was a practice that promised to enfranchise the magazine's middle-class readers from the social system in which they were so uncomfortably placed. The middle classes were aware of a need to maintain their difference from the ranks below, and aware, too, of the scorn with which their social manners were viewed by the ranks above. They might achieve a new social confidence if they could be trained to become the interpreters of the sign systems within which, when they had been merely unconscious participants, they had been trapped.[30] Klancher's suggestion has the virtue of explaining why it was that the *New Monthly* chose to include so many articles, many of them written by the brothers Horace and James Smith,[31] that might seem on the face of it likely to alienate their readers. The magazine, for example, clearly set out to appeal to literary women,[32] but felt free to offer for their enjoyment a paper such as Horace Smith's 'Miss Hebe Hoggins's account of a literary society in Houndsditch'.[33]

---

[28] *New Monthly Magazine*, 11 (July 1824), 17–21; Howe, 11, 141–7. In its review of *The Spirit of the Age*, *Blackwood's* singled out the essay on Eldon for its 'familiarity' and 'ape-like impudence'. See *Blackwood's Edinburgh Magazine*, 17 (March 1825), 361–5, 362.

[29] 'On Londoners and Country People', *New Monthly Magazine*, 8 (August 1823), 171–9; Howe, 12, 66–71.

[30] Jon P. Klancher, *The Making of English Reading Audiences, 1790–1832* (Madison: University of Wisconsin Press, 1987), 62–8, and Mark Parker, *Literary Magazines and British Romanticism*, 135–56.

[31] For a good discussion of Horace Smith's contributions to the *New Monthly*, see Mark Parker, *Literary Magazines and British Romanticism*, 142–6.

[32] As pointed out by Nanora Sweet, 'The *New Monthly Magazine* and the Liberalism of the 1820s', in *Romantic Periodicals and Print Culture*, ed. Kim Wheatley (London and Portland, Oregon: Frank Cass, 2002), 147–62.

[33] *New Monthly Magazine*, 7 (February 1823), 160–3.

In his long-running series, 'Grimm's Ghost', James Smith is always ready to mock the vulgarities of London cits who are represented as the direct descendants of Mr Smith and the Branghtons in Fanny Burney's *Evelina*. He seems wholly unconscious of the possibility of responses like those of 'a linen-draper in the City' who owned to Hazlitt that he had never much cared for these scenes in the novel: 'I fancy myself a sort of second Mr Smith, and am not quite easy at it!'[34]

The magazine's readers were flattered, perhaps, to be invited to assume a posture of superiority to such characters, but it may also be that it is flattering to come upon a representation of oneself in print no matter how mocking. One contributor, Eyre Evans Crowe, observed, 'It is the want of link with the soil, of attachment to a particular spot, which gives the life of a metropolitan that ideal insignificance so happily embodied in the term Cockney.'[35] The *London* and the *New Monthly* shared a concern to redeem metropolitan life from its 'ideal insignificance' by showing how the city might offer an experience as thick and as deep as the English shires, for all that the man who lives in the city 'does not know his next-door neighbour'. Wordsworth, Hazlitt allowed, believed that city life inevitably stunted the humanity of those who lived it, but in his Elia essays Lamb had shown how London's public and semi-public spaces, the Inns of Court, the South Sea House, Christ's Hospital, Drury Lane, are places that can stage emotions as intense and as intimate as any that may be experienced in country churchyards. A series such as Henry Roscoe's 'Literary Recollections of London' is designed to link metropolitan experience with the writers who have lived in the city. To walk through the city as Roscoe describes it is to feel oneself rooted in the nation's literature.[36] If this is the case, then it may be that even those who felt themselves implicated in Horace Smith's account of Miss Hebe Hoggins of Houndsditch could take a certain consolation from the sketch: to be elevated into a comic stereotype is, however galling, still to be redeemed from insignificance by being imprinted on the consciousness of the magazine's readership. The *New Monthly* had a series of 'London Lyrics', light verse on topics such as 'Bridge-street, Blackfriars',[37] which seem many of them similarly divided, torn between an impulse to reclaim everyday London scenes for poetry, and to expose their absurd unfitness for the purpose.

Washington Irving's accounts of English life in *The Sketch Book* were remarkably well received in Britain by reviewers and readers alike. In his 'Account of Himself', Irving (writing as Geoffrey Crayon) explains that he travelled to Europe in search of 'storied and poetical association', in search of places and people possessed of a historical depth that somehow makes them more

[34] 'On Londoners and Country People', *New Monthly Magazine*, 8 (August 1823), 176; Howe, 12, 72–3.
[35] *New Monthly Magazine*, 2 (November 1821), 449.
[36] *New Monthly Magazine*, 4 (January 1822), 29–34, and 5 (August 1822), 118–24.
[37] *New Monthly Magazine*, 11 (November 1824), 449–50.

substantial than the people and places of America.[38] Hazlitt thought, reasonably enough, that Irving was approved by the English because they found his representation of them flattering,[39] but it may also have been the case that many of Irving's English readers, and especially his deracinated metropolitan readers, shared his plight. The lives of Cockneys had in common with the lives of Americans an ideal insignificance for which Irving provides an antidote. In reading him Cockneys could discover the unexpected depth of their own everyday experience. Little Britain must have seemed a rather unprepossessing district of London until Geoffrey Crayon's account of it, which invests it with historical depth. Even the glass panes of Irving's lodging house windows are scrawled with 'scraps of very indifferent gentleman-like poetry' celebrating 'the charms of many a beauty of Little Britain, who has long, long since bloomed, faded, and passed away' (213). In Little Britain the national life is maintained in the form of 'pancakes on Shrove Tuesday, hot-cross-buns on Good Friday, and roast goose at Michaelmas'. In Little Britain, Valentine cards are sent, bonfires are lit on 5 November, girls are kissed under the mistletoe, roast beef and plum pudding are 'held in superstitious veneration', and in consequence of all this Little Britain transcends its status as one of the cheaper districts of London to become 'the strong-hold of true John Bullism', not only in its name but in its nature a just epitome of the whole nation (213–14).

In reading *The Sketch Book* Cockney readers might find that 'attachment to a particular spot' through which human lives achieve their substance. In the quietly mock-heroic voice that inflects essays such as 'Little Britain' they could find authority, too, for their recognition that in the modern urban world no such attachments are really possible, because every spot changes too ceaselessly and too rapidly for it ever to achieve particularity. One reason that the magazines of the period felt themselves so modern was that they were so conscious of themselves as ephemeral:

Each of our monthly appearances may be considered as a death-blow to the one which preceded it. We lay no claims to posterity; or, if we look to a longer immortality than 'one calendar month', it is through the friendly instrumentality of a good bookbinder.

In 'a stout Russia back' and 'two thick pieces of pasteboard' the magazine may graduate from the drawing room to the library, but with the result only that it will there be 'as thoroughly neglected as authors of much more weight and merit'.[40] The periodical writer is distinguished from writers of a more elevated kind principally, it seems, in being less deceived. The library of Westminster

---

[38] Washington Irving, *The Sketch-Book of Geoffrey Crayon, Gent.*, ed. Susan Manning (Oxford: Oxford University Press, 1996), 12. Subsequent page references are included in the text.

[39] Howe, 11, 183. The sketch of Washington Irving in *The Spirit of the Age* had not previously appeared in the *New Monthly Magazine*.

[40] 'The Literary World', *New Monthly Magazine*, 10 (April 1824), 364–8, 368. The contributor was Sir Thomas Charles Morgan.

Abbey prompts Irving to similar reflections. Is it, he asks, because the language is so like its capital city, so 'subject to changes and intermixtures', that English literature is 'so mutable, and the reputation built upon it so fleeting' (116), or is it that, again like the city, the literature is expanding so rapidly that no one has time to get to know more than a fraction of it?: 'Many a man of passable information, at the present day, reads scarcely anything but reviews', and very soon it will be impossible to read even reviews of all the good books that are published: their titles alone will engage all the student's leisure hours and 'a man of erudition will be little better than a mere talking catalogue' (118).

The 'storied and poetical association' that Irving found in Britain is most fully displayed to him in a country house visit, during his stay at Bracebridge Hall. It was the product of the nation's social as well as its historical depth, a social depth that allowed the simplest action, a knock at the door, for example, to assume in Britain an extra resonance, to become a sign. In 'A Sabbath in London' a man returning to his home town after seven years abroad is put out to discover that 'a single knock at the door' has become 'an official announcement that the hand which struck it was plebeian'.[41] But it is the mutability as much as the ubiquity of such signs that fascinates the *New Monthly*. The magazine offers a regular commentary on the comical race that the upper orders run against their bour-geois imitators. James Smith notes how the 'people of ton' have been exiled from all their old haunts. Bath and Brighton have already become intolerably déclassé:

To what Libyan desert, what rocky island in the watery waste, is high life now to retreat? Saint Helena may do, the distance is too great to allow of men of business frequenting it; they cannot well run down from Saturday to Tuesday.[42]

The consequences of continuing to visit the same resorts are traced in 'Every-day People' which records the consternation of the correspondent's 'Aunt Edwards', who lives in Fitzroy-square, when she finds that the family whose company she has enjoyed so much at Ramsgate lives in Gower-street.[43] James Smith recalls the piece when he fabricates the annual report of a 'Society for the Propagation of Gentility'. The publication of that particular paper, he claims, prompted more than one resident of Gower-street to terminate their leases.[44] It is one of a number of pieces in the *New Monthly* that seem to hold up to ridicule the magazine's own enterprise. The magazine appealed to those with cultural aspir-ations by incorporating papers on topics such as classical artefacts, European literature, the British galleries, and the old literature of England, and yet inter-spersed among them were articles that seem to mock all such pretensions, papers

    [41] 'A Sabbath in London, by a seven years absentee', *New Monthly Magazine*, 5 (December 1822), 502–7, 502. The contributor was Thomas Grattan.
    [42] 'Grimm's Ghost no 11', *New Monthly Magazine*, 7 (January 1823), 38–40.
    [43] *New Monthly Magazine*, 10 (June 1824), 527–31.
    [44] *New Monthly Magazine*, 11 (December 1824), 562–5.

such as James Smith's that humorously maps the spread of gentility east from the 'few streets and square' to which it was once confined. The Society's report notes with approval that 'gentility is greatly on the increase in Moorfields', that 'a book-club has sprung up in Trinity-square, and the dinner-hour in the Minories is half past six for seven'. Such papers are less simple than they seem. When, for example, Smith reports that a man was ejected from a meeting of the Society because he 'drank hock out of a white glass, and claret out of a green one', his mockery is oddly undiscriminating, embracing the absurdly arbitrary nature of all such social rules, the triviality of the class that established them, and the equal or greater triviality of the class that aspires to adopt them, but, because the rules have been learned rather too late in life, is always likely to get them wrong. It is precisely in its dividedness, I suspect, that the *New Monthly* contrives so accurately to reflect the cast of mind typical of its readership.

It may be that this readership enjoyed Irving's *Sketch Book* not so much because it found Irving's representation of Britain flattering, but because it recognized in Irving similarly divided impulses. In 'English Writers on America' Irving notes the futility of responding in kind to defamatory accounts of the United States by British travellers: 'Our retorts are never republished in England; they fall short, therefore, of their aim' (56). Irving's solution, though it may well have been unconsciously arrived at, was to develop a prose so finely poised that it is often impossible to determine whether the tone is satirical or celebratory. His essays, it may be, are like the 'inscriptions' scrawled on the walls of the 'squalid chambers' of the house where Shakespeare was born, a 'striking instance of the spontaneous and universal homage' that greatness, the greatness of the poet and of his nation both, inspires (225). And yet these are essays written by a man who prides himself on being the product of 'a society where there are no artificial distinctions', and of a nation that, because it is free from the burden of the past, having 'sprung into national existence in an enlightened and philosophic age', is uninfected by 'the inveterate diseases of old countries, contracted in rude and ignorant ages' (52 and 56). It may be that the essays have more in common than they ever acknowledge with the very different graffiti that Irving notes when he inspects the royal tombs in Westminster Abbey which have been 'all more or less outraged and dishonoured', and have some of them been 'covered with ribaldry and insult' (156).

In the *London* John Scott denounced *Blackwood's* for accommodating contradictions within its pages, a brutal attack on Wordsworth and Coleridge, and a fawning tribute to them in successive numbers, both written, Scott believed, by the same hand. The magazine, as John Scott and the editors of *Blackwood's* agreed, was distinguished from other periodicals such as reviews precisely because of its refusal of 'unity of mind', but Scott was surely right to believe that Wilson's alternating accounts of Wordsworth and Coleridge cannot be explained simply by the need to give the magazine the variety it needs. They display in extreme form conflicting responses that are common to most magazines of the period.

The claim to stand independent of and superior to the literary market that the magazines attributed to Wordsworth and Coleridge inspired at once respect and derision. When he accepted in the *New Monthly* that periodical writers could look forward only to 'an immortality of a month, after which we are tragically left to an eternity—of oblivion', Horace Smith seemed to acknowledge the superior status of those like the Lake Poets who were prepared to sacrifice present popularity for a permanent reputation. But the concession is no sooner given than withdrawn: 'if we must perish and be forgotten, it is better to die of a monthly essay than an annual epic'.[45] Cockneys, Americans, and magazine writers have in common a tendency at once to acknowledge and resentfully to deny their own inferior status. It is a volatile combination of feelings. It so infected the relationship between Britain and the United States according to Washington Irving as to threaten that the war of 1812 might initiate a series of such conflicts (53–4). John Scott's death provides the most striking evidence that it fatally infected the relationship between writers, too.

CONSUMING LITERATURE

One might have expected the relations between John Murray and his aristocratic poet, the sixth Baron Byron, to be free from such complications. Murray, especially in the early stages of the relationship, was apt to play up the class differences between the two men. He excused himself for including, without Byron's warrant, an extra poem in the seventh edition of *Childe Harold* on the grounds that '[his] <u>sordid</u> propensities got the better of [him]', and he gloatingly recorded the success of the stratagem: 'I sold my lord at once nearly a <u>Thousand</u> Copies of this New Edition.' He had decided to publish the third canto of *Childe Harold* and *The Prisoner of Chillon* separately in 'two brochures at 5/6 each—to ensure my Pelf—& thy popularity'.[46] Byron was just as flamboyant, although his protestations lacked the ironic edge of Murray's, in insisting on his role as the gentleman poet: 'whenever I avail myself of any profit arising from my pen—depend upon it it is not for my own convenience'.[47] But the relationship soon became more nuanced. Murray was capable of claiming for himself the disinterest appropriate to the man of letters. When he wrote to Byron explaining that he did not intend to publish *The Prophecy of Dante* and the translation of Pulci immediately, he added, 'I do beseech you not to conceive it possible the mere L. S. D. have any thing to do with the business.' When Byron implied that

---

[45] 'The Library,' *New Monthly Magazine*, 7 (May 1823), 430–4. Smith echoes *Don Juan*, 10, 97, in which Byron observes that the public has come to expect 'An epic from Bob Southey every spring.'

[46] *The Letters of John Murray to Lord Byron*, 79 and 181.

[47] *Byron's Letters and Journals*, ed. Leslie A. Marchand, 4 (London: John Murray, 1975), 14–15.

Murray had tried to bilk him by paying in pounds a sum that had been agreed in guineas, Murray was clearly wounded: 'I sometimes feel a deep regret that in our pretty long intercourse I appear to have failed to shew, that a man in my situation may possess the feelings & principles of a Gentleman.'[48] But by this time Byron was finding it difficult to maintain the pretence that his own gentlemanly status required that he refuse to make a profit from his pen. It was an affectation that had begun to irritate Murray. When Kinnaird told him that 'Byron's friends' expected 2000 rather than the 1500 guineas that Murray had offered for the third canto of *Childe Harold*, Murray wrote to Byron that the poem was 'so much beyond any thing in modern days that I may be out in my Calculation—it requires an etherial mind like the Authors to cope with it'. His choice of word, 'etherial', seems scarcely innocent. But Kinnaird, who, unlike Hobhouse, kept Murray in mind of the social distance that separated them (in a letter to Byron of January 1815, he refers to him as 'the merchant Murray'), always rubbed him up the wrong way: 'Hobhouse . . . is very gentlemanly but I don't know you when I negotiate with Mr Kinnaird.'[49] Here it is the pronoun, 'you', that seems pointed, intimating that Murray was quite aware that Byron allowed his friends to act for him as a way of preserving his own affected indifference to L. S. D.

Even Byron, the most famous poet of the day and a peer of the realm, was reduced to shuffling inconsistencies by the relationship between poetry and payment. For those like Hazlitt who were 'paid by the sheet' matters were still more vexed. In its review of Hazlitt's *Spirit of the Age*, *Blackwood's* wrote of Hazlitt, 'He may be said to live in the very lowest society, for he has for years absolutely *been upon the Press*',[50] which leaves one wondering where the writers for *Blackwood's* imagined that they had been. Writers for periodicals, precisely because they wrote for money, were often particularly sensitive to the charge that they wrote only in order 'to purchase bread'. De Quincey was induced to write his *Confessions* for publication in the *London Magazine* only by reason of 'dire necessity'. When he was a seventeen-year-old runaway in Wales, he had been reduced to living on 'blackberries, hips, haws', except when he earned money by writing 'letters of business for cottagers' or 'love-letters to their sweethearts for young women who had lived as servants in Shrewsbury',[51] and in his gloomier moments it must have seemed to him that very little had changed. Even a professional writer (perhaps I should say, especially a professional writer) who depended for his survival on the money that he earned by writing for the periodicals could not escape from the notion that aesthetic value was properly defined by its independence of economic value. For Hazlitt, for example, the

---

[48] *The Letters of John Murray to Lord Byron*, 177; *Byron's Letters and Journals*, ed. Leslie A. Marchand, 5 (London: John Murray, 1976), 254; *The Letters of John Murray to Lord Byron*, 241.
[49] *The Letters of John Murray to Lord Byron*, 177, 124, and 388.
[50] *Blackwood's Edinburgh Magazine*, 17 (March 1825), 362.
[51] 'Confessions of an English Opium-Eater,' *London Magazine*, 4 (September 1821), 293–312, 301; Lindop, 2, 20.

song of a thrush is more beautiful than a Mozart aria because 'one is paid for, and the other is not'. The thrush sings 'to relieve the overflowings of its own breast' whereas 'Madame Fodor sings the air of *Vedrai Carino* in *Don Giovanni* so divinely because she is hired to sing it; she sings it to please the audience, not herself, and does not always like to be *encored* in it.'[52]

Hazlitt is intent for the most part on securing the difference between works of art and commodities. Fonthill Abbey, for example, is 'a cathedral turned into a toy-shop', and whereas the tendency of a cathedral is to 'aggrandise the species', the tendency of such a place as Fonthill is to 'aggrandise none but the individual'. The whole place is a celebration of ownership: its contents 'come under the head of property, or showy furniture, which are neither distinguished by sublimity nor beauty, and are estimated only by the labour required to produce what is trifling or worthless, and are consequently nothing more than obtrusive proofs of the wealth of the immediate possessor'. To admire such objects is really just to admire the wealth that can command the labour required to produce them. The essay derides Fonthill—Hazlitt had far rather visit the Escorial 'where the piles of Titians lie'—and yet it is William Beckford, not Charles II of Spain, as the essay recognizes, who better represents the beau idéal of the reader of Hazlitt's article. Beckford is the modern consumer apotheosized, the shopper as Romantic genius. The Fonthill Abbey catalogue, according to Hazlitt, is itself a work of art, even if a meretricious one: it 'reads so like Della Cruscan poetry'.[53] Hazlitt's editors, both John Scott at the *London* and Thomas Campbell at the *New Monthly*, shared his sensitivity to the difference between culture and commodity. In the *London*, for example, the busy contemporary matter, the chronicles of market prices, the lists of new publications, the commercial reports, and the summaries of intelligence tend in each issue to be counteracted by a series of articles on 'Traditional Literature', a plate with commentary of a classical sculpture, or, it may be, an article on the 'Ambrosian Codex of Homer'.[54] But it was hard in the pages of a magazine to preserve a secure distinction between literature and commerce.

The magazine was an unstable genre. It fell, as it were, between the review and the newspaper, not just by virtue of its appearance once a month rather than weekly or quarterly, but by virtue of its status. Magazines occupied a place in-between the permanence of literature and newspapers that scarcely survive the day or week of their issue. The magazine occupies a place neatly defined by Lamb in his 'Detached Thoughts on Books and Reading' when he advises on how a set of magazines should be bound: 'I would not dress a set of Magazines, for instance, in full suit. The dishabille, or half-binding (with Russia backs ever),

---

[52] 'Pope, Lord Byron, and Mr Bowles,' *London Magazine*, 3 (June 1821), 593–607, 602; Howe, 19, 76–7.
[53] 'Fonthill Abbey, *London Magazine*, 6 (November 1822), 405–11; Howe, 18, 173–80.
[54] I take all my examples from a single issue: *London Magazine*, 3 (March 1821).

is *our* costume.'[55] A magazine article differed from a newspaper article in its semi-permanence. Even as it was being written its author may have imagined for it a more permanent existence, as when De Quincey, in the second episode of his *Confessions* in the *London* correctly predicts 'the next edition of my Opium Confessions revised and enlarged'. De Quincey defends himself against the charge that he is 'too confidential and communicative of [his] own private history' by claiming that as he writes he thinks of himself as being read 'fifteen or twenty years ahead of this time' by 'those who will be interested about me hereafter'.[56] He knows that Wordsworth's poem on his own mind is written but will not be given to the public until a decent lapse of years has deprived the poem of any indecorous personality, and he makes a similar, if more modest, claim for himself. But the claim comes oddly in the October 1821 edition of the *London Magazine*, in an article scarcely written before it was set into print.

Lamb in his essays is endlessly fascinated by shops, by the 'endless selection of knacks and gewgaws, and ostentatiously displayed wares of tradesmen, which make a week-day saunter through the less busy parts of the metropolis so delightful': his particular favourites are the book-stalls and print-shops. When an essay specifies that a folio Beaumont and Fletcher cost sixteen shillings and a print after 'Lionardo' rather less, readers are unlikely to forget that magazines, like prints and old folios, are items for sale, and that Lamb is being paid for his contribution.[57] An essay such as 'Old China' is a lyrical celebration of commodities. One implication of all this is, no doubt, that Lamb recognizes the likeness between an Elian essay and a china tea-cup, not just because they are both beautiful, but because both are commercial articles, sold by their makers and available to be bought by the consumer.[58] It may have been 'thirty-five years ago' that Lamb depended for the 'supplementary livelihood' that supplied him 'in every want beyond mere bread and cheese' on the sixpences that Daniel Stuart, editor of the *Morning Post*, paid for a witty topical paragraph not to exceed seven lines, but the anecdote inevitably invites the reader to ask what the difference may be, apart from the length and the level of remuneration, between those newspaper paragraphs and the magazine essay in which they are recalled.[59] In just as many essays Lamb insists on distinguishing economic value from value of other kinds. He protests, for instance, against the practice of charging for entrance to Westminster Abbey, and in essay after essay he distinguishes the ledgers that occupied him at India House from the literature that he read and wrote in the evenings and on holidays. The distinction is never more emphatic than when he

---

[55] 'Detached Thoughts on Books and Reading', *London Magazine*, 6 (July 1822), 33–6, 33.
[56] *London Magazine*, 4 (October 1821), 364 and 369; Lindop, 2, 54 and 62.
[57] 'The Superannuated Man,' *London Magazine*, n.s. 2 (May 1825), 67–73.
[58] 'Old China', *London Magazine*, 7 (March 1823), 269–72.
[59] 'On the total Defect of the faculty of Imagination, observed in the works of modern British Artists', *Englishman's Magazine*, 2 (October 1831), 137–42, 138. The essay was published in *The Last Essays of Elia* under the title 'Newspapers Thirty-Five Years Ago'.

claims that the ledgers have a better title to be called his 'works' than his contributions to literature.[60] Lamb clings tenaciously to a sense of his own in-betweenness. His proper place is 'The South-Sea House', which is a trading house, at the heart of the city, close to the Bank of England in Threadneedle Street, and yet also a place that the busy man hurrying about his business will overlook, a dust-covered place, a great commercial house transformed into a 'memorial', a museum.[61] It is that odd status that makes it the proper object for Elia to meditate upon, for Elia is at once a successful magazine writer, the best-paid such writer in the country, and a figure whose charm is dependent on his distance from the city streets that he walks. Implicit in all those essays in which Lamb focuses on enclosed places such as the South Sea House and the Inner Temple, places secluded from the busy streets of the city that they so closely neighbour, is the contrast that Hazlitt makes explicit in his 'On Reading Old Books': 'the dust, and smoke, and noise of modern literature have nothing in common with the pure, silent air of immortality'.[62]

Thomas Love Peacock seems to have found the 'dust and smoke and noise' especially disagreeable, retreating from them to Greek literature so enthusiastically that Thomas Taylor knew him as 'Greeky Peaky'. In 1820 Shelley described him as a 'strain too learned for a shallow age'.[63] In 1839 James Spedding too insisted on the exclusiveness of Peacock's appeal. His books are 'above the taste of ordinary readers', and 'it may be doubted whether they will ever attain a place in our circulating literature'.[64] A taste for Peacock has remained ever since a mark of a refined reader. As Leavis put it in *The Great Tradition*, his novels are 'indefinitely re-readable—for minds with mature interests'.[65] It is the kind of reputation that Peacock seems to have wished for himself. His own reading was uncompromisingly serious and classical, as might be expected of a self-educated man.

For six weeks in the scorching summer of 1818 Peacock kept a journal briefly recording his boating expeditions and his reading: *Don Quixote*, some Pindar odes, Nonnus's *Dionysiaca*, Stanley's *History of Philosophy*, Statius's *Thebaid*, Bacon's *Novum Organum*, the *Dictionnaire Philosophique*, Buffon's *Histoire Naturelle*, Smith's *Wealth of Nations*, and Bacon's *Essays*.[66] This seems to place him at

[60] 'Letter of Elia to Robert Southey, Esquire', *London Magazine*, 8 (October 1823), 405–7 (the essay was published in modified form in *The Last Essays of Elia* as 'The Tombs in the Abbey'), and 'A Character of the Late Elia,' *London Magazine*, 7 (January 1823), 21.
[61] 'Recollections of the South Sea House', *London Magazine*, 2 (August 1820), 142–6.
[62] 'On Reading Old Books', *London Magazine*, 3 (February 1821), 129; Howe, 12, 221.
[63] 'Letter to Maria Gisborne', *Percy Bysshe Shelley: The Major Works*, ed. Zachary Leader and Michael O'Neill (Oxford: Oxford University Press, 2003), l. 242.
[64] *Headlong Hall. Nightmare Abbey. Maid Marian. Crotchet Castle* (Standard Novels, No. 57), *Edinburgh Review*, 68 (January 1839), 432–59, 435.
[65] F. R Leavis, *The Great Tradition* (London: Chatto and Windus, 1948), 18 (note).
[66] 'Marlow Journal, 7 July–26 [September] 1818', *The Letters of Thomas Love Peacock*, ed. Nicholas A Joukovsky, 2 vols. (Oxford: Clarendon Press, 2001), 1, 134–44.

a far remove from the Honourable Mr Listless of *Nightmare Abbey*, who has a parcel of books posted to him express which

> proved to contain a new novel, and a new poem, both of which had long been anxiously expected by the whole host of fashionable readers; and the last number of a popular Review, of which the editor and his coadjutors were in high favour at court, and enjoyed ample pensions for their services to church and state.[67]

The package contains, we are expected to deduce, a novel by Scott, a poem by Byron, and the latest number of the *Quarterly Review*. This is the taste that Peacock inveighs against in his 'Essay on Fashionable Literature', the books that 'furnish forth the morning table of the literary dilettante', consisting of the 'newspaper of the day, the favourite magazine of the month, the review of the quarter, the tour, the novel, and the poem which are most recent in date and most fashionable in name' (8, 265). The Minerva Press is offered as proof that there is a ready sale for books 'completely expurgated of all the higher qualities of mind', but there are readers for whom even a Minerva Press novel is too weighty, 'that not innumerous class of persons who make the reading of reviews and magazines the sole business of their lives' (8, 265–6). And yet even in the summer of 1818 Peacock did not confine himself to Nonnus, Statius and the like. He read the *Examiner*, and Cobbett's *Political Register*, the second series of Scott's *Tales of My Landlord*, and in the latest copy of the *Edinburgh Review* he read several articles, including the notice of the fourth canto of *Childe Harold*. In *Crotchet Castle* the Revd Dr Folliott clearly speaks for Peacock when he classes Scott's novels with Covent Garden pantomimes: 'The one is the literature of pantomime, the other is the pantomime of literature' (4, 116–17). But he speaks for Peacock too when he insists that pantomimes are his delight. In January 1818, Peacock wrote to Shelley, 'There is a very splendid pantomime at Covent Garden founded on the adventures of Baron Munchausen: I have seen it twice.'[68]

Modern magazines and reviews are particular targets of Peacock's contempt, because, although they number amongst their contributors people of 'great individual talent', they are superficial, offering, in comparison with their predecessors, 'more of that kind of knowledge which is calculated for shew in general society, to produce a brilliant impression on the passing hour of literature, and less, far less, of that solid and laborious research which builds up in the silence of the closet, and in the disregard of perishable fashions of mind, the strong and permanent structure of history and philosophy' (8, 267). The novels of talk satirize precisely the 'perishable fashions of mind' catered for by modern magazines. The contempt Peacock so often expresses for periodicals is most often

---

[67] *Halliford Edition of the Works of Thomas Love Peacock*, ed. H. F. B. Brett Smith and C. E. Jones, 10 vols. (London: Constable, 1944), 3, *Nightmare Abbey*, 38. All subsequent references to Peacock's novels and essays are to this edition. Volume and page references are included in the text.
[68] *The Letters of Thomas Love Peacock*, 1, 164.

prompted by the notion that because periodical writers write for money their opinions are not disinterested. As Mr Escot puts it in *Headlong Hall*:

I look upon periodical criticism in general to be a species of shop, where panegyric and defamation are sold, wholesale, retail, and for exportation. I am not inclined to be a purchaser of these commodities, or to encourage a trade which I consider pregnant with mischief.   (1, 43)

In *Crotchet Castle* the Revd Dr Folliott describes the *Edinburgh* reviewers as 'a sort of sugar-plum manufacturers to the Whig aristocracy' (4, 51). The article that they produce is a commodity and without real nutritional value: on both counts it fails to qualify as literature. In this, articles in the *Edinburgh* resemble Miss Philomela Poppyseed's novels, which are read by 'the young ladies of the age, whom she taught to consider themselves as a sort of commodity, to be put up at public auction, and knocked down to the highest bidder' (1, *Headlong Hall*, 62). It is a moral that she enforces in her plots, in which, presumably, happiness is secured by marriage to a rich young man, but also in her practice, because to write as she does for money is a variety of intellectual prostitution. She is one of those who have transformed their minds into 'high-pressure steam engines for spinning prose by the furlong, to be trumpeted in paid-for paragraphs in the quack's corner of newspapers: modern literature having attained the honourable distinction of sharing with blacking and macassar oil, the space which used to be monopolized by razor strops and the lottery' (4, *Crotchet Castle*, 166).

Wordsworth and Southey, by accepting government pensions have transformed themselves into Mr Paperstamp and Mr Feathernest, and disgraced their profession so grossly that the stain has spread from themselves to their poems. It even contaminates the landscape that they celebrate, 'the romantic scenery of the northern lakes, where every wonder of nature is made an article of trade, where the cataracts are locked up, and the echoes are sold: so that even the rustic character of that ill-fated region is condemned to participate in the moral stigma which must dwell indelibly on its poetical name' (2, *Melincourt*, 277–8). In *Headlong Hall* Mr MacLaurel may argue very differently—'ye mun alloo, sir, that poetry is a sort of ware or commodity, that is brought into the public market wi' a' other descreptions of merchandise, an' that a mon is pairfectly justified in getting the best price he can for his article' (1, 47)—but this only serves to expose MacLaurel for what he is, a purveyor of political economy for the *Edinburgh Review*. It is a good deal odder that Peacock should deploy similar arguments when he seems to be speaking in his own person. In 'The Four Ages of Poetry' he insists that poetry, like all other trades, 'takes its rise in the demand for the commodity, and flourishes in proportion to the extent of the market'. It is a passage in which he contrives to sound very like Mr MacLaurel (8, 4). This is an essay that has been suspected of irony, but Peacock often fields similar arguments. In 'L'Épicier', for example, he points out the futility of Wordsworth's sonnet, 'Milton! thou shouldst be living at this hour':

Every variety of the human mind takes its station, or is ready to do so, at all times in the literary market; the public of the day stamp the currency of fashion on that which jumps with their humour. Milton would be forthcoming if he were wanted; but in our time Milton was not wanted, and Walter Scott was.

The public always gets the writers that it deserves, because the nature of the demand determines the character of the supply. It was pointless for Wordsworth to wish that another Milton might be forthcoming because at that hour 'there was no more market for him than for Cromwell'[69] (9, 294). The political economists that figure so largely in Peacock's fictions are at once objects of his derision, and exponents of an analytical technique that delights him by its bracing rigour.

The reduction of ideas to commodities and the pretence that they are ever anything other than commodities are positions equally likely to win Peacock's approval and to secure his contempt, which is why the symposium is the form that best suits him. Squire Headlong and Mr Crotchet buy in two kinds of provision, intellectual and material. Squire Headlong secures provisions of the first kind by distributing his invitations to the 'men of taste and philosophers' that he locates by 'beating up in several booksellers' shops, theatres, exhibition-rooms, and other resorts of literature and taste' (1, *Headlong Hall*, 7–8). At Headlong Hall the men of taste and philosophers arrive together with a multitude of packages of a quite different kind. These have come

by land and water, from London, and Liverpool, and Chester, and Manchester, and Birmingham, and various parts of the mountains: books, wine, cheese, globes, mathematical instruments, turkeys, telescopes, hams, tongues, microscopes, quadrants, sextants, fiddles, flutes, tea, sugar, electrical machines, figs, spices, air-pumps, soda-water, chemical apparatus, eggs, French-horns, drawing books, palettes, oils and colours, bottled ale and porter, scenery for a private theatre, pickles and fish-sauce, patent lamps and chandeliers, barrels of oysters, sofas, chairs, tables, carpets, beds, looking-glasses, pictures, fruits and confections, nuts, oranges, lemons, packages of salt salmon, and jars of Portugal grapes. (1, *Headlong Hall*, 13–14)

It is at dinner that the provisions of both kinds are best displayed, the one in conversation, and the other by being eaten and drunk, and the two activities maintain a running commentary on each other. When the Revd Dr Folliott and Mr Mac Quedy debate the rival claims of nature and nurture, the discussion is repeatedly interrupted by more pressingly material matters: 'I will thank you for a slice of lamb, with lemon and pepper' (4, *Crotchet Castle*, 51). It is, not by coincidence, the same effect that Byron several times reproduces in *Don Juan* and that William Maginn rehearses in an episode of the *Noctes Ambrosianae*. Ensign Odoherty berates Byron for making sport of 'the holiest ties—the most sacred

---

[69] On Peacock's fascination with political economy, see James Mulvihill, '"A Species of Shop": Peacock and the World of Goods', *Keats–Shelley Journal*, 49 (2000), 85–113.

feelings—the purest sentiments. In a word, with every thing—the bottle is with you—with every thing which raises a man above a mere sensual being.'[70] Peacock does not keep separate from one another the material and the intellectual, commodities and works of art, any more than Byron, or the magazines that he despised. It is one of the things that makes his novels of talk so representative of their time.

THE PROFESSION OF LETTERS

John Scott died because the profession of letters occupied an uncertain position: it neither guaranteed, like the church, the higher ranks of the armed services, and the higher branches of the law and medicine, the gentlemanly status of its followers, nor did it preclude that status. One illustration of this is that neither John Scott nor his second P. G. Patmore were quite familiar with the protocol of duels. It was because of this, surely, rather than innate bloodthirstiness, that Patmore failed to put an end to the duel when he had the opportunity. Scott died believing that he was the victim of Patmore's bungling. That was sad for him, but worse for Patmore, who carried the imputation with him for the rest of his life. Twenty-five years later Thackeray referred to him as 'that murderer'.[71]

Certainly, Patmore had blundered. A year later two British Dukes gave a lesson in how such matters should be conducted. The Duke of Buckingham challenged the Duke of Bedford when he refused to retract his charge that the Duke of Buckingham had sacrificed his political principles to his financial convenience, anxious to cling on to the emoluments that he and his family received from the Government. The two men met in Kensington Gardens, and the outcome was widely reported. *The Examiner* borrowed its account from *The Courier*:

Both parties fired together at the distance of twelve paces, on a word given, but without effect; when the Duke of Buckingham, observing that the Duke of Bedford fired into the air, advanced to his Grace, and, remarking that for that reason the thing could go no further, said, 'My Lord Duke, you are the last man I wish to quarrel with; but you must be aware that a public man's life is not worth preserving unless with honour.' Upon which the Duke of Bedford declared, 'Upon his honour, that he meant no personal offence to the Duke of Buckingham, nor to impute to him any bad or corrupt motive whatsoever.' The parties then shook hands, and the whole business was terminated most satisfactorily.[72]

[70] *Blackwood's Edinburgh Magazine*, 3 (July 1822), 103.
[71] Edmund Gosse reports, on Robert Browning's authority, that Thackeray refused to be introduced to Coventry Patmore in 1846, saying, 'I won't touch the hand of a son of that murderer.' Edmund Gosse, *Coventry Patmore* (London: Hodder and Stoughton, 1905), 2.
[72] *The Examiner*, no. 745, 5 May 1822, 282.

One Duke had accused the other of sacrificing principle for gain, which is precisely the charge that John Scott had brought against Lockhart. It galled him as he lay dying, his wife and children unprovided for, that his own affair could have been terminated just as satisfactorily. But he was a mercer's son from Aberdeen, and he had chosen as his second the son of a man who kept a jewellery shop in Leadenhall Street. They neither of them had that exact knowledge of the punctilio of duels that came so easily to two dukes. They were trying to conform to a social code without being quite sure of the code, and the results were fatal.

The social position of the periodical writer seems to have been particularly anxious, with the predictable result that magazines concerned themselves almost obsessively with questions concerning the appearance and reality of gentlemanliness. Jon Klancher and others have explored the role that magazines played in educating their upwardly mobile readers in the knowledge that would allow them to pass muster in the social circles to which they aspired, but one reason that the magazines were so well equipped to offer this kind of education is that they tended to be written by those who shared the social insecurities of their readers. As Hazlitt's points out in his sixth 'Table Talk' for the *London Magazine*, 'On the Look of a Gentleman', it was 'a very delicate subject'. Gentlemen, according to Hazlitt, should be sharply distinguished from professional men: 'the professor of any art or science' is master 'of a particular instrument', whereas the gentleman is 'master of his own person', and 'directs it to what use he pleases and intends'. Alcibiades, who threw away his flute when he found that playing it 'discomposed his features', showed a proper grasp of the manner in which following a particular profession deforms the mind just as grievously as 'laborious trades' deform the body.[73] Hazlitt's essay appeared in the *London* in January 1821, just a month before John Scott's death, and there is no better evidence of the vexed relationship between professional men of letters and the code of gentlemanly behaviour of which John Scott's death was one unfortunate result.

Even more pressingly than Byron, Walter Scott was obliged to confront the fraught relationship in the post-war decade between literature and money. It sometimes seems that he was impelled to invent the historical novel out of nostalgia for a time when the barriers separating different orders of men were more carefully maintained. Michael Lambourne in *Kenilworth*, for example, is an ambitious, upwardly mobile young thug, but he is an Elizabethan thug, and hence he is surprisingly willing to grant the difference between gentlemen to the manner born and the likes of himself:

I will say, and I care not who hears me, there is something about the real gentry that few come up to who are not born and bred to the mystery. I wot not where the trick lies; but although I can enter an ordinary with as much audacity, rebuke the waiters and drawers as

---

[73] 'On the Look of a Gentleman,' *London Magazine*, 3 (January 1821), 39–45; Howe, 12, 209–20.

loudly, drink as deep a health, swear as round an oath, and fling my gold as freely about as any of the jingling spurs and white feathers that are around me,—yet, hang me if I can ever catch the true grace of it, though I have practised for an hundred times.

But in fact, in *Kenilworth* as in the other novels, Scott never allows the chivalrous societies he depicts quite to obscure the modern, commercial world that he inhabits. Every now and then modernity intrudes, in a simile it may be, as when Amy Robsart's father, a country squire, is said to have the 'fidgetty anxiety about the exact measurement of time' peculiar to those 'who have a great deal of that commodity to dispose of, and find it lie heavy on their hands,—just as we see shopkeepers amuse themselves with taking an exact account of their stock at the time there is least demand for it'.[74] Or when, in *The Monastery*, Sir Piercie Shafton is as ignorant of the effect of his eloquence on Mysie Happer, the miller's daughter, as 'a first-rate beauty in the boxes' who never 'dreams of the fatal wound which her charms may inflict on some attorney's romantic apprentice in the pit' (266). Or in *The Abbot*, when Henry Warden, at a time when the pulpit was 'the same powerful engine for affecting popular feeling which the press has since become,' exploits the privilege it gives him to discuss the 'private faults' of individuals who have offended him 'specifically, personally, and by name'.[75] Or in *The Fortunes of Nigel*, when Nigel's coming into the presence of King James armed with pistols is compared with the mishap that befell the Earl of Glegarry in 1821 at the coronation of George IV. He wore full Highland dress and was arrested when a nervous marchioness, seeing his ornamental pistols and fearing an assassination attempt, screamed.[76] At such moments Scott's fictional worlds come into brief collision with the world out of which his fictions were produced and to which they were addressed. The effect is discordant, but moments like these, though they are common enough and characteristic, are fleeting. More often, Scott tries in the novels to realize an ideal world, a world that never existed, in which the ancient and the modern, or, more precisely, the chivalrous and the commercial, might be revealed as long-lost brothers. In his first novel Scott's hero may be Edward Waverley of Waverley-Honour, but in his sixth, *Rob Roy,* his place is taken by Frank Osbaldistone, who is equally chivalrous but the son not of a Jacobite squire but of the head of a thriving metropolitan trading company.

The Edinburgh in which Scott grew up, where he attended the city's High School, a near contemporary of political opponents such as Francis Jeffrey, Henry Cockburn, and Henry Brougham, was the city in which the new

---

[74] Walter Scott, *Kenilworth: A Romance*, ed. J. H. Alexander (Edinburgh: Edinburgh University Press, 1993), 20 and 112–13.
[75] Walter Scott, *The Abbot*, ed. Christopher Johnson (Edinburgh: Edinburgh University Press, 2000), 39.
[76] Walter Scott, *The Fortunes of Nigel*, ed. Frank Jordan (Edinburgh: Edinburgh University Press, 2004), 306. Subsequent page references are included in the text.

professional class to which all these men belonged, the class which during the nineteenth century came increasingly to dominate the life of the whole nation, first came to prominence. The cultural, political, and intellectual life of the city was dominated by Edinburgh's lawyers, academics, and divines. They boasted, many of them, Scott included, of family links with the Scottish aristocracy, and Scott in his novels was apt to represent the two classes as united in fond admiration each of the other. In *Redgauntlet,* for example, Alan Fairford is the true representative of the new class: his father, like Scott's, was a writer to the signet, but he has himself risen to be an advocate. Asked by a man he takes to be a disguised priest—he later turns out to be the Pretender—whether he could 'count kindred' with 'a family of birth and rank called Fairford', he admits that he has 'not the honour to lay such a claim', that his 'father's industry has raised his family from a low and obscure situation', and that he has 'no hereditary claim to distinction of any kind'.[77] Darsie Latimer, on the other hand, is directly descended from 'Fitz-Aldin' 'a valiant knight of Norman descent' and from 'Alberick Redgauntlet, 'the first of his house so termed', who was eminent in the baronial wars (190). Yet Fairford and Latimer are united in a friendship so close and so passionate that Latimer can offer to resign all claim to the woman he has fallen in love with if Fairford feels about her in the same way: 'my love for Alan Fairford surpasses the love of woman' (113). The more than brotherly love that Fairford and Latimer share is formally registered at the close of the novel when Fairford marries Latimer's sister. But even in *Redgauntlet* Scott registers at odd moments that the old aristocracy might not be so wholly sympathetic to the new professionals as all this might imply, as when Redgauntlet himself fears that Latimer, who lodged with Fairford's family while the two young men were law students together, might reveal 'the grovelling habits of a confined education, among the poor-spirited class that [he was] condemned to herd with' (317). In fact, Latimer, although we are allowed to imagine that he welcomes Fairford's marriage to his sister, has so keen a horror of miscegenation that 'his very flesh creep[s] with abhorrence' when he learns that Cristal Nixon, a man without family, has aspired to his sister's hand (313). Historical distance seems to allow Scott to hold together these uncomfortably contradictory prejudices, although sensitive readers such as Coleridge were alert to their dissonance. For Coleridge, Scott's is 'an age of anxiety from the crown to the hovel, from the cradle to the coffin; all is an anxious straining to maintain life, or *appearances*—to *rise,* as the only condition of not falling',[78] and this is the age that Scott represents no matter the historical period during which the novels are set.

[77] Walter Scott, *Redgauntlet,* ed. G. A. M. Wood with David Hewitt (Edinburgh: Edinburgh University Press, 1997), 277. Subsequent page references are included in the text.

[78] Written on the fly-leaf of *Peveril of the Peak,* quoted from *Scott: The Critical Heritage,* ed. John O. Hayden (London: Routledge and Kegan Paul, 1970), 183.

In *The Monastery*, for example, the action takes place in the Borders in the mid-sixteenth century, at a time when Scotland is divided between the upholders of the old faith and the Protestant reformers, but as in all the novels Scott understands the past through the present. When the Sub-Prior of the Abbey meets Henry Warden, a Protestant evangelist second in reputation only to John Knox, he recognizes him as Henry Wellwood. The two had been 'ancient and intimate friends in youth at a foreign university', and, despite their divisions, 'their hands were for a moment locked in each other', in remembrance of their youthful friendship (288). Scott, it seems evident, is re-creating his own relationship with those famous Whigs such as Jeffrey and Cockburn who were his schoolfellows at Edinburgh High School and his fellow students at the city's university. He casts back into the sixteenth century the disputes of his own day between those who championed the claims of rank and those who recognized only the claims of merit, and he seems entirely conscious of this, so much so that he is prepared to allow the Sub-Prior to appear at times as a knowing, self-deprecating caricature of a Tory such as Scott himself, as when he denounces 'all that is mutable and hot-headed in this innovating age' (290). But the Earl of Murray seems equally to speak for Scott when he discounts Halbert Glendinning's low birth: 'Nay, nay—leave pedigrees to bards and heralds—in our days, each man is the son of his own deeds' (324).

It seems a claim easier to make of Scotland in the early nineteenth than the mid-sixteenth century, but it serves to remind us that Scott's leading characters are far more often of doubtful or obscure descent than his assertive Toryism would lead one to expect. The Earl of Murray is himself illegitimate, and it is entirely characteristic that the mother of Sir Piercie Shafton, the novel's most emphatic spokesman for the claims of birth, is revealed at the last to be a tailor's daughter (349–50). The novel ends with the marriage of Halbert and Mary of Avenel, who is of noble birth, but, as the Earl of Murrray notes, has been 'bred up under the milk-pail' (345). People of obscure or hidden parentage are, of course, stock characters in the novel of the period, but Scott's interest in a character such as Halbert Glendinning seems more intimate, as if Scott can accommodate in a sixteenth-century Border warrior, as he could not in a contemporary, the troubled sense that he was himself, like Glendinning, the 'son of his own deeds', the product of the professionalized meritocracy of Edinburgh rather than the Border laird that he tried to make himself into.

The Fortunes of Nigel (1822) is set in Jacobean London, at a time when the cities of London and Westminster were far more distant from one another than in his own day 'when the toe of the citizen presses so close on the courtier's heel' (94). The observation is contradicted by almost every event in a novel in which the happiness of the hero is secured by the joint activities of the king and the goldsmith, George Heriot. Nigel, Lord Glenvarloch, the novel's hero, wins as his bride Margaret Ramsay, the daughter of the watch and spectacle maker, Davie Ramsay. On the occasion of the marriage the king provides Davie Ramsay with a comically appropriate coat-of-arms consisting of 'his paternal coat, charged with the crown-wheel of a watch in chief, for a difference' (398). Even Nigel's loyal but absurd servant, Richie Moniplies, finds himself in the novel's final paragraph knighted by the king and bidden to 'rise up, Sir Richard Moniplies, of Castle Collop!' (406). Different ranks seem as easily and as happily combined as the ingredients in the king's favourite cock-a-leekie soup. But even here the comedy overlays anxieties, as is revealed most vividly in the 'Ordinary' run by Monsieur Beajeu, an institution imported from France in which fine dining is the preamble to gaming. It differs from existing institutions chiefly in 'being open to all whom good clothes and good assurance combined to introduce there' (141). At the tables courtiers mix with young lawyers and London apprentices, amongst them Davie Ramsay's apprentice, Jenkin Vincent or Jin Vin, who is all but ruined by the experience. Such anxieties are both more evident and less easily accommodated in the one novel that Scott set in the Scotland of his own day.

Lockhart writes that 'several circumstances of Sir Alexander's [that is, Sir Alexander Boswell's] death are exactly reproduced in the duel scene in *St Ronan's Well*'.[79] He does not elaborate and the reproduction seems at most approximate, but it does signal that the only novel by Scott set in the nineteenth century—the action takes place in a small Scottish spa town during the Peninsular war—offers Scott's impression of an exactly contemporary Scotland, the Scotland of the 1820s.[80] According to Lockhart the novel was prompted by William Laidlaw remarking to Scott, 'I have often thought that if you were to write a novel, and lay the scene *here* in the very year you were writing it, you would exceed yourself.' At the time Lockhart, Laidlaw, and Scott were riding along the brow of Eildon hill overlooking Melrose. Scott responded by suggesting a novel in which he would 'never let the story step a yard beyond the village below us yonder', and Laidlaw agreed: 'The very thing I want; stick to Melrose in July 1823.'[81] In fact, Scott had begun the novel two months before, but the anecdote at least serves to signal that Lockhart, who was perhaps the best reader Scott ever had, thought of it as a novel set in an exactly contemporary Scotland.

St Ronan's, which is divided between the 'Aultoun' and the recently built spa, is a comically diminutive version of an Edinburgh similarly divided between its old and new towns. Meg Dods, who presides over the Cleikum inn, maintains the old ways and a fierce opposition to modernity in all its forms, but especially in the form of the Spa hotel. Again the effect is gently to mock the intensity of Edinburgh's party political conflicts by reproducing them in miniature. But, however comically diminished, disputes at St Ronan's are just as violent. At the

---

[79] J. G. Lockhart, *Memoirs of Sir Walter Scott* (London: Macmillan, 1900), 3, 528.

[80] The novel's modern editor, Mark A. Weinstein concludes that '1809–12 is the most likely time in which to place the action of *Saint Ronan's Well*.' See *Saint Ronan's Well* (Edinburgh: Edinburgh University Press and Columbia University Press, 1995), 442–3.

[81] J. G. Lockhart, *Memoirs of Sir Walter Scott*, 4, 114.

Spa the Highlander Captain MacTurk, 'the Peace-maker', ensures that each man has a proper concern for his own honour. When he goads the reluctant Sir Bingo Binks into challenging Francis Tyrrel, a duel is only averted because on his way to the ground Tyrrel meets and exchanges shots with his half-brother. The novel ends bleakly with a meeting between John Mowbray, the Laird of St Ronan's, and the villainous Lord Etherington. Mowbray avenges his sister by shooting Etherington through the heart: 'He sprung a yard from the ground, and fell down a dead man.'[82] The people of the Spa are, as Clara Mowbray warns her brother, addicted to such quarrels: 'I never go down there but I hear of some new brawl; and I never lay my head down to sleep, but I dream that you are a victim of it' (102). The Spa residents quarrel out of boredom, because they have nothing else to do. But there is more to it than that. The Spa, like other watering places, is a symptom of a society in which different ranks no longer maintain their social exclusivity. Meg Dods approves of the old manners in which the gentry had their balls that were attended by 'the auld folks in their coaches, wi' lang-tailed black horses, and a wheen gaillard gallants on their hunting horses', and the farmers had their balls 'wi' the tight lads of yeomen with the brank new blues and buckskins'. When 'they danced farmers wi' farmers' daughters, at the tane, and gentles wi' gentle blood, at the t'other', social gatherings seemed to Mrs Dods 'decent', but at the dances held at the Spa Clara Mowbray keeps company 'wi' a' that scauff and raff of students, and writers' 'prentices, and bagmen, and sic-like trash as are down at the Well yonder' (22).

Saint Ronan's Well is a novel about the confusion of ranks. Its marriages are all of them mismatches. The Englishman, Sir Bingo Binks, is trapped into marriage with Miss Rachael Bonnyrig, committed by his ignorance of Scots marriage law to marrying a woman he is too ashamed to introduce to his family. The antagonism between the half-brothers Francis Tyrrel and Lord Etherington has its origin in their father's private marriage with a beautiful French orphan, Tyrrel's mother. Only later did he more publicly, and, as it emerges, bigamously, marry Etherington's mother. The enmity between the two brothers is confirmed when Etherington persuades a naive Church of Scotland minister that it is he rather than his brother who has seduced Clara Mowbray and should be allowed to marry her in secret. Mismatchings are complicated by misnamings. In *Redgauntlet* it is not in itself disgraceful to have two names. Redgauntlet himself, because he is a proscribed Jacobite, sometimes passes under his maternal name as Herries of Birrenswork. Alan Fairford may not take Thomas Trumbull's advice to assume an alias when he ventures across the Solway, but the advice seems canny rather than dishonourable: 'thou who art to journey in miry ways, and amongst a strange people, may'st do well to have two names, as thou hast two shirts, the one to keep the other clean' (242–3). But in *Saint Ronan's Well*, naming is

[82] Walter Scott, *Saint Ronan's Well*, ed. Mark A. Weinstein (Edinburgh: Edinburgh University Press, 1995), 370. Subsequent page references are included in the text.

a more fraught business. Etherington wants to legitimize his fraudulent marriage with Clara Mowbray because marrying into her family will allow him to inherit a rich property from a relative who had made a fortune in trade but, suffering under 'the vulgar name of Scrogie' (171), has assumed his mother's name of Mowbray as being at once more euphonious and more aristocratic. Old Scrogie has disowned his own son, who 'thought Scrogie sounded as well as Mowbray, and had no fancy for an imaginary gentility, which was to be attained by the change of one's natural name, and the disowning, as it were, of one's actual relations' (341)—admirable sentiments, but scarcely consistent with the son's decision subsequently to abandon the name Scrogie for the name Touchwood.

Saint Ronan's Well is, for Scott, an unusually sour novel. It may have been because he found the spectacle of social confusion of this kind so uncomfortable that he never repeated the experiment of setting a novel in his own century, and he seems almost as uncomfortable with another aspect of modern Britain. The mixed society of the nineteenth century was also an intensely literary society. Society at the Well acknowledges two rival leaders. The interests of Mowbray's set centre on alcohol, gambling, and field sports. They are in competition with a set presided over by Lady Penelope Penfeather, a bluestocking whose interests, as her name suggests, are primarily literary. She gathers around her 'painters, and poets, and philosophers, and men of science, and lecturers, and foreign adventurers, *et hoc genus omne*' (27). Only Latin, it seems, can accommodate a snort of disdain intense enough to meet the case. For Scott, nothing seems so completely to seal the vulgarity of spa society as the presence 'in the very centre of the parade, (for so is termed the broad terrace walk which leads from the inn to the well)' of a 'bookseller's shop', kept by a 'Mr Pot,' which 'also served as post-office and circulating library' (292). When a young stranger arrives who is suspected of being an 'illustrious poet', 'all names were recited—all Britain scrutinized, from Highland hills to the Lakes of Cumberland—from Sydenham Common to St James's Place' (35). Samuel Rogers lived in St James's Place, Thomas Campbell in Sydenham, Wordsworth and the poet laureate, Southey, in the Lakes, and Walter Scott had made the Highlands his own. This is a joke, but it is for Scott a rather bitter one. He finds it humiliating, it seems, to think of his own name and the names of his friends being bandied about in social circles presided over by the likes of Lady Penelope Penfeather.

Scott's decision to publish his novels anonymously, as it turned out a marketing stratagem of genius, surely had its origin in this sensitivity. When Francis Tyrrel appears at St Ronan's and is taken first for a famous poet and then for a talented artist, he is referred to as the 'Unknown' (33), the self-reference is, one suspects, a good deal less insouciant than it appears. When Tyrrel is found not to be a poet but a man who admits of his sketches, 'I gain my livelihood of them', Mowbray is left to glory in his own acuteness in having identified him as a 'raff from the beginning' (46). Even the artless Maria Digges can only bring herself to compare him with that fashionable anomaly, the untaught poet: she claims that his eyes are 'quite deep and dark, and full of glow, like what you read to us in the letter from that lady, about Robert Burns' (59). The whole novel seems soured by Scott's contempt for the particular social world, with its strong literary interests supported by institutions such as the circulating libraries, that had secured Scott's wealth and fame. Part of him seems to have believed that his dependence on that world threatened to exclude him, in his own mind if not in that of others, from the social class with which he most closely identified, the Scottish gentry. It was uncomfortable feeling of a similar kind that ended in the duel in which John Scott was killed.

John Scott recognized that a 'printing-press is a more deadly weapon than a pistol or a small-sword',[83] and he showed in his own practice that it might also function as a horsewhip. Lockhart, by retreating to Scotland, had made himself 'only a fit subject for that public castigation, by means of the instrument he has venally abused, which I have already effectually applied, and shall be ready to apply again, should I see occasion for it'.[84] Hostile literary criticism is regularly described in the period as a kind of whipping, and the critics as 'whipsters'.[85] Chastisement may be with the schoolmasterly cane that Lockhart, writing as 'Z', imagines himself applying to Keats's posteriors, or it may be the still more savage flogging that Wilson imagines that Wordsworth has received from Jeffrey: 'he writhes under the lash which that consummate satirist has inflicted on him, and exhibits a back as yet sore with the wounds which have been in vain kept open, and which his restless and irritable vanity will never allow to close'.[86] Hazlitt is advised not to attempt any retaliation against Gifford: 'It shows little knowledge of human nature . . . thus to direct public attention, in hopes of exciting public sympathy, to the tingling, inflamed, discoloured, and perhaps raw parts, round which the lash of the Q (almost as sharp as that of Z himself) had so flourishingly played its periodical gambols.'[87] Such metaphors have a good deal to say about the less fortunate effects of the British schooling system, but they also serve to define a particular point in the evolution of print culture.

When James Stuart accosted the printer of *The Beacon* and demanded to know the author of the attacks on him, Stevenson referred him to the newspaper's editor, who would supply the name on the usual condition, that is, if Stuart agreed to pursue his grievance in person rather than through the courts. *The Beacon* had contrived it, *The Scotsman* complained, that every Whig was 'to be assailed with the most rancorous personal abuse and loaded with every vulgar epithet that can be selected from the flowers of Billingsgate oratory', and, if he objected, would be invited 'to seek redress from the pistols of an acknowledged slanderer'.[88] In the end *The Beacon* folded, unable to sustain the number of law

---

[83] 'The Mohock Magazine', *London Magazine*, 2 (December 1820), 666–85, 671.
[84] *Mr Scott's Second Statement, Feb. 2, 1821* (London: Baldwin, 1821), 8.
[85] 'Preface', *Blackwood's Edinburgh Magazine*, 19 (January 1925), xxv.
[86] *Blackwood's Edinburgh Magazine*, 1 (June 1817), 265.
[87] *Blackwood's Edinburgh Magazine*, 17 (March 1825), 363.
[88] *The Scotsman*, no. 244, 22 September 1821, 297.

suits brought against it, but Stuart was not content with victory in the courts: hence the attempt to horsewhip Stevenson and the challenge to Boswell when he was exposed as author of similar attacks in *The Sentinel.* Literary duels and horsewhippings were an inevitable consequence of a literary profession that now 'mingled all orders', and had no formal qualifications for membership. Claims had to be proved at the point of a pen, or, when sensitivities became too enflamed, through the barrel of a duelling pistol.

Blackwood's understood that the problem had to do with the rapid growth in the size of the reading public. Print had once been the preserve of gentlemen, a medium produced and consumed primarily by a group who shared a gender, an education, and a certain social standing. When two members of such a group fell out they might have recourse to pistols. If the offence was given by someone whose entitlement to gentlemanly status was refused then the proper recourse was to the horsewhip rather than the pistol. The distinction between the two weapons was a primitive attempt to organize those who worked within the new and rapidly expanding print industry into two categories. But by the early decades of the nineteenth century the literary world had become too large and too various to be divided so simply, and the social uncertainties that resulted, as John Scott found, could be fatal. The choice between duelling and horsewhip-ping might serve to distinguish gentlemen from plebeians, but both activities suggest a need violently to insist that print was so intimately connected with the fleshly body of its author that the offences of the one might properly be visited upon the other. It was a need that seems to have become more urgent the more the two bodies diverged, the more distant the physical body of the author became from the body of text that he produced.

8

Disunity of Mind: The Novel as Magazine

Magazines were distinguished from other periodicals by their miscellaneous character. As the *British Lady's Magazine* put it, 'Contrary to the Review, which requires in its conduct a general accordance of leading opinion, variety in the character of mind, is essential to the magazine.'[1] Lockhart agreed, pointing out in *Blackwood's* that 'the notion of unity of mind, in a Journal like this, is a thing quite below our contempt'.[2] Odoherty makes the same point to Byron in the episode of *Noctes Ambrosianae* 'transferred (by poetic licence) to Pisa'. Christopher North's magazine is

a classical work, which happens to be continued from month to month; a real Magazine of mirth, misanthropy, wit, wisdom, folly, fiction, fun, festivity, theology, bruising, and thingumbob. He unites all the best materials of the Edinburgh, the Quarterly, and the Sporting Magazine—the literature and good writing of the first—the information and orthodoxy of the second, and the flash and trap of the third.[3]

Magazines had always been miscellaneous. The *Blackwood's* innovation was to refuse a decorous division of its various contents into different sections. The fun, the theology, and the thingumbob were allowed to jostle against one other. Poetry, for example, was not separated from the prose, an editorial decision that the magazine advertised by noticing the objection of a doubtless fictitious clergyman:

> A Berkshire Rector has been pleased to wonder
> Why we've dismissed the primitive arrangement,
> He hates, he says, from verse to prose to blunder,
> Our quick transitions seem to him *derangement*.
>
> Begging our good friend's pardon, we prefer
> To mix the *dulce* with the *utile*,
> And think it has in fact a charming air
> Such different things in the same page to see.

---

[1] *British Lady's Magazine*, 1 (January 1815), 3.
[2] *Blackwood's Edinburgh Magazine*, 17 (February 1825), 132, in a paper on Byron by Lockhart.
[3] *Blackwood's Edinburgh Magazine*, 12 (July 1822), 105–6.

> A sonnet there, a good grave essay here,
> Chalmers, Rob Roy, Divorce-law, the New Play,
> Next (our divan, amid their toils to cheer)
> Some squib upon our neighbours o'er the way.[4]

Blackwood's abandoned arrangement in favour of 'derangement', and the *London*, and, after some time, the *New Monthly* followed suit.[5] The effect was to make the relationship between a magazine's various contents more volatile.

When James Stuart saw accusations of cowardice migrate from the political columns of *The Sentinel* into the poetry columns in 'A New Whig Song', he found the experience particularly wounding. The December 1820 issue of the *London* is still more revealing. The greater part of 'The Lion's Head', the magazine's editorial, is taken up by an apology offered by Charles Lamb to his friend, George Dyer, who had been distressed by Elia's representation of 'G. D.' in his essay 'Oxford in the Vacation' in the October number. Dyer had been especially upset by the suggestion that the schoolmaster who had once employed him as an usher never willingly paid his salary, and that Dyer had ever since supported himself by working as an underpaid bookseller's hack. Lamb admits to carelessness but denies that he had been guilty of a 'heartless jest' designed 'to set off his own wit or ingenuity'.[6] The same issue contained John Scott's 'The Mohock Magazine', the attack on *Blackwood's* that finally persuaded Lockhart to travel to London and deliver his challenge (though not before he had been assured by William Maginn, in a letter to Christopher North under the signature Dr Olinthus Petrie, that he was 'quite above the range of such a paper-shot as this').[7] Magazine 'derangement' made it difficult to distinguish between jokes and libels, or between banter and blackguardism. But in these years it was not only magazine writers who preferred to derange rather than arrange their material.

By 1813 Jane Austen was already conscious that the novel, always the loosest of literary forms, was becoming markedly more miscellaneous. Her own *Pride and Prejudice*, she felt, or pretended to feel, was rather too 'light & bright & sparkling;—it wants shade;—it wants to be stretched out here & there with a long Chapter—of sense if it could be had, if not of solemn specious nonsense—

---

[4] 'Notices to Correspondent', *Blackwood's Edinburgh Magazine*, 2 (March 1818), no page numbers. The verses, probably written by Lockhart, were prefixed to the March number, and preface the second volume of the magazine. The 'neighbours o'er the way' are those who write for Archibald Constable's publications, principally the *Edinburgh Review*. Thomas Chalmers, the Church of Scotland minister, was often targeted by the magazine which was suspicious of his interest in social reform.

[5] In early issues of the *New Monthly* 'Original Papers' were clearly distinguished from material included in the 'Historical Register'. The two sections of the magazine were separately paginated, and designed so that each year the Historical Register might be bound up as a separate volume. This practice was discontinued in the 1830s.

[6] See 'The Lion's Head', *London Magazine*, 2 (December 1820), 595–6.

[7] *Blackwood's Edinburgh Magazine*, 8 (December 1820), 207.

about something unconnected with the story; an Essay on Writing, a critique on Walter Scott, or the history of Bonaparte—or anything that would form a contrast & bring the reader with increased delight to the playfulness and Epigrammatism of the general stile'.[8] Susan Ferrier is sometimes called the Scottish Jane Austen, and like Austen she decorously concealed as best she could the fact of her authorship. In 1816 she wrote to her closest friend, Charlotte Clavering, 'I have been reading "Emma", which is excellent.' There was 'no story whatever', and the heroine was 'no better than other people', but the characters were so 'true to life' and the style so 'piquant' that it did not matter.[9] By then she was already at work on her own first novel, and would have recognized in Austen's Miss Bates an English cousin of her own Miss Grizzy, but it is the differences between the two novelists that are more interesting.

Like Austen, Ferrier is at once satirist and moralist, but whereas Austen tries to hold together her two literary characters, Ferrier is happy to allow them to diverge. When her heroine, Mary Douglas, begins to wrestle with moral dilemmas—for example, her mother refuses her permission to attend Sunday service, and she concludes that the duty to obey her parent must be subordinated to the duty to obey her God[10]—Ferrier has to introduce another character, a cousin Lady Emily, to make all those observations that seem too acerbic for the increasingly pious Mary. The friendship between the two young women, interrupted as it is by moments when Lady Emily gives way to spasms of irritation with her pious cousin, seems a proper expression of the divided character of the author. The formal differences between Ferrier's novel and Jane Austen's are still more revealing. In *Marriage* the narrative is repeatedly interrupted by sententious remarks—'In every season of life, grief brings its own peculiar antidote along with it' (231)—by free-standing sketches such as the account of the bluestocking salon presided over by 'Mrs. Bluemits' (414–25), by poems, many of which may have been supplied by Ferrier's friend, Charlotte Clavering, who certainly contributed to the novel the lengthy 'History of Mrs. Douglas', an account of the life of Mary's mother that seems scarcely connected with the rest of the novel (73–92), and by extracts of some length from other books. A 'pretty and well known' lyric by Moore, 'Careless and Faithless Love', is given in its entirety (321–2), and the gourmand, Dr Redgill, is allowed two substantial quotations in the original French from the first ever restaurant guide, Grimod de la Reynière's *Manuel des Amphitryons*, first published in Paris in 1808 (392–3). The fourth chapter of volume 3 epitomizes Ferrier's method. Mary sings to Colonel Lennox, the man she will marry, accompanying herself on the harp (32). The song is

---

[8] *Jane Austen's Letters*, ed. Deirdre Le Faye, 3rd edn (Oxford: Oxford University Press, 1995), 203.

[9] *Memoir and Correspondence of Susan Ferrier, 1782–1854*, ed. J. A. Doyle (London: John Murray, 1898), 128.

[10] Susan Ferrier, *Marriage*, ed. Herbert Foltinek (London: Oxford University Press, 1971), 146–52. Subsequent page references are included in the text.

George Herbert's 'Virtue'. The colonel knows the poem from its inclusion in Isaac Walton's *Compleat Angler*, which prompts him to quote several hundred words of Walton's prose (332–3), and this in turn prompts his blind mother to ask for a passage in which Walton celebrates the blessings of sight (334). This is a novel that flaunts rather than seeks to control its heterogeneity. The novel displays a tendency that Charlotte Clavering's aunt, Lady Charlotte Bury, takes to its logical conclusion in her *Journal of the Heart*, which does without any continuous narrative at all, frankly confessing its miscellaneous character. It brings together stories, travel pieces, Christian homilies, mood pieces, and poems, some of them contributed by Matthew Lewis.[11]

'Marriage' is the institution that gives the novel its theme, and marriage in this novel often yokes together ill-sorted individuals. Even the happy marriages flout boundaries, most often the boundary between Scotland and England. This is why *Marriage* is usually presented by modern critics as a national tale, but the cross-border marriages so frequent in the novel are not offered as a sign that the two nations have settled into a comfortable union one with another. The English according to Mary's Aunt Grizzy are 'a very dissipated unprincipled set. They all drink and game, and keep race-horses; and many of them, [she's] told, even keep play-actresses' (192). For Mary's mother, Lady Juliana, on the other hand, 'all Scotchwomen' are 'vulgar': 'They have red hands and rough voices; they yawn, and blow their noses, and talk, and laugh loud, and do a thousand shocking things' (189). Ferrier celebrates the differences between the two nations rather than their unity.

It is through the novel's language that Ferrier makes her strongest claims for cultural hybridity. Her Scottish gentry may speak Scots or English, or alternate between the two, her Scottish servants speak a more localized Scots, and the gentry at Bath speak an English fashionably sprinkled with French. Ferrier can move between all these worlds but her mobility is, she implies, a function of her own Scottishness. The fullest account that the novel offers of the Edinburgh society with which Ferrier was familiar appears in the section of the novel written by Charlotte Clavering. In comparison with London, Edinburgh is a small world, but precisely because it is so small, its society is more various; the fashionable, the intellectual, and the commercial classes mix together in Edinburgh as they do not in London:

The circle is so confined that its members are almost universally known to each other; and those various gradations of gentility, from the city's snug party to the duchess's most crowded assembly, all totally distinct and separate, which are to be met with in London, have no prototype in Edinburgh. There the ranks and fortunes being more on an equality,

[11] See *The Journal of the Heart* (London: Colburn and Bentley, 1830). *Journal of the Heart, second series* (London: James Cochrane, 1835) followed five years later. The two novels, if novels is the right description, are published as by 'the Author of "Flirtation"', and are sometimes ascribed, I think mistakenly, to Lady Caroline Lucy Scott.

no one is able greatly to exceed his neighbour in luxury and extravagance. Great magnificence, and the consequent gratification produced by the envy of others being out of the question, the object for which a reunion of individuals was originally invented becomes less of a secondary consideration. Private parties for the actual purpose of society and conversation are frequent, and answer the destined end; and in the societies of professed amusement are to be met the learned, the studious, and the rational; not presented as shows to the company by the host and hostess, but professedly seeking their own gratification.   (88)

The friendship with Charlotte Clavering out of which *Marriage* grew is itself the best clue to the character of such a society, for Susan Ferrier was a lawyer's daughter, whereas Charlotte Clavering was the granddaughter of the fifth Duke of Argyll, who employed Ferrier's father as his agent. The novel celebrates a world in which such friendships are possible. *Marriage* is then a typical product of Edinburgh in the early decades of the nineteenth century, as typical in its way as the *Edinburgh Review* and *Blackwood's Magazine*. But, as the success of the two periodicals shows, in these years the cultural forms that Edinburgh produced had an appeal throughout Britain, and that appeal had much to do with their miscellaneousness. *Emma* is a far more shapely novel than *Marriage*, but, after it was first published in 1816, no new edition was called for until it appeared as one of Bentley's Standard Novels in 1833. *Marriage* was not published as part of the same series until 1841, but by then there had been, since the novel's first publication in 1818, a second edition the following year, and a third edition in 1826.

    Susan Ferrier moved in Scott's social circle and Scott's novels, too, his reviewers began to intimate, were like magazines. They appeared almost as regularly, and they seemed scarcely more unified. Indeed it was rumoured that the novels, like magazines, were the work not of an individual but of a committee, 'a few master spirits, each perfect in its part and calling'.[12] The first novel that appeared under Scott's own name, *Chronicles of the Canongate*, makes the similarity explicit. Chrystal Croftangry, Scott's narrator, has retired with a modest independence to Edinburgh's Canongate after he has wasted his inheritance as a spendthrift young man and slowly recovered his fortunes abroad.[13] Needing to find a way to pass his time, it occurs to him that he might be 'capable of sustaining a publication of a miscellaneous nature, as like to the Spectator, or the Guardian, the Mirror, or the Lounger, as my poor abilities may be able to accomplish'. Croftangry refers to the magazines of the eighteenth century because he is an antiquarian, but he goes on to complain of the stiff 'swagger' of Johnson's prose in the *Rambler* essays in a way that reveals that his own affinities

---

[12] *Knight's Quarterly Magazine*, 1 (June 1823), 203. The suggestion is canvassed in a review of *Quentin Durward*.
[13] On Scott's narrator, see Frank Jordan, 'Chrystal Croftangry, Scott's Last and Best Mask', *Scottish Literary Journal*, 7 (1980), 185–92.

are with the periodical writers of Scott's own day.[14] Croftangry decides against periodical publication because he does not 'like to be hurried', and because 'a periodical paper is not easily extended in circulation beyond the quarter in which it is published' (51–2), but Scott gives his novel many of the other characteristics of the monthly miscellany.

Three fictions, two of them, 'The Highland Widow' and 'The Two Drovers', short stories, and the third, 'The Surgeon's Daughter', a short novel, are interspersed with chapters in which Croftangry describes how sourly he was received when he re-visited the house where he was raised, how he decided to settle himself in his retirement in the Canongate, the life he lives there, and his anxieties as a tyro author. The novel is designed like a magazine, so that it can be read from cover to cover or dipped into: 'Dearest reader, if you are tired, pray pass over the next four or five pages' (58).[15] The three stories that it includes might be read independently, or as a group, and, like magazine fiction, they display a keen sensitivity to literary fashion. 'The Highland Widow' and 'The Two Drovers' are Highland stories, but, Croftangry admits that, although 'the Highlands *were* indeed a good mine', it may be a mine that has been 'fairly wrought out' (principally, of course, by 'the author of *Waverley*') (67). The stories are concise, as if fearing to strain the reader's patience. Only in the third tale, 'The Surgeon's Daughter', does the narrative pace slow to the more leisurely rhythms of the novel. Although it begins in a village in Central Scotland so typical that it is called Middlemas, the story ends in an excitingly new literary landscape, the India of the East India Company, where, at the story's close, the villainous Captain Middlemas is executed by being crushed to death by a royal elephant. When Croftangry reads the story to his lawyer and his family he is pleased to notice that 'the extinction of the lover in a way so horribly new' had its effect in 'awakening the imaginations' of his 'fair auditors', the lawyer's daughters (287). The rapid transition between the parochial and the exotic, the delight in the sensational, and the heightened alertness to gender all suggest the magazine writing of the 1820s.

Of all the major novelists of the period Hogg was the most closely associated with magazines. His greatest novel, *The Private Memoirs and Confessions*, was anticipated or advertised in a letter to *Blackwood's* printed in August, 1823, under the heading 'A Scots Mummy',[16] the bulk of which is reproduced in the novel. Lockhart may have insisted that 'the notion of unity of mind, in a Journal like this, is a thing quite below our contempt,' but in *Private Memoirs* Hogg, who had learned from the appearances of the Ettrick Shepherd in the *Noctes*

[14] Walter Scott, *Chronicles of the Canongate*, ed. Claire Lamont (Edinburgh: Edinburgh University Press, 2000), 51. Subsequent page references are included in the text.
[15] In the collected editions of Scott's novels that appeared after his death its contents were broken up, its tales used as makeweights in the volumes containing Scott's shorter novels.
[16] *Blackwood's Edinburgh Magazine*, 14 (August 1823), 188–90.

Ambrosianae what it was to have a double, took disunity of mind as his central theme. It is a topic he is just as concerned with in his other fiction. In *The Three Perils of Man*, for example, it seems at first merely conventional that Hogg should present himself as the editor of a manuscript written by 'Isaac, the curate',[17] but the device allows Hogg to present his novel as a palimpsest in which a pre-modern sensibility underlies a sensibility that is markedly contemporary. A recent editor of the novel, Douglas Gifford, suggests that it is 'essentially a comic romance rather than a nineteenth-century novel',[18] but in fact it is both, and it is by being both that it achieves its own peculiar, magazine-like modernity. Black Douglas is a romance hero who, when he believes his mistress, the Princess Margaret, to be dead, kneels 'before the holy rood' and swears that, since he 'has been bereaved of the sovereign mistress of [his] heart . . . never shall another of the sex be folded in the arms of Douglas, or call him husband!' (422) He is also a man who 'never once conceived of giving up the enterprise', the siege of the castle of Roxburgh, whatever the risk to Margaret, because failure would result in the loss of 'his broad domains', and, besides, 'the king had more daughters, though none like his beloved and accomplished Margaret' (354). The novel does not so much oscillate between different moral perspectives as between different systems of representation. Hence it is entirely appropriate that it refuses a single language, accommodating verse and prose, the broad Scots of characters such as Charlie Yardbyre, an English imitated from chivalric romances, the biblical pastiche in which the Friar speaks, and the aggressively disenchanted voice of the editor.

In Hogg's sequel, *The Three Perils of Woman*, the effect is still more marked. The novel is made up of two independent tales, one contemporary, the other historical, one domestic, the other national, and it switches abruptly between genres. The first tale begins by lightly satirizing the 'modern manners' that prevent Agatha Bell from confessing to the man she loves the state of her feelings, but it becomes a sentimental novel when her rival in love, her cousin Cherry, dies of a broken heart, and then moves into supernatural Gothic mode, when Agatha dies a holy death only to be jerked back into ghastly life by the refusal of her father to accept God's dispensation. It is a scene that seems to borrow from *Frankenstein*:[19]

The body sprung up with a power resembling that produced by electricity. It did not rise up like one wakening out of a sleep, but with a jerk so violent that it struck the old man on

---

[17] In fact, the Editor works from a copy or edited version of the manuscript left by Isaac, further complicating the notion of textual authenticity. See Penny Fielding, *Writing and Orality: Nationality, Culture, and Nineteenth-Century Scottish Fiction* (Oxford: Clarendon Press, 1996), 93–4.

[18] James Hogg, *The Three Perils of Man: War, Women and Witchcraft* (Edinburgh: Scottish Academic Press, 1989), x. Subsequent page references, given in the text, are to this edition.

[19] Walter Scott's 'Remarks on Frankenstein' had appeared in *Blackwood's Edinburgh Magazine*, 2 (March 1818), 613–20.

the cheek, almost stupefying him; and there sat the corpse, dressed as it was in its dead-clothes, a most appalling sight as man ever beheld.[20]

Hogg's novels all of them prompt the unsettling thought that the world encountered in fiction is a world determined by the way in which it is written down.

The story of Agatha's courtship and marriage is intercut with the story of Richard Rickleton's marriage. Rickleton is a Northumberland sheep-farmer, a giant embodiment of corporeal masculine energy quite undiluted by mind, and the tale ends with a series of letters in which Rickleton describes his pursuit of his wife's lover, the father of her child. Rickleton is a poor penman and dictates his letters to a series of amanuenses with the result that his own dialect—'Hast thou no beef and mwottong, shooger and tey?' (228)—bizarrely alternates with passages composed by his secretaries. One is literary: Rickleton's wife 'looked very timorous and wistful, as if the sun of truth dreaded to peer from behind the dark cloud of moral turpitude that overshadowed it' (229). Another is a devout Presbyterian, who phrases a challenge thus: 'come thou forth with thy sword in thine hand, that we may look one another in the face, at such place as the son of Rimmon shall appoint' (243). The literary man protests when he transcribes Rickleton's speech that he is 'not accountable for the grammar or orthography of what follows' (228), but the whole series of letters seems designed to suggest that every system of grammar and orthography creates its own world, and that Hogg rests his authority as a novelist simply on the number of rival systems that he is able to command. Hogg was an accomplished parodist,[21] but he was also a magazine writer, and those who wrote for magazines quickly learned that authority, and even identity were, in the end, matters of style.

Blackwood's had changed the status of the magazine, and it had done so by taking as its subject matter not 'literature' but 'human life'.[22] That was the crucial decision, and it is echoed in other productions characteristic of the post-war years, by *Don Juan* most obviously—'It may be profligate but is it not *life*, is it not *the thing*?'[23]—but also by a novel such as Pierce Egan's *Life in London* in which the project that the novel shares with Tom and Jerry, its heroes, is presented in bold capitals, 'SEEING LIFE'.[24] The same, of course, might be said of Wordsworth whose poems so manifestly aspire to 'see into the life of things'.

---

[20] James Hogg, *The Three Perils of Woman; or, Love, Leasing, and Jealousy*, ed. David Groves, Antony Hasler, and Douglas S. Mack (Edinburgh: Edinburgh University Press, 1995), 200. Subsequent page references are included in the text.
[21] For Hogg's verse parodies, see James Hogg, *Poetic Mirrors: Comprising the* Poetic Mirror (*1816*) *and* New Poetic Mirror (*1829–31*), ed. David Groves (Frankfurt: Peter Lang, 1990).
[22] *Blackwood's Edinburgh Magazine*, 8 (October 1820), 100/104–5. The page numbering in this volume is defective.
[23] *Byron's Letters and Journals*, ed. Leslie A. Marchand, 6 (London: John Murray, 1976), 232.
[24] Pierce Egan, *Life in London; or, The day and night scenes of Jerry Hawthorn, esq. and his elegant friend Corinthian Tom, accompanied by Bob Logic, the Oxonian, in their rambles and sprees through the metropolis* (London: Sherwood and Jones, 1823), 24. Subsequent page references are included in the text.

But 'life' for Wordsworth is characterized by so deep an interiority that differences are lost within it, whereas it is precisely those differences that Byron and Egan and *Blackwood's* delight in.

According to Egan, every one of London's streets is like an issue of *Blackwood's*: 'There is not a street in London, but what may well be compared to a large or small volume of intelligence, abounding with anecdote, incident, and peculiarities' (24). Egan, much more obviously than Ferrier, or Scott, or Hogg, transformed the novel, as Byron transformed the epic poem, into a kind of magazine, and not only because *Life in London* was the first prose fiction to be published in monthly numbers.[25] He makes it pointedly, wilfully heterogeneous, not just by tracing the movements of its heroes from the saloon of Covent Garden, to a gin-shop, a coffee-shop, and then, when they are arrested after a brawl, to the watch-house, but by interspersing the story of their doings with the plates by the Cruikshanks, on the merits of which Egan often comments. There are long notes which supplement the fiction with historical and topical anecdotes the surprising range of which is summarized by J. C. Reid, Egan's biographer:

These notes are full of diverting details of contemporary social life, scandalous anecdotes, glosses on slang, character-sketches and home-spun eighteenth-century philosophizing and jokes. There is a long section on Junius, a eulogy of R. B. Sheridan, a description of Dutch Sam, a pugilist of note, a biography of the genteel pickpocket, George Barrington, a blistering attack on the Duchess of Macclesfield for her desertion of her son, the unfortunate poet, Savage, a splendid account of the place of pawnbrokers in the economy of the poor, praise for the industry of Mr Thrale and Mr Rothschild and a contemptuous comment on dandies.[26]

The notes help to give the novel its magazine-like character, a character that Egan himself notices when he appeals for inspiration in writing his novel to 'my *Mag* of BLACKWOOD', a '*chiel* of Satire' whose 'lively sallies and "laughing-in-the-sleeve" greatness' Egan admires, as much as he admires—and the catholicity of the taste is itself magazine-like—the work of the radical pamphleteer William Hone (6).

Much of *Life in London* is devoted to vigorous description of various London social events. London is construed as a gigantic metropolitan theatre and Egan presents himself as its chief reviewer. As in his *Boxiana* Egan is always as fascinated by the character of the audience or crowd as by the doings of the chief participants, but his crowds share a particular character. This, for example, is the company at Tattersall's:

---

[25] The first monthly instalment appeared in September 1820. It was not issued in book form until July 1821.
[26] J. C. Reid, *Bucks and Bruisers: Pierce Egan and Regency England* (London: Routledge and Kegan Paul, 1971), 59.

The company, I admit, is a *mixture* of persons of nearly all ranks in life; but, nevertheless, it is that sort of *mixture* which is pleasingly interesting: there is no *intimacy* or *association* about it. A man may be well known here, he may also in his turn *know* almost every body that visits TATTERSALL'S, and yet be quite a *stranger* to their habits and connexions with society. (238)

This is a crowd brought together by the chance of a shared interest, a crowd that has nothing but the interest in common. It includes men from quite different social ranks, and all participate on equal terms in the judging of the finer points of the horses, the buying and the selling, and the laying of bets, and yet the social hierarchy remains quite unthreatened. It is an almost entirely masculine group— the only women present are likely to be prostitutes—and the men who compose it are in company at once with those who are their familiars and total strangers. It is, in Canning's terms, merely an 'aggregation', that is a 'multitude of individuals' who have 'no permanent relation to each other, no common tie, but what arises from their concurrence as members of that meeting'.[27] In all these respects such crowds figure the new reading public, which was the public that a magazine such as *Blackwood's* both addressed and helped to bring into being.

It was a readership that Thomas Love Peacock seems heartily to have despised, which makes it odd that it is in Peacock's work that the novel should make its closest approach to the magazine. In his essay on 'French Comic Romances' Peacock distinguishes between comic fictions like 'those of Henry Fielding' 'in which the characters are individuals, and the events and actions those of actual life', and comedies in which 'the characters are abstractions or embodied classifications, and the implied or embodied opinions the main matter of the work'. It is the second kind of fiction to which Peacock's own novels seem clearly to belong. Its masters, according to Peacock, are 'Aristophanes, Petronius Arbiter, Rabelais, Swift, and Voltaire',[28] certainly an impressive lineage, except that Peacock's novels do not resemble very closely the work of any of them. All five of Peacock's novels of talk centre on chapters in which the characters converse as they dine. The novels are held together by a conventional courtship narrative that ends equally conventionally in a perfunctory marriage ceremony, usually involving several couples. In *Headlong Hall* we are told in the final chapter that Squire Headlong 'did not suffer many days to elapse, before the spiritual metamorphosis of eight into four was effected by the clerical dexterity of the Reverend Doctor Glaster' (1, 150). By the time the third of the novels, *Nightmare Abbey*, was published in 1818 the form was fully developed. The closest counterpart to Peacock's novels of talk is surely the *Noctes Ambrosianae*, the first episode of

[27] From a speech by Canning quoted in *Blackwood's Edinburgh Magazine*, 7 (April 1820), 15.
[28] *Halliford Edition of the Works of Thomas Love Peacock*, ed. H. F. B. Brett-Smith and C. E. Jones, 10 vols. (London: Constable and Co., 1926), 5, 258. All subsequent quotations from Peacock's novels and essays are taken from this edition, and references by volume and page number included in the text.

which did not appear in *Blackwood's* until March 1822. It is unlikely that Lockhart, who wrote it, William Maginn who occasionally contributed an episode, or John Wilson, who eventually made the series his own, was indebted to Peacock, but it is surely not coincidental that Peacock and the *Blackwood's* writers should have happened within so short a space of time on the same form, the record of the conversation of a male gathering (there are sometimes women at Peacock's tables but they take little part in the conversation, and even happily married men such as the Revd Dr Folliott in *Crotchet Castle* and the Revd Doctor Opimian in *Gryll Grange* do not take their wives with them when they go to dinner), in which the talk extends from literature to philosophy to the topics of the day but is repeatedly interrupted by references to what is being eaten and what drunk. In *Gryll Grange*, Dr Opimian seems to speak for Peacock himself when he praises the symposium: 'Consider how much instruction has been conveyed to us in the form of conversations at banquets, by Plato and Xenophon and Plutarch. I read nothing with more pleasure than their Symposia: to say nothing of Athenaeus, whose work is one long pamphlet' (5, 197). The Oxford- educated Lockhart and Wilson, and Maginn who had been a prize-winning student at Trinity College, Dublin, were almost as ready as the self-educated Peacock to make a display of their classical scholarship, which makes it unsurprising that they should together have revived a classical form. But it still needs to be explained why the symposium should have been the form that attracted them.

As I have argued earlier, it was a form that allowed its readers, the consumers of a mass-produced commodity, the benign illusion that in reading they were granted entry to a brilliant social group. Reading, the favourite activity of lonely people, the resource of that new clerical class that lived, so many of them, solitary lives in rented rooms, might still afford a virtual experience of social gatherings in which the wit flows as freely as the wine. The readers of these pieces were not of course deluded: rather, they were invited to enjoy the experience offered to them in full recognition that it was illusory. In the *Noctes*, for example, Wilson addresses the problem of how it could be possible to offer in the magazine a verbatim transcription of an evening's conversation between men who are often tipsy at the beginning of the evening, and sometimes drunkenly asleep at its close. He imagines that the shorthand writer, Nathan Gurney, has been hired by William Blackwood, and is secreted in a cupboard under instructions to take down the conversation for reproduction in the magazine.[29] It is one of the many ways (another is the Shepherd's dialect) in which the series seems deliberately to call attention to the difference between writing and speech. Peacock does the same. He insists, for example, on allowing his speakers to use in conversation a vocabulary that is never found except in print. In *Gryll Grange*, the Revd Doctor Opimian uses the word 'agistor' to describe a particular kind of forest officer, and

---

[29] *Blackwood's Edinburgh Magazine*, 21 (April 1827), 478.

Peacock acknowledges in a footnote explaining the meaning of the word that he has 'read the word, but never heard it' (5, 27). Words of this kind are inserted into the conversation in almost all the novels, as if to call attention to the beguiling absurdity of printed talk that, for all that it reproduces conversational cadences, is too exactly phrased to allow the reader to suppose that it was ever other than written. Peacock may even footnote his conversations, treating every speech as if it were a pamphlet. So, in *Melincourt*, the abilities and manners of Sir Oran Haut-Ton, Peacock's gentlemanly primate, are elaborately glossed in notes that quote from Delisle de Sales, Buffon, Rousseau, and, most of all, Lord Monboddo. The political opinions of Mr Anyside Antijack and his poetical friends Mr Feathernest and Mr Paperstamp are just as elaborately annotated with references to an article in the *Quarterly* by Southey on parliamentary reform (2, 200–15).[30] His speakers are not so much embodied opinions as embodied texts, which makes it oddly appropriate that when Mr Feathernest and Mr Derrydown duel their chosen weapons should be seventeenth-century folios by George Chapman and Jeremy Taylor. They turn away from one another, 'the one flourishing his Chapman and the other his Jeremy with looks of defiance' (2, 197).

The authors chosen are characteristically recherché. Peacock affects a lofty superiority to popular fiction of all kinds. He may mimic in all his fictions the plot of the conventional romantic novel, but his is a wholly condescending imitation. In *Nightmare Abbey*, Mrs Hilary tells her niece that 'propriety, and delicacy, and decorum, and dignity, &c. &c. &c., would require them to leave the Abbey immediately', and Peacock appends a note to the third '&c': 'We are not masters of the whole vocabulary. See any novel by any literary lady' (3, 30). He has in mind novelists such as Miss Philomela Poppyseed of *Headlong Hall*. In his 'Essay on Fashionable Literature' Peacock counts among the 'half dozen' jokes that have proved sufficient to fill the 'two hundred thousand pages of sheer criticism' that the reviews have published in the seventy years since their first introduction the assertion that 'the work in question is a narcotic, and sets the unfortunate critic to sleep' (7, 287–9). It was a joke, as the name 'Poppyseed' shows, that he was not above repeating.

He despised magazines as much as he despised sentimental novels, and yet just as he borrowed his plots from the sentimental novelists, he borrowed the content of his novels from the magazines. The novels of talk at once satirize and delight in the 'perishable fashions of mind,' on which, Peacock complains, magazines draw for their content. In their dining rooms men such as Squire Headlong and Mr Crotchet bring magazines to life. As the Revd Dr Folliott says, 'all the arts and sciences are welcome here: music, painting, and poetry; hydrostatics, and political economy; meteorology, transcendentalism, and fish for breakfast'

---

[30] The references are all to Southey's review essay on the state of public opinion, *Quarterly Review*, 16 (October 1816), 225–78. This issue was in fact published on 11 February 1817.

(4, *Crotchet Castle*, 28). Guests talk at rather than to one another. All discussions end 'as most controversies do, by each party continuing firm in his own opinion, and professing his profound astonishment at the blindness and prejudices of the other' (1, *Headlong Hall*, 148). In consequence, the disputatious characters remain quite insulated one from another, as if they were not guests sharing a table, but rival contributors appearing between the covers of the same magazine. The magazine that Peacock's novels most resemble is, perhaps, *The Pamphleteer*, a periodical that appeared irregularly between 1813 and 1828. It was a rather solemn periodical, dedicated to both houses of Parliament. It re-printed pamphlets and also included some original papers. Peacock took *The Pamphleteer* and in his short-lived journal he records reading the 23rd number on 10 and 11 August 1818, and finding an article on gold coinage 'sensible' (*The Pamphleteer* specialized in political economy).[31] *The Pamphleteer* had distinguished contributors; Jeremy Bentham, George Dyer, Basil Montagu, Nicholas Vansittart. It was non-partisan, but unusually accommodating to radical voices such as Bentham's and Dyer's. In its prospectus it positioned itself between the magazine and the review, 'neither imitating the miscellaneous and chaotic confusion of the first, nor the analytical and judiciary processes of the last'.[32] But simply by bringing together in a single issue pamphlets so disparate it arrives at its own kind of chaos. Brought together in number xv, for example, are the first instalment of 'A Dissertation on the Eleusinian and Bacchic Mysteries' by Peacock's friend, Thomas Taylor, a piece by Polidori, 'On the Punishment of Death', humanely arguing against the death penalty in the case of any but the most serious crimes, and a scholarly pamphlet by Sir Joseph Banks, 'Some Remarks on the Mildew of Wheat.'[33] However worthy in themselves such pieces become absurd in their association. *The Pamphleteer* also found room for contributions that Peacock could only have found delightfully dotty, as for example the 'New Theory of the Two Hemispheres: Whereby it is attempted to explain, on Geographical and Historical Facts, the Time and Manner in which America was Peopled' (the difficulties that have perplexed earlier commentators disappear if we suppose that Eurasia and the Americas were separated not at the time of the Flood but some years later, as a delayed consequence of the inundation).[34] Peacock's novels make fun of the anarchic intellectual energy of Regency culture, its magazine quality, and yet they are also entranced by it. Peacock was introduced to J. F. Newton, the prototype of more than one of his characters, by Shelley when he was living at Bracknell:

He was an estimable man and an agreeable companion, and he was not the less amusing that he was the absolute impersonation of a single theory, or rather of two single theories

---

[31] *The Letters of Thomas Love Peacock*, ed. Nicholas A. Joukovsky (Oxford: Clarendon Press, 2001), 138.
[32] *The Pamphleeter*, 1 (1813), vi.
[33] *The Pamphleteer*, 8 (1816), no. xv.
[34] A piece by G. A. Thompson, *The Pamphleteer*, 5 (1815), 543–61.

rolled into one. He held that all diseases and all aberrations, moral and physical, had their origin in the use of animal food and of fermented and spirituous liquors; that the universal adoption of a diet of roots, fruits, and distilled water, would restore the golden age of universal health, purity, and peace; that this most ancient and sublime morality was mystically inculcated in the most ancient Zodiac, which was that of Dendera; that this Zodiac was divided into two hemispheres, the upper hemisphere being the realm of Oromazes or the principle of good, the lower that of Ahrimanes or the principle of evil; that each of these hemispheres was again divided into two compartments, and that the four lines of division radiating from the centre were the prototype of the Christian cross. (8, 'Memoirs of Percy Bysshe Shelley', 71–2)[35]

Newton seems not to have contributed to *The Pamphleteer*, but he might have done.

Marilyn Butler has rightly dismissed the notion that Peacock may properly be represented as an intellectual bystander, a man who delights in a clash of opinions from which he remains himself aloof.[36] In all his earlier fiction he clearly associates himself with the reformist principles that he ascribes to the Shelley-like Mr Forester in *Melincourt*. His peculiarity is that he just as clearly associates himself with many of the principles of Mr Forester's antagonist, the Malthus-like Mr Fax. Peacock seems from his fictions, from his letters, and from his essays to have been a robustly opinionated man, unusual only in his ability to hold opinions on most things, as on political economy, of a flatly contradictory kind, and it is this that makes his fictions so characteristic a product of the age of magazines. After all, the defining characteristic of the magazine was, according to Lockhart, that it was 'not bound to maintain any one set of opinions, in regard to any one set of objects, throughout the whole of its pages'.[37] It seems entirely appropriate that in 1860 *Gryll Grange*, the very last of Peacock's fictions should have been first published in a magazine, *Fraser's*.

Scott wrote of *Chronicles of the Canongate*, 'I intend the work as an *olla podrida* into which any species of narrative or discussion may be thrown',[38] and his metaphor reveals that he intended his novel to emulate the virtues of the magazine. In the post-war decade the *olla podrida* became the favourite literary dish. In October 1817, Hogg had advised Blackwood, who was preparing to re-launch his magazine, 'A general miscellany should exactly be such an olio that when a man has done with a very interesting article he should just pop his nose into another quite distinct but as good of its kind.' The reader should have 'no rule to go by but the table of contents'.[39] In these years it was not just the novel

---

[35] Peacock used the Zoroastrian theology himself in his unfinished poem, 'Ahrimanes'.

[36] Marilyn Butler, *Peacock Displayed: A Satirist in his Context* (London: Routledge and Kegan Paul, 1979).

[37] J. G. Lockhart, *Peter's Letters to his Kinsfolk*, 3 vols. (Edinburgh: Blackwood, 1819), 2, 224.

[38] *The Journal of Sir Walter Scott*, ed. W. E. K. Anderson (Oxford: Clarendon Press, 1972), 151.

[39] *The Collected Letters of James Hogg*, ed. Gillian Hughes, 3 vols. (Edinburgh: Edinburgh University Press, 2004–8), 1, 305.

that aspired to the condition of the magazine. So did certain kinds of poetry, as Byron intimates in his Preface to *Don Juan,* when he invites the reader to imagine that his poem is told by a Spanish gentleman who sits 'at the door of a *posada*' at a small table 'containing the relics of an *olla-podrida*'. This is the kind of poetry that I will discuss in my next chapter.

9

Practical Asyndeton: The Poem as Magazine

Sir Alexander Boswell was in an odd state in the days before he died. For most of that time he was the cool, determined duellist. His first thought had been that the duel should take place across the Channel: 'If I should be the successful shot, he says, I would not like the after proceedings of a Court of Justice.' His next was that he and Stuart should meet across the border in England. Only when he was assured that he would be 'safer in the hands of the Lord Advocate, who is a gentleman [and also, of course, a close political ally], than before a grand jury', did he agree to meet Stuart in Scotland. At Stuart's trial, Henry Cockburn, his defence counsel, established all this in his opening statement. He needed to show that Stuart had every reason to believe that Boswell was in deadly earnest when he accepted Stuart's challenge, and that when Stuart 'stepped from his carriage to the appointed field, he firmly believed he stepped on what would be his grave'. But as he made the journey in his carriage from North Queensferry to Auchtertool, Boswell spoke very differently. His second, John Douglas, gave evidence: 'He said that he had no ill will against Mr Stuart—that perhaps in an unhappy moment he had injured him—that he had no wish to put his life in jeopardy, and therefore was determined to fire in the air.' Douglas agreed that this would be the best course, and when Boswell fell, mortally wounded, his only anxiety was that 'he was very much afraid that he had not made his fire in the air as decided as he could have wished'.[1] He was a desperado who revealed himself at the last as a quietly decent man, a nonchalant duellist who was also a loving husband and father. He died not so much for writing squibs as because he failed to reconcile the different aspects of his character. The same might be said of John Scott, who at the moment that he fell was a gentleman standing on his honour, a professional man of letters, and a man who was about to leave a wife and two young children quite unsupported. I dare say that a similar diagnosis would fit most duellists since the system of duelling began, but the failure to establish working relations between different aspects of the self seems to have been a character trait particularly common in this period.

---

[1] *A full report of the trial of James Stuart, Esq. younger of Dunearn, before the High Court of Justiciary, 10th June 1822; with an appendix containing documents, etc.* (Edinburgh 1822), 19–20, and 35–6.

The clever young men who wrote *The Etonian* gave it a name. It was 'Practical Asyndeton', that is, the habit of living life by alternating between, rather than resolving, inconsistent identities. This is the characteristic that distinguishes the most representative modern heroes, Scott's Marmion and Byron's Manfred. Its classical type is Alcibiades, who 'moralized like a philosopher, jested like a mountebank, fought like a hero, lied like a scoundrel, lived like a knowing one, and died like a fool'.[2] But, despite the representative character of Marmion and Manfred, the chivalric romance and the Faustian drama are not the literary forms that most easily incorporate experience of this kind. It is more easily represented in genres that tend towards the serio-comic, itself a term that only became established in this period (the *OED* dates its use from the 1780s). For a brief period after Waterloo it served to designate the most fashionable aesthetic ideal. For *The Etonian* it is an ideal embodied in the most desirable women such as 'charming Leonora', who is 'like a chess-board which is chequered with black and white squares alternately,—or a melodrama, in which the tears of Tragedy are relieved by the follies of Farce—or a day in April, which blends rain with sunshine, Summer with Winter'. At last we arrive at the expected conclusion: what Leonora best resembles is the very magazine in which this passage appears, '"The Etonian", in which the Serious is united with the Absurd, and Pathos is intermingled with Puns'.[3] *The Etonian* was written in flattering imitation of *Blackwood's*, and, as *Gold's London Magazine* remarked, *Blackwood's* was a magazine in which 'a serio-comic vein pervades almost every description of men and manner that strikes to the mind with an impression of the deepest originality'.[4] It was the achievement that John Wilson was himself to offer as the most decisive proof of the magazine's originality, or rather it was a claim that he placed in the mouth of James Hogg (the Shepherd is speaking to Christopher North):

Afore you and her [*Blackwood's*] came out, this wasna the same warld it has been sin syne. Wut and wisdom never used to be seen linkin' alang thegither, han' and han' as they are noo, fra ae end o' the month to the ither—there was na prented a byuck that garred ye break out ae page into grief, and at anither into a guffaw.[5]

But an insistence on the proximity of grief and guffaws was unusually common in the writing of the period.

In Hogg's *The Perils of Woman*, Richard Rickleton's wife, Kate, is told that she must choose between her husband and her illegitimate child. Her response is characteristic: 'her crying turned by degrees into something like laughter, and that of the most violent kind; and then it changed into crying again, and then

---

[2]   *The Etonian* (London: Charles Knight, 1824), 1, 225–32, 231, and 229.
[3]   *The Etonian*, 2, 282.
[4]   *Gold's London Magazine and Theatrical Inquisitor*, 3 (January 1821), 18.
[5]   *Blackwood's Edinburgh Magazine*, 21 (March 1827), 345.

into laughing, I know not how oft.'[6] For Hogg, the abrupt transition between laughter and tears is the authenticating hallmark of all strong emotion, and the thought was widely enough shared to make of the serio-comic, or, as Thomas Hope described it, the 'strange mixture of the sweet and the bitter',[7] the dominant literary style in the decade after the Napoleonic wars. But perhaps it would be better to identify the serio-comic not as a style but as the most characteristic expression of the distinctively modern aesthetic that characterized this period. For John Scott, Walter Scott's novels offer decisive proof of how closely related are 'the comic and the affecting': 'Those who can go deep into human nature find where their roots entwine.'[8] It was a perception most closely associated not with the novel but with magazines like John Scott's own *London*.

Magazines were by virtue of their miscellaneous character serio-comic by definition, but it was also the manner cultivated by the most successful magazine writers. It was the manner claimed by Charles Lamb who points out in his epitaph on himself how he was wont to 'interrupt the gravest discussion with some light jest', and who, another contributor noted, 'delighted in antithetical presentments: thou lovest to exhibit thy tragic face in its most doleful gloom, that thou mayst incontinently turn upon us the sunshine of thy comic smile'.[9] Hazlitt, too, it was agreed, favoured the serio-comic mode: his admirers, according to the *London Magazine* 'see, and enjoy, all the rapid changes of humour and intention, which, like clouds, pass over his mind in the course of contemplating his subject ... their feelings correspond with his in an instant, when his serious tone runs off into irony, or is coupled with gaiety of remark'.[10] *Blackwood's*, despite its detestation of Hazlitt, agreed. In the series 'Characters of Living Authors, By Themselves' Eyre Evans Crowe has Hazlitt describe himself as 'of that mongrel humour, which deals out philosophy with flippant air, and cracks jests with coffin visage'.[11] De Quincey's *Confessions* share the alertness to the close kinship between laughter and tears characteristic of the magazine writer. His narrative begins when he runs away from school, the servant who is helping him with his trunk drops it, and it thunders down the stairs crashing into the door of the sleeping headmaster. Both the servant and the young De Quincey, despite their terror, burst into laughter: it is an incident that he 'cannot yet recall without smiling', 'so blended and intertwisted in this life are occasions of

---

[6] James Hogg, *The Three Perils of Woman*, ed, David Groves, Antony Hasler, and Douglas S. Mack (Edinburgh: Edinburgh University Press, 1995), 254.

[7] Thomas Hope, *Anastasius, or, Memoirs of a Greek: Written at the Close of the Eighteenth Century* (London: John Murray, 1820), 3, 430.

[8] *London Magazine*, 1 (January 1820), 13.

[9] 'A Character of the Late Elia', *London Magazine*, 7 (January 1823), 21, and 'Death—Posthumous Memorials—Children', 3 (March 1821), 250, a piece written by Horace Smith.

[10] *London Magazine*, 1 (February 1820), 186, in John Scott's review of Hazlitt's *Lectures on the Literature of the Age of Elizabeth*.

[11] *Blackwood's Edinburgh Magazine*, 10 (August 1821), 72.

laughter and of tears'.[12] The 'very reprehensible way of jesting at times in the midst of [his] own misery' that de Quincey acknowledged in the next instalment of his Confessions was the capacity that specially fitted him to become a periodical writer, because such abrupt transitions are the stuff out of which magazines are made.[13] It is unsurprising that a magazine writer should have introduced the manner into poetry. Hazlitt praised *The Story of Rimini* for its manner of 'blending tears with smiles, the dancing of the spirits with sad forebodings, the intoxication of hope with bitter disappointment, youth with age, life and death together'.[14] Abrupt transitions defined the new acting style that Kean brought to the stage. Hazlitt remarked on 'the rapidity of his transitions from one tone and feeling to another'.[15] They are also the stuff from which Byron fashioned *Don Juan*: it was 'the sudden transition of this author from grave to humorous poetry' that best showed 'the compass of his power':[16] 'If he, or any man can be said to resemble Shakespeare in any particular', George Darley wrote in the *London*, 'it is in the faculty of passing from the solemn to the ludicrous, of dropping from the empyreal heights of fancy to the low concerns of reality,—in one stroke of the wing'.[17]

Don Juan was the most widely read poem of the age. As the *Monthly Magazine* allowed, 'scarcely any poem of the present day has been more generally read, or its continuation more eagerly and impatiently awaited',[18] which makes it odd that it should have been reviewed so seldom. In August 1821, the *Edinburgh Magazine* complained that 'two years have passed away, and such a publication has not been reprobated by either of the two leading Journals of the day'.[19] Murray's review, the *Quarterly*, could scarcely notice a poem that Murray himself disowned, withholding his name as publisher from the title page, but Jeffrey, too, judged the poem too scandalous to notice in the *Edinburgh*. *Blackwood's* offered the most striking exception to this policy of studied neglect. It noticed the poem repeatedly, not just reviewing each instalment as it was published, but returning to it again and again. J. G. Lockhart's reaction to the poem was so intense that it overflowed the columns of *Blackwood's* and issued in a separate publication, *John Bull's Letter to Lord Byron*. The *Blackwood's* responses are distinctive, too, by virtue of their being so very Byronic. They are, for example, startlingly inconsistent. Denunciations of *Don Juan* are themselves denounced in a subsequent number, and sometimes, as in

---

[12] *London Magazine*, 4 (September 1821), 298; Lindop, 2, 16–17.
[13] *London Magazine*, 4 (October 1821), 356; Lindop, 2, 43.
[14] *Edinburgh Review*, 26 (June 1816), 477. The review was first identified as Hazlitt's by Duncan Wu, *New Writings of William Hazlitt*, 2 vols. (Oxford: Oxford University Press, 2007).
[15] 'Mr Kean's Shylock', Howe, 5, 179.
[16] *Edinburgh Monthly Review*, 2 (October 1819), 481.
[17] *London Magazine*, n.s. 1 (January 1825), 82.
[18] *Monthly Magazine*, 56 (September 1823), 112. William St Clair estimates that it 'was read by more people in its first twenty years than any previous work of English literature'. See *The Reading Nation in the Romantic Period* (Cambridge: Cambridge University Press, 2004), 333.
[19] *Edinburgh Magazine and Literary Miscellany*, 9 (August 1821), 107.

John Bull's Letter, a single contribution veers erratically between the two postures. It was, of course Byron himself who had insisted on the virtue of holding opinions which are 'twin opposites': for 'if a writer should be quite consistent, / How could he possibly show things existent?' (*Don Juan*, 15, 87, 7–8).

Lockhart points out in *John Bull's Letter to Lord Byron* that Blackwood ('the *man* Blackwood, not the *thing* Blackwood,—the biblipole, not the magazine') had refused to stock *Don Juan* in his Edinburgh shop (Blackwood was motivated, it may be, less by moral considerations than a desire to retaliate against John Murray, who had withdrawn from his partnership with Blackwood because of his magazine's 'shameful personality'),[20] whereas, had Byron sent the poem to 'that well-known character Christopher North, Esq., with a request to have the Don inserted in his Magazine,—lives there that being with wit enough to keep him from putrefying, who doubts the great KIT would have smiled a sweet smile, and desired the right honourable guest to ascend into the most honourable place of the upper chamber of immortality?'[21] All the same, Lockhart rather often gives the impression that he agrees with William Blackwood's decision. The central charge that he brings against Byron is the accusation most commonly brought against *Don Juan*: 'With you heroism is lunacy, philosophy folly, virtue a cheat, and religion a bubble.'[22] But it is an odd charge when placed in a magazine that so often represents its mission as the deflation of pomposity and the exposure of humbug, pious humbug included. In *Beppo*, Lockhart insists in his *Blackwood's* review, Byron is guilty of indecorum, but again the charge is odd when it appears in a magazine that delights in breaches of decorum at least as flagrant. The point was well made in a review of Lockhart's *Letter to Lord Byron*, and it seems wholly appropriate that it should have been made in the review that appeared in *Blackwood's* itself. The reviewer remarks of the treatment of *Don Juan* in the magazine that 'furious paragraph after furious paragraph is written against a book nearly as clever as if they had written it themselves'.[23] Lockhart regularly responded to *Don Juan* with rage, but the rage was Caliban's on glimpsing his own reflection, and Lockhart seems half aware of it. It is significant that in summing up Byron's career some months after his death Lockhart concludes, 'There is no trick of self-love more common than that of ridiculing in others, the fault which we feel, and which we would fain have others not detect, in ourselves.'[24]

---

[20] *The Letters of John Murray to Lord Byron*, ed. Andrew Nicholson (Liverpool: Liverpool University Press, 2007), 319.

[21] J. G. Lockhart, *John Bull's Letter to Lord Byron*, ed. Alan Lang Strout (Norman: University of Oklahoma Press, 1947), 85.

[22] *Blackwood's Edinburgh Magazine*, 3 (June 1818), 326.

[23] *Blackwood's Edinburgh Magazine*, 9 (July 1821), 426. The review, in which Wilson scans Lockhart's pamphlet for evidence that its author is senile, impishly revises Lockhart's charge that in *Blackwood's* 'furious paragraph after furious paragraph is written against a book of which the whole knot would have been happy to club their brains to write one stanza'. *John Bull's Letter to Lord Byron*, 86.

[24] *Blackwood's Edinburgh Magazine*, 17 (February 1825), 136.

Blackwood's was at its most Byronic in the *Noctes Ambrosianae*. George Gilfillan claims of the *Noctes* that each is 'a miniature *Don Juan*, jerking you down at every point from the highest to the lowest reaches of feeling and thought', and more recent critics have agreed with him.[25] The series was launched in March 1822, with an episode written by Lockhart, in which he versifies the letter from Byron to his publisher in which Byron had defended *Cain* and insisted that the whole responsibility for the publication rested with him rather than with Murray. In his letter Byron protested, 'If "Cain" be "blasphemous," Paradise Lost is blasphemous, and the very words of the Oxford Gentleman [a pamphleteer who had attacked *Cain*], "Evil be thou my good," are from that very poem, from the mouth of Satan.'[26] This is sensible, but somewhat flat. Lockhart relegates the letter to a footnote, and re-writes it in the main text in couplets:

> But my poor shoulders why throw *all* the guilt on?
> There's as much blasphemy, or more, in Milton.[27]

This is not just sharper and more economical than Byron's prose, it is—and the effect is unnerving—more Byronic. The *Noctes Ambrosianae* repeatedly signal the affinity of the series with *Don Juan*. In the episode for April 1829, for example, Wilson characteristically registers a fond disgust at the visibility of Hogg's tongue, so 'deeply, darkly, beautifully red'. On the face of it, the expression parodies Southey's description of dolphins in *Madoc* as 'darkly, deeply, beautifully blue',[28] but the point of the joke is lost if the reader does not remember that Byron had borrowed the expression, misremembering how Southey had applied it:

> Oh 'darkly, deeply, beautifully blue',
>   As someone somewhere sings about the sky,
> And I, ye learned ladies, sing of you.
>
>   (*Don Juan*, 4, 110, 1–3)

The redness of Hogg's tongue is as lively an expression of Hogg's fleshly masculinity as the colour blue is of intellectual womanhood.

---

[25] See George Gilfillan, *A Gallery of Literary Portraits*, ed. W. Robertson Nicoll (London: Dent, 1927), 30; *The Tavern Sages*, ed. J. H. Alexander (Aberdeen: Aberdeen University Press, 1992), xii; and Robert Morrison, '*Blackwood's* Berserker, John Wilson and the Language of Extremity', *Romanticism on the Net*, 20 (November 2000) [accessed 24 July 2008] http://users.ox.ac.uk/ ~scat0385/20morrison.html; and *Blackwood's Magazine, 1817–25: Selections from Maga's Infancy*, 6 vols. (London: Pickering and Chatto, 2006), 3, *Noctes Ambrosianae, 1822–23*, ed. Mark Parker, Introduction, viii.

[26] *Byron's Letters and Journals*, ed. Leslie A. Marchand, 9 (London: John Murray, 1979), 103, but I quote the passage as given by Lockhart in the magazine.

[27] *Blackwood's Edinburgh Magazine*, 11 (March 1822), 376.

[28] *Blackwood's Edinburgh Magazine*, 25 (April 1829), 526, and Robert Southey, *Madoc*, Part 1, 993.

In the episode of the *Noctes Ambrosianae* for July 1822, in which Byron appears in person, Odoherty takes the opportunity to tax Byron with 'that very immoral work Don Juan': 'how you therein sport with the holiest ties—the most sacred feelings—the purest sentiments. In a word, with every thing—the bottle is with you—with every thing which raises a man above a mere sensual being.' As Mark Parker points out, the tiny parenthesis, 'the bottle is with you', does its work so well that it is no surprise at all when Odoherty later confesses that he would rather have written a stanza of *Don Juan* than the whole of *Childe Harold*.[29] The parenthesis reveals that for all Odoherty's concern for the 'holiest ties' he remains attentive to the needs of the body. Liquor marks the schism between mind and flesh on which the comedy of the *Noctes Ambrosianae*, like the comedy of *Don Juan*, is founded, though in Byron it is more often erotic desire that proves so wonderfully resistant to the mind's control:

> Love, constant love, has been my constant guest,
> And yet last night, being at a masquerade,
> I saw the prettiest creature, fresh from Milan,
> Which gave me some sensations like a villain.
>
> (*Don Juan*, 2, 209, 5–8)

Odoherty soon reverts to the darling topic of *Blackwood's*, its own excellence. Byron raises his glass to the 'immortal Kit North!!! !!! !!!', who has exposed the 'humbug' of all previous reviews and periodicals, and Odoherty explains how the feat was achieved: 'by doing all that ever these folks could do in one Number, and then undoing it in the next,—puffing, deriding, sneering, jeering, prosing, piping, and so forth'. In other words, it is precisely the capacity to advance an opinion—that *Don Juan* is an immoral work, say—and immediately afterwards to hold that kind of moralism up to ridicule, that marks *Blackwood's* superiority, and marks, too, its affinity with *Don Juan*. But *Blackwood's* was not the only magazine that registered its affinity with Byron's poem. John Scott, for example, writing in the *London*, denounced in the poem 'a sort of violence' produced by 'the quick alteration of pathos and profaneness,—of serious and moving sentiment and indecent ribaldry',[30] but he can scarcely have been wholly unaware that these are precisely the kind of quick alterations to which magazines, his own not least, regularly subject their readers, as their eyes are invited swiftly to scan the pages from one article to another.

Magazines are by definition miscellaneous. The *Blackwood's* innovation was to make the transition between contributions of different kinds sudden and unexpected. It was an effect that, as *Blackwood's* recognized, its chief competitors were anxious to imitate. As Mark Parker points out, John Scott's imitation of

---

[29] See *Blackwood's Edinburgh Magazine*, 12 (July 1822), 100–14, and *Blackwood's Magazine, 1817–25: Selections from Maga's Infancy*, 6 vols. (London: Pickering and Chatto, 2006), 3, *Noctes Ambrosianae, 1822–23*, ed. Mark Parker, Introduction, xxviii–xxix.

[30] *London Magazine*, 3 (January 1821), 56.

Blackwood's in the *London* extended even to format: both magazines consisted of 128 pages of double columns, and they used an identical type face.[31] Just as indebted was Thomas Campbell, editor of the *New Monthly* which owed its 'very breath, and being, and form, and substance, and life, to *imitation of Blackwood'*.[32] But Campbell, though he tries, fails to match his original for lack of able contributors:

> Then the New Monthly in its pomp appears,
> But weak, weak, weak—the thing will never do:—
> 'Essay on Hats,' and 'Chapter on Long Ears,'
> 'Sonnets,' 'The State of Learning in Peru,'
> 'Verses on Seeing a Lady Bathed in Tears;'
> Oh, gentle Campbell! What a thick-skull'd crew
> Art thou combin'd with!—it must surely grieve,
> To have such ninnies pinn'd upon your sleeve.[33]

The *New Monthly* can imitate the heterogeneousness of *Blackwood's*, but not its piquancy, and the point is made by casting its contents into the stanza of *Don Juan*. It is another tacit confession that magazines and Byron's poem shared an aesthetic, but, writers in *Blackwood's* seem sometimes to intimate, it was the magazine that got there first. Hence the frequency with which they cast doubt on Byron's claims to originality.

Sometimes they are content pointedly to refer to 'this new style of Frere's',[34] but on other occasions they trace a much more extended genealogy for the manner. On one occasion, Chaucer's *Troilus and Criseyde* is offered in proof of the contention that 'to the merit of originating the serio-comic style, or even of introducing it first to English literature, the noble author has no claim'.[35] To nominate Chaucer as the founder of the style carries, of course, another useful implication. Since Chaucer's position as the founding father of English poetry was unchallenged, the style that *Blackwood's* shared with *Don Juan* became, by implication, a style as distinctively English in the history of English letters as tragi-comedy in the tradition of English drama. Sometimes Byron was allowed his originality. For Lockhart, for example, the style of *Don Juan* is 'not much like the style of any other poem in the world'. It is 'utter humbug' to say that Byron

---

[31] Mark Parker, *Literary Magazines and British Romanticism* (Cambridge: Cambridge University press, 2000), 21.

[32] *Blackwood's Edinburgh Magazine*, 14 (August 1823), 230.

[33] D. M. Moir, 'Christmas Chit-Chat', *Blackwood's Edinburgh Magazine*, 10 (December 1821), 498, stanza 31.

[34] *Blackwood's Edinburgh Magazine*, 3 (July 1818), 404. The reference is to Frere's *The Monks and the Giants*, an imitation of the Italian ottava rima comic romances published by Frere in 1817 as the work of the brothers 'William and Robert Whistlecraft'. Byron was happy to acknowledge the influence of Frere's poem on his own.

[35] *Blackwood's Edinburgh Magazine*, 10 (October 1821), 5–8.

borrowed it from the Italians 'because they have nothing but their merriment' whereas Byron's fun is 'delightfully intermingled with and contrasted by all manner of serious things', and it is 'mere *humbug*' to accuse [Byron] of having plagiarized it from 'Mr Frere's pretty and graceful little Whistlecrafts'.[36] But here too the passage functions as a defence of the originality of Lockhart's magazine as much as of the poem.

The best indication of the affinity of the magazines with *Don Juan* is that so many of them began to produce their own Juanesque ottava rima poems so soon after July 1819, when the first two cantos of Byron's poem were published. In fact, the first of them, Lockhart's *The Mad Banker of Amsterdam*, began to appear even earlier, in July 1818, in the month that Byron began to write *Don Juan*, and a full year before the publication of its first two cantos.[37] There is no mystery here—Byron had published *Beppo* in February and Lockhart had denounced the poem in the June issue of *Blackwood's*: 'You have transferred into the higher departments of poetry (or you have at least endeavoured to transfer) that spirit of mockery, misanthropy, and contempt, which the great bards of elder times left to preside over the humbler walk of the satirist and the cynic.'[38] But even as he wrote this he must have recognized that Byron's new manner was ideally suited to the magazine. He points out in the first instalment of his poem one reason that this was so:

> But to return—(in this new style of Frere's
> A phrase which oft hath been, and oft must be.)[39]

Lockhart identifies the phrase 'to return' as the hallmark of the new style but only when introducing it into his poem for the third time. It is a phrase that characterizes the new kind of magazine just as well as the new kind of poem, and not just because the manner of both is digressive. 'The Mad Banker of Amsterdam' itself, for example, will return in the following issue, or after an absence of one, two or more issues, as will a piece of prose fiction, or all those other magazine features such as the *Noctes Ambrosianae* which appeared in an irregular series.

Lockhart's, or, in the fiction of the magazine, William Wastle's 'The Mad Banker of Amsterdam' transports its reader to Amsterdam, 'capital of smugness, and the Dutch', years before Byron's Juan was to pass through the 'waterland of Dutchmen and of ditches' (*Don Juan*, 10, 63, 2). Lockhart offers Amsterdam as the comic antithesis of Byron's Venice. It is a city where feminine beauty is

---

[36] J. G. Lockhart, *John Bull's Letter to Lord Byron*, 90–1.

[37] The poem appeared in four episodes; the first two cantos in *Blackwood's Edinburgh Magazine*, 3 (July 1818), 402–7; the fourth (the third was 'suppressed') in 3 (August 1818), 530–3; the fifth in 4 (February 1819), 563–7; and the last, the 'eighth' in 4 (March 1819), 729–34.

[38] *Blackwood's Edinburgh Magazine*, 3 (June 1818), 325.

[39] 'The Mad Banker of Amsterdam,' 2, xix, 1–2, *Blackwood's Edinburgh Magazine*, 3 (July 1818), 407.

understood to be in direct relation to girth, and where courtship takes place in a smoke-filled 'treckshuyt' rather than a gondola:

> it appears to me extremely funny,
>   To think one can't kiss any thing but Greeks,
> And Jewesses, and dark Italian dames,
>   Merely because they are Lord Byron's flames.[40]

But the story of a Dutch banker's courtship of a stout Dutch widow does not hold Lockhart's attention for long. The poem soon drifts back to Edinburgh. Its fourth canto (the third having been 'suppressed') revises the title as given in the first two, which had promised 'A Poem in Four Cantos', noting that this was a mistake for 'Twenty-Four'.[41] In the event, after one additional elegiac canto, numbered the eighth, on the downfall of Scotland and the Stuarts, it breaks off. But not before Lockhart has anticipated a number of the most distinctive features of *Don Juan*, not least its ever-expanding length:

> I thought, at setting off, about two dozen
>   Cantos would do; but at Apollo's pleading,
> If that my Pegasus should not be foundered,
>   I think to canter gently through a hundred. (*Don Juan*, 12, 55, 5–8)

More importantly, Lockhart matches Byron in self-consciousness. His poem may be offered as the work of 'William Wastle', but it includes a sketch of the membership of an Edinburgh club, 'The Dilettanti', among whom he identifies 'Lockhart (Gibson John) / So fond of jabbering about Tieck and Schlegel.' The joke is clinched in the following canto:

> The reading public very fiercely blame,
>   And with good reason too, as I opine,
> The introducing of one's real name
>   Into the pages of a magazine.[42]

Lockhart even predicts that the new manner will be disapproved of by the 'Blue-Stocking misses', who had done so much to secure Byron's popularity. They castigate Wastle for 'skipping you about from soft to hard, / Never perplexing him how one thing hinges / Upon another'.[43] Lockhart may claim that a taste for 'belles of large diameter' remains the same whether 'dressed in ottava-rima or hexameter',[44] but 'The Mad Banker of Amsterdam' demonstrates, as *Don Juan* will confirm, that on the contrary sentiments are never independent of the metre

---

[40] 'The Mad Banker of Amsterdam', 2, 19, 1–2, *Blackwood's Edinburgh Magazine*, 3 (June 1818), 325.

[41] *Blackwood's Edinburgh Magazine*, 3 (August 1818), 530 (note).

[42] ''The Mad Banker of Amsterdam', 2, 10, 1–4, *Blackwood's Edinburgh Magazine*, 3 (August 1818), 531.

[43] 'The Mad Banker of Amsterdam', 5, 1, 3–5, *Blackwood's Edinburgh Magazine*, 4 (February 1819), 563.

[44] 'The Mad Banker of Amsterdam', 1, 17, 7–8, *Blackwood's Edinburgh Magazine*, 3 (July 1818), 403.

in which they are expressed, although one trait distinctive of ottava rima is the disconcerting variety of sentiment that it is able to accommodate.

A letter 'postmarked Birmingham' appended to the fourth canto of 'The Mad Banker' (the playful suggestion is that it is from the radical Whig and classical scholar, Samuel Parr) claims that the new style was in fact invented by 'Ensign and adjutant Odoherty', but concedes that he has been surpassed by some of his imitators, in particular by 'Mr Frere, lord Byron, and a certain Scottish gentleman or laird, one Wastle'. Parr concludes, 'To this last I incline to refer the superiority, but they are all pleasant'.[45] The letter was doubtless supplied by Lockhart himself, but his confidence in his own performance did not survive the publication of *Don Juan*. Early in 1820 the 'Ettrick Shepherd' reports of Wastle that 'Don Juan has put him quite out of countenance with the Mad Banker, I now fear, he will never conclude.'[46] The challenge was taken up by other *Blackwood's* contributors, such as D. M. Moir, writing as Ensign Odoherty, who secured his independence of Byron by modifying the Byronic octave into a seven line stanza of his own (he has, we are probably meant to suppose, been infected with 'metromanie' by Keats):

> You see I'm tainted with the metromanie,
> And not a little proud of innovation;
> I'll have original verse as well as any,
> And not think there's any great occasion
> To write like Frere and Byron;—when the nation
> Talks of the seven line stanza, they shall cry,
> Aye—that's the stanza of Odoherty![47]

From Moir it passed to William Maginn who serialized in *Blackwood's* an Irish *Don Juan*, 'Daniel O'Rourke, an Epic Poem', written in collaboration with a Cork friend, Dr William Gosnell.[48] The poem tells the story in the desultory, Byronic manner of an evening in an Irish shebeen, the Mountain Daisy, and a trip to the moon that O'Rourke realizes at the last takes place only in a drunken dream. O'Rourke's journey prompts comparison with Wordsworth's aerial voyage in a boat shaped like a 'crescent-moon':

[45] *Blackwood's Edinburgh Magazine*, 3 (August 1818), 533.

[46] In a letter that appeared under Hogg's signature but was almost certainly written by Lockhart. See *Blackwood's Edinburgh Magazine*, 6 (January 1820), 390.

[47] Keats is diagnosed with 'Metromanie' in the fourth of Lockhart's papers on 'The Cockney School of Poetry,' *Blackwood's Edinburgh Magazine*, 3 (August 1818), 519. Moir's poem appears in *Blackwood's Edinburgh Magazine*, 8 (February 1821), 542.

[48] The poem appeared in six episodes, the first canto in *Blackwood's Edinburgh Magazine*, 7 (August 1820), 476–81; the second in 8 (October 1820), 40–5; the third in 8 (November 1820), 155–61; the fourth in 9 (April 1821), 77–85; the fifth in 9 (July 1821), 370–8; and the sixth in 10 (November 1821), 429–37.

(You'll find the flight described in Peter Bell,
    Published by Longman, Hurst, Rees, Orme, and Brown,
I own I like that poem passing well,
    Though by your wits 'tis laughed at and cried down.
Cheer up, Great Poet, loud thy fame will swell,
    When thy detractors' names shall be unknown,
When all forgotten is the tiny crew,
Who quiz thee in the Edinburgh review).[49]

The comedy comes from Wordsworth being celebrated rather than ridiculed in a Byronic octave, and it is heightened by the inclusion of details, the name of the publishing firm, that Byronic octaves digest so easily but that remain utterly incongruous with Wordsworth's own poetic manner.[50]

Maginn or Gosnell eventually brings the poem to a close because the Byronic metre has

              got much into disrepute,
    Since the last cantos of the Don were roll'd
    Forth on the world, good morals to pollute.[51]

But it was precisely the disrepute of *Don Juan* that seems to have attracted magazines to the measure. It is also, paradoxically, what gives the imitations their Byronic character. The author of the anonymous *Juan Secundus* is unqualified in his admiration for Byron:

His was a life of loneliness—and he
    Stood the proud monarch eagle of the rock,
His fearless eye fix'd on the raging sea
    That roar'd beneath, unruffled at the shock—
Viewing with scorn—with spirit bold as free,
    Dark hatred's frown—pale sick'ning envy's mock—
Greater 'mid every effort to confound him,
Brighter, thro' ev'ry cloud that low'r'd around him.[52]

It is precisely the single-mindedness of his hero-worship that makes it so thoroughly unByronic, or, at any rate, Byronic only in the manner that Byron dispenses with in *Don Juan*. *Blackwood's* treated the long-established and old-fashioned *Scots Magazine* with derisive condescension: 'The marriage list had a

---

[49] 'Daniel O'Rourke', Canto 3, stanza 17, *Blackwood's Edinburgh Magazine*, 8 (November 1820), 159.
    [50] References to Wordsworth constitute one of the running jokes of 'Daniel O'Rourke'. In a letter introducing the poem, its author 'Fogarty [misspelt Fagarty] O'Fogarty compares it to *Benjamin the Waggoner*. The moon in Fogarty's description of it recalls the pond in Wordsworth's 'The Thorn', 'Measuring across, exactly eight foot two / From side to side' ('Daniel O'Rourke, 4, 14, 3–4, *Blackwood's Edinburgh Magazine*, 9 (April 1821), 81).
    [51] 'Daniel O'Rourke', 6, 2, 2–4, *Blackwood's Edinburgh Magazine*, 10 (November 1829), 429.
    [52] *Juan Secundus* (London: John Miller, 1825), 17, stanza XXV.

high character, and, we believe, deservedly so—and the obituary was well conducted.'[53] But when the *Scots Magazine* made the assault on *Don Juan* that was to be expected of it, it did so in the form of a poem, 'The Silliad', and attacks on *Don Juan* that attempted the *Don Juan* stanza were always in danger of turning into embraces:

> Thou thinkst, whene'er thou wilt, to reascend
> By native vigour, and regain thy seat!
> Hope not!—for we no ear to thee will lend,
> Nor that illusion which was once so sweet
> Will more invest thy lays—there is an end!
> Britain no longer owns thee—'tis not meet
> Thou still should'st use her speech, but let thy line
> Run in the language of gross Aretine.
>
> Yes, grovel on in thy Venetian sty,
> Fit only to drain down the lowest dregs
> Of the corrupted cup of Italy:
> Go where loose courtesan loose sonnet begs—
> The poet of outlandish harlotry!—
> But now my verse is running off its legs—
> And meant for grave, may only produce laughter, all;—
> I wish the peccant Lord no mischief, after all.[54]

This is, as pastiche, delightfully incompetent, but precisely for that reason it shows more clearly than abler imitations the power of *Don Juan* to beguile its fiercest critics. Byron is solemnly disowned in one stanza only for the following stanza to make its peace with him. It is as if *Don Juan* unleashes a spirit of comic inclusiveness that seduces even those most outraged by the poem. A poem entitled in an intended irony *An Apology for 'Don Juan'* denounces Byron for his impiety, but, just like the writer in the *Scots Magazine*, its author finds the stanza turn against him:

> But, since ye boast of 'reason,' would ye use it
>   'Twould teach you that to him who made the soul,
> Ye owe obedience, and, should ye refuse it,—
>   Dispensing with such 'troublesome control,'
> Awhile ye triumph! But the Maker views it
>   With just displeasure—nor is this the whole:
> I'd have ye tremble for the consequences,
>   And think on what your future recompense is![55]

[53] *Blackwood's Edinburgh Magazine*, 8 (October 1820), 87.
[54] *The Scots Magazine and Edinburgh Literary Miscellany*, n.s. 84 (August 1819), 135.
[55] *An Apology for Don Juan* (London: T. Green, 1824), 14.

The couplet converts the stanza, evidently against its author's wishes, into a satire on the moral crudity of the 'Christian dogma rather rough' (*Don Juan*, 9, 25, 6) that sceptics should be consigned to hellfire. Or, to put the same thought differently, it is as if *Don Juan* cannot be repudiated single-mindedly in octaves because octaves refuse single-mindedness, which was exactly what persuaded so many magazines that they had a special affinity with 'this new style of Frere's'.

'Dan Duffe's Pilgrimage', which appeared in several issues of the *Edinburgh Magazine and Literary Miscellany* in 1823 travesties *Childe Harold* as well as *Don Juan* by transplanting the Byronic hero from the Mediterranean to the north east of Scotland, where, the climate being a good deal less sultry, Dan Duffe lives less expansively.[56] He attends King's College in Aberdeen, and then lives a reclusive bachelor life on land, fit for nothing but rough grazing, that he has inherited from an aunt. After living this life for forty years he embarks on a pilgrimage through his native region in the course of which he meets with remarkably few adventures. Duffe's celibacy counters Juan's more susceptible nature, Byron's citrus groves are replaced by the industrial landscapes of the Don valley with its 'mills for threads and mills for paper, / And iron foundries making uncouth noise'.[57] But here too parody is always likely to melt into admiring imitation:

> There is a cliff hard by, whose front appears
>   Proud in the bold presumption of its station,
> And in whose crannies, for a thousand years,
>   The sea-fowls have maintained their habitation.
> There the fond mother, in her season, rears
>   'Love's pledges,' by a patient incubation:—
> 'Tis a fine place to study ornithology,
> So, also, is the sea-beach for conchology.[58]

The Byronic sublime slips into the comic sentimentalism of the 'fond mother' whose chicks are 'Love's pledges', before the cliff and the beach it overlooks are transformed into magnets for all those educated nineteenth-century people wishing to indulge their newly acquired interest in natural history. It was Byron who had taught how a stanza might turn not so much on a landscape as on the different ways of looking at it, and it is a lesson to which the poet of 'Dan Duffe's Pilgrimage' is so receptive because of the particular literary apprenticeship he had served: 'Nurs'd in a weekly newspaper was he, / And in a magazine provincial cradled'.[59] His magazine training makes it no surprise that Duffe should be attuned to seeing the world not singly but as a miscellany.

---

[56] The poem appeared in four episodes; the first in the *Edinburgh Magazine and Literary Miscellany*, 12 (January 1823), 60–5; the second in 12 (March 1823), 310–15); the third in 12 (April 1823), 424–9; and the fourth in 13 (July 1823), 45–50.

[57] *Edinburgh Magazine and Literary Miscellany*, 12 (January 1823), 62.

[58] *Edinburgh Magazine and Literary Miscellany*, 12 (March 1823), 313–14.

[59] *Edinburgh Magazine and Literary Miscellany*, 12 (January 1823), 61.

John Moultrie's 'Godiva', when it was published in *The Etonian*, was thought by some too Juanish a poem to be safely included in a school magazine.[60] Moultrie inserted in a later number some newly discovered stanzas of the poem in which he reasserts his moral rectitude:

> This by the way. I sometimes step aside,
>   As Poets always should, to give advice;
> They are the world's instructors,—and should hide
>   In trope and figure many a precept nice;
> Morals and maxims they should all provide,
>   And homilies for every sort of vice;
> They should lash vice, and honour virtue too,
> In short do all that Byron scorns to do.[61]

Byron is repudiated, but what does it mean to repudiate Byron in a stanza that, as if in spite of itself, seems to qualify all its most upright assertions with an ironic disclaimer? Moultrie is an interesting case. After a brilliant youth at Eton and at Trinity, where his closest associates were his old school friend, W. M. Praed, Derwent Coleridge, and Macaulay, Moultrie first read for the Bar, but, finding himself unsuited to the profession, chose instead to take orders. In 1828 he became Rector of Rugby, a post that he retained for the rest of his life. In his manhood, after some years of silence, he began once again to write poems, encouraged by the example of Henry Alford, whose *School of the Heart*, a Wordsworthian autobiographical poem, inspired Moultrie's own Wordsworthian autobiographical *The Dream of Life*.[62] It is clear that he came to regret his youthful Byronic poems, 'Godiva' published in *The Etonian* and 'La Belle Tryamour' in *Knight's Quarterly Miscellany*.[63] In a poem to Alford he lamented the 'rash misuse' he had made of his gifts. Failing to recognize

> The obligation of a higher law
> Than my own will, I travell'd uncontroll'd
> Through all the fields of song, as fancy led,
> Or passionate caprice, from idle hearts
> Winning vain praise, and solacing my own
> With what was wasting all its better strength.[64]

It was a thought that had occurred to him even in his rash youth. He introduces the second canto of 'La Belle Tryamour' with stanzas promising that in future his 'song shall be attuned' to 'loftier music', failing which he will remain 'mute for

---

[60] See the review of *The Etonian* in the *Quarterly Review*, 25 (April 1821), 95–112.

[61] *The Etonian*, 3, 97.

[62] On *The School of the Heart*, see my *Romantic Victorians: English Literature, 1824–1840* (Basingstoke: Palgrave, 2002), 247–50.

[63] 'La Belle Tryamour' appeared, in *Knight's Quarterly Miscellany*, 1 (June 1823), 145–79 and 1 (October 1823), 378–418.

[64] From 'To Henry Alford,' in John Moultrie, *Poems* (London: William Pickering, 1837), 89.

ever'.[65] As early as 1823 he recognized that the moral climate was changing. Writing as 'Vyvyan Joyeuse' he comments on the change in a particularly sprightly octave:

> Your ladyship of course is well aware
>   That love and laughter, mirth and immorality,
> Satan and Shakespeare, sin and Adam Blair,
>   Are quite exploded from the folks of quality;
> The great, the gay, the learned and the fair,
>   Return at last to prudence and formality;
> And reverence, as their fathers did before 'em,
> Dry bread, dry talk, cold water, and decorum.[66]

As a young man Moultrie was an admirer of Shelley, a 'vast, though erring spirit,' and of Keats, 'him who sung so well—/ Of slain Lorenzo and his Isabel!'—rather than of Byron. Byron, by contrast with Keats and Shelley, was 'the jaded rake / The heartless bard, the hoary debauchee'.[67] But it is only when he writes under Byron's auspices that he is a poet to reckon with. This much is evident even when he is paying tribute to Wordsworth:

> 'Wisdom doth live with children round her knees,'
>   Says Wordsworth; and he says what's very true;
> But, then, to nurse the children, if you please,
>   I'd rather have the children's mother too.[68]

Moultrie wrote well for that brief period when he freed himself to write against his better judgement, and his was a cultural rather than simply a personal case. This whole book is an attempt to trace that same moment in the history of English literature.

One of the most representative poets of these years, though little read these days, is Barry Cornwall. Byron had kindly feelings for Barry Cornwall. Under his real name, Bryan Procter, he had been an 'old schoolfellow' of Byron's at Harrow. This was promising, but the promise was offset by his association with the Cockneys: 'Barry Cornwall will do better by & bye—I dare say—if he don't get spoiled by green tea—and the praises of Pentonville—& Paradise Row.' His problem was that, unlike Moore and Byron himself, 'the one by circumstances & the other by birth', who had 'entered into its pulses and passions', Cornwall and his ilk knew high life 'merely as *spectators*'.[69] But even becoming the object of a

[65] *Knight's Quarterly Magazine*, 1 (October 1823), 378–82.
[66] *Knight's Quarterly Magazine*, 1, 232. The stanza form suggests that this was written by Moultrie but the stanza may equally well have been supplied by Praed.
[67] *Knight's Quarterly Magazine*, 1 (October 1823), 385, 410, and 385.
[68] *Knight's Quarterly Magazine*, 1 (June 1823), 151.
[69] *Byron's Letters and Journals*, ed. Leslie A. Marchand, 8 (London: John Murray, 1978), 207.

condescension so lordly was not enough to persuade Barry Cornwall that the *Don Juan* manner was not for him.

A Sicilian Story, published in 1820, is a Cockney volume,[70] its title poem a less ghastly version of the same tale from Boccaccio that Keats uses for 'Isabella' (Cornwall substitutes for the head of the murdered lover a more decorous heart), but Cornwall also finds room in the volume for 'Gyges' and 'Diego de Montilla', two exercises in ottava rima. Cornwall insists that he will not so much as glance 'to the left and right, / To see how others touch this style and metre' ('Gyges', 10, 3–4):

> I'll even keep Lord Byron out of sight.
>   By the bye, Lord B. and I were school'd together
> At Harrow where, as here, he has a name.
>   I—I'm not even on the list of fame.
>
>   ('Gyges', 10, 5–8)

In fact, Byron never leaves his field of vision. Cornwall plunders rhymes from him—'boys suffering 'neath the lash of Cupid, / Are sometimes even more than sad, they're stupid' ('Diego de Montilla', 30, 7–8, compare *Don Juan*, 1, 55, 7–8)—although he does not manage to make off with the joke that Byron's rhyme points. A similar bathos results when he repeats Byron's rhyming of 'Cadiz' and 'ladies' (*Don Juan*, 1, 190, 7–8, and 2, 5, 1 and 5):

> And then he added he should go to Cadiz,
> To see the place, and how he lik'd the ladies.
>
>   ('Diego de Montilla', 41, 7–8)

But the pilfering of rhymes is only a minor symptom of Cornwall's imitative ambitions. He tries to rival Byron's confident sexual connoisseurship:

> I'd have her eyes dark as the summer night,
>   When Dian sleeps, and fair the planets roll
> Along their golden journeys: 'tis a sight
>   That comes like—like—I mean that, on the whole,
> It touches and, as 'twere, transports one quite,
>   And makes one feel that one must have a soul;
> And then our wits go wandering from their ways,
> Wild, and 'wool-gathering,' as the proverb says.
>
>   ('Gyges', 6)

He follows Byron in his mock-intimacies with the reader—'The Don Diego (mind this, Don Dieygo: / Pronounce it rightly)' ('Diego de Montilla' (14, 1–2))—and in his swift tonal shifts:

> I never saw a fault in women yet:
>   Their bodies and their minds are full of grace:
> Sometimes indeed their tongue—but I forget . . .
>
>   ('Gyges', 8, 1–3)

---

[70] Barry Cornwall, *A Sicilian Story* (London: C. and J. Ollier, 1820).

And of course he follows Byron in his digressive manner: 'But I am prating /
While th'reader and Diego, both, are waiting.' ('Diego de Montilla', 11, 7–8).
But he is not simply imitative. For example, he allows his own Cockneyisms to
infiltrate the Byronic. When Gyges accepts the King's invitation to gaze on his
naked Queen, the scene is rendered with an embarrassed and embarrassing erotic
intensity, in debt not to Byron but the Keats of 'The Eve of St Agnes':

> The boy came (guided by the king) to where,
>   In the most deep and silent hour of night,
> Stood Lais: quite unloos'd, her golden hair
>   Went streaming all about like lines of light
> And, thro' the lattice-leaves gusts of soft air
>   Sighed like perfume, and touched her shoulders white,
> And o'er her tresses and her bosom played,
> Seeming to love each place o'er which they strayed.
>
> Then sank she on her couch and drew aside
>   The silken curtains and let in the moon,
> Which trembling ran around the chamber wide,
>   Kissing and flooding the rich flowers which June
> Had fann'd to life, and which in summer-pride
>   Rose like a queen's companions. Lais soon,
> Touch'd by the scene, look'd as she had forgot
> The world: the boy stood rooted to the spot.
>
>   ('Gyges', 29–30)

When he imagines his ideal mate, Cornwall makes room for the kind of
celebration of suburban domesticities associated with Leigh Hunt:

> Oh! we would turn some pleasant page together,
>   And 'plaud the wit, the tale, the poet's tropes,
> Or, wandering in the early summer weather,
>   Talk of the past mischance and future hopes,
> Or ride at times, (and that would save shoe-leather,)
>   For nought so well with nervous humours copes
> As riding; i. e. taken by degrees;
> It warms the blood, and saves all doctor's fees.
>
>   ('Gyges,' 19)

The poem is, as Jeffrey pointed out in his review of it, 'an imitation of Don
Juan',[71] but it is also an experiment to gauge how far it is possible to accommodate within the Byronic manner a Cockney aesthetic that would seem to be
inimical to it. Except, of course, that, as Cornwall knew very well, it was *Don
Juan* itself that had created the fashion for poetical gallimaufries, hodgepodges
that brought together apparently incongruous materials:

[71] *Edinburgh Review*, 33 (January 1820), 154.

> Bards have a pleasant method, I must say,
> Of mixing up their songs in this lax age.
> Now, sweet and sharp and luscious dash'd with gay
> (Like Christmas puddings, laurell'd,) are the rage ...

> ('Gyges', 12, 1–4)[72]

In other words, *Don Juan* created a vogue for magazine poetry—not poetry that appeared in magazines, but poetry that offered the same piquant mixture that readers enjoyed in *Blackwood's*, and in the *London*, and in the *New Monthly*.

It seemed to many not so much a characteristic of Byron as of his stanza:

> The octave rhyme (Ital. ottava rima)
> Is a delightful measure made of ease
> Turn'd up with epigram.

> ('Diego de Montilla', 1, 1–3)

It is a stanza in which 'triplets chime / Smoothly' ('Gyges', 1, 4–5) only to be pulled up sharp by a couplet. That inbuilt dissonance between the first six lines and closing couplet of each stanza ensures that the measure may 'equally adapt to pleasure, / To war, wit, love, or grief, or mock-sublime' ('Gyges', 1, 5–6). Or rather it is a measure particularly well adapted to poems that make quick transitions between all of these. It is the proper measure of the brief period in which poems aspired to be like magazines.

---

[72] In fact, it was precisely this characteristic of the poetry that Byron objected to. *A Sicilian Story*, like Cornwall's *Marcian Colonna*, were 'spoilt by I know not what affectation of Wordsworth—and Hunt—and Moore—and Myself—all mixed up into a kind of Chaos'. *Byron's Letters and Journals*, 8, 56. *Blackwood's* was more sympathetic: Cornwall's two poems 'both aim at those sudden contrasts and mixtures of imagery and sentiment characteristic of the old models, and of Byron, Frere, and Wastle.' *Blackwood's Edinburgh Magazine*, 6 (March 1820), 147. Jeffrey thought likewise. Barry Cornwall may have 'flung himself fairly into the arms of Lord Byron, Coleridge, Wordsworth, and Leigh Hunt', and this might seem to make for 'rather a violent transition' but in fact 'the materials really harmonize very tolerably.' *Edinburgh Review*, 33 (January 1820), 144–5.

10

Cruel Mockeries

Had Walter Scott known of Lockhart's quarrel with John Scott before matters had gone too far, he would have advised against 'stirring such a dish of skim'd milk as this creature is with any proposal to an honourable action'. He adverted only truculently to the coincidence that Lockhart's antagonist was his namesake: 'As to my clan I comfort myself first that he is no true border Scot but some mongrel from about Aberdeen and secondly that our very true proverb says it is a poor Clan that has neither whore nor thief in it.' When Lockhart returned to Edinburgh, his challenge refused, Walter Scott gloatingly concluded that John Scott had shown himself to be a man who 'blusterd when at a distance and when Lockhart applied to him seriously shirked most pitifully and sate down under the handsome appellatives of scoundrel and liar'. Even John Scott's death failed to soften him:

It would be great hypocrisy in me to say I am sorry for John Scott. He has got exactly what he was long fishing for and I think it probable the incident will diminish the license of the periodical press so far as private character is concerned.[1]

Marion Lochhead, Lockhart's biographer, describes these letters as 'deplorable, and utterly unworthy of the most magnanimous of men',[2] but she is too severe. None of us has more than a limited stock of sympathy, and at this moment Scott was drawing heavily on his on behalf of his son-in-law, and of J. H. Christie, who had fired the fatal bullet and faced trial for murder. He spoke brutally of John Scott, because he could not, at the time, afford to respond more sensitively. He was writing private letters to close friends, and could dispense with proprieties.

A youthful Jane Austen wrote to her sister Cassandra, 'Mrs Hall of Sherbourn was brought to bed yesterday of a dead child, some weeks before she expected, owing to a fright.—I suppose she happened unawares to look at her husband.'[3] She was not betraying her callousness but making a special kind of joke, a joke that at once depended on and fostered an intimacy with her sister that guaranteed her against being misunderstood. In her published novels she avoids such

---

[1] *The Letters of Sir Walter Scott*, ed. H. J. C. Grierson, 12 vols. (London: Constable, 1932–7), 6, 342, 348, and 374.

[2] Marion Lochhead, *John Gibson Lockhart* (London: John Murray, 1954), 84.

[3] *Jane Austen's Letters*, ed. Deirdre LeFaye, 3rd edn (Oxford: Oxford University Press, 1995), 17.

remarks, except perhaps in *Persuasion* when she allows herself to mock a mother's grief for her dead son, or, as she puts it, Mrs Musgrove's 'large fat sighings over the destiny of a son, whom alive nobody had cared for'.[4] Had Austen lived, that sentence may have disappeared in revision, but there is a similar robustness in the response in *Emma* to the death of Mrs Churchill: 'Goldsmith tells us, that when lovely woman stoops to folly, she has nothing to do but to die; and when she stoops to be disagreeable, it is equally to be recommended as a clearer of ill-fame.'[5] It may be that in her last novels Austen was alert to a new callousness in the literary culture of the post-war years, that revealed itself in the production of writing that was apt to forge a bond with its readership by advertising its insensitivity.

The only novelist to rival Scott's success in these years was Pierce Egan, whose *Life in London*, first issued in monthly numbers in 1820–1, was, like so many of Scott's novels, as successful on the stage as it was in print. Sterne is the very first writer whose inspiration Egan begs in the preamble to his novel, and it ends, in a homage to *A Sentimental Journey*, with a sexual equivoque carried in a dash,[6] but Egan is, for all that, a pathologically unfeeling writer. His hero, Corinthian Tom, may dissolve into 'paroxysms of grief' when the death of his father leaves him an orphan, but Egan seems almost embarrassed to note it: 'None of my readers, I feel assured, will complain of a loss of time, in witnessing Tom shed a few drops of sensibility over the remains of the author of his existence' (80–1). Once that is established, neither Tom nor Egan give the father another thought. The novel is dedicated to the project of 'SEEING LIFE' (23), in particular the life of London, as it is exhibited by Tom to his country cousin Jerry Hawthorn, and it consistently invites the reader to inspect the sights of London with a cool, spectatorial detachment. The effect is enhanced by the plates by the Cruikshank brothers, which Egan repeatedly invites his readers to inspect and admire, and by Egan's frenetic typography. He claims to gather his inspiration from life rather than literature, or, as he puts it, to offer his readers (141)

That *grand living* BOOK of BOOKS
MAN!!!

[4] Jane Austen, *Persuasion*, ed. Janet Todd and Antje Blank (Cambridge: Cambridge University Press, 2006), 73.
[5] Jane Austen, *Emma*, ed. Richard Cronin and Dorothy McMillan (Cambridge: Cambridge University Press, 2005), 422.
[6] Jerry entrusts his cousin, Tom, with a message: 'Mention me in the kindest manner to the lovely SUE: tell her I am only gone into *training*, and in the course of a few weeks I shall most certainly return to London to enjoy a few more *Sprees* (which I have so unexpectedly been deprived of) and also to have with her the pleasure of another game of —', Pierce Egan, *Life in London; or, The day and night scenes of Jerry Hawthorn, esq. and his elegant friend Corinthian Tom, accompanied by Bob Logic, the Oxonian, in their rambles and sprees through the metropolis* (London: Sherwood, Jones and Co., 1823), 376. Subsequent page references are included in the text.

In seven words, he centres, uses italics, a triple exclamation mark, and capitals of three different sizes, and the effect is to negate the claim. The novel's readers are never allowed to forget that they are separated from the life of the metropolis by the medium through which they view it, through print, which, in Egan's hands, is very far from being a transparent medium.

The book has a rudimentary ethic—it subscribes to a simple, hearty code of masculine honour which allows a man to keep a mistress but not to seduce the wife or daughter of a friend, to father an illegitimate child but not to refuse the child financial support, to black a watchman's eye but to be prepared to pay him for the privilege. The 'sprees' Tom and Jerry enjoy are remarkably free from consequences. They both, it is true, become physically debilitated, but their doctor assures them that to recruit their health they need only repair to the country for a few weeks. Bob Logic ends the novel dunned and confined to the Fleet, but his predicament is simply a source of merriment both to himself and his friends. Tom quips, 'we shall always be sure now to find you "at home"' (348). London becomes in Egan's hands rather like the world that Lamb found in 'the artificial comedy of the last century', a place magically free from 'laws or conscientious restraints'.[7] Egan's method is to juxtapose scenes from high and low life, to move abruptly 'from the high-mettled CORINTHIAN of St James's, *swaddled* in luxury, down to the *needy* FLUE FAKER of Wapping, *born without a shirt*, and not *a bit of scran* in his cup to allay his piteous cravings' (24). Readers are encouraged to respond to scenes of both sorts with the undiscriminating pleasure displayed by Tom and Jerry themselves. Tom is a Corinthian because he is a citizen of the whole city, equally happy 'whether he was animatedly engaged in squeezing the hand of some lovely countess of St James's, or passing an hour with a poor custard-monger in the back settlements of St Giles's' (44). For Tom and Jerry all the sights of London seem somehow of equal interest; 'taking a turn in the evening to listen to Coleridge, Flaxman, and Soane' (29) is an activity on precisely the same level as a visit to Newgate on the morning of an execution, to the dog-pit to watch the famous monkey Jacoo take on the dogs, or to the Royal Academy exhibition at Somerset House, a visit to which is, as Bob Logic, Tom's Oxonian friend, insists, always 'a bob well laid out' (339).

Differences in *Life in London* are aesthetic rather than moral. They result in a kind of chiaroscuro: 'the contrasts' that give the book its one structural principle 'are so fine and delightful—so marked with light and shade' (36). Even scenes that seem to demand an ethical response contrive somehow to refuse it. In the plate depicting the Fleet, for example, Egan draws his reader's attention to 'the poor, honest, but almost broken-hearted TRADESMAN, near the door, upon whose face misery is so strongly depicted, surrounded by his unhappy, but faithful wife and two children'. The tradesman is 'listening to the affecting information that

---

[7] *London Magazine*, 5 (April 1822), 306. The paper, 'The Old Actors', was published in *The Essays of Elia* under the title 'On the Artificial Comedy of the Last Century'.

she has *pledged* the last article she had left (his waistcoat) for only eight-pence, in order to purchase her a loaf'. But any disposition the reader may have to be affected is at once checked: 'This is a rich little bit, and equal to any thing of *Hogarth's*, for its fidelity to nature and truth' (354).[8] Sometimes the reader's sympathies are more actively discouraged. Jerry's introduction to London life reaches its 'climax' (346) when Tom takes him to spend an evening with the cadgers, that is, the street beggars of the city. Every evening, we are given to understand, the cadgers return to their favourite public house, where they are free to dispense with their daytime identities: 'the *Beggar* who has been writhing to and fro all the day, in the public streets, in terrific agony, to excite your charity and torture your feelings, here meets his fellows to laugh at the flats, count over his gains, and sit down to a rich supper' (343). Both text and plate depict a scene of riotous mirth. One cadger, who spurns the scraps of food given him during the day, is 'blowing up the cook for sending in his rump-steaks without the garnish of pickles and horse-radish' (343–4). The absurd notion that the city's beggars are prosperous rogues, is supported solely by a note reporting that once, when a magistrate ordered a beggar to be searched, twenty-five shillings were found in his pockets (343–4), but it is a fiction on which the whole episode relies, because it frees the reader from any obligation to respond with pity to the beggars' predicament. Urban poverty, the great ugly fact of London life, is exposed as an elaborate mummery. When they dress in rags to spend an evening with the cadgers, Tom and Jerry are freed to become amused spectators, just as they were earlier when they attended a performance of *Don Giovanni* at Drury Lane. So, too, is the reader.

Life in London is an extreme case, but successful novels of the period often check the reader's sympathetic responses. In *Anastasius*, for example, Thomas Hope's narrator confesses that he has consistently 'sought the amusement of describing scenes beheld, rather than the occupation of analysing sentiments experienced', content to exhibit himself rather as 'an unconcerned spectator in the world's motley drama, than as an actor very deeply concerned in the plot'. He will not find readers, he acknowledges, in the crumbling Ottoman empire where the action of the novel takes place, but among 'those strangers of the west, who, from their distant corner of the globe, watch the inhabitants of the more genial zones, as children do a worm, to wonder at its motions, and to thank God that they are formed of other mould'.[9] The most popular novelist of them all, Walter Scott, though he could scarcely be accused of regarding his fellow human beings 'as children do a worm', often discourages excessive sympathy for his characters as an injurious self-indulgence. In the very first novel, *Waverley*, for example, he spares his young hero, when he casts a 'dubious look' backwards as he rides south

---

[8] In fact, the Cruikshanks do not supply a plate of this scene, though Egan seems to expect one.
[9] Thomas Hope, *Anastasius, or, Memoirs of a Greek Written at the Close of the Eighteenth Century* (London: John Murray, 1820), 3, 221–3.

from Carlisle, any glimpse of the impaled head of Fergus Mac-Ivor. As Alick Polwarth explains, 'The heads are ower the Scotch yate.' Instead, Fergus's memorial is a painting in which he appears with Waverley posed in 'a wild, rocky, and mountainous pass, down which the clan were descending': 'Raeburn himself (whose Highland Chiefs do all but walk out of the canvas) could not have done more justice to the subject.' Scott's point is that the happiness of his young hero and the stability of the nation alike depend on a principled forgetting of the violence through which history so often unfolds. The nation must repair itself, just as the Bears of Tully-Veolan must be 'renewed or repaired with so much care, that they bore no tokens of the violence which had so lately descended upon them'.[10] The London artist translates the executed Fergus into paint, just as Scott himself translates the savage history of the '45 into a picturesque novel. In both cases historical violence is aestheticized, but it is aestheticized so that it can be the more easily accommodated. Scott's procedure could not be confused with the impulse that leads Egan to describe the ruined tradesman and his wife as 'a rich little bit, and equal to any thing of *Hogarth's*', but it is akin.

Similar effects are repeated in much of Scott's fiction. The moment of deepest pathos in *The Antiquary* comes with the death and funeral of the young fisherman, Steenie Mucklebackit, who has perished at sea. Oldbuck, entering the cottage, sees the father sunk in a bitter grief that he cannot speak, the mother with an apron over her head that fails to conceal the 'convulsive agitation of her bosom', the children, their grief moderated by wonder at the strangeness of the spectacle, and the grandmother, who may, or may not grasp what has happened. But, as Oldbuck enters, the author addresses the reader: 'in the inside of the cottage was a scene, which our Wilkie alone could have painted, with that exquisite feeling of nature that characterizes his enchanting productions'.[11] At moments of high emotional intensity in Scott's novels the characters are often frozen into tableaux, and the reader invited to regard them as if they composed a genre painting, or as if they were characters disposed on a stage. The effect is oddly distancing: it teases the reader to recall that these are not real people at all, only figures in a novel. The historical distance, the lapse of years that separates the reader from the characters who inhabit the fiction, reinforces the effect, and, as Scott's extraordinary, unprecedented popularity indicates, it was an effect that his contemporaries prized. It was often imitated. In *Valerius*, his son-on-law, Lockhart, describes the heroic martyrdom of Tisias of Antioch, and then reviews the sketches in which a painter recorded the same event: 'the muscles showed powerfully when he knelt;—there again, you have his fingers as they were folded

---

[10] Walter Scott, *Waverley*, ed. Claire Lamont (Oxford: Oxford University Press, 1986), 329, 338, and 334.
[11] Walter Scott, *The Antiquary*, ed. David Hewitt (Edinburgh: Edinburgh University Press, 1995), 247.

on his breast—not much flesh, but the lines good—veins well expressed'.[12] This is lightly satirical but Lockhart's novel most often shares the painter's way of looking. It prizes second-century Christianity for its distanced, formal, aesthetic charm.

History is best contemplated by those able to moderate their emotional responses, and the same might be said, as *Life in London* suggests, of the city. Cities are most fully enjoyed by those who can regard them as a kind of theatre in the round, and this is so even for a writer so tempted by sentimentality as Charles Lamb. What Elia admires most in comic acting is a certain unreality, of a kind that allows a character in Congreve to admit that he had forgotten that his brother was dead without at all prompting the audience to flinch at his callous insensitivity,[13] and this is the taste that stays with him when he leaves the London theatres for the London streets. In an early letter he pays a characteristic tribute to London:

Streets, streets, streets, markets, theatres, churches, Covent Gardens, shops sparkling with pretty faces of industrious milliners, neat sempstresses, ladies cheapening, gentlemen behind counters lying, authors in the street with spectacles, George Dyers (you may know them by their gait), lamps lit at night, pastry-cooks' and silver-smiths' shops, beautiful Quakers of Pentonville, noise of coaches, drowsy cry of mechanic watchman at night, with bucks reeling home drunk.[14]

This, Lamb writes, is the 'furniture of [his] world—eye-pampering but satisfies no heart'. The 'but' is misleading: such sights pamper precisely because they do not make any uncomfortably peremptory appeals to the heart. Lamb can take that impartial pleasure in any and every spectacle that London affords only because his gaze remains heartless. In his later career as an essayist, he even regrets the removal from the London streets of beggars because they were 'among her shows, her museums, and supplies for ever-gaping curiosity', and it is precisely its provision of such supplies that defines for Elia what London is: 'and what else but an accumulation of sights—endless sights—*is* a great city; or for what else is it desirable?' A beggar who had lost both his legs in the Gordon riots is, for Elia, a prized museum exhibit, 'a grand fragment; as good as an Elgin marble'.[15]

Lamb's prose may be utterly different from Egan's, but the two men look at beggars in rather similar ways. In the plate depicting Tom and Jerry's evening with the Cadgers, the Cruikshanks included portraits of a number of well-known beggars who are identified by Egan in his text. These beggars found themselves quite literally made into pictures, and offered up to Egan's readers for their

---

[12] J. G. Lockhart, *Valerius: A Roman Story* (Edinburgh: Blackwood, 1869), 194.

[13] In 'On Some of the Old Actors,' *London Magazine*, 5 (February 1822), 178–9.

[14] *The Works of Charles and Mary Lamb*, ed. E. V. Lucas, 7 vols. (London: Methuen, 1905), 6, 194–5.

[15] 'A Complaint of the Decay of Beggars in the Metropolis, *London Magazine*, 5 (June 1822), 532–6.

delighted contemplation. In the most successful stage production of the novel, at the Adelphi, the effect was enhanced. In their plate the Cruikshanks had included amongst the cadgers 'Little Jemmy' Whiston, a cripple who propelled himself along the pavement using a little cart with wheels, a well-known figure who usually conducted his trade on Blackfriars Bridge. In the stage production the role was taken by an actor, and Whiston, it seems, was delighted, finding that his takings greatly increased. The Cruikshanks also depicted Billy Waters, a black beggar popularly reputed to have been born an African prince, and he was played on stage by himself, completing the identification of person and theatrical character.[16] Lamb shares this way of seeing. His chimney sweeps are not like Blake's pitiable victims, they are masquers in the great performance of London life: when a sweep smiles, and teeth, dazzlingly white by contrast, appear in the midst of his black face, it seems to Elia 'an allowable piece of foppery', and he is reminded of lines from a masque, from *Comus*: 'A sable cloud / Turns forth her silver lining on the night.'[17] Cyrus Redding seems to have Lamb particularly in mind when he numbers among the unfortunate characteristics of the Cockney school the notion that to 'suppress mendicity was to stifle the poetry of life and obliterate its picturesqueness'.[18]

Lamb was writing for magazines, and there was a close affinity between the magazine genre and the kind of writing that I am trying to describe. The new way of reading that magazines encouraged, skimming, dipping, skipping through the pages, obstructed deep responses, as did their miscellaneous character. The *London Magazine* had championed Keats against his detractors, and yet the solemnity with which the magazine recorded his death is unexpectedly qualified when the death is reported as the leading item in a column called 'Town Conversation'.[19] Magazines repeatedly reproduce such effects: it is, it may be, an inevitable by-product of the magazine format. The papers that they bring together remain discrete, so that they often impress the reader as heartlessly unaware of each other. In the *London* for April 1821, for example, the editorial, 'The Lion's Head', sadly reports John Scott's death and announces the subscription that has been set up for his wife and two children, and is immediately followed by 'All Fools' Day', in which Lamb celebrates 1 April as the day that memorializes each year the folly, the absurdity of the world.[20] In September 1821, the 'Monthly Register' reported the death of the Queen and then prepared to describe the enthusiastic reception of the King in Ireland: 'We have now to

[16] See J. C. Reid, *Bucks and Bruisers: Pierce Egan and Regency England* (London: Routledge and Kegan Paul, 1971), 80.

[17] 'The Praise of Chimney-Sweepers: A May-Day Effusion', *London Magazine*, 5 (May 1822), 405–8, 407. Lamb quotes Milton's *Comus*, 222–3.

[18] Cyrus Redding, *Fifty Years' Recollections, Literary and Personal*, 3 vols. (London: Charles J. Skeet, 1858), 2, 184.

[19] *London Magazine*, 3 (April 1821), 426–7.

[20] *London Magazine*, 3 (April 1821), 359–63.

turn from this scene of woe, to one of joy and festivity.'[21] Such sentences seem anxiously keeping a straight face, as if they are aware that conjunctions of this kind are precisely the stuff out of which magazines, novels, and the most fashionable poems, poems in 'this new style of Frere's', are made—poems such as John Moultrie's 'La Belle Tryamour', which reports in *Knight's Quarterly Magazine* how Arthur had to go to Ireland to look for his bride:

> King George the Fourth, you know, was luckier still;
> For *his* spouse left the world she'd long been troubling,
> Just as he anchor'd in the bay of Dublin.[22]

It is, as I have already argued, not at all coincidental that Juanesque poems of this kind appeared so often in the magazines of the period.

Magazines offered an opiate, or at least they reproduced one of the virtues that De Quincey claimed for opium. After taking a draught on a Saturday night he would visit the markets attended by the poor, and sympathize with their pleasure if the price of bread or onions or butter had fallen, but 'if the contrary were true' opium reconciled him to the misfortune, 'For opium (like the bee, that extracts its materials indiscriminately from roses and from the soot of chimneys) can overrule all feelings into compliance with a master key.'[23] Like the bee, and also like a magazine such as the *London*, in a paper for which De Quincey coins the simile. There is a kind of heartlessness in the sheer variety of the material that a magazine can accommodate.

Lamb was the most successful of all magazine writers, and yet he could on occasion elicit protests from even his greatest admirers. Crabb Robinson noted in his journal for 3 May 1823:

Read the *London Magazine* in bed. Lamb's 'Poor Relations'. It is not quite agreeable— some observations on poverty which it is painful to make.[24]

But in truth the essay is so funny precisely because it is so merciless. The only thing worse than a poor relation is 'a female Poor Relation':

She calls the servant *Sir*; and insists on not troubling him to hold her plate. The housekeeper patronises her. The children's governess takes upon her to correct her, when she has mistaken the piano for a harpsichord.[25]

The essay exhilarates by releasing its readers from the sentimental pieties that everyone from time to time finds galling. But the tactic is as likely to prompt outrage as exhilaration, as Crabb Robinson reminds us, and some of Lamb's contemporaries could be much more brutal than him. In *Blackwood's*, for

---

[21] *London Magazine*, 4 (September 1821), 330.
[22] *Knight's Quarterly Magazine* 1 (June 1823), 174.
[23] *London Magazine*, 4 (October 1821), 361; Lindop, 2, 50.
[24] Quoted by E. V. Lucas, *The Life of Charles Lamb*, 2 vols. (London: Methuen, 1921), 2, 623.
[25] 'Poor Relations', *London Magazine*, 7 (May 1823), 533–6.

example, in the eighth of the *Noctes Ambrosianae*, written by Lockhart, one of the
guests is 'Philip Kempferhausen', a scholarly German distinguished by his
philosophical and sentimental refinements, and a character who embodies
one aspect of Lockhart himself. Kempferhausen is appalled by Hogg's breezy
acknowledgement that he had come to Edinburgh to witness a hanging, which,
Hogg insists, echoing Burke, is 'worth a' the Tragedy Plays that ever were acted'.
It was a woman that was hanged, and Odoherty adds that 'of course a female exit
is the more piquant'.[26]

Magazines sometimes showed themselves alert to the dangers of gazing at life
merely as a spectacle. T. J. Wainewright was reminded by a Landseer painting of
a boar attacked by dogs of an unpleasant little anecdote: 'I was told the other day
of a living artist who when a child was run over by a cart, before its own loved
home, and the bankrupt mother stood rigid as stone, staring with maniac agony
on her crushed darling, calmly and deliberately gazed on her "to study the
expression", as he called it.'[27] But it was, as he must have known, an anecdote
that touched rather nearly a magazine writer such as himself. In 'On the Knock-
ing at the Gate in Macbeth', a paper that first appeared in the *London*, De
Quincey, takes the manner to a sardonic extreme when he recalls a notorious
murderer: 'At length, in 1812, Mr. Williams made his *début* on the stage of
Ratcliffe Highway, and executed those unparalleled murders which have pro-
cured for him such a brilliant and undying reputation.'[28] Three years later, in an
essay for *Blackwood's*, 'On Murder Considered as One of the Fine Arts', De
Quincey produced an essay that is at once the supreme instance and the supreme
parody of this aspect of magazine writing. The paper, supposedly a lecture
delivered to the Society of Connoisseurs in Murder, turns on a single joke, that
murder may, like any other topic, be treated not morally but aesthetically.
A member of the society refuses the general admiration for John Thurtell's
murder of William Weare (Thurtell makes a thinly disguised appearance, as a
boxing trainer rather than a murderer, in another splendid example of magazine
prose of the pointedly provocative kind, Hazlitt's 'The Fight'): 'Mere plagiarism—base plagiarism from hints that I threw out! Besides, his style is as harsh as
Albert Dürer, and as coarse as Fuseli.'[29]

The refusal of sentiment, the spectacularisation of all experience, even murder,
that De Quincey at once satirizes and exploits, was a feature of the magazines of

[26] *Blackwood's Edinburgh Magazine*, 13 (May 1823), 592.
[27] *London Magazine*, 3 (April 1821), 438. Wainewright seems to have in mind 'The Seizure of a
Boar' that was exhibited by the youthful Landseer at the British Institute in 1821. Its current
location is unknown. See Richard Ormond, *Sir Edwin Landseer* (Philadelphia: Philadelphia
Museum of Art, 1981), 60.
[28] *London Magazine*, 8 (October 1823), 353–6, 354; Lindop, 3, 151.
[29] *Blackwood's Edinburgh Magazine*, 21 (February 1827), 199–213, 212; Lindop, 6, 130.
Thurtell's trial prompted one of J. H. Reynolds's best papers for the *London*. See 'A Pen and Ink
Sketch of a Late Trial for Murder', *London Magazine*, 9 (February 1824), 165–85.

the period, and also of the newspapers. The character in a novel of the 1820s who admits that he could not live without 'the papers' is representative:

There's an account in the Traveller to-day, of a horrid murder, that amused me so much this morning at breakfast. The brains of a whole family knocked out; the maid-servant with her throat cut from ear to ear, and a butcher's knife found sticking in the small ribs of an infant in the cradle. I'll be happy to send you over the paper, ma-am, if you wish to see it.[30]

It was a heartlessness that was not confined to print, but seeped into the wider culture. Thurtell's murder of Weare offers a striking evidence of this. Even before Thurtell came to trial the murder was dramatized on the London stage in a play called *The Gamblers*, the allure of which was heightened by the use on stage of precisely the horse and gig in which Thurtell had accompanied Weare as they travelled from London to Radlett in Hertfordshire, where the murder took place.[31] But the most powerful expression of this aspect of early nineteenth-century culture was a poem rather than a novel, or a magazine contribution, or a play.

When Southey denounced in the Preface to *A Vision of Judgement* 'those monstrous combinations of horrors and mockery, lewdness and impiety, with which English poetry has, in our days, first been polluted', he had, as Byron himself immediately recognized, one poem in particular in mind, *Don Juan*. It is the author of *Don Juan* that Pierce Egan begs for inspiration as he begins *Life in London* (6), the author of *Don Juan* who was believed by many to have written *Anastasius*, and it was the same author who was, both in himself and through his poem, the inspiration of much magazine writing. In *The Champion* John Thelwall asked, 'who ever shed a tear over the works of Lord Byron?' The reason no one does, he suggests, is that 'the characters he delineates are never such as can excite any *moral* sympathy:—there is nothing about them which, speaking as moral agents, we can esteem and love'.[32] He supports his case by pointing to *The Corsair* and *The Bride of Abydos*, but he does so in a review of the first two cantos of *Don Juan*, and I doubt whether, before their publication, the point would have occurred to him.

In *Don Juan*, as in newspapers and magazines, the past is rigorously subordinated to the present. Juan's affections are buoyant, not weighed down by his former loves: Julia is not a ghostly presence at the feast he shares with Haidée. His sympathies are at once strong and short-lived. Juan feels for the highwayman that he kills, but he does not feel for long, and it is this more than any other trait that makes him close kin to the narrator: 'But Tom's no more—and so no more of

[30] Thomas Hamilton, *The Youth and Manhood of Cyril Thornton* (Aberdeen: Association of Scottish Literary Studies, 1990), 272. The novel was first published by Blackwood in 1829.

[31] See the entry on John Thurtell in the *Oxford Dictionary of National Biography*, contributed by Angus Fraser.

[32] *The Champion* (1 August 1819), 488.

Tom' (11, 20, 1). When Haidée dies the narrator's voice merges with the sound
of the sea-swell as it 'mourns o'er the beauty of the Cyclades', but only for a
moment before swiftly passing on:

> But let me change this theme, which grows too sad,
>   And lay this sheet of sorrows on the shelf;
> I don't much like describing people mad,
>   For fear of seeming rather touch'd myself—
> Besides I've no more on this head to add;
>   And as my Muse is a capricious elf,
> We'll put about, and try another tack
> With Juan, left half-kill'd some stanzas back.
>
>   (4, 74)

  Juan may be armoured against Gulbeyaz's advances by memories of Haidée's
'soft Ionian face' (*Don Juan*, 5, 117, 3). 'However strange,' Byron remarks, 'he
could not yet forget her' (5, 124, 3), which seems tartly ironic, except that
thoughts of his former love are of no avail that same night when Juan is put to
bed with Dudu in the harem. Only once more does Haidée enter the poem,
when Juan thinks to compare her with Aurora Raby. Aurora's character is

> High, yet resembling not his lost Haidée;
> Yet each was radiant in her proper sphere:
>   The Island girl, bred up by the lone sea,
> More warm, as lovely, and not less sincere,
>   Was Nature's all: Aurora could not be
> Nor would be thus;—the difference in them
> Was such as lies between a flower and gem.
>
>   (*Don Juan*, 15, 58, 2–8)

The comparison is coolly expert, suggesting the practised sexual connoisseur not
the mourning lover. Erik Gray, who writes so well about this aspect of Byron,
speaks of his 'Poetics of Tourism',[33] but I would want to suggest that at such
moments Byron is adopting a manner which, despite its individuality, can be
paralleled in much of the writing of the period.
  The death of Tom the highwayman is, for all its theatricality and for all the
brusqueness of Tom's dismissal, affecting. Juan offers to help take up the
wounded man:

> But ere they could perform this pious duty,
>   The dying man cried, 'Hold! I've got my gruel!
> Oh! for a glass of *max!* We've miss'd our booty—
>   Let me die where I am!' And as the fuel
> Of life shrunk in his heart, and thick and sooty
>   The drops fell from his death-wound, and he drew ill

---

[33] On this characteristic of the poem, see Erik Gray, *The Poetry of Indifference from the Romantics
to the* Rubáiyát (Amherst and Boston: University of Massachusetts Press, 2005), 74–7.

His breath,—he from his swelling throat untied
A kerchief, crying 'Give Sal that!'—and died.

(11, 16)

Tom is allowed a last grand gesture. It is an episode in which, as a reviewer in
the *Literary Chronicle* pointed out, 'Lord Byron, the British peer, and one of the
first poets of the day', showed himself 'as well versed in the vulgar tongue as
Pierce Egan',[34] and there are episodes in *Life in London* that might be compared
with it. There is, for example, Bill, not a highwayman but a coachman, who
brings a young woman before the magistrate for failing to pay the fare. She tells
an artless tale of a day spent going from door to door, rejected by all her
acquaintance including the man who had seduced her, before pulling from her
purse the last two shillings that she has in the world, only for the coachman
magnanimously to refuse them: 'it shall never be said that Bill—took the last
shilling from a woman in distress'. The magistrate himself insists on paying the fare
and in addition presents the young woman with three shillings. Egan points out
that 'it was a fine scene altogether,' 'one of NATURE'S richest moments', and goes on
to invite a comparison with Sterne: 'My UNCLE TOBY would have *hobbled* on
crutches one hundred miles to have witnessed it; and *Corporal* TRIM would never
have related the circumstances without *blubbering* over it for an hour' (187–8).
Egan avoids for once the flash out of which Byron so delightedly and delightfully
pieces together his highwayman's speech,[35] but his typography carries at least one
of its functions: it keeps the reader at a remove from the event, the admiring
spectator of 'a fine scene'. As his choice of the word blubbering indicates, Egan
lacks all Byron's delicacy, and yet the two episodes are akin.

For Lockhart the publication of the first cantos of *Don Juan* and the fourth of
Childe Harold in the same year constituted in itself a 'cruel mockery'.[36] Like
adjacent magazine articles the two poems inevitably reflected on one another,
and when they did so *Don Juan* revealed *Childe Harold* as an 'insulting deceit', its
claims to high emotion exposed as sham. But the charge that Byron is wilfully
practising on his readers a cruel mockery remains unconvincing. I would rather
suggest that in *Don Juan* Byron shares with several of his contemporaries an
interest in the economy of the emotions. Contemplating the violent upheavals of
history, or walking the streets of an early nineteenth-century city, how much
emotion is it politic or practical to expend? Byron may dismiss his highwayman
with comic brusqueness, 'But Tom's no more, and so no more of Tom', but he

---

[34] *The Literary Chronicle*, August 30, 1823, 554. Egan was not only celebrated for his 'slang-
whanging' style in *Boxiana* and *Life in London*: he was the compiler of the 1811 edition of the
Dictionary of the Vulgar Tongue.

[35] On the use of 'flash' in the period, see Gregory Dart, '"Flash Style": Pierce Egan and Literary
London, 1820–28', *History Workshop Journal*, 51 (2001), 180–205.

[36] 'Remarks on Don Juan,' *Blackwood's Edinburgh Magazine*, 5 (August 1819), 512–18. The
attribution to Lockhart is insecure.

dismisses him only when nothing more can be done for him. De Quincey's connoisseur of murder does, after all, have a point. If everything possible has been done to prevent a murder and to arrest the assailant—suppose that 'we have done our best, by putting out our legs, to trip up the fellow in his flight, but all to no purpose'—what then remains? The only sensible part is to 'make the best of a bad matter'. If the murder cannot be prevented, at least let it be enjoyed.[37] *Don Juan* repeatedly presents its reader with similar conundrums. Byron finds it hard to dismiss the death of the Italian Commandant, 'killed by five bullets from an old gun barrel', after he had been shot outside Byron's door and lifted into the house. The incident is less easily dismissed than the death of Haidée (it was, after all, 'a fact and no poetic fable'), but Byron interrupts himself almost as he had after recording Haidée's death,

> But let me quit the theme; as such things claim
> Perhaps even more attention than is due
> From me.
>
> (5, 38, 4–6)

Almost, but not quite. The rhythm is more hesitant than when dismissing Haidée, the tone abashed rather than jaunty. Byron is all too aware that the keen attention with which he watches a man that he had known pass almost imperceptibly from life to death is not at all altruistic. He returns to the scene even after he has promised to quit it, and at the last has to shake himself free of it: 'But let us to the story as before' (5, 39, 8). The commandant's death prompts reflection, but it is reflection that leads nowhere: it can only, sooner or later, be interrupted.[38]

Lockhart ends his 'Remarks on Don Juan', a review of the poem's first two cantos, with a prim question:

Will our readers believe that the most innocent of all the odious sarcasms is contained in these two lines?

> They grieved for those that perished in the cutter,
> And also for the biscuits, casks, and butter.[39]

It was a common enough response. Another reviewer wondered at 'the brutal inhumanity that could jest upon his fellow-beings drifting to their watery grave' by 'placing, for the sake of exciting a smile, (if at such an association any one can smile) the sinking of a boatful of them, to rise no more in this world, on a level

---

[37] 'On Murder considered as One of the Fine Arts', *Blackwood's Edinburgh Magazine*, 21 (February 1827), 201; Lindop, 6, 115.

[38] The incident occurred on 8 December 1820. Byron described it in letters to Thomas Moore and John Murray on 9 December, to his wife on 10 December, and to his half-sister Augusta on 21 December. See *Byron's Letters and Journals*, ed. Leslie A. Marchand, 7 (London: John Murray, 1977), 245–52.

[39] *Blackwood's Edinburgh Magazine*, 5 (August 1819), 518.

with the loss of "biscuit-casks and butter"'.[40] Clearly the lines raise a smile, but does the smile quite forbid a grim recognition that, for the survivors, the loss of the provisions was as serious a matter as the loss of their crewmates? The same defence could not be made of the complaint of the widows when the city of Ismail is taken:

> Some voices of the buxom middle-aged
>   Were also heard to wonder in the din
> (Widows of forty were these birds long caged)
>   'Wherefore the ravishing did not begin!'
> But while the thirst for gore and plunder raged,
>   There was small leisure for superfluous sin;
> But whether they escaped or no, lies hid
> In darkness—I can only hope they did.
>
> (8, 132)

The time-worn jest sits oddly with the canto's sense of the horror of a city under storm. But so too does the stanza just before it:

> Some odd mistakes too happened in the dark,
>   Which showed a want of lanthorns, or of taste—
> Indeed the smoke was such they scarce could mark
>   Their friends from foes,—besides such things from haste
> Occur, though rarely, when there is a spark
>   Of light to save the venerably chaste:—
> But six old damsels, each of seventy years,
> Were all deflowered by different Grenadiers.
>
> (8, 130)

In this canto styles trample over one another as brutally as the advancing troops. The sentimental ('quite refreshing' (8, 90, 2)) episode of Juan's rescue of Leila from 'two villainous Cossaques' jostles against the Grand Guignol of the Russian officer whose Achilles tendon is severed by the teeth of a dying Moslem: the operatic heroics of the Tartar who sees his five sons die before carelessly impaling himself on the bayonets that had killed them bumps into the brief pastoral interlude celebrating Daniel Boone:

> He was not all alone; around him grew
>   A sylvan tribe of children of the chase,
> Whose young, unwakened world was ever new.
>
> (8, 65, 1–3)

War, Byron accepts, is an 'awful topic,' and yet even in war 'our human lot' is 'checkered,' productive of 'melancholy merriment', and the poet must accept this if he is to 'sketch your world exactly as it goes'. But even in this stanza (8, 89), Byron does not rest his defence on realism. He prefers 'melancholy merriment'

---

[40] *The Investigator*, 5 (October 1822), 337.

because 'to quote / Too much of one kind would be soporific.' The writing I am describing, one might say, is hurried into casual cruelties out of a fear of being dull. But to say just this would be unfair. At its best, it is writing that recognizes that 'our human lot' demands the exercise of sympathetic feeling, and yet demands just as urgently a willingness when occasion requires to curtail that exercise, even to practise in its stead a strategic callousness. After Jane Austen's *Emma*, accompanied by Harriet, has made her visit to a distressed family, she observes to her young companion, 'I feel now as if I could think of nothing but these poor creatures all the rest of the day.' At once, Mr Elton appears and the poor creatures are immediately forgotten, but Emma is amused rather than abashed:

Well, (smiling,) I hope it may be allowed that if compassion has produced exertion and relief to the sufferers, it has done all that is truly important. If we feel for the wretched, enough to do all we can for them, the rest is empty sympathy, only distressing to ourselves.

Emma, Mrs Weston tells Knightley, is 'a picture of health', and it is, for Jane Austen, a health of the mind as much as of the body.[41]

[41] Jane Austen, *Emma*, 94 and 39.

11

Jack and Gill

CROSS-DRESSING THE NOVEL

Duelling was an assertion of manhood: entry to the field of honour was restricted to men. Occasionally, it is true, women fought duels. Most famously there was the 'petticoat duel' of 1792 in which Lady Almeria Braddock challenged Mrs Elphinstone, who had, Lady Almeria believed, made an insulting reference to her age. The two women fired at ten paces and survived unscathed, although a ball passed through Lady Almeria's hat. They then took to swords, and the dispute was resolved only after Mrs Elphinstone was wounded in the arm.[1] But this was exceptional. It was men who duelled. Women, as a contributor to the *British Lady's Magazine* insisted, had a crucial role to play, but only because it was their responsibility to put an end to the practice, which would not be eradicated until it became 'a *mark of infamy in woman* to admit a duellist to her bosom'.[2]

John Scott challenged Christie after Lockhart had posted him. As *The Scotsman* commented, J. H. Christie should perhaps have recognized that 'Scott's sense of honour would, for some time, be exceedingly tender'.[3] A similar tenderness seems to have been rather general among men of letters in these years. It was a symptom, I suspect, of a gathering suspicion that, in a literary marketplace increasingly dominated by women, male writers had come to occupy an uncomfortably feminine space. Walter Scott never felt impelled to fight a duel, although in his last years he expected a challenge from a Frenchman who felt himself defamed in Scott's *Life of Napoleon*, but no writer of the period took a greater interest in the topic.[4] Duels are fought in *Guy Mannering, The Antiquary, Saint Ronan's Well*, and *The Surgeon's Daughter*, and threatened in almost every novel he wrote. In a lengthy introduction to 'The Duel of Wharton and Stuart' in *Minstrelsy of the Scottish Border*, Scott traces the history of the

---

[1] For more on this and other duels involving women, see Robert Baldick, *The Duel: A History of Duelling* (London: Chapman and Hall, 1965), 169–78.

[2] *British Lady's Magazine*, 4 (July 1816), 3.

[3] *The Scotsman*, no. 214, 24 February 1821, 62.

[4] General Gaspar Gourgaud issued threats which, in the event, came to nothing. The episode is described in Edgar Johnson, *Sir Walter Scott* (London: Hamish Hamilton, 1970), 2, 1025–6. There were personal reasons for Scott's interest in duelling. He disowned his own brother, Daniel, when he believed him guilty of act of cowardice which may have involved his refusing a challenge.

institution and denies that it is even yet obsolete: duels 'long continued, they even yet continue, to be appealed to, as the test of truth; since, by the code of honour, every gentleman is still bound to repel a charge of falsehood with the point of his sword, and at the peril of his life'.[5] It is a point of view that Scott's Lord Glenvarloch despaired of making his citizen landlady understand. Nigel holds that 'a man's honour, which is, or should be, dearer to him than his life, may often call on and compel us to hazard our own lives, or those of others, on what would otherwise seem trifling contingencies'. But his landlady knows her Bible and has 'only read there that thou shalt not kill'.[6] The landlady seems so clearly to have the better of the argument that it is puzzling to see Scott all through his life clinging to a code of honour that he represents as obsolescent even in the seventeenth century, except that for Scott, as Hazlitt for one intimated, obsolescence might in itself be an attraction.

Scott's novels offer refuge in a masculine past to all those male readers of his who felt themselves at times rather uncomfortably trapped in a feminine modernity,[7] readers such as the Squire in Lockhart's *Reginald Dalton*. He suffers the conversation of a female relative who 'bothered him with prosing about new novels of which he had never heard, and when he, in his politeness, made any attempt to introduce Roderick Random, or Peregrine Pickle, she professed total ignorance of any such naughty books'.[8] From the first, Scott's heroes, like Edward Waverley, are enlisted into plots that oblige them to reconcile themselves with modern civility and to consign to history the fierce masculine codes that have seduced them, but one reason the novels were so successful was surely that in reading them the male reader of the early nineteenth century is allowed painlessly to yield to precisely the seduction that the hero must repent after much suffering.

If this is right, then the odd propensity of men of letters in the years immediately after the war to engage in duels may usefully be understood as one aspect of a concerted attempt to re-masculinize the literary world. The novel had become a dominantly feminine genre until Scott reclaimed it for his own sex. As Lamb put it, Scott's 'happier genius' 'expelled forever' the kinds of novel published by William Lane at the Minerva Press that had until recently supplied the 'scanty intellectual viands of the whole female reading public'.[9] The novel had been drained of all life by the women who had appropriated it: 'The Luximas, the

[5] Walter Scott, *Minstrelsy of the Scottish Border*, 3 vols. (Edinburgh: Longman and Rees, 1803), 3, 123–4.
[6] Walter Scott, *The Fortunes of Nigel*, ed. Frank Jordan (Edinburgh: Edinburgh University Press, 2004), 264.
[7] A point made by Hazlitt in 'On the Pleasure of Hating', in which he observes of the novels, 'As we read, we throw aside the trammels of civilization, the flimsy veil of humanity.' Howe, 12, 129.
[8] J. G. Lockhart, *Reginald Dalton* (Edinburgh: William Blackwood, 1823), 1, 138. Subsequent page references are included in the text.
[9] 'Popular Fallacies: *That great wit is allied to madness*', *New Monthly Magazine*, 16 (May 1826), 519. In *The Last Essays of Elia* the essay was re-published under the title, 'Sanity of True Genius'.

Wanderers, and the innumerable spawn of the Mysteries of Udolpho, were gradually sinking into the tomb of all the Capulets, when the author of the Scotch novels first appeared, like a giant refreshed with sleep.'[10] For the reviewers, *Waverley* was revolutionary in its manliness. The *Monthly Review* marvelled at how it stood out from 'sundry tomes of *Emmeline, Castel Gandolfo, Elegant Enthusiasts,* and *Victims of Sensibility*'.[11] It had an unexampled 'variety', which betrayed the masculine breadth of its author's experience; its allegiance was to the masculine world of fact, to history; and its learning too proved the novel to be a truly masculine production. It showed 'no moderate acquaintance with the arcana of the law' and it kept up 'a perpetual allusion to the English and Latin classics'.[12] It did not so much rival the feminine novel as supersede it. *Waverley* accommodated the romance plot of the woman's novel, resolved when Edward Waverley exchanges his fruitless infatuation with Flora McIvor for a calmer, more domestic attachment to Rose Bradwardine, but the romance plot is subordinated to the great plot of history which traces how a nation riven between two loyalties contrived to resolve its differences.

Peacock noted that Scott had 'the rare talent of pleasing all ranks and classes of men, from the peer to the peasant, and all orders and degrees of mind from the philosopher to the man-milliner'.[13] But for Byron Scott's chief distinction was that he wrote novels that could be read by men. In the book parcel he received from Murray in October 1820, Byron was irritated to find not just a volume of 'Johnny Keats's *piss-a-bed* poetry', but *Warbeck of Wolfenstein* by Margaret Holford, 'a spinster whom I thought we had sent back to her spinning', and Felicia Hemans's *The Sceptic*. The absence of the book that he most wanted provoked him into a couplet:

> I'm thankful for your books dear Murray
> But why not send Scott's Monastery?[14]

Scott, it was rather generally felt, had saved the novel, once the chosen form of writers such as Defoe, Smollett, and Fielding, from colonization by women, and it was an achievement of which Scott himself was well aware. In *Saint Ronan's Well*, Clara Mowbray playfully promises to support herself by her own labours: 'The needle or the pencil is the resource of all distressed heroines, you know; and I promise you, though I have been idle of late, yet, when I do set about it, no

[10] 'On the Living Novelists,' *Gold's London Magazine*, 2 (1820), 265.
[11] *Monthly Review*, 75 (November 1814), 279–80.
[12] *British Critic*, 2 (August 1814), 209.
[13] *The Works of Thomas Love Peacock*, ed. H. F. B. Brett-Smith and C. F. Jones, 10 vols. (London: Constable and Co, 1934), 8, 266.
[14] *Byron's Letters and Journals*, ed. Leslie A. Marchand, 7 (London: John Murray, 1977), 200.

Emmeline or Ethelinde of them all ever sent such loads of trumpery to the market as I shall, or made such wealth as I will do.' Scott refers to two of Charlotte Smith's better-known heroines, one suspects, precisely to signal his breach with the feminine tradition. Novels written by women, he comes close to implying, are not of much greater value than the 'landscapes with sap-green trees, and such mazareen-blue rivers' by the manufacture of which their heroines so often contrive to earn a pittance.[15] A taste for reading novels was, as Jane Austen complained, regularly represented even by novelists themselves as a surrender to feminine lassitude.[16] According to John Scott the Scotch novels offered the nation precisely the therapy of which it was most in need. As we read them, 'health and manliness are made to circulate through our frames'. The reader is 'excited by [Scott's] inspiring tally-ho': reading him is almost like engaging in a field sport.[17]

Other male novelists were determined to emulate Scott's achievement. In *Reginald Dalton* Lockhart draws a contrast between the austerely masculine rooms of Dalton's tutor, whose notion of 'modern literature' extends no further than 'Burke's Reflections or Johnson's Lives of the Poets', and those of the Provost of his Oxford college, where 'the Courier, a number of the Quarterly, and a novel of Miss Edgeworth' are to be seen 'reposing on a ROSE-WOOD TABLE'. The character of the reading matter is defined by the room's other appurtenances; the 'small Persian carpet', the 'parrot cage by the window', and the 'plump pet poodle upon the hearth-rug'.[18] A taste for novels, the passage implies, is effeminate, which is why Lockhart persistently tries to arm his own novels against the charge. The first, *Valerius*, makes an elaborate display of the classical learning that was largely confined to men. For one reviewer the novel owed its impressiveness to a prose 'so thickly interwoven with Latin idioms' that it achieved 'an air of stiffness resembling that of a Latin translation'.[19] In the second, *Adam Blair*, Lockhart chooses a subject matter, the sexual fall of a Minister of the Church of Scotland, that, as he must have anticipated, disqualified the novel for many women readers, and in his third he not only rehearses at some length Reginald Dalton's Oxford education, from which all women were excluded, he does so in a manner that displays his classical education almost as ostentatiously as he does in *Valerius*: 'they reached the snug little *habitaculum* where the Squire was established in the "otium

[15] Walter Scott, *Saint Ronan's Well*, ed. Mark Weinstein (Edinburgh: Edinburgh University Press, 1995), 100–1.
[16] Even the novel heroine, Austen remarks, 'if she accidentally take up a novel, is sure to turn over its insipid pages with disgust'. See Jane Austen, *Northanger Abbey*, ed. Barbara M. Benedict and Deidre Le Faye (Cambridge: Cambridge University Press, 2006), 30.
[17] *London Magazine*, 1 (January 1820), 13. On Scott's masculine re-colonization of the novel, see Ina Ferris, *The Achievement of Literary Authority: Gender, History, and the Waverley Novels* (Ithaca and London: Cornell University Press, 1991), especially 79–104.
[18] J. G. Lockhart, *Reginald Dalton* (Edinburgh: William Blackwood, 1823), 1, 303, and 313. Subsequent page references are included in the text.
[19] *Knight's Quarterly Magazine*, 1 (June 1823), 29.

cum dignitate" of his customary disorder' [gout] (1, 115). Thomas Hope's *Anastasius* is a novel even more uncompromisingly masculine than are Scott's. Anastasius's Juanish exploits are impelled by the disgust that he feels for all women once he has slept with them: his stabler and tenderer relationships are always with men. Hope's 'Oriental' novel is at a far remove from Pierce Egan's *Life in London*, but Egan's novel, too, is emphatically masculine in its celebration of the simple male pleasures such as drinking and fighting and of the masculine friendship shared by the two cousins, Tom and Jerry, and their Oxford associate, Bob Logic. Tom's true partner is his cousin Jerry. The role of 'Corinthian Kate', his consort, is by comparison vestigial: her function is simply to supply one more proof of Tom's masculine credentials.

There was, then, a concerted attempt in these years to masculinize the novel, but the novel can be masculinized only if it is admitted to be feminine, and the femininity of the novel in the early nineteenth century was all but guaranteed by a readership that included in its numbers so many women. Thomas Hamilton, brother of the philosopher, Sir William Hamilton, was a *Blackwood's* contributor, the inventor of one of its key characters, the lifelong bachelor Ensign Morgan Odoherty, and when he came to publish *The Youth and Manhood of Cyril Thornton* in 1827 he planned to make it a novel as uncompromisingly masculine as the magazine. It would trace Thornton's youth as a student at Glasgow University and his manhood as a soldier in the Peninsular campaign, and would end with Thornton's death in the storming of St Sebastian. That would make, he assured his publisher, William Blackwood, 'a striking conclusion'. But Blackwood knew that 'a happy termination to a work of this kind is most popular', and the published novel had a very different ending. Thornton, frightfully wounded, one arm amputated and his face disfigured by a scar that severs his upper lip, is abandoned by his flighty, aristocratic lover and finds happiness with Laura Willoughby, a very different, far more domestic woman. It is, as Hamilton wrote to Blackwood, a 'rather humdrum' conclusion, but it was the conclusion on which Blackwood insisted. The women readers of the novel were being invited to accept its hero's disfigurement. They could not be expected to tolerate in addition so 'melancholy' a conclusion as Hamilton had planned, 'the description of [Thornton's] grave in a grove of cork trees in the neighbourhood' of San Sebastian.[20] The novel, Hamilton was taught by his publisher, remained for all Scott's efforts a feminine form. It was a lesson that Hamilton shared with his hero who in his convalescence is entertained by the woman he

---

[20] See the introduction to Thomas Hamilton, *The Youth and Manhood of Cyril Thornton*, ed. Maurice Lindsay (Aberdeen: Association of Scottish Literary Studies, 1990), ix–x. Subsequent page references to the novel are included in the text.

will marry, who 'would sing, for [him], to the accompaniment of her harp, or read aloud a novel by Miss Austen or Miss Edgeworth' (377).

Even Scott sometimes registers an amused sense that in writing novels he has strayed into a literary area more properly inhabited by women. At the end of *Old Mortality*, for example, he acknowledges in the guise of Peter Pattieson, the supposed author of the tale, that he had thought to 'waive the task of a concluding chapter' until he was 'honoured with an invitation to drink tea with Miss Martha Buskbody', the Gandercleugh mantua-maker. Miss Buskbody speaks with the benefit of 'the experience which she must have acquired in reading through the whole stock of three circulating libraries in Gandercleugh and the two next market-towns', and she insists on 'a glimpse of sunshine in the last chapter', and full particulars of 'the marriage of Morton and Edith, and what became of the other personages of the story', from Lady Margaret down to Goose-Gibbie. Pattieson humbly complies.[21] This seems urbanely self-mocking, but Scott's suavity conceals, I suspect, a consciousness that in writing novels he is engaged in women's business, more embarrassed than he cares to admit. Scott was generous in acknowledging debts to predecessors such as Jane Porter and Maria Edgeworth, and in a late work, *Chronicles of the Canongate*, he seems to admit the sense of obligation into the fiction. He represents the book as a miscellany compiled by 'Chrystal Croftangry' in his years of retirement in Edinburgh's Canongate, but Croftangry commences author under the tutelage of a fellow Canongate resident, Mrs Bethune Baliol. It is Mrs Baliol who teaches him the 'singular art of dismissing all the usual protracted tautology respecting time, place, and circumstance, which is apt to settle like a mist upon the cold and languid tales of age, and at the same time of bringing forward, and illustrating, those incidents and characters which give point and interest to the story'. She teaches him the art of writing fiction, first through the anecdotes she tells him, and later through the manuscript that she leaves him after her death, from which he draws the material for his first tale.[22]

In the earlier fiction Scott seems less comfortable in acknowledging that he stands within a female line. *Guy Mannering*, for example, his second novel, flaunts its masculinity. The novel celebrates the bonding of Dandie Dinmont, the colossal Border farmer, and Harry Bertram, himself a stoutly built young man and 'remarkably tall'.[23] Between them, the two overcome the evil, though

---

[21] Walter Scott, *The Tale of Old Mortality*, ed. Douglas Mack (Edinburgh: Edinburgh University Press, 1993), 349–50.

[22] Walter Scott, *Chronicles of the Canongate*, ed. Claire Lamont (Edinburgh: Edinburgh University Press, 2000), 62. Frank Jordan describes Mrs Baliol as Scott's 'portrait of the artist' as 'female in sex and feminine in temperament,' although this description may simplify Scott's response to the predominantly feminine character of the novel as he inherited it. See Frank Jordan, 'Chrystal Croftangry, Scott's Last and Best Mask', *Scottish Literary Journal*, 7 (1980), 185–92, 192.

[23] Walter Scott, *Guy Mannering*, ed. P. D. Garside (Edinburgh: Edinburgh University Press, 1999), 173. Subsequent page references are included in the text.

similarly big-built, Dutch smuggler, Dirk Hatteraick. Young Hazledene is slighter, but earns his admission into this company by the manly way in which he refuses to take offence when Bertram accidentally shoots him during a scuffle. The most impressive female character, Meg Merrilies, is herself of masculine stature, being 'full six feet high' (14). But even *Guy Mannering* finds a place for the feminine novel. Young Bertram is in love with Julia Mannering, and it is Julia who narrates the progress of their love in letters to 'Miss Matilda Marchmont', a young lady she had met during a stay at a 'seminary for female education' so brief that she had only had time to 'form an eternal friendship'. (91) Chapters 17 and 18 consist of extracts from Julia's letters. These chapters are awkwardly poised, at once imitating the epistolary novel that women novelists had inherited from Richardson and burlesquing it in the manner of Eaton Stannard Barrett's *The Heroine*.[24]

That awkwardness suggests Scott's awareness that for all the surface masculinity of his novels, they take their place within a female tradition. His young heroes such as Roland Graeme in *The Abbot* are naive, often awkward and embarrassed, and, despite their prickliness, are much given to blushing. They seem in a more direct line of descent from Evelina than from Tom Jones.[25] In *Rob Roy*, for example, Frank Osbaldistone parts, he fears for ever, from Diana Vernon:

At length tears rushed to my eyes ... I wiped them mechanically, and almost without being aware that they were flowing, but they came thicker and thicker—I felt the tightening of the throat and breast, the *hysterica passio* of poor Lear; and sitting down by the wayside, I shed a flood of the first and most bitter tears which had flowed from my eyes since childhood.[26]

The feminized heroes are sometimes brought into confrontation with unusually masculine heroines. In *Rob Roy*, Frank Osbaldistone's taste for poetry and his distaste for trade seem to his father equally effeminate postures and the novel's heroine, Diana Vernon, agrees. When Frank wonders whether his bent is for original poetry or translation she assures him that he 'might employ [his] time to

---

[24] Scott may have been guided in his choice of which feminine cliché to mock by Barrett. Barrett's heroine, Cherubina, swears an 'eternal friendship' with a young woman she has only just met. See *The Heroine* (London: Colburn, 1813), letter 35. On the distinction between the 'masculine' mode of the novel derived from Fielding and the 'feminine' mode derived from Richardson, see Jane Spencer, *The Rise of the Woman Novelist: From Aphra Behn to Jane Austen* (Oxford: Blackwell, 1986), 90.

[25] Ina Ferris suggests a similar lineage when she observes that a hero such as Edward Waverley is 'best understood as a Gothic heroine in male form' in *The Achievement of Literary Authority: Gender, History and the Waverley Novels*, 100. Fiona Wilson argues that Scott's heroes of this kind—Frank Osbaldistone of *Rob Roy* is her preferred example—should be understood as male hysterics. See Fiona Wilson, 'He's come undone: Gender, Territory, and Hysteria in *Rob Roy*', in *Romanticism's Debatable Lands*, ed. Claire Lamont and Michael Rossington (Basingstoke: Palgrave Macmillan, 2007), 52–63.

[26] Walter Scott, *Rob Roy*, ed. David Hewitt (Edinburgh: Edinburgh University Press, 2008), 285. Subsequent page references are included in the text.

far better purpose than in either'. He has to concede not only the 'childishness' of his own conduct but the 'superior manliness of Miss Vernon's' (132). Diana Vernon does not just on occasion don masculine dress, she insists on being treated as a man. 'Call me Tom Vernon', she suggests to Frank, irritated by his empty compliments (46). It is her habit to talk to him 'in the style one gentleman uses to another' (106).

Diana is intended never to be less than delightful—she is after all the woman that Frank will marry. Her baleful counterpart is Helen MacGregor, the wife of Rob Roy. Helen, it seems, though Scott mumbles the matter, has been raped by her husband's persecutors (211), an experience which has rendered her more savage than any man. After a skirmish, Frank notes 'the specks of blood on her brow, her hands, and naked arms, as well as on the blade of the sword which she continued to hold in her hand' (260), and it is Helen who orders the killing of the craven English double-agent, Morris, who is drowned in the loch like an unwanted puppy:

The victim was held fast by some, while others, binding a large heavy stone in a plaid, tied it around his neck, and others again eagerly stripped him of some parts of his dress. Half-naked, and thus manacled, they hurled him into the lake, there about twelve feet deep, drowning his last death-shriek with a loud halloo of vindictive triumph, above which, however, the yell of mortal agony was distinctly heard.   (267)

There is no more savage scene in all of Scott, and it is orchestrated by a woman. Helen MacGregor inspires in Scott a holy terror. She reminds him of Old Testament heroines such as Deborah and Judith (260), and she can no more be reclaimed for civil society than one of her closest counterparts in Scott's fiction, Elspat MacTavish. Elspat is 'The Highland Widow', who so inflames her own son by her taunts of cowardice that he shoots dead a soldier sent to arrest him and dies by firing squad. Elspat is left to live out her life as unaccommodated as Martha Ray in Wordsworth's 'The Thorn'.

In several of the novels, but in *Rob Roy* especially, Scott ascribes to his Highland speakers an odd style of speech in which everyone, man or woman, is referred to by feminine pronouns. A Highlander refuses to restore his shoes to Andrew Fairservice, Frank's comical Calvinist manservant, on the ground that 'she's nae gentle body, I trow' (260). In the speech forms of the Highlands, it seems, genders are indeterminate,[27] and what is true of the Highlands, it may be, is also true of the novel. Scott set out confidently to masculinize the novel, but his novels seem haunted by a suspicion that the masculine novel may simply be the

---

[27] Scott is following a literary convention, also espoused by Hogg, according to which 'she' might be substituted for 'I', 'you', or 'he'. This seems to have been simply a literary convention that does not reflect any actual Gaelic speech habit. See Mairi Robinson, 'Modern Literary Scots: Ferguson and After', in *Lowland Scots: Papers Presented to an Edinburgh Conference*, ed. A. J. Aitken (Edinburgh: Association for Scottish Literary Studies, 1973), 38–55.

novel in drag. It may be this rather than a simple admiration for Shakespeare that underlies Scott's curious interest in cross-dressing.

In *Redgauntlet* Darsie Latimer's acknowledgement that his 'love for Alan Fairford surpasses the love of woman'[28] serves only to underwrite his masculinity, but can the same be said of the oddity that Darsie travels to the final rendezvous with Charles Stuart disguised, at his uncle's insistence, as a woman, his face hidden by 'one of those silk masks which ladies frequently wore to preserve their complexions when exposed to the air during long journeys on horseback'? Despite his remonstrances, his uncle insists that he also wear a 'riding-skirt' (322). In *The Abbot*, even more surprisingly, the young hero, Roland Graeme, is unable to distinguish the young woman he loves, Catherine Seyton, from her brother, Henry, an odd incapacity for which he has at least the excuse that, when he first meets Catherine's brother, Henry Seyton is dressed as a woman. This seems surprising behaviour in a young nobleman, but his sister reports that it is one of the 'mad pranks' for which he is well known.[29] Rather oddly, Scott writes as if he is just as unable to penetrate Henry's disguise as his hero. Even as Henry protests that 'the moon shines bright enough surely to know the hart from the hind', Scott persists in referring to him by feminine pronouns (280). *The Abbot* is set at a time when both England and Scotland are ruled by Queens, though Mary's rule is contested, and Scott can reasonably claim that at such a period genders will be unusually fluid and confusing.[30] 'Times which make men out of women, are least of all fitted for men to become women', says Henry Seyton, but he says it to Roland while wearing female dress and while he is still being mistaken by Roland for his sister. Immediately afterwards Seyton breaks into song:

> Oh, some do call me Jack, sweet love,
>   And some do call me Gill;
> But when I ride to Holyrood,
>   My name is Wilful Will.

(257)

Cross-dressing, it may be, offers Scott a device that allows him at once to register and make light of an anxious sense that in writing novels he is himself cross-dressing. Roland Graeme is brought up by the Lady of Avenel as her page, and when he threatens a fellow-servant with a dagger, he is denounced in a sermon by the fiery Protestant divine, Henry Warden, who describes the poniard as a

---

[28] Walter Scott, *Redgauntlet*, ed. G. A. M. Woof with David Hewitt (Edinburgh: Edinburgh University Press, 1997), 113. Subsequent page references are included in the text.

[29] Walter Scott, *The Abbot*, ed. Christopher Johnson (Edinburgh: Edinburgh University Press, 2000), 326. Subsequent page references are included in the text.

[30] Judith Wilt persuasively argues that in the Waverley novels both men and women 'must journey through the experience of the other, the outlawed, gender, before either one can choose and re-fix the male or female identity appropriate to the new age'. See Judith Wilt, *Secret Leaves: The Novels of Walter Scott* (Chicago: University of Chicago Press, 1985), 117.

'treacherous and malignant instrument, which is therefore fit to be used, not by men or soldiers, but by those who, trained under female discipline, become themselves effeminate hermaphrodites, having female spite and female cowardice added to the infirmities and evil passions of their masculine nature' (40). Scott was very well aware that, as a novelist, he had himself been 'trained under female discipline', and that even the most masculine novelists might be vulnerable to the charge that they were nothing more than 'effeminate hermaphrodites'.

The more strenuously the novels of the period insist on their masculinity the more likely they are to compromise it. In this the novel rather resembled the duel. Men fought duels as an assertion of their masculinity, but, in the unfortunate event that they killed their opponent, they were required to complement their display of manly courage with an equally flamboyant demonstration of their capacity for feminine sensibility. At James Stuart's trial Jeffrey, in cross-examining Stuart's second, was anxious to establish two points; first that Stuart's behaviour on the field had been that of 'a person of constancy and manly', and second that, when the news reached him in Calais that Boswell had died, Stuart had at once 'burst into tears'.[31] It is as if masculinity, if it is emphatically enough displayed, has a tendency to be transformed into something like its opposite. In this it is rather like the moustache lovingly cultivated by Thomas Hope's Anastasius:

An hour every day was the shortest time admitted to the culture of his adored mustachios, and to the various rites which these idols of his vain-glorious heart demanded—such as changing their hue from a bright flaxen to a jetty black, perfuming them with rose and amber, smoothing their straggling hairs, and giving their taper ends a smart and graceful curve. Another hour was spent in refreshing the scarlet dye of his lips, and tinting the dark shade of his eye-lids, as well as his practising the most fascinating smile which the Tirzhana [admiralty] could display. (1, 261)

Like *Life in London*, *Anastasius* is a novel about the relationships between men, but it is set in the East, and in the East it is possible more frankly to allow that the homosocial might shade into the homoerotic. In James Hogg's Scotland, gender boundaries were more strictly patrolled. Like Scott, Hogg seems to write rather emphatically masculine novels. Richard Rickleton in *The Three Perils of Woman*, a close relation of Scott's Dandie Dinmont, seems a typical hard-drinking, loud-laughing, simple-minded, comical embodiment of ideal masculinity until he learns that his wife, when she married him, was pregnant by another man. The child she bears is the son of a married lawyer, her longstanding lover. Rickleton, goaded by his male advisers, casts her off, but quickly repents of it, and finds to his surprise that he has a heart large enough lovingly to accept both mother and

---

[31] *A Full Report of the Trial of James Stuart, Esq. younger of Dunearn, before the High Court of Justiciary, 10th June 1822; with an appendix containing documents, etc.* . . . (Edinburgh, 1823), 30 and 58.

child. His only misgiving concerns his neighbour, Simey Dodd. Rickleton has kept up for many years the kind of fierce masculine rivalry with Simey Dodd that offers a bachelor like him a viable alternative to marriage, and he is terrified that Dodd will ridicule him for accepting another man's child. But when he learns what Rickleton has done, Dodd congratulates him: he has shown himself for 'all [his] obstreperous oddities, to be possessed of a more gentle, forgiving, and benevolent heart, than almost any other of [his] sex'.[32] Rickleton has shown himself to be more of a man that Simey Dodd had suspected, and he has done so by displaying virtues more commonly associated with women. Hogg's hero and the novel in which he appears are not quite so unreflectingly masculine as they pretend: both reveal, at the last, an unexpected delicacy.

BYRON AND THE BLUES

Byron praised Scott for having rescued the novel from women, and Byron himself was intent on performing a similar rescue act for poetry. Byron's hero Don Juan becomes a great favourite of the Blues, not just the youthful prodigy Miss Araminta Smith, but Lady Fitz-Frisky and Miss Maevia Mannish, and is admitted to all their 'Coteries' (*Don Juan*, 11, 53–4). The same was not true of the poem in which he appeared. *Don Juan,* as many reviewers noted, brazenly advertised its inadmissibility into a woman's library. The *British Critic*, reviewing the poem's first two cantos, warned that it 'would have the worst opinion indeed of any man, upon whose family table this volume were to lie exposed'.[33] It was poetry, according to the *Eclectic*, 'such as no brother could read aloud to his sister, no husband to his wife'.[34] Even in its obituary notice of Byron the *Literary Gazette* insisted that 'no man of the least experience could have been unconscious, that many passages, not only in Don Juan, but in other of Lord Byron's poems, must, of necessity, sully that native purity, and impair that instinctive delicacy, which are among the greatest charms, and the surest safe-guards of the sex'.[35] *The Examiner* was edited by Byron's friend and admirer, Leigh Hunt, but even he mildly suggested of *Don Juan* that 'poems of this kind may not be the best things to put abruptly into the hands of young ladies',[36] and Constable's *Edinburgh Magazine* more robustly described it as a poem 'such as no man of pure taste can read a *second* time, and such as no woman of correct principles can

---

[32] James Hogg, *The Three Perils of Woman*, ed. David Groves, Antony Hasler, and Douglas S. Mack (Edinburgh: Edinburgh University Press, 1995), 257.

[33] *British Critic*, n.s. 12 (August 1819), 204.

[34] *Eclectic Review*, 16 (October 1821), 118.

[35] *Literary Gazette and Journal of Belles Lettres*, 416 (8 January 1825), 39. The *Gazette* is re-printing remarks from the *Annual Obituary* for 1825.

[36] *The Examiner*, 14, no. 708, 29 July 1821, 473.

read the *first*.[37] That it was a forbidden text might itself act as an attraction to women readers, of course, as even the staid *Scots Magazine* recognized, when it allowed irony to shadow its claim that 'No Scotian fair e'er read the book I know!'[38] All the same, the many women who doubtless did contrive to read the poem would have read as trespassers, conscious that they were intruding into a text the indelicacies of which clearly marked it as forbidden territory.[39] As Miss Prudence Morton (a Blue as her name suggests) puts it in a piece by John Hamilton Reynolds, 'Have you read Don Juan? I have not: but I think it abounds with beautiful passages, though it is a sad wicked book.'[40]

For the poem's admirers the poem's masculinity was the key indicator of its superiority to the earlier work. The heroes of the early poems, 'humbug Harolds' as Lockhart calls them, may have converted many into becoming 'devout believers in the amazing misery of the black-haired, high-browed, blue-eyed, bare-throated, Lord Byron', but the majority of those so beguiled are members of the class best represented by Jane Austen: 'Now, tell me, Mrs Goddard, now tell me, Miss Price, now tell me, dear Harriet Smith, and dear, dear, Mrs Elton, do tell me, is not this just the very look, that one would have fancied for Childe Harold?' They are women, and only middling women at that.[41] The *British Lady's Magazine* was much more polite, but otherwise in full agreement. In 1815 it insisted that the 'compositions of Lord Byron appear, by the tone of their versification, the novel softness of their subjects, and the peculiarities of their language, to have captivated ladies' hearts with a success far above all other productions of the present day'.[42] When he began to publish *Don Juan*, Byron, as he was well aware, was turning against the sex that made up a very large part of his own readership ('There has been an eleventh commandment to the women not to read it—and what is still more extraordinary they seem not to have broken it.').[43] It was an important matter, because, as Ugo Foscolo pointed out (in a

[37] *Edinburgh Magazine and Literary Miscellany*, 9 (August 1821), 106.
[38] *Scots Magazine*, 9 (September 1821), 252.
[39] On this, see Andrew Elfenbein, *Byron and the Victorians* (Cambridge: Cambridge University Press, 1995), 72–3. Elfenbein quotes Amelia Opie's confession: 'And when I heard some highly virtuous and modest women tell me they had read it, and were "not ashamed," and when I recollected that I had read Prior, Pope, Dryden and Grimm, I thought I would e'en add to my list of offences that of reading "Don Juan." I must say that the account of its wickedness is most exaggerated.' Moyra Haslett concludes that the poem 'was addressed conspiratorially to masculine intimates, but was not unaware that women would overhear'. *Byron's* Don Juan *and the Don Juan Legend* (Oxford: Clarendon Press, 1997), 191.
[40] 'Greenwich Hospital,' *London Magazine*, 4 (November 1821), 530.
[41] J. G. Lockhart, *John Bull's Letter to Lord Byron*, ed. Alan Lang Strout (Norman: University Of Oklahoma Press, 1947), 80. It is a point that Lockhart reiterates in his novel, *Reginald Dalton*, when Reginald observes 'a small circle of blue-stockings that were gathered round a certain lyrical poet, who sat in an ottoman among them, with something of the air of a little Turkish Bashaw luxuriating in the seclusion of his own haram, evidently considering every whisper of his as a compliment—every smile as a seduction' (3, 85).
[42] *British Lady's Magazine*, 1 (January–June 1815), 175.
[43] *Byron's Letters and Journals*, ed. Leslie A. Marchand, 6 (London: John Murray, 1976), 237.

review of the most important precursor of *Don Juan*, Frere's *Whistlecraft*) the commercial success of poems was determined by 'the suffrages of the ladies, who, in every country, and particularly in England, are, after all, the supreme arbiters of the destiny and reputation of the new poetry'.[44]

In these years women were increasingly important not just as consumers but as producers of poetry, and Byron had been chosen as the Muse of the new school of women poets. Angela Leighton, in a fine reading of Felicia Hemans's 'The Chamois Hunter's Love', points out that the chamois hunter, who loves the perilous, stormy heights, is almost a metonym for the Byronic, that is, the Romantic Byron of *Manfred*.[45] In Landon's *The Improvisatrice* Lorenzo, the object of the improvisatrice's passion is described at the moment that she first sees him, with his 'dark and flashing eye' that yet betrayed an 'almost female softness', his pale cheek, 'raven curls', 'high and haughty brow' as white as the mountain snow, and his heart-stopping eloquence. We learn later that he has 'thick-clustering curls' and a 'smile which past like lightning o'er / The curved lip'.[46] It is a description that, as all her early readers would have recognised, is derived directly from the idealized prints of Byron's portraits that were so popular, especially in the years immediately following his death. Byron had once admired Felicia Hemans, but, by September 1820, as her popularity grew, his comments on her become ever more grudging: 'I do not despise Mrs. Heman [the missing "s" is, I fear, a joke, rather than, as Byron's editor, Leslie Marchand, charitably imagines, an oversight]—but if [she] knit blue stockings instead of wearing them it would be better.' A month earlier he had begged Murray to be spared any more 'poesy' by 'Mrs. Hewoman' or any other 'female or male Tadpole of Poet Turdsworth's'.[47] His spleen was vented at last in an elaborate squib, *The Blues*, which was published in the third number of *The Liberal*.

Byron turned violently against a school of women poets that he had himself done much to inspire, and he was not alone. Keats, for all that Byron thought him an effeminate producer of '*piss-a-bed* poetry',[48] had already discovered that there was 'nothing in' the poetry of Mary Tighe that he had once admired, that 'the Dress Maker, the blue Stocking and the most charming sentimentalist differ but in a Slight degree and are equally smokeable', and was announcing to his friend Richard Woodhouse that he wished to write only for men.[49] The male

---

[44] *Quarterly Review*, 21 (April 1819), 508–9.

[45] Angela Leighton, *Victorian Women Poets: Writing Against the Heart* (London: Harvester Wheatsheaf, 1992), 24–5.

[46] L.E.L., *The Improvisatrice and Other Poems*, 3rd edn (London: Hurst Robinson and Co., 1825), 29–30, and 63.

[47] *Byron's Letters and Journals*, ed. Leslie A. Marchand, 7 (London: John Murray, 1977), 182 and 158.

[48] *Byron's Letters and Journals*, 7, 200.

[49] *The Letters of John Keats*, ed. Hyder Edward Rollins (Cambridge: Cambridge University Press, 1958), 2, 18–19, and 163. Woodhouse adds that in his revisions to 'The Eve of St Agnes' Keats 'affected the "Don Juan" style of mingling up sentiment & sneering'.

poets of the period seemed to respond as aggressively as the male novelists to the threat that the nation's literary, unlike its political, leaders might be at the mercy of the 'suffrages of women', and in both cases it was an aggression sharpened by anxiety.

Byron and Keats exemplify a rather general tendency amongst male poets to protect themselves against women readers, and to brand any women who persisted in reading their work as trespassers. The popularity in the period of plots in which male characters intrude into enclosed females spaces is perhaps best understood as a reflex of this project. Juan, cross-dressed in order to gain entry to the seraglio, is an oddly representative figure. In 'The Eve of St Agnes', Porphyro hides himself away in Madeline's closet, spies on her as she undresses, and, as soon as she closes her eyes, emerges into her bedroom. His behaviour, as has often been pointed out, recalls Iachimo's in *Cymbeline*. In 'Gyges' Barry Cornwall tells a very similar story. King Candaules is so vain of his wife's beauty that he invites Gyges, a young courtier, to spy on her as she prepares for bed. Cornwall makes the Shakespearean allusion specific:

> There was a mark on Lais' swan-like breast,
>   (A purple flower with its leaf of green,)
> Like that the Italian saw when on the rest
>   He stole of the unconscious Imogene,
> And bore away the dark fallacious test
>   Of what was not, altho' it might have been,
> And much perplex'd Leonatus Posthumus;
> In truth he might have puzzled one of us.[50]

Cornwall writes in ottava rima and his couplet is Byronic, but when the hidden Gyges gazes on the Queen's beauty, he models himself, as I pointed out in a previous chapter, on Keats. For Barry Cornwall, Byron and Keats are complementary, both of them offering him a model for the composition of poems of a challengingly masculine cast. John Moultrie seems to have felt similarly. Jeffrey thought that, unlike *Don Juan*, Cornwall's poem was free from 'profligacy'.[51] The daringly Byronic ottava rima poem that appeared in *The Etonian*, 'Godiva', struck the *Quarterly* reviewer as a good deal less innocent.[52] He flinched perhaps from the inclusion in a school magazine of the description of the waltz:

> I must say I enjoy it—'tis a pleasure
>   *Good-natured* fair ones grant to amorous swains;
> I like to whirl to that bewildering measure,
>   Which, 'just like love',—or brandy, turns one's brains:
> I like to view my partner's charms at leisure,

---

[50] Barry Cornwall, *A Sicilian Story* (London: C. and J. Ollier, 1820), 'Gyges', stanza 23.
[51] *Edinburgh Review*, 33 (January 1820), 153.
[52] See the review of *The Etonian* in the *Quarterly Review*, 25 (April 1821), 95–112.

> Till scarce a secret for the bride remains;
> While round her waist each wanton finger strays,
> And counts the whalebones in her panting stays.

The final line adds to the erotic mix the touch of 'buffoonery' that clinches its Byronic character, but Moultrie has affinities with the Cockneys too. The only close parallel to his story, he writes, is 'That of Candaules—handed down to us / By Barry Cornwall, and Herodotus', and at the poem's erotic climax Cornwall or Keats rather than Byron seems to be the model:

> A moment's pause—and then she deeply blush'd,
> As, trembling, she unclasp'd her rich attire,
> And shrinking from the sunlight, shone confest
> The ripe and dazzling beauties of her breast.[53]

The Cockneys, Byron and the Eton poet are united in their fascination with plots in which men intrude into female preserves, plots that assert by confounding the separateness of male and female spheres.[54]

MAGAZINES AND MASCULINITY

Of the magazines it was *Blackwood's* that most vigorously asserted its role as the champion of the new masculinity. Readers of *Blackwood's* were invited to join a boisterous, lively, exclusively male gathering of the kind that Wilson and others brilliantly epitomized in the alcohol-fuelled public house dinners consumed with such gusto in the series *Noctes Ambrosianae*. Readers of *Blackwood's* were assumed to be addicted to masculine pleasures. When summer arrives they are encouraged to make the most of the season:

Hunt, shoot, fish, course, leap, run, walk, ride, wrestle, box (with the gloves of course,) et cetera. Let the ladies amuse themselves lady-like; but not the slightest approach to blue-stockingism, which is a vile vice. Do not drink overmuch in the warm weather,—say, not above two bottles per diem.[55]

Blackwood's defence of masculinity involved it in an evangelical mission against 'blue-stockingism', and it was a mission that the magazine delighted to proclaim. Before *Blackwood's*, Wilson boasted,

blue-stockingism was in its cerulean altitude. Every female leg was azure—absolutely painted blue like a post. A slight beard was becoming visible on young women still

---

[53] 'Godiva', stanza 39, stanza 41, 7–8, and stanza 57, 5–8, *The Etonian* (London: Henry Colburn, 1824), 1, 197, 198, and 203.
[54] A point astutely made of *Don Juan* by Susan Wolfson, '"Their She Condition": Cross-Dressing and the Politics of Gender in *Don Juan*', *ELH*, 54 (1987), 585–617.
[55] *Blackwood's Edinburgh Magazine*, 9 (July 1821), 465.

marriageable—a certain consequence of incipient literary habits; so you may imagine the upper lip of well-informed women of forty. A single number of the Magazine was equivalent to a thousand razors—for as our friends gave up book-reading, that of which we found so much reason to complain subsided into a pleasing down.[56]

As Lisa Niles has pointed out, *Blackwood's* represented itself emphatically as a 'space for the single man', presided over by the septuagenarian bachelor, Christopher North. North claims to be the successor of his fellow-bachelor, Addison's 'Mr Spectator', but his single status registers a far more emphatic rejection of the female sex in general, and female intellectual ambition in particular.[57] *Blackwood's*, Wilson claims, is the most effective deterrent against women falling into the unfortunate habit of book-reading. In the *Noctes Ambosianae* series, the exclusively male conversation of a group of hard-drinking men figures the kind of conversation in which the magazine as a whole invites its readers to join, and it is self-consciously distinguished by Morgan Odoherty from the mixed society of 'Conversazioni':

> Conversazioni—are not for my money,
>   Where Blue Stockings prate about Wylie and Pen;
> I'd rather get tipsy with *ipsissimi ipsi*—
>   Plain women must yield to plain sense and plain men.[58]

In its uncompromising masculinity Lockhart's *Peter's Letters to his Kinsfolk* is a legitimate by-product of the magazine. Peter Morris is delighted to record that in Edinburgh 'the infection of blue-stockingism' is less rife than in England. Morris himself prefers the kind of 'very snug party' at which a select group of men sit over their claret, but on one occasion he attends a party that includes several Edinburgh bluestockings, lured by the prospect of Jeffrey's presence. Jeffrey is ambushed by six of them, 'pinioned up against the wall', and subjected to a merciless literary interrogation—'don't you agree with me, in being decidedly of opinion, that Mr Scott is the true author of Tales of my Landlord?' He is subjected to 'query upon query, about the conduct of Lord Byron, in deserting his wife', and stridently reminded of the merits of *Peter Bell*: 'Can you be blind to the pathetic incident of the poor ass kneeling under the blows of the cruel, hard-hearted, odious Peter?' Jeffrey listens 'with a greater expression of misery' than Morris had thought him capable of, but he is not entirely a figure recommended to our pity. The implication is that he has brought the ordeal on himself by failing adequately to safeguard the *Edinburgh Review* against feminine

[56] *Blackwood's Edinburgh Magazine*, 8 (October 1820), 99.

[57] See Lisa Niles, '"May the married be single, and the single happy": *Blackwood's*, the Maga for the Single Man', in *Romantic Periodicals and Print Culture*, ed. Kim Wheatley (London and Portland, Oregon: Frank Cass, 2002), 102–21.

[58] *Blackwood's Edinburgh Magazine*, 3 (May 1822), 614. Wylie and Pen are characters in novels by John Galt and James Hook, who join the company at Ambrose's no doubt because both novelists were published by Blackwood.

encroachments. Although he stands near Jeffrey in the room, John Wilson is left unmolested, in happy conversation with Henry Mackenzie, two anglers discussing the merits of a particular fly.[59]

Women were admitted to *Blackwood's* most often as contributors of poetry. Caroline Bowles was a regular and Felicia Hemans an occasional contributor. For the most part, though, the magazine maintained its masculine character. In *Blackwood's* the readers of the magazine tend to be represented as the members of a club, an intimate and exclusively male gathering. The magazine offered its readers the literary equivalent of the room in Ambrose's tavern in which the magazine represented its contributors as gathering: it was a space magically free from female intrusion. *Blackwood's* was appealing to a new sense that men were a beleaguered sex, marooned in the feminized cultural modernity of the early nineteenth century, a modernity from which Ambrose's tavern represented an escape, as did the magazine that the frequenters of the tavern produced.

It was a feature of the magazine that the young men who wrote *The Etonian* enthusiastically imitated. Although *The Etonian* only accepted contributions from those who were or had recently been pupils at the school, the editor represents himself as badgered by young women who aspired to become contributors: 'Letitia wanted to bore us with some poetry;—obliged to tell her we received no contributions from ladies.'[60] Praed went on to edit *Knight's Quarterly Magazine* in which he advertises John Moultrie's 'La Belle Tryamour' as a poem just as unacceptable to women readers as *Don Juan*. The fear of the financial consequences that he affects quite fails to disguise his pleasure in the outrage of feminine feelings:

> And alas! who will read us, or buy us, or fund us?
> Madam looks serious, Miss looks away!
> And fat Lady Lumber has burned the first Number,
> And the murder is out, and the devil's to pay!
> And poor Mr. Knight will look terribly white
> When Benbow and Dugdale shall fly to their function;
> When our exquisite meats shall be hawk'd in the streets,
> And the Chancery lawyers dissolve the injunction.[61]

The best-selling magazine of them all, the *New Monthly*, was so successful because it was more sensitive to the feelings of Madam, Miss, and 'fat Lady Lumber'.

[59] J. G. Lockhart, *Peter's Letters to his Kinsfolk* (Edinburgh: Blackwood, 1819), 1, 307–10.
[60] *The Etonian*, 1, 311.
[61] *Knight's Quarterly Magazine*, 1 (June–October 1823), 233. Benbow and Dugdale were publishers who had both produced pirated editions of *Don Juan*, which they correctly judged that they could do with impunity because works deemed immoral were not granted copyright protection by the courts.

It may be that Charles Lamb, the magazine's best-paid contributor developed Elia as a pointed retort to the emphatic masculinity of *Blackwood's*. Elia with his shyness, his childhood lameness, somehow so different from Christopher North's gout, his stammer, living his bachelor life not raucously in Ambrose's Tavern but decorously and domestically in the house that he shares with his cousin, Bridget Elia, ten years his senior, seems designed as the antithesis of the fictitious editor of *Blackwood's*. Elia is at ease in feminine spaces, at the card table presided over by Mrs Battle, or in the 'china-closet' that, when he visits an old house, he always asks to inspect before the picture gallery (he confesses to 'an almost feminine partiality for old china').The world of the essays is a little like the world of china tea-cups, made up of 'men with women's faces' and 'women, if possible, with still more womanish expressions'.[62] He represents himself as less than fully masculine, a 'boy-man' on whose shoulders the '*toga virilis* never sat gracefully',[63] but this is less a disability than a passport: it allows him access to the kind of enclosed feminine space to which the likes of Christopher North would never gain admission. He celebrates the old-fashioned gallantry of Joseph Paice, who did not have '*one* system of attention to females in the drawing-room, and *another* in the shop or at the stall', and who 'never lost sight of sex, or overlooked it in the casualties of a disadvantageous situation'.[64] Elia might make the same claim for himself: the essays, even when they reflect on male institutions, Christ's Hospital or the Inner Temple, never lose sight of sex: they remain gallantly aware of their women readers. Lamb's more emphatically masculine colleagues tend not to lose sight of sex either, but in them this is not an expression of their gallantry, but rather the reverse.

The most visible symptom of the new masculinism of the post-war years was the cult of the prize fight. When Tom and Jerry pay a visit to 'Gentleman' Jackson's Rooms in Bond Street they are following a fashion long-established, by amongst others Byron, who advertised his attendance in his verse, referring in a note to his translation of Pulci to his 'old friend and master, Jackson' and advising in *Hints from Horace* 'men unpractised in exchanging knocks' to 'go to Jackson's ere they dare to box'.[65] It was a fashion that was not confined to Regency Dandies. Hazlitt and John Hamilton Reynolds were both enthusiastic members of 'The Fancy', and even though Keats thought that a street quarrel was a hateful thing he still found that 'the energies displayed in it are fine'.[66]

Of the magazines, *Blackwood's* was the great champion of the sport. John Wilson had himself been an accomplished boxer, but it was also an aspect of

---

[62] See 'Mrs Battle's Opinions on Whist,' *London Magazine*, 3 (February 1821), 161–5, and 'Old China,' *London Magazine*, 7 (March 1823), 269–72.

[63] 'A Character of the Late Elia,' *London Magazine*, 7 (January 1823), 21.

[64] 'Modern Gallantry', *London Magazine*, 6 (November 1822), 453–5.

[65] *The Liberal*, 2 (April 1823), 216, and *Hints from Horace*, 597–8.

[66] *The Letters of John Keats*, 2, 80.

Blackwood's populism and its celebration of muscular Britishness that it gave extensive coverage to a pastime far below the notice of the great quarterlies. Pierce Egan, author of *Boxiana*, is perhaps the only writer of whom, at least until he included an essay by Hazlitt in one of his collections, *Blackwood's* had not a bad word to say. *Blackwood's* introduced its own 'Boxiana' series in which the history of boxing is traced through the development of its different 'schools'. The ex-slave Tom Molineaux, for example, led 'The Sable School of Pugilism'.[67] The various schools of boxing paralleled the different schools into which *Blackwood's* delighted to divide the nation's poets; the Lake School, the Cockney School, 'The Leg of Mutton School of Poetry' (made up of poets who specialize in complimentary poems written to secure dinner invitations from those complimented),[68] and so on. It was a running joke in *Blackwood's* to compare the history of poetry with the history of prize-fighting. So, Pierce Egan's *Boxiana* is compared with a history of poetry:

Our readers will understand what our opinion of it is, when we say that it may be classed with Campbell's Specimens of English Poetry. There is the same 'springy force' in all our author says, and as in reading what Mr Campbell writes on poetry, we feel that he is himself a poet, so in the perusal of Boxiana we trace the hand of a pugilist.[69]

Six months later the joke had become more extravagant. Egan has 'all the elegance and feeling of a Percy—all the classical grace and inventive ingenuity of a Warton—all the enthusiasm and zeal of a Headley?—all the acuteness and rigour of a Ritson—all the learning and wit of an Ellis—all the delicacy and discernment of a Campbell; and at the same time, his style is perfectly his own, and likely to remain so, for it is as inimitable as it is excellent'.[70] The style that Jack Broughton introduced into the ring is offered as a proof of what 'has been well said by Mr Coleridge, that a great poet must create the taste capable of enjoying his works', and again the joke seemed good enough to repeat: 'the Game Chicken's left-handed lounge on the jugular, Belcher's cross-buttock, and Randal's one-two—all created a taste in the public mind which was not there before'.[71] The comparison might be reversed: men of letters might be described as boxers. Byron's many detractors, for example, 'entered the ring in very bad condition, and immediately got a-piping, like hot mutton pies—fell on their own blows, and knapped it every round, till they shewed the white feather and

---

[67] *Blackwood's Edinburgh Magazine*, 8 (October 1820), 60.
[68] *Blackwood's Edinburgh Magazine*, 9 (June 1821), 345–66.
[69] *Blackwood's Edinburgh Magazine*, 5 (July 1819), 442.
[70] *Blackwood's Edinburgh Magazine*, 6 (March 1820), 611.
[71] *Blackwood's Edinburgh Magazine*, 8 (October 1820), 61 and 62. Many years later the joke still seemed fresh enough for De Quincey, in 'On Murder Considered as One of the Fine Arts', to extend it from pugilists to murderers. He notes of the perpetrator of the Ratcliffe Highway murders, John Williams, that he 'as Mr Wordsworth observes, has in a manner "created the taste by which he is to be enjoyed."' *Blackwood's Edinburgh Magazine*, 21 (February 1827), 200.

bolted'.[72] The joke culminated in May 1820, when *Blackwood's* produced the '"Luctus" on the Death of Sir Daniel Donnelly, Late Champion of Ireland', an elaborate memorial to the recently deceased Irish champion, which includes a letter from Byron including the opening stanzas of his new poem, 'Child Daniel', and a letter from 'Mr W. W.' enclosing an extract from his 'Great Auto-Biographical Poem':

> Yea, even I,
> Albeit, who never 'ruffian'd' in the ring,
> Nor know of 'challenge,' save the echoing hills;
> Nor 'fibbing', save that poesy doth feign;
> Nor heard his fame, but as the mutterings
> Of clouds contentious on Helvellyn's side,
> Distant, yet deep, agnize a strange regret,
> And mourn Donnelly—Honourable Sir Daniel.[73]

The *Westminster Review* recognized Wilson's leading role in promoting the analogy between poetry and prize-fighting in an unusually facetious review of a poem called *The Danciad* written by a Thomas Wilson, a professor of dancing that the *Westminster* chose to identify with Professor Wilson of Edinburgh University. The real Professor Wilson had contrived it that 'Crib and Tom Moore, Rogers and White-headed Bob, Dolly Smith and Wordsworth' became so 'mingled in the imagination' that 'the Art of Poetry and the Art of Self Defence seemed one and the same thing'. Wilson is congratulated on signalling, with the publication of a poem on dancing, that the fashion is at end, and that it might now be possible to 'ask a poet to see you without the risk of having your claret drawn'.[74]

It seems a harmless enough jest, but there is a serious edge to the humour. It is a comedy that reinvents the world of letters as uncompromisingly masculine, just as masculine as the world of the ring. There were those who objected. In *The Liberal*, in his poem 'The Choice', Leigh Hunt claimed to enjoy sports such as golf, quoits, and cricket:

> But, as for prize fights, with their butchering shows,
> And crowds of black-legs, I'd have none of those;—
> I am not bold in other people's blows.[75]

---

[72] *Blackwood's Edinburgh Magazine*, 8 (October 1820), 81.
[73] *Blackwood's Edinburgh Magazine*, 7 (May 1820), 186–205.
[74] *Westminster Review*, 2 (July 1824), 213. The joke was more pointed for those who recognized the piece as by John Hamilton Reynolds, who, as a close friend of Keats, was antagonistic to *Blackwood's*, but who delighted in the analogy between literature and prize-fighting almost as much as John Wilson.
[75] *The Liberal*, 2 (July 1823), 272. As might be expected, in 'Mr North's Lecture on "The Choice"', on which the eleventh episode of the *Noctes Ambrosianae* centres, this passage is picked out for ridicule, Christopher North wonders what would be the response if 'Bill Gibbons should some day pitch the ring for a fight between the Bush-Cove and the Cabbage . . . in Mr Hunt's Park?' *Blackwood's Edinburgh Magazine*, 14 (August 1823), 202.

For *Blackwood's* it was one more proof of his Cockney effeminacy. Other editors found it much harder to resist the new fashion. In the *London* Thomas Wainewright might defend his own dandyism—'We want more macaroni and champagne; less boxing and bull beef'[76]—but his editor decided that *Blackwood's* could not be allowed to enjoy a 'monopoly' of manly sports. The *London* entered into direct rivalry with the Scottish magazine by offering its own tribute to the 'poetry' of Egan's prose: 'There is in the language of Mr Egan, a beautiful indistinctness—a sort of gentle twilight—that softens all objects to the same endurable appearance.'[77] Reynolds, who wrote this, had already in May 1820, contributed a paper 'On Fighting' by 'a young gentleman of the Fancy' which provoked letters 'questioning the propriety of inserting *pugilistic articles*', but the complaints were reported in the issue for August 1820, which included another such article, and in July the *London* had reviewed Reynolds's *The Fancy*, a spoof selection of the 'Poetical Remains' of the Irish boxer, Peter Corcoran.[78] Of the major magazines the *New Monthly* had from the first been the most attentive both to women writers and to women readers, which made it the more remarkable that it was the *New Monthly* that published in February 1822, the greatest of all pugilistic articles, Hazlitt's 'The Fight'.[79] Cyrus Redding, Campbell's assistant editor, recalled that Campbell had been against its inclusion:

There were considerable doubts about admitting such a paper. The subject was so thoroughly 'blackguard,' and it was giving currency to a disgraceful, demoralising species of vulgar exhibition that branded England as the bull-fight does Spain with disgrace in the sight of all civilised nations—an exhibition, too, that its advocates pretend kept up the national courage, while the real motive was the gain made of it, as of all similar shows, by blacklegs and thieves. Campbell hesitated a good while. I suggested that the paper, disgraceful as its theme was, afforded too true a picture of existing manners, and would, in the course of things, soon become a mere record of our past barbarities. The poet, too, did not like to refuse, at so early a period, a paper of Hazlitt's, because he felt it might be charged to his personal dislike of the writer: so it was agreed, the barbarism should appear in a publication very differently characterised in its other articles.[80]

But Hazlitt had already incorporated in the piece an awareness of its incongruity with the rest of the magazine's contents.

He begins, 'Ladies! It is to you I dedicate this description.' The mixed, domestic readership that Thomas Campbell had so carefully nurtured is invited to savour an extravagantly violent, exclusively masculine blood sport. Hazlitt's

[76] *London Magazine*, 1 (June 1820), 631.
[77] *London Magazine*, 2 (August 1820), 155–6.
[78] *London Magazine*, 1 (May 1820), 519–25; 2 (August 1820), 122, and 'The Jewels of the Book', 155–61; and 2 (July 1820), 71–5.
[79] *New Monthly Magazine*, 4 (February 1822), 102–12; Howe, 17, 72–86.
[80] *New Monthly Magazine*, 79 (February 1847), 245.

journey to Hungerford in Berkshire where the fight between the Gasman, Thomas Hickman, and Bill Neate took place—a seat outside on the coach as far as Reading where an inside place became available, sitting up all night at the Crown in Newbury, and then in the early morning 'the nine mile march to Hungerford'—is recounted in a raffishly jaunty prose. The fight itself is brutal. In the twelfth round Hickman is floored:

His face was like a human skull, a death's head, spouting blood. The eyes were filled with blood, the nose streamed with blood. The mouth gaped blood.

Still Hickman fought on: 'Ye who despise the Fancy, do something to shew as much *pluck*, or as much self-possession as this, before you assume a superiority which you have never given a single proof of by any one action in the whole of your lives!' In a ploy that oddly recalls how *Blackwood's* had denounced the Cockneys, Hunt and Hazlitt himself chief among them, those who disapprove of prize-fighting are branded effeminate. Hazlitt, despite admitting that this was his '*first fight*', ostentatiously signals his membership of the Fancy. He is familiar with the 'Hole in the Wall' in Chancery Lane, kept by Jack Randall, 'the Nonpareil', acquainted with the trainer Tom Turtle (John Thurtell), with whom he discusses training methods, can recall how Jem Belcher and Henry Pearce, the Game Chicken, comported themselves in the ring, reports a remark made by Jack Scroggins, and refers familiarly to John Gully, the ex-prize-fighter and boxing aficionado. But Hazlitt is just as ostentatious in presenting himself as a man of letters. 'I was going down Chancery-lane, thinking to ask Jack Randall's where the fight was to be, when looking through the glass-door of the *Hole in the Wall*, I heard a gentleman asking the same question at Mrs Randall, as the author of Waverley would express it.' It was a tic of Scott's to ask questions at someone rather than of them, as in *Marmion*—'Blithe would I battle, for the right / To ask one question at the sprite'[81]—but the real function of the remark is to identify the essay's speaker as a man of letters. In an essay of just ten pages Hazlitt manages to echo at least six plays by Shakespeare, some of them, *Hamlet, Julius Caesar*, and *Othello*, more than once, Etherege's *The Man of Mode*, Dryden's *The Indian Emperor, Paradise Lost*, Chaucer's 'Prologue', Cowper's *Task*, Spenser's *Muiopotmos*, and the 'Ballad of Chevy Chase'. The irruption into his inn of some London tradesmen prompts a quotation from the *Aeneid*, and the bloodied Gasman resembles 'one of the figures in Dante's *Inferno*' (at the start of the bout he had seemed like Diomed confronting in Bill Neate a 'modern Ajax'). The essay's exaggerated literariness is a device that allows Hazlitt to proclaim himself a cultural democrat, a man equally at home in the republic of letters and the world of the ring. Distinctions between high and low culture are not so much questioned as held up to mockery. But another distinction seems still more

---

[81] *Marmion*, Canto 3, stanza 29, 10–11, *The Poems of Sir Walter Scott*, ed. J. Logie Robertson (London: Oxford University Press, 1904).

absolute. Hazlitt comments in his essay 'On Personal Character', 'The character of women (I should think it will at this time of day be granted) differs essentially from that of men, not less so than their shape or the texture of their skin',[82] and the character of literature as it is represented in 'The Fight' aligns it emphatically with men. The republic of letters, Hazlitt implies, is as exclusively masculine as the crowd that gathers to watch Hickman and Bill Neate.

Hazlitt saves his most telling jibe to the last. He had travelled to Newbury by mail-coach with Joe Toms (Joseph Parkes), he returns by post-chaise with Jack Pigott (P. G. Patmore), two men of very different character: 'Toms is a rattle-brain; Pigott is a sentimentalist.' During lulls in the conversation Pigott reads. Hazlitt asks what the book is and learns 'to [his] peculiar satisfaction that it was a volume of the New Eloise': 'Ladies, after this, will you contend that a love for the FANCY is incompatible with the cultivation of sentiment?' Even women, the suggestion is, should not scorn prize-fighting enthusiasts if they include within their number an admirer of Rousseau. But this suggestion conceals another, that literature of the kind that women had claimed for their own, the sentimental novel, is, truth be told, no less distinctively masculine than Dante, Chaucer, Milton, and the 'Ballad of Chevy Chase'. The proper reader of *La Nouvelle Heloise* is a man like Jack Pigott, who has a proper appreciation at once of Rousseau's prose, of the Gasman's pluck, and of Tom Neate's right hand.

Stewart C. Wilcox, in his study of the manuscript of 'The Fight', has calculated that some five hundred words were deleted from the first eight leaves. He deduces from the deleted passages that have been preserved that all these cuts had to do with the infatuation with Sarah Walker that Hazlitt records in *Liber Amoris*.[83] As he walks past Hyde Park Corner on his way to catch the mail-coach to Newbury, Hazlitt thinks of it as his Rubicon, the stream that marks the boundary between the world of sentiment, the world presided over by Sarah Walker, and the masculine camaraderie of the world of boxing. In a deleted passage, he writes, 'Oh! thou dumb heart, lonely, sad, shut up in the prison house of this rude form, that hast never found a fellow but for an hour & in very mockery of thy misery, speak, find bleeding words to escape thy thoughts, break thy dungeon-gloom, or die pronouncing the name of thy Clarissa!' The deletions suggest that 'The Fight' began as a very different essay, a paper that dramatized the conflict within Hazlitt between the reader of Richardson and the member of the Fancy, between the sentimentalist and the exponent of an aggressive masculinity. Even in the piece as published traces of the earlier article remain visible, as when Hazlitt thinks of the life lived by a prize-fighter, an instinctual, bodily life, blissfully free from self-reflection:

---

[82] *London Magazine*, 3 (March 1821), 291; Howe, 12, 234.
[83] *Hazlitt in the Workshop: The Manuscript of 'The Fight'*, ed. Stewart C. Wilcox (Baltimore: John Hopkins University Press, 1943).

Is not this life more sweet than mine? I was going to say; but I will not libel any life by comparing it to mine, which is (at the date of these presents) bitter as coloquintada and the dregs of aconitum!

Hazlitt echoes *Othello*, the play that repeated allusions identify as the ur-text of *Liber Amoris*. As David Higgins points out, Hazlitt made 'The Fight' 'much more coherent by cutting most of the digressions relating to Sarah Walker.' Hazlitt realized, he guesses, that 'his positioning of himself within the masculinist, patriotic language of pugilism was totally undermined by including passages of sentimental confession'.[84] But the effect, surely, might operate in reverse. It might be that it is the sentimental that is undermined by the jaunty, brutal masculinity which is, after all, the dominant style of the whole essay. In 'The Fight' the two styles work to undermine each other, as if sentimentality and masculine heartiness were at once and equally theatrical, guises that the essay does not so much exploit as parody.

Only traces of the sentimental remain in the published essay, but the contrast is relocated rather than refused, because the issue of the *New Monthly* for February 1822 includes two essays by Hazlitt. 'The Fight' appeared over the signature, 'Phantastes', and 'On Great and Little Things' appeared as 'Table-Talk No. II',[85] but both were immediately recognizable as Hazlitt's, and in the second essay, as if suffering from a compulsive disorder, Hazlitt repeatedly digresses from his topic to his relations with women in general and to Sarah Walker in particular. As in the passages deleted from 'The Fight', Hazlitt appears as a sentimentalist, as a man writing in the Richardsonian tradition, although it is the 'Pamelas' rather than the 'Clarissas' that 'make [his] blood tingle'. This is not, though it might seem so, a tribute to the attractions of the servant class:

Poets chuse mistresses who have the fewest charms, that they may make something out of nothing. They succeed best in fiction, and they apply this rule to love. They make a Goddess of any dowdy.

In 'The Fight', as in most pugilistic pieces, aesthetic as well as cultural values are exclusively masculine. The ideal of beauty is embodied in the male body. Hazlitt is interrupted in his disapproval of Tom Hickman's swaggering entrance to the ring when the Gas-Man strips and reveals a body glistening 'like a panther's hide'. Women can function as Muses, it seems, only because their physical imperfections prompt a more energetic exercise of the artistic imagination.

Hazlitt also prefers to choose his women from the servant class because such women are more likely to accept their exclusion from the literary realm. As one might expect, they have no appreciation of philosophy: Hazlitt claims that the 'only thing [he] ever piqued himself upon was the writing the *Essay on the*

[84] David Higgins, 'Englishness, Effeminacy, and the *New Monthly Magazine*: Hazlitt's "The Fight" in Context', *Romanticism*, 10 (2004), 173–90, 178–9.
[85] *New Monthly Magazine*, 4 (February 1822), 127–39; Howe, 8, 226–42.

Principles of Human Action—a work that no woman ever read'. More surprising-ly, they are just as unappreciative of sentimental literature: Hazlitt recalls how he has written love letters '*d'un pathetique à faire fendre les rochers*, and with about as much effect as if they had been addressed to stone'.[86] The women he wrote to only laughed 'and said "those were not the sort of things to gain the affections"'. Sentimental writing is produced by men, and addressed not to women as they are, but to women as men like to imagine them, and hence when Hazlitt offers a specimen of it himself—'Oh! if I am deceived, let me be deceived still. Let me live in the Elysium of those soft looks; poison me with kisses, kill me with smiles; but still mock me with thy love!'—he adds a note inviting the reader to 'consider the passage merely as a specimen of the mock-heroic style, and as having nothing to do with any real facts or feelings'. Given his assumptions, all sentimental writing is parody, whether the parody is intended or otherwise.

Hazlitt is writing here, quite clearly, under intense personal pressure, but if that were simply the case it would have only biographical significance. It seems more important to point out that Hazlitt is exhibiting with unusual intensity a set of cultural rather than psychological symptoms. Male writers in the late teens and early twenties of the nineteenth century register anxieties that have to do with a nervous sense of their emergent professional status. The production of literature was no longer securely a gentlemanly vocation: it had become an employment for which a writer expected and required payment. The increasing importance of women writers, first as novelists, but more recently as poets too, threatened this new status by suggesting that literary earnings might properly be thought of as amounting to no more than 'Pin Money' (which was incidentally the title of an 1831 novel by the most popular woman novelist of her era, Catherine Gore). It was a situation that left male writers anxious to assert their own masculinity, as John Scott did by engaging in the duel in which he died, and as Keats and Byron did by insisting on their wish to write for men rather than for women. Magazines are the most sensitive cultural barometers of the period, which makes it unsurprising that *Blackwood's* from very early on should have flamboyantly adopted so ultra-masculine a character. The appear-ance of 'The Fight' in the *New Monthly* for February 1822, is in some sense even more significant evidence, for of all the major magazines the *New Monthly* had been most emphatic in its decision to address itself to a mixed, domestic audience. From the first a series of more or less sympathetic articles on women, women writers, even bluestockings, carefully maintained this character. But in January 1822, the most recent in this series, 'Women', took on a new character.[87] James Smith, the contributor, begins by insisting that there must be a 'natural' difference between men and women, because difference in education was in itself insufficient to explain why 'women, in all ages and in all countries, have held only

---

[86] The quotation is from Rousseau's *Confessions*.
[87] *New Monthly Magazine*, 4 (January 1822), 141–4.

a subordinate station in society', and goes on somewhat feebly to suggest that the unquestionable pre-eminence of men 'in arts and arms, and science and philosophy, in foresight and grandeur of soul' is adequately offset by the thought of 'how vastly inferior he is in all the softer graces, in tenderness, delicacy, and sentiment!' As he concludes his paper Smith registers in a remark addressed to the editor his concern that he may have raised 'some matters at which your fair readers may probably cavil', but he takes nothing back, and his contribution was allowed to appear. It was, perhaps, less of a surprise than it might seem that the very next month Thomas Campbell agreed to publish Hazlitt's 'The Fight'.

Conclusion: Two Cultures

The duels in which John Scott and Sir Alexander Boswell died were unusual. Most literary quarrels were resolved without loss of blood, let alone loss of life. Far more typical was the rencontre between Francis Jeffrey and Thomas Moore who met at Chalk Farm on 11 August 1806, almost fifteen years before John Scott and Jonathan Christie came together on the same spot with such unhappy consequences. In the July issue of the *Edinburgh Review* Jeffrey had denounced Moore's *Epistles, Odes, and Other Poems* using language that seems grossly personal and insulting. Moore 'takes care to intimate to us, in every page, that the raptures which he celebrates do not spring from the excesses of an innocent love, or the extravagance of a romantic attachment; but are the unhallowed fruits of cheap and vulgar prostitution, the inspiration of casual amours, and the chorus of habitual debauchery'.[1] Moore read the offending article while he was staying at an inn in Worthing, and when he returned to town he learned from Samuel Rogers that Jeffrey himself was at that moment in London. He immediately sent Jeffrey an uncompromising message: 'You are a liar: yes, sir, a liar.' It was a year almost to the day since the death of Jeffrey's wife had left him 'inwardly sick of life'. He accepted Moore's challenge. In the event the proceedings were dramatically interrupted. A friend, Lord Fincastle, heard of the meeting and, anxious to avoid bloodshed, informed the authorities. Two Bow Street Officers arrived in the nick of time. One of them struck Jeffrey's pistol from his hand as he was in the very act of taking aim, and the other disarmed Moore. Both men were bound over to keep the peace. There was some talk of the two escaping from British jurisdiction by repairing to Hamburg, but neither man seemed anxious to take things so far. Samuel Rogers brought them together at one of his breakfasts. Jeffrey explained that his review had reference only to the morality of Moore's book and that he had 'intended to assert nothing as to the personal motives or personal character of the author', Moore promised that he would in future write more chastely, and the matter was happily resolved when the two men 'breakfasted together very lovingly'.[2]

Moore and Jeffrey were spared injury, but they did not escape ridicule. *The Times* reported as fact a rumour that Jeffrey's pistol 'was not loaded with ball',

[1] *Edinburgh Review*, 8 (July 1806), 458.
[2] My account of the duel is based on the accounts given by Howard Mumford Jones, *The Harp That Once—A Chronicle of the Life of Thomas Moore* (New York: Henry Holt, 1937), 92–9, and

and that Moore's 'had nothing more than a pellet of paper', so that if the police had not appeared 'this alarming duel would have turned out to be a game at pop-guns'. The *Morning Post* versified the same allegation in a piece entitled 'The Paper Pellet Duel; or, Papyro-Pelleto-Machia, An Heroic Ballad':

> 'The pistols draw,' the Justice cried,
>   'Produce the balls of death;
> 'And prove how these dire men of pride
>   'Would stop each other's breath.'
>
> They search'd each pistol, some afraid,
>   But glad were they to tell it,
> They found instead of deadly lead,
>   Naught but a paper pellet!

The affair had an odd pendant. Three years later in *English Bards and Scotch Reviewers*, Byron made a reference to the duel and to Moore's 'leadless pistol', adding in a note that 'on examination, the balls of the pistols, like the courage of the combatants, were found to have evaporated'.[3] On New Year's Day, 1810, Moore responded, very much as he had to Jeffrey, with a letter demanding to know whether Byron 'took responsibility for this *lie*'. Byron was in Greece. Francis Hodgson, who was handling his correspondence, guessed Moore's letter to be a challenge and thoughtfully decided not to forward it. By the time that Byron returned to England, Moore's temper had cooled, and the two men were reconciled. Yet again it was Samuel Rogers who brought them together. In both cases an averted duel initiated a lifelong friendship.[4]

It is these duels rather than those in which John Scott and Sir Alexander Boswell died, that best represent the period, and not just because so few duels ended fatally. The practice of duelling might seem the proper index of an intensity in literary antagonisms that led some contemporaries to compare their time with the time of Queen Anne, but when Moore wrote to Byron on his return to England he seemed unsure whether he intended to repeat his challenge or to claim Byron's acquaintance. It is an uncertainty that nicely illustrates a paradox central to the duelling code, a duel being at once an expression of murderous antagonism and an acknowledgement that the two combatants belong to the same social circle, and it may also offer an insight into the literary character of the period. Two of the fiercer and more prolonged episodes of literary animosity will serve to illustrate my point. In the very first

---

Henry Cockburn, *Life of Lord Jeffrey: With a Selection from his Correspondence*, 2 vols. (Edinburgh: A. and C. Black, 1852), 1, 134 and 136–8.

[3] *English Bards and Scotch Reviewers*, l. 466, and Lord Byron, *The Complete Poetical Words*, ed. Jerome J. McGann, 1 (Oxford: Clarendon Press, 1980), 407.

[4] On this averted duel, see Howard Mumford Jones, *The Harp That Once—A Chronicle of the Life of Thomas Moore*, 140–2, and Leslie A. Marchand, *Byron: A Biography*, 3 vols. (New York: Arnold A. Knopf, 1957), 1, 245 and 299–301.

number of the *Edinburgh Review* Francis Jeffrey identified Wordsworth as the instigator of 'the most formidable conspiracy that has lately been formed against sound judgement in matters poetical'. *Poems in Two Volumes* were described in 1807 as 'an insult to the public taste'. *The Excursion* prompted the exclamation, 'This will never do!', and in the following year *The White Doe of Rylstone* was allowed 'the merit of being the very worst poem we ever saw imprinted in a quarto volume'.[5] In intervening issues of the *Review* similar sentiments were very regularly expressed. Jeffrey implicitly compared his campaign against the Lake Poets with Britain's war against revolutionary France. It lasted almost as long, and it was deeply resented by Wordsworth. In October 1817, when John Wilson and J. G. Lockhart became the chief writers for *Blackwood's*, Jeffrey found himself the target of a campaign at least as intense if not sustained for quite so long. In the same issue appeared the first of Lockhart's papers on 'The Cockney School of Poetry'. The coincidence reveals clearly enough that Lockhart and Wilson felt a hostility to Jeffrey of a kind that did not exclude imitation, because the single most significant precedent for their attack on the Cockney School was Jeffrey's series of assaults on the Lakers. At times, as in the dedicatory stanzas to Jeffrey that precede the tenth volume, the admiration remains clearly visible through all the ironies:

> Were I forced by some dread demoniacal hand,
>   To change heads (what a fate!) with *some* Whig in the land,
>   I don't know but I'd swap with yourself my old Gander.

As the years passed a similar rough affection began to infiltrate even the references in *Blackwood's* to the leader of the Cockney School, the 'King of Cockaigne', Leigh Hunt.[6]

Literary antagonism, like the duel, seemed as likely to culminate in friendship as in enmity. Even in the quarrel that ended in his death, the quarrel begun when he denounced the *Blackwood's* writers as constituting the 'Reekie School of Criticism', John Scott flatteringly made use of weapons borrowed from his antagonists. Scott attacked Lockhart for the same reason that Lockhart himself had attacked Jeffrey. In each case the aggression of a newly established periodical was directed against a more established competitor.[7] It was one of the ways in

---

[5] *Edinburgh Review*, 1 (October 1802), 64; 11 (October 1807), 222; 24 (November 1814), 1; 25 (October 1815), 355.

[6] See the account of the relationship between Hunt and the magazine by Kim Wheatley, 'The *Blackwood's* Attacks on Leigh Hunt', *Nineteenth-Century Literature*, 47 (June 1992), 1–31. For an argument that Leigh Hunt was a principal model for Lockhart and Wilson in their development of *Blackwood's*, see David Stewart, 'Filling the Newspaper Gap: Leigh Hunt, *Blackwood's*, and the Development of the Miscellany', *Victorian Periodicals Review* (forthcoming).

[7] As was recognized at the time. Lockhart, for example, wrote of *Blackwood's*: 'The history of this Magazine may be considered . . . as the struggle, namely, of two rival booksellers, striving for their respective shares in the profits of periodical publications', *Peter's Letters to his Kinsfolk*, 3 vols. (Edinburgh: Blackwood, 1819), 2, 226.

which a new magazine might choose to compete for its share of the rapidly expanding market for periodicals, but it was also, like the challenge offered by a duellist, a demand for recognition, a demand that Jeffrey refused by studiously resisting the temptation ever to respond to the jibes of *Blackwood's* in the pages of the *Edinburgh*, and a demand to which Lockhart yielded, though surely not in the manner that John Scott had anticipated, when he hurried down to London to confront his attacker.

In periodical writing insult was always and transparently a back-handed compliment, but the same might not be granted of the attacks by periodical writers on poets. Jeffrey's attacks on Wordsworth, for example, or Lockhart's attacks on the Cockney poets reveal, it may be, the rancour that those who practise the secondary art of criticism are apt to feel for the practitioners of the more creative art on which they are dependent. Lucy Newlyn has spoken of 'the embattled relationship between poetry and prose which dominated periodical culture' in these years,[8] and her view seems to be rather emphatically supported by the regular denunciations by Romantic poets of their critics, most famously by Byron in *English Bards and Scotch Reviewers*. But in fact Byron's attention is rather soon diverted from Jeffrey's presumptions to those of the poets, some of whom (Wordsworth for one) he ridicules in a manner that seems to follow Jeffrey rather than correct him. The poem's primary target may be Jeffrey, but the figure most strongly commended is Jeffrey's chief competitor, the editor of the rival review, William Gifford. Byron's poem ends by all but dissolving the opposition between bards and reviewers from which it begins, which makes it somehow appropriate that Byron should have taken the opportunity afforded by Jeffrey's admiring review of the first cantos of *Childe Harold* to begin a friendship with him that was quite unruffled by Jeffrey's later attacks on *Cain* and *Don Juan*. Jerome Christensen has described *English Bards* as a poem that belongs 'as much to the history of English duelling as to the history of English literature'.[9] If so, it was a duel like Jeffrey's with Moore that reached its proper end when the two men 'breakfasted together very lovingly'.

Byron touches on a more nervous distinction when he attacks Walter Scott for forfeiting 'the poet's sacred name' by agreeing to 'descend to trade', that is, by lowering himself to write for money (*English Bards and Scotch Reviewers*, 175–7). After the publication of *Childe Harold*, it was an objection that was rather frequently brought against Byron himself. In 1814 Wordsworth asked Samuel Rogers, 'Mr Scott and your friend lord B flourishing at the rate they do, how can an honest *Poet* hope to thrive?'[10] Hazlitt reports that when Wordsworth was

[8] Lucy Newlyn, *Reading, Writing, and Romanticism: The Anxiety of Reception* (Oxford: Oxford University Press, 2000), 188.

[9] Jerome Christensen, *Lord Byron's Strength: Romantic Writing and Commercial Society* (Baltimore: Johns Hopkins University Press, 1995), 33.

[10] *The Letters of William and Dorothy Wordsworth*. Vol. 3: *The Middle Years, Part II. 1812–1820*, ed. Mary Moorman and Alan G. Hill (Oxford: Clarendon Press, 1969), 148.

asked how long Byron's reputation would survive his death, he replied, 'Not three days, Sir.'[11] In the third chapter of the *Biographia* Coleridge denounces his treatment and the treatment of his friends in the 'reviews, magazines, and news-journals of various name and rank', the readers of which, he believes, make up 'nine-tenths of the reading of the reading public', and he links the reviewers with 'satirists with or without a name, in verse or prose, or in verse-text aided by prose-comment'.[12] He has in mind, perhaps, Canning's *The New Morality*, in which, when it was published anonymously in 1798, in the final issue of the *Anti-Jacobin*, he and his friends had first been subjected to public ridicule, but also, it may be, *English Bards and Scotch Reviewers*. Such poems can be conflated with 'periodical works' because they are addressed to the same readership, colourfully defined by Coleridge as 'the multitudinous PUBLIC, shaped into personal unity by the magic of abstraction'. This is the depersonalized readership, brought into existence by the mass production of print, that, Coleridge believes, now 'sits nominal despot on the throne of criticism'. Its tyranny is merely nominal because it only 'echoes the decisions of its invisible ministers', the reviewers (1, 59). Wordsworth regularly makes a very similar distinction between 'the PEOPLE', and 'the PUBLIC', that is, the readership made up of anonymous consumers that had ensured the success of Scott and Byron. Wordsworth is confident that the people would have a proper relish of a poem such as *Peter Bell*,[13] but in fact the people remained unreachable, so that Wordsworth needed to console himself with the thought that he would find a fit readership in posterity.[14]

Byron and Thomas Moore made their peace with Jeffrey, Wordsworth did not, and this might suggest that the radical division in the period was not between poets and prose writers but between those writers who addressed the reading public, and that other group of writers who refused or failed to do so. Romantic literature, when I was first taught it, had to do principally with that second group. My own book, like many recent studies of the period, is much more concerned with the first, but in this last chapter I turn to the relationship between the two groups of writers, in order to suggest that it, too, displays some of the characteristics of the relationship between the combatants in a duel.

The point seems obvious enough. Coleridge begins his denunciation of the reviewers by confessing that it is 'to anonymous critics in reviews, magazines, and news-journals of various name and rank' that he owes 'full two thirds of whatever

---

[11] 'On Reading New Books', *Monthly Magazine*, n.s. 4 (July 1827), 23 (footnote); Howe, 17, 209 (note).

[12] Samuel Taylor Coleridge, *Biographia Literaria or Biographical Sketches of My Literary Life and Opinions*, ed. James Engell and Walter Jackson Bate, 2 vols. (Princeton: Princeton University Press, 1983), 1, 48. Subsequent page references are included in the text.

[13] *The Letters of William and Dorothy Wordsworth*. Vol. 3: *The Middle Years, Part I. 1806–1811*, ed. Mary Moorman and Alan G. Hill (Oxford: Clarendon Press, 1970), 194.

[14] On this, see Andrew Bennett, *Romantic Poets and the Culture of Posterity* (Cambridge: Cambridge University Press, 1999).

reputation and publicity' he happened to possess (1, 48). He exaggerates how little he had published in these years, but accurately identifies a disproportion between the number of his publications and the number of his appearances in the periodical press in which he found himself hauled up for judgement 'year after year, quarter after quarter, month after month (not to mention sundry petty periodicals of still quicker revolution, "or weekly or diurnal")' (1, 50).[15] Coleridge's success as a lecturer in these years was clearly heavily dependent on the celebrity that those frequent references in the periodical press conferred on him, so that he found himself in the odd position of being dependent for the bulk of his earnings on a reading habit that he judged the intellectual equivalent of 'swinging, or swaying on a chair or gate; spitting over a bridge; smoking; snuff-taking; tête-à-tête quarrels after dinner between husband and wife; conning word by word all the advertisements of the daily advertiser in a public house on a rainy day, etc. etc. etc.' (1, 49, Coleridge's note). It seems likely that Coleridge's contemporary reputation was sustained by his quarrel with the periodical press rather in the same way that some marriages rely for their continuance on after dinner disagreements, and his was not an isolated case.

After the modest success of *Lyrical Ballads* Wordsworth's volumes were produced in small print runs (Longman produced only 500 copies of *The Excursion* and the collected *Poems* of 1815), and these proved more than enough to meet the demand. The single exception was *Peter Bell*, which went into a second edition in 1819, the year of its publication, the explanation for which is not surely that this was a volume more admired than *The Excursion* or the collected *Poems*, but that it was a volume more heartily ridiculed, both in John Hamilton Reynolds's parody that appeared a few days before Wordsworth's original (Shelley's *Peter Bell the Third* was not published until 1839), and in the reviews of the poem, many of which took full advantage of Reynolds's promptitude.[16] 'The sale, in every instance of Mr Shelley's works has been very confined', his publisher, Charles Ollier wrote the year after his death,[17] and yet his scanty sales did not prevent him from establishing a reputation wide enough for popular magazines to take it for granted that their readers would recognize his name, and might know something even of his personal life and the character of his opinions. *Blackwood's* expressed an admiration for the poetry as intense as the distaste for the opinions, whereas the *Quarterly* detested the poetry and the opinions equally, but both reviewed Shelley's poems at length, bringing them to the attention of a readership that would never have considered buying any of

---

[15] The editors of the *Biographia* have identified over ninety articles and reviews appearing between 1798 and 1814 in which Coleridge makes a prominent appearance. See *Biographia Literaria*, 1, 50 (note).

[16] On Wordsworth's publishing history, see Lee Erickson, *The Economy of Literary Form: English Literature and the Industrialization of Publishing, 1800–1850* (Baltimore and London: Johns Hopkins University Press, 1996), 49–69.

[17] Quoted by William St Clair, *The Reading Nation in the Romantic Period* (Cambridge: Cambridge University Press, 2004), 650.

Shelley's volumes. Byron wrote to Murray of one *Quarterly* attack, 'it has sold an edition of the *Revolt of Islam*, which, otherwise, nobody would have thought of reading'.[18] Byron was mistaken. The volume sold so poorly that Browning remembered finding a pile of copies of the first edition on a bookseller's stall when he was a young man, but the poem was widely read in the pages of the *Quarterly*. Keats similarly was widely known by the time of his death not because of Leigh Hunt's championing of him in the *Examiner*, but because of the fury of Croker's attack on him in the *Quarterly* and the long-running campaign against him in *Blackwood's* as a member of the Cockney School. It was a period in which many of the poets who are now best remembered were more indebted for their contemporary reputation to their detractors than their admirers. Jeffrey may have written of *The Excursion*, 'This will never do!', but when he did so he was addressing more than fifty times as many readers as bought the poem. Had Hobhouse thought of this he would not have been so puzzled at Hazlitt's annoyance when, at Hobhouse's suggestion, Byron removed from *Don Juan* an appendix that had incorporated an attack on Hazlitt: 'Hazlitt is going to attack me for cutting out the notice against him in Don Juan—strange. He says I did it to sink him!!'[19] Jeffrey in his attacks on Wordsworth, and Lockhart and Croker in their attacks on Leigh Hunt and Keats seem all to have been engaged in a spectacularly misconceived enterprise through which they contrived to call attention to the very writers that they were recommending to oblivion.

Kim Wheatley has suggested that the period is distinguished by its 'paranoid politics', one of the distinguishing features of which is that its practitioners authenticate their political positions in the act of repudiating some demonized other. Southey, for example, in his articles for the *Quarterly* can only establish his political character through the violence of his denunciations of Henry Hunt and Cobbett. Hunt and Cobbett become the dark mirrors without whom he would be unable to secure his own political identity.[20] Some of the novels of the period, Mary Shelley's *Frankenstein*, Hoffmann's *The Devil's Elixir* in its translation by Gillies, and Hogg's *Private Memoirs and Confessions of a Justified Sinner* offer sharp analyses of the mechanisms of this kind of paranoia, which was not, as Wheatley indicates, confined to politics. *Blackwood's* offered the corpulent, gout-ridden, seventy-year-old bachelor, Christopher North, as the fleshly embodiment of the character of the magazine, but Christopher North seems to have been conceived as the antithesis of the yellow-breeched, tea-drinking editor of *The Examiner*, Leigh Hunt, and of the spry, mentally nimble editor of the *Edinburgh*,

---

[18] *Byron's Letters and Journals*, ed. Leslie A. Marchand, 6 (London: John Murray, 1976), 83. Byron is referring to the remarks on Shelley in a review of Leigh Hunt's *Foliage*, *Quarterly Review*, 18 (January 1818), 324–35.

[19] From a diary entry quoted by Duncan Wu, *William Hazlitt: The First Modern Man* (Oxford: Oxford University Press, 2008), 270.

[20] See Kim Wheatley, *Shelley and his Readers: Beyond Paranoid Politics* (Columbia and London: University of Missouri Press, 1999), especially 13–57.

Francis Jeffrey,[21] and the magazine confesses as much by the frequency with which it returns to the attack on the two rival editors.

Jeffrey himself seems much less happy when expressing his own aesthetic principles through an examination of one of the poets he supposes to share them—Crabbe, for example—than when returning, as he so often does, to the work of the poet most flagrantly in breach of them, Wordsworth. Jeffrey's ideal seems always most powerfully articulated for him in its Wordsworthian negative definition. Some such notion seems necessary to explain his persistent attention in the most influential periodical of the time to a poet who published so infrequently, and whose publications until 1824 met with such little success. A similar explanation offers itself for the frequency of Byron's references in *Don Juan*, by far the best-selling poem of the day, to Wordsworth, whose volumes even in print runs of 500 so rarely went into a second edition. It seems that Byron, after being dosed by Shelley with Wordsworth all through the summer of 1816, found that he could best develop his new poetic manner by understanding it through its difference from Wordsworth's.[22] Wordsworth, it may be, functioned for Byron as he did for Jeffrey as a repudiated other self, 'He, Juan, (and not Wordsworth)' (*Don Juan*, 1, 91, 1).

But Wordsworth was not consistently derided by those writing in genres (periodical criticism, popular poetry) that he despised. As early as 1800, in his Preface to *Lyrical Ballads*, Wordsworth had associated the production and consumption of writing in these genres with 'the increasing accumulation of men in cities'. For both Jeffrey and Byron Wordsworth's own life of rural retirement, his 'long seclusion / From better company ... At Keswick' (*Don Juan*, Dedication, 5, 1–3), was the key indicator of his poetic deficiencies. But for others it was the source of his superiority. Thomas Noon Talfourd, writing in *The Pamphleteer*, identifies in the poems virtues that were only available to Wordsworth because he lived 'secluded from the anxieties and dissipations of the world'.[23] Wordsworth's geographical isolation seems praiseworthy to Talfourd as the proper index of his healthy indifference to the reception of his work. He prefaces another reverential account of Wordsworth with the assurance, 'To him our eulogy is nothing.'[24] John Scott similarly records that he had seen 'in the same number' of *Blackwood's* 'lampoons on the poet, and high commendations

---

[21] The primary point of an odd Swiftian vignette in *Peter's Letters to his Kinsfolk* seems to be to point the contrast between Jeffrey and the lame, corpulent editor of *Blackwood's*. Morris reports that at Craigcrook, Jeffrey's country retreat outside Edinburgh, Jeffrey and his guests prepare for dinner by engaging in a leaping contest: 'they all jumped wonderfully; and Jeffrey was quite miraculous considering the brevity of his stride'. J. G. Lockhart, 3 vols. *Peter's Letters to his Kinsfolk* (Edinburgh: Blackwood, 1819), 1, 66.

[22] For an argument to this effect, see my 'Words and the Word: The Diction of *Don Juan*,' in *Romanticism and Religion from William Cowper to Wallace Stevens*, ed. Gavin Hopps and Jane Stabler (Aldershot, Ashgate, 2006), 137–54.

[23] *The Pamphleteer*, 5 (1815), 462.

[24] *New Monthly Magazine*, 14 (November 1820), 498.

of his genius', and has 'had occasion personally to hear the poet express his calm contempt for both!'[25] But *Blackwood's*, too, admired the serene distance that Wordsworth maintained from petty literary quarrels. In a sonnet by D. M. Moir he is celebrated for living 'from the strife / Far distant, and the turmoil of mankind', even though his seclusion ensures that his poems remain unappreciated by 'the men of cities'.[26] Even periodicals, it seems, found it necessary to recognize that there were some authors who breathed the 'pure, silent air of immortality', far above 'the dust, and smoke, and noise' of the urban world in which periodicals themselves and those who wrote for them had their existence.[27] This was the role that Wordsworth had rather vociferously claimed for himself. More surprisingly, it was a role that a number of periodical writers were willing to grant him. It was as if every periodical writer, like De Quincey, had 'a phantom-self—a second identity' that lived far from the presses of London or of Edinburgh in the 'sweet solitudes' of Westmoreland.[28]

Periodicals felt a need to embrace even or perhaps especially those writers who contemned them. Wordsworth would not admit a copy of *Blackwood's* into his house, and the contemporary taste for novel-reading struck him as not much more respectable than the taste for magazines. He would certainly have sympathized with Coleridge's belief that circulating libraries offer their subscribers 'a sort of beggarly day-dreaming, during which the mind of the reader furnishes for itself nothing but laziness and a little mawkish sensibility' (1, 19, Coleridge's note). But it was not an antipathy that the novelists seem to have returned. The shelves of the circulating libraries began more and more often to admit novels that found room for advertisements for Wordsworth's poems. Wordsworth and Scott were friends, but it was, at least on Wordsworth's side, an edgy friendship. At their very first meeting Scott had shocked Wordsworth by his easy confidence that literature might be a more lucrative profession than the law: 'he was sure he could, if he chose, get more money than he would ever wish from the booksellers'.[29] Scott's writings filled far more space on the circulating library shelves than those of any other writer, and at least five of the novels accommodated quotations from Wordsworth. In the Advertisement to *The Antiquary*, in which Jonathan Oldbuck anachronistically expresses his nostalgia for his lost youth by quoting from 'The Fountain', Scott goes so far as to present his novels as an extension of Wordsworth's project in *Lyrical Ballads*. He has chosen many of his principal characters from the 'lower orders' because they are 'less restrained by the habit of suppressing their feelings, and because [he] agree[s] with [his] friend Wordsworth, that they seldom fail to express them in the strongest and most

[25] *London Magazine*, 2 (November 1820), 512.
[26] *Blackwood's Edinburgh Magazine*, 8 (February 1821), 542.
[27] William Hazlitt, 'On Reading Old Books', *London Magazine*, 3 (February 1821), 134.
[28] *Tait's Edinburgh Magazine*, n.s. 6 (January 1839), 1; Lindop, 11, 44.
[29] Quoted by Edgar Johnson, *Walter Scott: The Great Unknown*, 2 vols. (London: Hamish Hamilton, 1970), 1, 214.

powerful language'.[30] Where Scott led the way others quickly followed. By the 1820s even the sight of a punch bowl might remind a novelist of Wordsworth: 'Within its beautiful and hallowed sphere, are buried no "thoughts that do lie too deep for tears."'[31] The habit crossed the Atlantic. In John Neal's *Randolph*, the reader is introduced to the Baltimore writer, Paul Allen, whose poetry is 'never so simple, so affecting, or so awful, as that of Wordsworth; nor is it ever so feeble and childish'.[32] Still earlier and perhaps still more remarkably, it percolated to Hampshire where Jane Austen imagined the poetaster Sir Edward Denham assuring Charlotte Heyman, 'Montgomery has all the fire of poetry, Wordsworth has the true soul of it.'[33] Clearly it was not Wordsworth's popularity that prompted these references but his posture. His claim, admitted by his admirers and detractors alike, to write without any reference at all to the reading public or to the venial reviewers that controlled its taste gave his work a peculiar value for those busily addressing the very reading public that he claimed to ignore. He successfully claimed for himself and his writings a semiotic value. They came to represent the notion that literature should be defined as the kind of writing that had an existence independent of the market, and, as these novelists indicate, that was itself an eminently marketable notion.[34] It was so marketable that it was mimicked with increasing frequency by writers whose earnings were wholly dependent on the circulating libraries. Lady Charlotte Bury's literary pretensions, for example, were much less lofty than her social connections (she wrote for Henry Colburn), but she was quite prepared to claim kinship with the kind of writer who 'magnanimously scorns to be the slave of what is called (odious, degrading term!) the taste of the day'.[35]

Some such notion seems necessary to explain the otherwise unaccountable prominence of Wordsworth in periodical writing, which, as Lee Erickson has shown, offered higher and more secure remuneration than writing of any other kind in the period from 1815 to the late 1830s.[36] David Higgins remarks in a study to which I am indebted, 'Magazine accounts of genius were caught between the supposedly debased literary culture in which they were produced and read,

---

[30] Walter Scott, *The Antiquary*, ed. David Hewitt (Edinburgh: Edinburgh University Press, 1995), 75 and 3.

[31] Thomas Hamilton, *The Youth and Manhood of Cyril Thornton* ed. Maurice Lindsay (Aberdeen: Association for Scottish Literary Studies, 1990), 418. The novel was first published in 1826.

[32] John Neal, *Randolph: A Novel* (Baltimore: Published for Whom it May Concern, 1823), I, 136.

[33] *Sanditon*, Jane Austen, *Later Manuscripts*, ed. Janet Todd and Linda Bree (Cambridge: Cambridge University Press, 2008), 175.

[34] For an incisive statement of this point focused on De Quincey, see David Stewart, 'Commerce, Genius and De Quincey's Literary Identity', *Studies in English Literature, 1500–1900* (forthcoming).

[35] [Lady Charlotte Bury], *Journal of the Heart* (London: Colburn and Bentley, 1830), 91.

[36] See Lee Erickson, *The Economy of Literary Form*, 71–103.

and the supposedly pure realm of autonomous creativity that they often sought to describe.[37] Periodical writers might emphasize the wide disparity between the two realms, or they might insist on their continuity. Moir's complimentary sonnet emphasizes the discrepancy between the poet and the magazine in which Moir celebrates him. In his review in the *Edinburgh* of Coleridge's *Biographia Literaria*, Hazlitt reverses the tactic, insisting that the only tolerable passages in the book approach the excellence of the personal essay, which was the form that he, like the other leading magazine writers of the period, most favoured. Coleridge's tenth chapter is 'more likely to be popular than any other part'. The story of how Coleridge launched *The Watchman* is 'an easy, gossiping, garrulous account of youthful adventures—by a man sufficiently fond of talking of himself'.[38] Coleridge and Southey, Hazlitt points out in his *Edinburgh* essay on periodical literature, had been the victims of periodical abuse ever since the days of the *Anti-Jacobin*: 'What has been the effect? Why, that these very persons have, in the end, joined that very pack of hunting tigers that strove to harass them to death.' The response seems unnatural, but, Hazlitt argues, it is not, because Southey and Coleridge recognize that the periodicals supply in this age the 'one royal road to reputation'. The age of genius has departed. This is the age of criticism: 'Therefore, let Reviews flourish—let Magazines increase and multiply—let the Daily and weekly Newspapers live for ever!'[39]

Hazlitt, characteristically, pushes his argument to a paradoxical extreme. Typically the magazines were more ambivalent, especially in a characteristic group of articles in which the private life of the retiring poet is displayed for the entertainment of the magazine's readers. The third of John Wilson's letters from the Lakes, 'translated from the German of Philip Kempferhausen', offers a portrait of Wordsworth domesticating with his family, respectfully saluted by the local peasantry as he walks to church, and guiding his German visitor to the 'small lake or tarn of deepest solitude' where 'he had meditated, and even composed, much of his poetry'.[40] The tone throughout is reverential, but, as Wilson must have anticipated, the piece annoyed Wordsworth.[41] The 'aversion to intrude on the privacy of a great poet' that Kempferhausen protests serves to underline, not to mitigate, Wilson's offence. In the second of the letters, Kempferhausen, in reporting how he had been received into Southey's family,

---

[37] David Higgins, *Romantic Genius and the Literary Magazine: Biography, Celebrity, Politics* (London and New York: Routledge, 2005), 1.

[38] *Edinburgh Review*, 28 (August 1817), 498–9.

[39] *Edinburgh Review*, 38 (May 1823), 349–78, 373, and 358.

[40] *Blackwood's Edinburgh Magazine*, 4 (March 1818), 735–44.

[41] Wordsworth complained to Francis Wrangham, 'the articles in B's *Magazine* that disgusted me so, were personal'. *The Letters of William and Dorothy Wordsworth*. Vol. 3: *The Middle Years, Part II 1812–1820*, 524.

admits that he was 'acting in the character of a well-intentioned spy',[42] but it is in the letter on Wordsworth that his duplicity becomes fully apparent. The letter is at once an act of homage and an act of treachery The double motive is fully acknowledged by De Quincey in the first of his 'Lake Reminiscences' of Words-worth when he admits that his 'filial devotion' to Wordsworth coincides with 'a rising emotion of hostility' that is 'nearly akin to vindictive hatred', and adds that he 'might even make the same acknowledgement on the part of Professor Wilson (though [he has] no authority for doing so)'.[43] Kempferhausen describes himself as 'perfectly at ease' in Southey's household. In Wordsworth's, though he does not acknowledge it, he seems conscious of a constraint. The conflicting emotions that De Quincey acknowledges and Wilson betrays have their origins very evidently in the sense the two men share that Wordsworth had failed adequately to return the friendship they had offered him, but I want to claim that their ambivalence has a cultural as well as a personal significance.

For Wilson and for De Quincey, Wordsworth is not a poet so much as a synecdoche for poetry (compare Hazlitt remembering how, when he first met him, Coleridge seemed the very 'face of Poetry').[44] In comparison with Words-worth, according to Wilson, 'other poets, at least all that [he has] ever known, are poets but on occasions'. Wordsworth's seclusion in the Lake District has sym-bolic value. His is a poetry properly composed beside a 'small lake or tarn of deepest solitude' because such a setting aptly figures the indifference to public opinion that allows Wordsworth to walk 'alone, through a world almost exclu-sively his own'. Wilson evidently and self-consciously composed his *Blackwood's* paper as a prose version of an episode from *The Excursion*, but he also acknow-ledges that, looked at in another way, the relationship between poetry as it is realized in the person of Wordsworth and his own magazine article is antithetical. His is, however he might disguise it, an instance of periodical criticism, and 'of the periodical criticism of Britain [Wordsworth] spoke with almost unqualified contempt'. Wordsworth speaks out of wounded vanity, but not just that. The periodical essayist writes 'avowedly and professionally to the public'. The peri-odical writer must 'please' or 'startle' or 'astonish' or he will 'acquire no character at all'. Poetry, by contrast, is defined as a kind of writing that, if addressed to anyone is addressed to the self: it is writing that, as Mill would put it, is only ever overheard by its reader. In his poetry as in his conversation Wordsworth 'solilo-quizes'. Kempferhausen feels 'perfectly at ease' with Robert Southey and his family, in part perhaps because Southey, like Wilson himself, is a poet content to earn his living as a periodical writer. His relationship with Wordsworth by contrast is tense, incorporating at once admiration and latent hostility, and in doing so it reveals not just the complexity of Wilson's relationship with

---

[42] *Blackwood's Edinburgh Magazine*, 4 (January 1819), 401.
[43] *Tait's Edinburgh Magazine*, n.s. 6 (January 1839), 11; Lindop, 11, 62.
[44] *The Liberal*, 2 (April 1823), 35.

Wordsworth but the complex relationship in the period between periodical writing and poetry.

Wordsworth's hostility extended to all writing that addresses itself to the reading public. He was incapable, De Quincey records, of recognizing the talents of Harriet Lee, and had never, it is De Quincey's 'firm persuasion', 'read one page of Sir Walter Scott's novels'. He had, 'by some strange accident', read Radcliffe's *The Italian*, 'but only to laugh at it'.[45] On Hazlitt's first meeting with him, he expressed his contempt for a performance of Lewis's *Castle Spectre* by remarking, 'it fitted the taste of the audience like a glove'.[46] He scorns those who address a taste that the public has already acquired. This disapproval is inflected by a closely associated scorn for those who write for money,[47] which, as De Quincey bitterly points out, Wordsworth is well able to indulge, because at every point of his life when he stood in need of money, as if by magic, money was forthcoming, 'in the shape of a bequest from Raisley Calvert', when Lord Lonsdale repaid the debt owed to Wordsworth's father, when a legacy fell to his wife, when he became distributor of stamps for Westmoreland, and when the death of the Cumberland distributor increased the value of the post. If Wordsworth never 'acquired any popular talent of writing for the current press', it was partly because he, unlike De Quincey, never needed to.[48] De Quincey and Wilson speak on behalf of a literary culture that at once accepts and resents Wordsworth's claim to belong to a culture at once very different and far superior. Their responses are further complicated by their acute sense that Wordsworth's claims are not wholly to be trusted. As his long involvement in the campaign to extend the term of legal copyright demonstrates, he was far from indifferent to his literary earnings, the serene acceptance that he professed of the failure of his poems to sell more widely only inadequately covered his resentment, and the 'unqualified contempt' that he expressed for periodical criticism coincided with a trembling sensitivity to it.[49]

---

[45] *Tait's Edinburgh Magazine*, n.s. 7 (October 1840), 635; Lindop, 11, 257–8.

[46] *The Liberal*, 2 (April 1823), 40; Howe, 17, 188.

[47] In 1799 he had been ready to acknowledge that he published *Lyrical Ballads* 'for money and money alone,' and that he took note of his reception by reviewers if only because he understands how their opinions might help him 'to pudding,' but he had since refined his position. See *The Letters of William and Dorothy Wordsworth: The Early Years, 1787–1815*, ed. Ernest de Selincourt, rev. Chester L. Shaver (Oxford: Clarendon Press, 1967), 267–8.

[48] *Tait's Edinburgh Magazine*, n.s. 6 (April 1839), 248–50; Lindop, 11, 98–101. As David Higgins notes, Hazlitt, De Quincey, and Hunt wrote their literary reminiscences under economic pressure. Hazlitt was under house arrest for debt when he wrote 'My First Acquaintance with Poets', Hunt published *Lord Byron and Some of his Contemporaries* in settlement of a debt to Colburn, and De Quincey envied Wordsworth's financial security in a series of magazine papers written whilst he was on the run from his creditors. See David Higgins, *Romantic Genius and the Literary Magazine*, 74.

[49] See, for example, Wilson on Wordsworth's response to Jeffrey's criticism of Burns (Wordsworth claims to know it only in quotation in order to maintain the fiction that he did not read the *Edinburgh Review*): 'it is not Robert Burns for whom he feels,—it is William Wordsworth. All the while that he is exclaiming against the Reviewer's injustice to Burns, he writhes under the lash which that consummate satirist has inflicted upon himself, and exhibits a back yet sore with the

Even in the fraught complexity of their responses, Wordsworth and the periodical writers contrive to mirror one another.

The best of these reminiscences, Hazlitt's 'My First Acquaintance with Poets',[50] is characteristic of all these pieces in its fusion of gratitude with resentment, but Hazlitt's gratitude seems more heartfelt. He owes it to Coleridge that his 'understanding' did not remain 'dumb and brutish' but found 'a language to express itself', and Wordsworth, when he remarked how the sun set on a yellow bank, taught him to be alert ever after to how 'the sun-set stream[s] upon the objects facing it'. He is no more prepared than De Quincey to allow the two poets to inhabit a disembodied, ideal world, but De Quincey's way of reminding Wordsworth of his material physicality is broadly farcical: 'His legs were pointedly condemned by all the female connoisseurs in legs that ever I heard lecture upon that topic; not that they were bad in any way which *would* force itself on your notice—there was no absolute deformity about them.'[51] Hazlitt more delicately points to the material of the poets' clothing, the 'short black coat (like a shooting-jacket) which hardly seemed to have been made for him' that Coleridge wore as he descended from the coach at Shrewsbury, or the 'brown fustian jacket and striped pantaloons' that Wordsworth sported when he visited Coleridge at Nether Stowey. Hazlitt does not deny his disillusion. Coleridge's 'small, feeble' nose now seems to him 'nothing—like what he has done', and his habit of 'shifting from one side of the foot-path to another' seems now a fit emblem of his 'instability of purpose'. But Hazlitt knows that his disillusion is as much in himself as in his friends. He casts his whole essay in a Wordsworthian register, as an elegy for dizzy raptures that the grown man can never hope to reproduce, so that even in the manner that he marks his separation from Wordsworth and Coleridge he pays them homage.

It is an aspect of his disillusion that Hazlitt wonders how much the charm of the two men's poems was dependent on their voices, Coleridge's 'loud, deep, and distinct' as though it might have 'floated in solemn silence through the universe', and Wordsworth's with its 'strong tincture of the northern *burr*, like the crust on wine'. 'There is', Hazlitt remembers 'a *chaunt* in the recitation both of Coleridge and Wordsworth, which acts as a spell upon the hearer, and disarms the judgement', which is no doubt one reason why their reputation should be highest in the narrow circle of their friends, amongst those who have been held in thrall by their voices. It is as if they are poets from a pre-print culture, poets at any rate quite without 'the popular talent of writing for the current press' on which a periodical writer such as Hazlitt relied for his income. They presented that inability, of course, as a mark of their superiority, and it was a superiority that

wounds which have in vain been kept open, and which his restless and irritable vanity will never allow to close.' *Blackwood's Edinburgh Magazine*, 1 (June 1817), 26?.

[50] *The Liberal*, 2 (April 1823), 23–46; Howe, 17, 106–22.
[51] *Tait's Edinburgh Magazine*, n.s. 6 (January 1839), 7; Lindop, 11, 55.

Hazlitt, like most periodical writers, was on occasion inclined to allow, but he ends this essay by recalling his first meeting, at Godwin's with Charles Lamb. Coleridge and Holcroft were disputing 'which was the best—*Man as he was, or man as he is to be*', and Lamb capped both of them: '"Give me," says Lamb, "man as he is *not* to be."' The moment marked the beginning of a friendship between Lamb and Hazlitt that, he believes, 'still continues'. So the essay ends, not with Wordsworth and Coleridge, but with Lamb and Hazlitt, not with the poets but with the two great essayists of the age.

It may not be quite fanciful to read that conclusion as making a quiet claim that the magazine essay, as practised by Hazlitt and by Lamb, has as much claim as *Peter Bell*, the poem that Hazlitt remembers Wordsworth reciting, to represent the literature of the period. It was a time when those who wrote for posterity and those who wrote for 'the current press' often seemed irreconcilably opposed one to another, but, as the duels of the period remind us, antagonism may be entirely compatible with sympathy. When John Scott fell, Christie grasped his hand and said, 'I would rather that I was in your situation and that you were in mine.' That is a touching sentiment, but it was also a thoroughly conventional one, repeated in one form or another by a very large number of successful duellists. In the more common kind of duel in which no one was injured, a duel of the kind in which Moore and Jeffrey engaged, it was again entirely conventional that the contest should end not in conflict but in sympathetic communion, with the two men breakfasting together 'very lovingly'. The two literary cultures of the period, the one most closely identified with Wordsworth, the other with the periodical writers, shared, it may be, a similar symbiotic relationship. Each supplied the mirror within which the other recognized its own features.

The issue of the *London* that appeared in March 1821, as the magazine's editor, John Scott, lay dying, when Keats, although it was not yet known in England, was already dead, included a 'Sketch of the Life of Perrinson, the Poet'. The contributor was very possibly John Hamilton Reynolds.[52] The paper turns on the joke that none of Perrinson's poems survives, except a fragmentary effort in couplets in praise of the beauty of his mistress which, like Coleridge's *Christabel* for so many years, survives in the memory of a friend who had heard it recited. Perrinson is an oddly representative figure. His apprenticeship to a grocer in Exeter, where 'after raisin-hours, he buried himself in the classic poets', suggests Keats as the likes of Lockhart caricatured him. During his apprenticeship he composes in his head an epic on the Fall of Man that his brother shopmen think superior to Milton, but the death of his master occurs so abruptly that the entire poem slips from his mind before he has written it down, a mishap surely designed to recall the accident that led to Coleridge forgetting the

---

[52] *London Magazine*, 3 (March 1821), 322–9. Reynolds's authorship is suggested by Frank P. Riga and Claude A. Prance, and seems to me persuasive. See their *Index to the London Magazine* (Garland: New York and London, 1978), 31.

bulk of 'Kubla Khan'. The whole article parodies the genre that Southey had done most to popularize in the 'Life' that he prefixed to his edition of *The Remains of Henry Kirk White*, the biography of the poet who had not lived to secure his reputation, the life of one of those poets that Shelley refers to as the 'inheritors of unfulfilled renown'. Perrinson's last attempt at a major poem, six cantos on the Holy Wars, is lost when the ship on which he was emigrating to St Vincent founders off the Goodwin Sands 'and poor Perrinson and his poem perished altogether', a fate that cannot parody Shelley's because it anticipates it by more than a year. Perrinson is a representative product of the literary culture of the Regency, a culture in which the celebrity of poets might bear little or no relation to the circulation of their poems: in which Keats and Shelley might become famous names despite the scantiness of their sales. But Perrinson is an appropriate representative of the other culture, too, of those who wrote for 'the current press'. During a short residence in London, he had written 'several papers in the Magazines,—but the signatures by which they were distinguished were never known' and in consequence 'all trace of them is lost'. It is the fate of most periodical writing, even of a paper so alert and witty as the 'Sketch of the Life of Perrinson, the Poet', which may have been written by Keats's friend, J. H. Reynolds, but then again may not. Perrinson had been gathering materials for an epic poem on Alfred the Great, undeterred by the warning example of Joseph Cottle, when a disappointment in love and an offer from the editor of a periodical of 'two guineas per sheet for what he might write' prompted him to leave Exeter for London. Perrinson was torn between two cultures, but so was Keats when he made his short-lived resolution to 'acquire something by temporary writing in periodical works', confident that he could 'cheat as well as any literary Jew of the Market and shine up an article on any thing without much knowledge of the subject, aye like an orange',[53] and so was Coleridge when he wrote to William Blackwood offering his services as a contributor to the magazine.[54] So, too, was Hazlitt when he thought of the difference between 'the dust, and smoke, and noise' out of which his own writing was produced and the 'pure, silent air of immortality'. It was a period in which the conflicts between writers mimicked the conflicts within them, and it is those conflicts that have been the subject of my book.

[53] *The Letters of John Keats*, ed. Hyder Edward Rollins, 2 vols. (Cambridge: Cambridge University Press, 1958), 2, 178–9.

[54] *The Collected Letters of Samuel Taylor Coleridge*, ed. Earl Leslie Griggs, 6 vols. (Oxford: Clarendon Press, 1956–71), 5, 167–71. The letter was published in *Blackwood's Edinburgh Magazine*, 10 (October 1821), 253.

Bibliography

PERIODICALS CITED:

The Atlas
The Beacon
Blackwood's Edinburgh Magazine
British Critic
British Lady's Magazine
British Review
The Champion
Cobbett's Political Register
Court Journal
Eclectic Review
Edinburgh Magazine and Literary Miscellany
Edinburgh Review
Englishman's Magazine
The Etonian
The Examiner
Gentleman's Magazine
Gold's London Magazine and Theatrical Inquisitor
The Investigator
John Bull
Knight's Quarterly Magazine
Lady's Magazine
The Liberal: Verse and Prose from the South
Literary Chronicle
Literary Gazette and Journal of Belles Lettres
Literary Register
London Magazine
London Weekly Review
Monthly Magazine
Monthly Review
New Monthly Magazine
The Pamphleteer
Quarterly Review
Scots Magazine and Edinburgh Miscellany
The Scotsman
The Sentinel
Tait's Edinburgh Magazine
The Times
Westminster Review

Anon., *An Apology for Don Juan* (London: T. Green, 1824).

—— *Juan Secundus* (London: John Miller, 1825).

Alexander, J. H., ed., *The Tavern Sages* (Aberdeen: Aberdeen University Press, 1992).

Austen, Jane, *Jane Austen's Letters*, ed. Deirdre Le Faye, 3rd edn (Oxford: Oxford University Press, 1995).

—— *Emma*, ed. Richard Cronin and Dorothy McMillan (Cambridge: Cambridge University Press, 2005).

—— *Northanger Abbey*, ed. Barbara M. Benedict and Deirdre Le Faye (Cambridge: Cambridge University Press, 2006).

—— *Persuasion*, ed. Janet Todd and Antje Blank (Cambridge: Cambridge University Press, 2006).

—— *Later Manuscripts*, ed. Janet Todd and Linda Bree (Cambridge: Cambridge University Press, 2008).

Baldick, Robert, *The Duel: A History of Duelling* (London: Chapman and Hall, 1965).

Barnard, John, 'Hazlitt's *Liber Amoris; or, the New Pygmalion* (1823): Conversations and the Statue', in *Translating Life: Studies in Transpositional Aesthetics*, ed. Shirley Chew and Alistair Stead (Liverpool: Liverpool University Press, 1988), 181–98.

Barrett, Eaton Stannard, *The Heroine* (London: Henry Colburn, 1813).

Bennet, Andrew, *Romantic Poets and the Culture of Posterity* (Cambridge: Cambridge University Press, 1999).

—— *Wordsworth Writing* (Cambridge: Cambridge University Press, 2007).

Blessington, Marguerite Gardiner, Countess of, *Conversations of Lord Byron with the Countess of Blessington* (London: Henry Colburn, 1834).

Boswell, Alexander, *The Poetical Works of Alexander Boswell*, ed. Robert Howie (Glasgow: Maurice Ogle and Co., 1871).

Boswell, James, *Boswell's Life of Johnson*, ed. G. B. Hill, revised L. F. Powell, 3 vols. (Oxford: Clarendon Press, 1934–50).

Bowles, William Lisle, *The Invariable Principles of Poetry* (London: Longman, Hurst, Rees, Orme and Brown, 1819).

—— *A Final Appeal to the Literary Public, relative to Pope, in reply to certain observations of Mr. Roscoe, in his edition of that poet's works* (London: Hurst, Robinson and Co., 1825).

Bradley, Arthur and Alan Rawes, eds, *Romantic Biography* (Aldershot: Ashgate, 2003).

Bury, Lady Charlotte, *Journal of the Heart* (London: Colburn and Bentley, 1830).

Butler, Marilyn, *Peacock Displayed: A Satirist in his Context* (London: Routledge and Kegan Paul, 1979).

Byron, George Gordon, Lord, *Byron's Letters and Journals*, ed. Leslie A. Marchand, 12 vols. (London: John Murray, 1973–81).

—— *The Complete Poetical Works*, ed. Jerome J. McGann, 7 vols. (Oxford: Clarendon Press, 1980–93).

—— *The Complete Miscellaneous Prose*, ed. Andrew Nicholson (Oxford: Clarendon Press, 1991).

Cafarelli, Annette Wheeler, *Prose in the Age of Poets: Romanticism and Biographical Narrative from Johnson to De Quincey* (Philadelphia: University of Pennsylvania Press, 1990).

Carlyle, Thomas, *The Works of Thomas Carlyle*, 29 vols. (London: Chapman and Hall, 1896–9).

Carruthers, Gerard and Alan Rawes, eds. *English Romanticism and the Celtic World*, (Cambridge: Cambridge University Press, 2003).

Christensen, Jerome, *Lord Byron's Strength: Romantic Writing and Commercial Society* (Baltimore and London: Johns Hopkins University Press, 1993).

Clare, John, *Poems of the Middle Period*, ed. Eric Robinson, David Powell, and P. M. S. Dawson, 4 vols. (Oxford: Clarendon Press, 1996–8).

Cockburn, *Life of Lord Jeffrey: With a Selection from his Correspondence*, 2 vols. (Edinburgh: A. and C. Black, 1852).

Coleridge, Samuel Taylor, *The Collected Letters of Samuel Taylor Coleridge*, ed. Earl Leslie Griggs, 6 vols. (Oxford: Clarendon Press, 1956–71).

—— *Biographia Literaria or Biographical Sketches of My Literary Life and Opinions*, ed. James Engell and Walter Jackson Bate, 2 vols. (Princeton: Princeton University Press, 1983).

Coleridge, Sara, ed. *Notes and Lectures upon Shakespeare and Some of the Old Poets and Dramatists with Other Literary Remains of S. T. Coleridge*, 2 vols. (London: Pickering, 1849).

Cook, Jon, *Hazlitt in Love: A Fatal Attachment* (London: Short Books, 2007).

Cornwall, Barry (Bryan Procter), *A Sicilian Story* (London: C. and J. Ollier, 1820).

—— *An autobiographical fragment and biographical notes, with . . . sketches of contemporaries, unpublished lyrics, etc.* (London, 1877).

Crabbe, George, *The Complete Poetical Works*, ed. Norma Dalrymple-Champneys and Arthur Pollard, 3 vols. (Oxford: Oxford University Press, 1988).

Cronin, Richard, *Romantic Victorians: English Literature, 1824–1840* (Basingstoke: Palgrave, 2002).

—— 'Words and the Word: The Diction of *Don Juan*', in *Romanticism and Religion from William Cowper to Wallace Stevens*, ed. Gavin Hopps and Jane Stabler (Aldershot: Ashgate, 2006).

Dart, Gregory, '"Flash Style": Pierce Egan and Literary London, 1820–28', *History Workshop Journal*, 51 (2001), 180–205.

Davis, Leith, Ian Duncan, and Janet Sorensen, ed., *Scotland and the Borders of Romanticism* (Cambridge: Cambridge University Press, 2004).

De Quincey, Thomas, *Works of Thomas De Quincey*, 21 vols., gen. ed. Grevel Lindop (London: Pickering and Chatto, 2000–3).

D'Israeli, Isaac, *Quarrels of Authors, or some Memoirs for our Literary History*, 3 vols. (London: John Murray, 1814).

Duncan, Ian, 'Hogg's Body', *Studies in Hogg and His World*, 9 (1998), 1–15.

—— *Scott's Shadow: The Novel in Romantic Edinburgh* (Princeton: Princeton University Press, 2007).

Egan, Pierce, *Life in London; or, The day and night scenes of Jerry Hawthorn, esq. and his elegant friend Corinthian Tom, accompanied by Bob Logic, the Oxonian, in their rambles and sprees through the metropolis* (London: Sherwood and Jones, 1823).

Elfenbein, Andrew, *Byron and the Victorians* (Cambridge: Cambridge University Press, 1995).

Erickson, Lee, *The Economy of Literary Form* (Baltimore and London: Johns Hopkins University Press, 1996).

Ferrier, Susan, *Memoir and Correspondence of Susan Ferrier, 1782–1854*, ed. J. A. Doyle (London: John Murray, 1898).

—— *Marriage*, ed. Herbert Foltinek (London: Oxford University Press, 1971).

Ferris, Ina, *The Achievement of Literary Authority: Gender, History, and the Waverley Novels* (Ithaca and London: Cornell University Press, 1991).

Fielding, Penny, *Writing and Orality: Nationality, Culture, and Nineteenth-Century Fiction* (Oxford: Clarendon Press, 1996).

Frere, John Hookham, *The Monks and the* Giants, ed. R. D. Waller (Manchester: Manchester University Press, 1926).

Galt, John, *The Steam Boat* (Edinburgh: Blackwood, 1822).

——*Life of Lord Byron* (London: Colburn and Bentley, 1830).

——*Annals of The Parish; and The Ayrshire Legatees* (Edinburgh: Mercat Press, 1994).

Gardner, John, 'Hobhouse, Cato Street, and *Marino Faliero*', *Byron Journal*, 31 (2003), 23–37.

Garside, Peter D., '*Old Mortality*'s Silent Minority', in *Critical Essays on Sir Walter Scott: The Waverley Novels*, ed. Harry E. Shaw (New York: G. K. Hall, 1996), 149–64.

Garside, Peter and Rainer Schöwerling, eds., *The English Novel 1770–1829: A Bibliographical Survey of Prose Fiction Published in the British Isles*, 2 vols. (Oxford: Oxford University Press, 2000).

Gilfillan, George, *A Gallery of Literary Portraits*, ed. W. Robertson Nicoll (London: Dent, 1927).

Gillies, R. P., trans., *The Devil's Elixir: from the German of E. T. A. Hofmann*, 2 vols. (Edinburgh: Blackwood, 1824).

Gordon, Mary Wilson, '*Christopher North*': *A Memoir of John Wilson* (Edinburgh: Edmonston and Douglas, 1862).

Gosse, *Coventry Patmore* (London: Hodder and Stoughton, 1905).

Graham, Peter W., ed., *Byron's Bulldog: The Letters of John Cam Hobhouse to Lord Byron* (Columbus: Ohio University Press, 1984).

Gray, Erik, *The Poetry of Indifference from the Romantics to the Rubáiyát* (Amherst and Boston: University of Massachusetts Press, 2005).

Green, Sarah, *Scotch Novel Reading; Or, Modern Quackery. A Novel Really Founded on Facts* (London: A. K. Newman, 1824).

Greene, Donald, ed., *Samuel Johnson: The Major Works* (Oxford: Oxford University Press, 2000).

Grierson, H. J. C. ed., *The Letters of Sir Walter Scott*, 12 vols. (London: Constable, 1932–7).

Griggs, Earl Leslie, ed., *The Collected Letters of Samuel Taylor Coleridge*, 6 vols. (Oxford: Clarendon Press, 1956–71).

Gross, Jonathan, 'Hazlitt's Worshipping Practice in *Liber Amoris*', *SEL*, 35 (1995), 707–21.

Hamilton, Thomas, *The Youth and Manhood of Cyril Thornton*, ed. Maurice Lindsay (Aberdeen: Association for Scottish Literary Studies, 1990).

Haslett, Moyra, *Don Juan and the Don Juan Legend* (Oxford: Clarendon Press, 1997).

Hazlitt, William, *The Complete Works of William Hazlitt*, ed. P. P. Howe, 21 vols. (London and Toronto: J. M. Dent and Sons, 1930–4).

——*Hazlitt in the Workshop: The Manuscript of 'The Fight'*, ed. Stewart C. Wilcox (Baltimore: Johns Hopkins University Press, 1943).

——*The Selected Writings of William Hazlitt*, ed. Duncan Wu, 9 vols. (London: Pickering and Chatto, 1998).

Hart, Francis R., *Lockhart as Romantic Biographer* (Edinburgh; Edinburgh University Press, 1971).

Hayden, John O., ed., *Scott: The Critical Heritage* (London: Routledge and Kegan Paul, 1970).

Higgins, David, 'Englishness, Effeminacy, and the *New Monthly Magazine*: Hazlitt's "The Fight" in Context', *Romanticism*, 10 (2004), 173–90.

——*Romantic Genius and the Literary Magazine: Biography, Celebrity, Politics* (London and New York: Routledge, 2005).

Hill, G. B. ed., revised L. F. Powell, *Boswell's Life of Johnson*, 3 vols. (Oxford: Clarendon Press, 1934–50).

Hogg, James, *The Three Perils of Man: War, Women and Witchcraft*, ed. Douglas Gifford (Edinburgh: Scottish Academic Press, 1989).

——*Poetic Mirrors: Comprising the* Poetic Mirror *(1816) and* New Poetic Mirror *(1829–31)*, ed. David Groves (Frankfurt: Peter Lang, 1990).

——*The Three Perils of Woman, or, Love, Leasing, and Jealousy: A Series of Domestic Scotch Tales*, ed. David Groves, Antony Hasler, and Douglas. S. Mack (Edinburgh: Edinburgh University Press, 1995).

——*Anecdotes of Scott*, ed. Jill Rubinstein (Edinburgh: Edinburgh University Press, 1999).

——*The Private Memoirs and Confessions of a Justified Sinner*, ed. P. D. Garside (Edinburgh: Edinburgh University Press, 2002).

——*The Collected Letters of James Hogg*, ed. Gillian Hughes, 3 vols. (Edinburgh: Edinburgh University Press, 2004–8).

Hope, Thomas, *Anastasius, or, Memoirs of a Greek: Written at the Close of the Eighteenth Century*, 3 vols. (London: John Murray, 1820).

Howe, P. P., ed., *The Complete Works of William Hazlitt*, ed. P. P. Howe, 21 vols. (London and Toronto: J. M. Dent and Sons, 1930–4).

Howie, Robert, ed., *The Poetical Works of Alexander Boswell* (Glasgow: Maurice Ogle and Co., 1871).

Hunt, Leigh, *Lord Byron and Some of his Contemporaries* (London: Henry Colburn, 1828).

Irving, Washington, *The Sketch-Book of Geoffrey Crayon, Gent.*, ed. Susan Manning (Oxford: Oxford University Press, 1996).

Jack, Alison M., *Texts Reading Texts, Sacred and Secular*, Journal for the Study of the New Testament Supplement Series 179 (Sheffield: Sheffield Academic Press, 1999).

Jamieson, John, *An Etymological Dictionary of the Scottish Language* (Edinburgh: Constable, 1818).

Johnson, Edgar, *Sir Walter Scott: The Great Unknown*, 2 vols. (London: Hamish Hamilton, 1970).

Johnson, Samuel, *The Major Works*, ed. Donald Greene (Oxford: Oxford University Press, 2000).

——*Lives of the English Poets*, ed. Roger Lonsdale, 4 vols. (Oxford: Clarendon Press, 2006).

Johnston, Kenneth R., *The Hidden Wordsworth: Poet, Lover, Rebel, Spy* (London and New York: W. W. Norton and Co., 1998).

Jones, F. L., ed., *The Letters of Percy Bysshe Shelley*, 2 vols. (Oxford: Clarendon Press, 1964).

Jones, Howard Mumford, *The Harp That Once—A Chronicle of the Life of Thomas Moore* (New York: Henry Holt, 1937).

Jones, Leonidas, 'The Scott-Christie Duel', *Texas Studies in Literature and Language*, 12 (Winter 1971), 605–29.

—— *The Life of John Hamilton Reynolds* (Hanover and London: University Press of New England, 1984).

Jones, Stanley, *Hazlitt: A Life from Winterslow to Frith Street* (Oxford: Oxford University Press, 1989).

Jones, Steven E., *Satire and Romanticism* (New York: St Martin's Press, 2000).

Jordan, Frank, 'Chrystal Croftangry, Scott's Last and Best Mask', *Scottish Literary Journal*, 7 (1980), 185–92.

Keats, John, *The Letters of John Keats*, ed. Hyder Edward Rollins, 2 vols. (Cambridge: Cambridge University Press, 1958).

Ketcham, Michael G., *Transparent Designs: Reading, Performance, and Form in the* Spectator *Papers* (Georgia: University of Athens Press, 1985).

Kiernan, V. G., *The Duel in European History: Honour and the Reign of Aristocracy* (Oxford: Oxford University Press, 1988).

Klancher, Jon P., *The Making of English Reading Audiences, 1790–1832* (Madison: University of Wisconsin Press, 1987).

Lamb, Lady Caroline, *A New Canto*, ed. Peter Cochran, http://www.hobby-o.com/newcanto.php.

Lamb, Charles, *The Works of Charles and Mary Lamb*, ed. E. V. Lucas, 7 vols. (London: Methuen, 1905).

Landale, James, *Duel: A True Story of Death and Honour* (Edinburgh: Canongate, 2005).

Landon, Letitia (L. E. L.), *Improvisatrice and Other Poems*, 3rd edn (London: Hurst Robinson and Co, 1825).

Lang Andrew, ed., *The Life and Letters of John Gibson Lockhart*, 2 vols. (London: John C. Nimmo, 1897).

Leavis, F. R., *The Great Tradition* (London: Chatto and Windus, 1948).

Leighton, Angela, *Victorian Women Poets: Writing Against the Heart* (London: Harvester Wheatsheaf, 1992).

Levin, Susan M., *The Romantic Art of Confession* (Columbia SC: Camden House, 1998).

Levinson, *Keats's Life of Allegory: The Origins of a Style* (Oxford: Oxford University Press, 1989).

Lochhead, Marion, *John Gibson Lockhart* (London: John Murray, 1954).

Lockhart, John Gibson, *Peter's Letters to his Kinsfolk*, 3 vols. (Edinburgh: Blackwood, 1819).

—— *Statement: Mr Lockhart very unwillingly feels himself again under the necessity of obtruding himself upon the public notice* (Edinburgh: 1821).

—— *Reginald Dalton* (Edinburgh: William Blackwood, 1823).

—— *The History of Matthew Wald* (Edinburgh: William Blackwood, 1824).

—— *Memoirs of the Life of Sir Walter Scott, Bart*, 7 vols. (Edinburgh: Robert Cadell, 1837).

—— *Valerius: A Roman Story* (Edinburgh: Blackwood, 1869).

—— *The Life and Letters of John Gibson Lockhart*, ed. Andrew Lang, 2 vols. (London: John C. Nimmo, 1897).

—— *John Bull's Letter to Lord Byron*, ed. Alan Lang Strout (Norman: University of Oklahoma Press, 1947).

——*Some Passages in the Life of Mr Adam Blair, Minister of the Gospel at Cross-Meikle* (Edinburgh: Edinburgh University Press, 1963).

Lonsdale, Roger ed., *Samuel Johnson, Lives of the English Poets*, 4 vols. (Oxford: Clarendon Press, 2006).

Lucas, E. V., ed. *The Works of Charles and Mary Lamb*, 7 vols. (London: Methuen, 1905).

——*The Life of Charles Lamb*, 2 vols. (London: Methuen, 1921).

Luttrell, Henry, *Advice to Julia: A Letter in Rhyme. A New Edition* (London: John Murray, 1820).

MacCarthy, Fiona, *Byron: Life and Legend* (New York: Farrar, Strauss and Giroux, 2002).

McGann, Jerome J. ed., *Lord Byron, The Complete Poetical Works* (Oxford: Clarendon Press, 1980–93).

Manning, Peter, 'Detaching Lamb's Thought' in *Romantic Periodicals and Print Culture*, ed. Kim Wheatley (London and Portland, Oregon: Frank Cass, 2002), 137–46.

Marchand, Leslie, A., *Byron: A Biography*, 3 vols. (New York: Albert A. Knopf, 1954).

——ed., *Byron's Letters and Journals*, 12 vols. (London: John Murray, 1973–81).

Mason, Nicholas, 'Building Brand Byron: Early Nineteenth-Century Advertising and the Marketing of *Childe Harold's Pilgrimage*', *Modern Language Quarterly*, 63 (December 2002), 411–40.

——gen. ed. *Blackwood's Magazine, 1817–25: Selections from Maga's Infancy*, 6 vols. (London: Pickering and Chatto, 2006).

Mitchell, W. J. T., *Picture Theory: Essays on Verbal and Visual Representation* (Chicago: Chicago University Press, 1994).

Mole, Tom, *Byron's Romantic Celebrity: Industrial Culture and the Hermeneutic of Intimacy* (Basingstoke: Palgrave Macmillan, 2007).

Moore, Thomas, *The Epicurean: A Tale* (London: Longmans, 1827).

——*Memoirs, Journal, and Correspondence of Thomas Moore*, ed. Lord John Russell, 8 vols. (London: Longmans, 1853–6).

[Morgan, Lady (Sydney Owenson)], *The Mohawks: A Satirical Poem with Notes* (London: Colburn, 1822).

Morrison, Robert, '*Blackwood's* Berserker, John Wilson and the Language of Extremity', *Romanticism on the Net*, 20 (November 2000), http://users.ox.ac.uk/~scat0385/20morrison.html.

Moultrie, John, *Poems* (London: William Pickering, 1837).

Mulvihill, James, '"A Species of Shop": Peacock and the World of Goods', *Keats–Shelley Journal*, 49 (2000), 85–113.

Murphy, Peter, 'Impersonation and Authorship in Romantic Britain', *English Literary History*, 59 (1992), 625–49.

Murray, John, *The Letters of John Murray to Lord Byron*, ed. Andrew Nicholson (Liverpool: Liverpool University Press, 2007).

[Napier, Macvey], *Hypocrisy Unveiled and Calumny Detected in a Review of Blackwood's Magazine* (Edinburgh: 1818).

——*Correspondence on the Subject of Blackwood's Magazine*, bound up with *Hypocrisy Unveiled and Calumny Detected in a Review of Blackwood's Magazine*, 2nd edn (Edinburgh: 1818).

Neal, John, *Randolph: A Novel* (Baltimore: Published for Whom it May Concern, 1823).

Newlyn, Lucy, *Reading, Writing and Romanticism: The Anxiety of Reception* (Oxford: Oxford University Press, 2000).

Nicholson, Andrew, ed., *Lord Byron: The Complete Miscellaneous Prose* (Oxford: Clarendon Press, 1991).

——ed., *The Letters of John Murray to Lord Byron* (Liverpool: Liverpool University Press, 2007).

Niles, Lisa, '"May the married be single, and the single happy": *Blackwood's*, the Maga for the Single Man', in *Romantic Periodicals and Print Culture*, ed. Kim Wheatley (London and Portland, Oregon: Frank Cass, 2002), 102–21.

O'Leary, Patrick, *Regency Editor: Life of John Scott* (Aberdeen: Aberdeen University Press, 1983).

Ong, Walter J., *Interfaces of the Word: Studies in the Evolution and Consciousness of Culture* (Ithaca: Cornell University Press, 1977).

Ormond, Richard, *Sir Edwin Landseer* (Philadelphia: Philadelphia Museum of Art, 1981).

Owen W. J. B., and Jane Worthington Smyser, eds. *Prose Works of William Wordsworth*, 3 vols. (Oxford: Clarendon Press, 1974).

Paine, Thomas, *Rights of Man* (Harmondsworth: Penguin, 1985).

Parker, Mark, *Literary Magazines and British Romanticism* (Cambridge: Cambridge University Press, 2000).

Patmore, P. G., *My Friends and Acquaintances* (London: Saunders and Otley, 1854).

Paulin, Tom, *The Day-Star of Liberty: William Hazlitt's Radical Style* (London: Faber and Faber, 1988).

Peacock, Thomas Love, *Halliford Edition of the Works of Thomas Love Peacock*, ed. H. F. B. Brett Smith and C. E. Jones, 10 vols. (London: Constable, 1944).

—— *The Letters of Thomas Love Peacock*, ed. Nicholas A Joukovsky, 2 vols. (Oxford: Clarendon Press, 2001).

Peterkin, Alexander, *Review of the Life of Robert Burns and of Various Criticisms on His Character and Writings* (Edinburgh: Macredie, Skelly, and Mackersy, 1815).

Pittock, Murray, *Scottish and Irish Romanticism* (Oxford: Oxford University Press, 2008).

Place, Francis, *The Autobiography of Francis Place*, ed. Mary Thrale (Cambridge: Cambridge University Press, 1972).

Playfair, Giles, *The Flash of Lightning: A Portrait of Edward Kean* (London: Kimber, 1983).

Procter, Bryan (Barry Cornwall), *An Autobiographical fragment and biographical notes, with . . . sketches of contemporaries, unpublished lyrics, etc.* (London: Bell, 1877).

Redding, Cyrus, *Fifty Years' Recollections, Literary and Personal*, 3 vols. (London: Charles J. Skeet, 1858).

Reid, J. C., *Bucks and Bruisers: Pierce Egan and Regency England* (London: Routledge and Kegan Paul, 1971).

Reiman, Donald H. and Neil Fraistat, eds, *Shelley's Poetry and Prose* (New York: Norton, 2002).

Riga, Frank P. and Claude A. France, *Index of the London Magazine* (New York and London: Garland Publishing, 1978).

Robertson, Fiona, *Legitimate Histories: Scott, Gothic and the Authorities of Fiction* (Oxford: Clarendon Press, 1994).

Robinson, Charles E., 'Percy Bysshe Shelley, Charles Ollier, and William Blackwood', in *Shelley Revalued: Essays from the Gregynog Conference* (Leicester: Leicester University Press, 1983), 183–226.

Robinson, Mairi, 'Modern Literary Scots: Ferguson and After', in *Lowland Scots: Papers Presented to an Edinburgh Conference*, ed. A. J. Aitken (Edinburgh: Association for Scottish Literary Studies, 1973), 38–55.

Rollins, Hyder Edward, ed., *The Letters of John Keats*, 2 vols. (Cambridge: Cambridge University Press, 1958).

Russell, Lord John, ed., *Memoirs, Journal, and Correspondence of Thomas Moore*, 8 vols. (London, Longmans, 1853–6).

St Clair, William, *The Reading Nation in the Romantic Period* (Cambridge: Cambridge University Press, 2004).

Scott, John, *Statement, etc. by Mr John Scott in his Dispute with Mr John Gibson Lockhart* (London: 1821).

—— *Mr Scott's Second Statement, February 2, 1821* (London: 1821).

Scott, Sir Walter, *Minstrelsy of the Scottish Border*, 3 vols. (Edinburgh: Longman and Rees, 1803).

—— *The Poems of Sir Walter Scott*, ed. J. Logie Robertson (London: Oxford University Press, 1904).

—— *The Letters of Sir Walter Scott*, ed. H. J. C Grierson, 12 vols. (London: Constable, 1932–7).

—— *The Journal of Sir Walter Scott*, ed. W. E. K. Anderson (Oxford: Clarendon Press, 1972).

—— *Kenilworth*, ed. J. H. Alexander (Edinburgh: Edinburgh University Press, 1993).

—— *The Tale of Old Mortality*, ed. Douglas Mack (Edinburgh: Edinburgh University Press, 1993).

—— *The Antiquary*, ed. David Hewitt (Edinburgh: Edinburgh University Press, 1995).

—— *Saint Ronan's Well*, ed. Mark A. Weinstein (Edinburgh: Edinburgh University Press, 1995).

—— *Redgauntlet*, ed. G. A. M. Wood with David Hewitt (Edinburgh: Edinburgh University Press, 1997).

—— *Guy Mannering*, ed. P. D. Garside (Edinburgh: Edinburgh University Press, 1999).

—— *The Abbot*, ed. Christopher Johnson (Edinburgh: Edinburgh University Press, 2000).

—— *Chronicles of the Canongate*, ed. Claire Lamont (Edinburgh: Edinburgh University Press, 2000).

—— *The Monastery*, ed. Penny Fielding (Edinburgh: Edinburgh University Press, 2000).

—— *The Antiquary*, ed. Nicola J. Watson (Oxford: Oxford University Press, 2002).

—— *The Fortunes of Nigel*, ed. Frank Jordan (Edinburgh: Edinburgh University Press, 2004).

—— *The Heart of Midlothian,* ed. David Hewitt and Alison Lumsden (Edinburgh: Edinburgh University Press, 2004).

—— *Waverley*, ed. Peter D. Garside (Edinburgh: Edinburgh University Press, 2007).

—— *Rob Roy*, ed. David Hewitt (Edinburgh: Edinburgh University Press, 2008).

Shelley, Mary, *Frankenstein; or, the Modern Prometheus*, ed. Nora Crook (London: William Pickering, 1996).

Shelley, Percy B., *The Letters of Percy Bysshe Shelley*, ed. F. L. Jones, 2 vols. (Oxford: Clarendon Press, 1964).

—— *Shelley's Poetry and Prose*, ed. Donald H. Reiman and Neil Fraistat (New York: Norton, 2002).

Shelley, Percy B., *Percy Bysshe Shelley: The Major Works*, ed. Zachary Leader and Michael O'Neill (Oxford: Oxford University Press, 2003).

Sher, Richard, *The Enlightenment and the Book: Scottish Authors and Their Publishers in Eighteenth-Century Britain, Ireland, and America* (Chicago and London: University of Chicago Press, 2006).

Simonsen, Peter, *Wordsworth and Word-Preserving Arts: Typographic Inscription, Ekphrasis and Posterity in the Later Work* (London: Palgrave Macmillan, 2007).

Smiles, Samuel, *A Publisher and his Friends: Memoir and Correspondence of the Late John Murray, with an account of the Origin and Progress of the House, 1768–1884*, 2 vols. (London: John Murray, 1891).

Southey, Robert, *The Doctor, etc.* (London: Longman, Brown, Green and Longmans, 1849).

——*Selections from the Letters of Robert Southey*, ed. J. W. Warter, 4 vols. (London: Longman, 1856).

Spencer, Jane, *The Rise of the Woman Novelist: from Aphra Behn to Jane Austen* (Oxford: Blackwell, 1986).

Stabler, Jane, *Byron, Poetics and History* (Cambridge: Cambridge University Press, 2002).

Stauffer, Andrew M., *Anger, Revolution, and Romanticism* (Cambridge: Cambridge University Press, 2005).

Stewart, David, *The Age of the Magazine: Literary Consumption and Metropolitan Culture, 1815–1825*, a doctoral thesis submitted to the University of Glasgow, August 2008.

—— 'Commerce, Genius and De Quincey's Literary Identity', *Studies in English Literature, 1500–1900* (forthcoming).

——'Filling the Newspaper Gap: Leigh Hunt, *Blackwood's*, and the Development of the Miscellany', *Victorian Periodicals Review* (forthcoming).

Strout, Alan Lang, 'James Hogg's "Chaldee Manuscript"', *Publications of the Modern Language Association of America*, 65 (1950), 695–718.

——*A Bibliography of Articles in Blackwood's Magazine* (Lubbock, Texas: Texas Tech Press, 1959).

Stuart of Dunearn, James, *Correspondence between James Stuart, Esq. and the printer of the Beacon* (Edinburgh, 1821).

—— *Correspondence between James Stuart, Esq. younger of Dunearn, and the Lord Advocate* (Edinburgh, 1821).

—— *Correspondence between James Stuart, Esq. younger of Dunearn, and the Earl of Morton, Lord Lieutenant of the county of Fife: relative to Mr. Stuart's resignation of his commission in the Royal Fifeshire Yeomanry Cavalry* (Edinburgh, 1822).

——*A Full Report of the Trial of James Stuart, Esq. younger of Dunearn, before the High Court of Justiciary, 10th June 1822; with an appendix containing documents, etc.* (Edinburgh, 1823).

Sutherland, John, *Life of Walter Scott: A Critical Biography* (Oxford: Blackwell, 1995).

Sweet, Nanora, 'The *New Monthly Magazine* and the Liberalism of the 1820s', in *Romantic Periodicals and Print Culture*, ed. Kim Wheatley (London and Portland, Oregon: Frank Cass, 2002), 147–62.

Treadwell, James, *Autobiographical Writing and British Literature, 1783–1834* (Oxford: Oxford University Press, 2005).

Trott, Nicola Z., 'North of the Border: Cultural Crossing in the *Noctes Ambrosiane.*' *Romanticism On the Net* 20 (November 2000), http://users.ox.ac.uk/~scat0385/20trott.html.

Warter, J. W. ed., *Selections from the Letters of Robert Southey*, 4 vols. (London: Longman, 1856).

Wheatley, Kim, 'The *Blackwood's* Attacks on Leigh Hunt', *Nineteenth-Century Literature*, 47 (June 1992), 1–31.

—— *Shelley and his Readers: Beyond Paranoid Politics* (Columbia and London: University of Missouri Press, 1999).

——ed. *Romantic Periodicals and Print Culture* (London and Portland, Oregon: Frank Cass, 2002).

Wilson, Ben, *Decency and Disorder: The Age of Cant 1789–1837* (London: Faber and Faber, 2007).

Wilson, Fiona, 'He's come undone: Gender, Territory, and Hysteria in *Rob Roy*', in *Romanticism's Debatable Lands*, ed. Claire Lamont and Michael Rossington (Basingstoke: Palgrave Macmillan, 2007), 52–63.

Wilson, Frances, ed., *Byromania: Portraits of the Artist in Nineteenth- and Twentieth-Century Culture*, ed. Frances Wilson (London: Macmillan, 1999).

Wilson, John, *Correspondence on the Subject of Blackwood's Magazine* (Edinburgh, 1818).

—— *Lights and Shadows of Scottish Life* (Edinburgh: Blackwood, 1822).

—— *The Trials of Margaret Lindsay* (Edinburgh: Blackwood, 1823).

—— *Noctes Ambrosianae*, ed. Professor James Farrier, 4 vols. (Edinburgh and London: William Blackwood and Sons, 1855).

Wilt, Judith, *Secret Leaves: The Novels of Walter Scott* (Chicago: University of Chicago Press, 1985).

Wolfson, Susan, '"Their She Condition": Cross-Dressing and the Politics of Gender in *Don Juan*', *ELH*, 54 (1987), 585–617.

Wordsworth, William, *The Letters of William and Dorothy Wordsworth: The Early Years, 1787–1805*, ed. Ernest de Selincourt, rev. Chester L. Shaver (Oxford: Clarendon Press, 1967).

—— *The Letters of William and Dorothy Wordsworth*. Vol. 3: *The Middle Years, Part I. 1806–1811*, ed. Mary Moorman and Alan G. Hill (Oxford: Clarendon Press, 1969).

—— *The Letters of William and Dorothy Wordsworth*. Vol. 3: *The Middle Years, Part II. 1812–1820*, ed. Mary Moorman and Alan G. Hill (Oxford: Clarendon Press, 1969).

—— *Prose Works of William Wordsworth*, ed. W. J. B. Owen and Jane Worthington Smyser, 3 vols. (Oxford: Clarendon Press, 1974).

Wu, Duncan, ed., *The Selected Writings of William Hazlitt*, 9 vols. (London: Pickering and Chatto, 1998).

—— *Hazlitt: The First Modern Man* (Oxford: Oxford University Press, 2008).

Index